Southeast Asia's Chinese Businesses in an Era of Globalization

The **Institute of Southeast Asian Studies (ISEAS)** was established as an autonomous organization in 1968. It is a regional research centre dedicated to the study of socio-political, security and economic trends and developments in Southeast Asia and its wider geostrategic and economic environment.

The Institute's research programmes are the Regional Economic Studies (RES, including ASEAN and APEC), Regional Strategic and Political Studies (RSPS), and Regional Social and Cultural Studies (RSCS).

ISEAS Publications, an established academic press, has issued more than 1,000 books and journals. It is the largest scholarly publisher of research about Southeast Asia from within the region. ISEAS Publications works with many other academic and trade publishers and distributors to disseminate important research and analyses from and about Southeast Asia to the rest of the world.

Southeast Asia's Chinese Businesses in an Era of Globalization
Coping with the Rise of China

Edited by
Leo Suryadinata

Institute of Southeast Asian Studies
Singapore

First published in Singapore in 2006 by ISEAS Publications
Institute of Southeast Asian Studies
30 Heng Mui Keng Terrace
Pasir Panjang, Singapore 119614
E-mail: publish@iseas.edu.sg
Website: http://bookshop.iseas.edu.sg

ISEAS Library Cataloguing-in-Publication Data

Southeast Asia's Chinese businesses in an era of globalization : coping with the rise of China / edited by Leo Suryadinata.
   1. Chinese—Southeast Asia—Economic conditions.
   2. Minority business enterprises—Southeast Asia.
   3. China—Economic conditions—2000–
   4. China—Foreign economic relations—Southeast Asia.
   5. Southeast Asia—Foreign economic relations—China.
   I. Suryadinata, Leo, 1941–
HD2358.5 A9S72   2006

ISBN-13: 978-981-230-398-1 (soft cover — 13 digit)
ISBN-10: 981-230-398-7 (soft cover — 10 digit)

ISBN-13: 978-981-230-401-8 (hard cover — 13 digit)
ISBN-10: 981-230-401-0 (hard cover — 10 digit)

Typeset by Superskill Graphics Pte Ltd
Printed in Singapore by Photoplates Pte Ltd

Contents

The Contributors

Teresita Ang See is the President of ISSCO (International Society for the Studies of Chinese Overseas); founding President of Kaisa Para Sa Kaunlaran, a non-government organization addressing Chinese-Filipino concerns; and Executive Trustee of Kaisa Heritage Center, which runs the Bahay Tsinoy-Museum of the Chinese in Philippine Life, a data bank and research center, and an extensive specialized library on Chinese overseas.

Sujoko Efferin is Dean and Lecturer of the Faculty of Economics, Universitas Surabaya, Indonesia and head of the Focus Group Business and Investment, Indonesian Economists Association (ISEI), Surabaya Chapter. He specializes in Chinese business and organizational culture.

Go Bon Juan is the vice president for research and member of the Council of Advisers of Kaisa Para Sa Kaunlaran, a non-government organization that undertakes research and publication on Chinese-Filipino concerns. He is also news editor and columnist for the Chinese-language daily *World News* and has extensive writings on the Philippines and Chinese-Filipino issues.

Ho Khai Leong is Associate Professor of Public Administration and Political Science at the Nanyang Technological University, Singapore. He was a Fellow at the Institute of Southeast Asian Studies and Senior Lecturer in the National University of Singapore.

Lee Kam Hing was professor of history at the University of Malaya from 1994 to 1997. Since then he has been with Star Publications as Research Editor and he has also helped set up the Asian Centre for Media Studies.

Lee Poh Ping is Professor and Senior Fellow in the Institute of Malaysian and International Studies (IKMAS), Universiti Kebangsaan Malaysia. Previously he was Professor and Head of Department, Department of Administrative and Political Studies, University of Malaya.

Leong Kai Hin was Associate Professor of Finance at the University of Nottingham, Malaysia Campus. Currently, he lectures at the University of Malaya in the post-graduate business programmes. He is Deputy Chairman of the Socio-Economic Research Committee of the Associated Chinese Chamber of Commerce and Industry of Malaysia.

Ng Beoy Kui is Sub-Dean/Associate Professor of the School of Humanities and Social Sciences, Nanyang Technological University, Singapore. He was formerly attached to the Economics Department of the Central Bank of Malaysia (Bank Negara Malaysia) and the Southeast Asian Central Banks Research and Training Centre (SEACEN Centre). His current research interests include money and banking, macroeconomic management, Chinese economy and overseas Chinese business.

Ellen H. Palanca is Professor of Economics and Director of the Chinese Studies Program at the Ateneo de Manila University. Her area of research includes China's economy, regional economic integration, and ethnic Chinese business.

Pavida Pananond is Assistant Professor in the Department of International Business, Logistics and Transport Management, Thammasat Business School, Thammasat University in Bangkok.

Wiyono Pontjoharyo is Lecturer, Faculty of Economics and head of the Masters Management programme, Graduate School, Universitas Surabaya, Indonesia. He specializes in strategic management, Chinese business, and management accounting.

Djisman S. Simandjuntak is Chairman, Executive Board, CSIS Foundation, Jakarta; Member, Board of Directors, Prasetiya Mulya Business School; Chairman, Board of Advisors, Indonesian Institute of Corporate Directorship; teaching at the Prasetiya Mulya Business School; and Member representing Indonesia in the EU-ASEAN Vision Group and Expert Group on East Asia Free-Trade Area.

Leo Suryadinata is Director of the Chinese Heritage Centre, Singapore and adjunct Professor, Nanyang Technological University. He was former Professor at the Department of Political Science, National University of Singapore and Senior Research Fellow, Institute of Southeast Asian Studies.

Thee Kian Wie is Senior Economist at the Economic Research Centre, Indonesian Institute of Sciences (P2E-LIPI), Jakarta.

Sarasin Viraphol is currently Executive Vice President (responsible for business development), Charoen Pokphand Group. The Thai multinational company operates businesses globally, which include agribusiness, retailing, and telecommunications. Prior to joining the business sector, he served in Thailand's Ministry of Foreign Affairs, attaining the rank of Ambassador. He was also previously an Assistant Professor at Thailand's Chulalongkorn University.

John Wong, Professor, is Research Director at the East Asian Institute (EAI) of the National University of Singapore. He was formerly Director of the Institute of East Asian Political Economy.

Introduction

Leo Suryadinata

GLOBALIZATION, CHINA AND THE ETHNIC CHINESE IN SOUTHEAST ASIA

In the last decades of the twentieth century, there have been two significant international developments: the rise of globalization and the emergence of China as an economic power. Globalization has reduced the physical distance of regions and countries all over the world and resulted in intensive interaction. These interactions occurred not only between regions but also between countries. The impact is of course tremendous and multi-dimensional. It is also obvious that smaller and developing countries are likely to receive more impacts than the larger and more developed ones. We in Southeast Asia, a collection of small and medium countries and still developing, have really felt this impact, initially from the West but lately from China.

Our northern neighbour, China, has rapidly become a major economic power. It has become the "dynamo" of Asia and some even see it as the "world factory" for mass production, flooding the Southeast Asian markets. Both globalization and the rise of China have resulted in a profound socio-political and economic change in the region of Southeast Asia and offer an opportunity for scholars to study. The Institute of Southeast Asian Studies (ISEAS) in Singapore decided to hold a workshop focusing on the rise of China and its economic rather than political and socio-cultural impacts on Southeast Asia, with special reference to the economic position of the ethnic Chinese in general, and ethnic Chinese businesses in particular. The study is put in the context of an era of globalization where changes have taken place. The book that you are reading is the result of the workshop which was held in late April 2005.

About 75 per cent of the ethnic Chinese outside China live in Southeast Asia. They have made significant contributions to the development of the region, particularly in the areas of economy and business. With the rise of China as an economic power, it would be interesting to study what role the ethnic Chinese in the region would play. What would be the impact of the rise of China on Southeast Asia in general and on ethnic Chinese in particular? Would it be positive or negative for the economic development of the countries in the region? What have been and will be the attitude and position of the Southeast Asian governments towards both China and the local ethnic Chinese? What is the current situation of Chinese businesses, including both conglomerates and SMEs?

In light of the above questions, the workshop was divided into three sub-topics: the rise of China and its impact on Southeast Asia's economies and businesses, especially on those of ethnic Chinese; Southeast Asian government policies, particularly their economic and business policies, towards local ethnic Chinese; and Southeast Asian Chinese businesses in an era of globalization. This has been the order of the sub-topics. We did it in this way so that we would be able to discuss the subject matters from the general to the specific.

Before discussing the chapters presented in this volume, some observations on the various terms regarding the Chinese in Southeast Asia should be mentioned. The most frequently used English terms to refer to the Chinese in Southeast Asia are "Chinese Overseas" and "Overseas Chinese".

People in certain Southeast Asian countries may feel somewhat sensitive with regard to terms like "Overseas Chinese" and "Chinese Overseas", because both terms are China-centric. The terms imply that these Chinese are "overseas", and Southeast Asia is not their home. Worse still, the term "Overseas Chinese" (not "Chinese Overseas") was used to refer to *huaqiao*, that is, Chinese nationals residing temporarily outside China. In fact, China itself uses the terms *huaqiao* (overseas Chinese) and *huaren* (ethnic Chinese) to refer to two types of Chinese: *huaqiao* for Chinese nationals and *huaren* for ethnic Chinese who are non-Chinese nationals. In view of the historical connotation of the term Overseas Chinese, Wang Gungwu uses "Chinese Overseas" rather than "Overseas Chinese" to refer to the Chinese outside China.

It is clear that there is no general agreement on the use of the terms to refer to the Chinese outside China and Taiwan. I personally prefer the English term "ethnic Chinese" to refer to all Chinese outside China regardless of their citizenship and culture, but I do not want to restrict the usage of other terms as I am also aware of individual preferences and the complexity of the issue, hence all the chapter writers were allowed to use their own terms in this volume. However, one point that readers should remember is that the majority of the so-called "Overseas Chinese" or "Chinese Overseas" are citizens of the Southeast Asian states.

THE RISE OF CHINA AS AN ECONOMIC POWER

The last decades of the twentieth century saw the rise of China as a major economic power, if not a political power, in the region and beyond. In fact, China has become the "world factory" which is able to produce cheap goods. The chapter by John Wong, a Singapore economist, is on China's economy and its impact on the Southeast Asian region. He describes a general picture of the economic rise of China since 1979 following the open-door policy: within twenty-five years, it has become one of the largest economies in the world. He has detailed the economic growth of China and the strength of its economies in various sectors, showing very impressive growth of this Eastern giant. He acknowledged that initially the original ASEAN countries benefited from the open-door policy but with the rapid growth of China and the Asian economic crisis, China became a competitor of the ASEAN states, especially for the foreign direct investment (FDI). Nevertheless, he believes that the impact of the rise of China on ASEAN is overall positive and ASEAN will be able to benefit from this growth. He did not discuss the negative aspects encountered by the ASEAN states in facing the economic growth of China nor did he discuss the impact on the Chinese communities and their businesses.

Sarasin Viraphol, a Sino-Thai historian and former Thai foreign ministry high official who is now a corporate leader, also discussed the economic growth of China but with special reference to the impact on ethnic Chinese businesses in Southeast Asia. Similar to John Wong, Sarasin also noted the rapid economic growth of the Middle Kingdom and its benefits to the ASEAN countries. However, unlike Wong, he discussed the responses of the Chinese (especially in Thailand) to the rise of China as an economic power. He maintained that:

> ASEAN is a central piece in China's "win-win" strategy, given its traditional amicable contacts, its geographical proximity and strategic location, as well as its resources and market. In this "soft approach", one cannot overlook the role of Southeast Asian

businessmen of Chinese origin (*huaren*), given their resources and resourcefulness as well as ethnicity, in the continuing evolution of China's economic ascendancy.

He further maintained that ethnic Chinese in ASEAN would serve as "connectors and bridge" between the region and China. He also noted that publicly listed companies, mainly owned by Sino-Thais, captured the opportunity to do business with China and benefited from the dealings. One often wonders if the impact of a rising China on the SMEs in Thailand has also been equally positive. Unfortunately Sarasin did not discuss this group of ethnic Chinese businessmen.

IMPACT ON SOUTHEAST ASIAN STATES

a) Indonesia

Djisman S. Simandjuntak, an Indonesian economist, addressed the issue of the rise of China and its impact on Southeast Asia with special reference to Indonesia. He was of the view that China's rise was the most important event in the last one hundred years. He saw the growth of China as a major economic and political power a challenge as well as an opportunity to the archipelagic state. He acknowledged that Indonesia is a plural society where there is a dichotomy between the "indigenous people" and Chinese Indonesians, with the former holding political powers and the latter owning businesses. He argued that "Given their leading position in business Chinese Indonesians have more ways to benefit from the rise of China than indigenous Indonesians do. Nothing is mysterious in such facts." Unfortunately the wide gap in business ownership has become a "fertile soil for criticism or even suspicion that the rise of China is unfairly exploited by Chinese Indonesians".

He disagreed, however, with the introduction of the "affirmative actions" against Chinese Indonesians as these measures had failed in the past and would not benefit the Indonesians in general. Simandjuntak also maintained that Chinese Indonesians are tough and survived several onslaughts over a long period of time and are the entrepreneurs who would withstand the wave of globalization. They are in fact an integral part of Indonesia who would be able to help Indonesia develop economically in this global era. In his view, most important for Indonesia is not an affirmative policy but how to design ways to achieve rapid economic growth since the past affirmative measures encountered failure. "A faster growth in China and Indonesia is bound to make ethnicity less and less contentious in the world of commerce." This view is refreshing but may not be subscribed to by many less successful "indigenous" businessmen and politicians.

However, Thee Kian Wie, an Indonesian economist of Chinese descent, examined the Indonesian Government's policies towards the ethnic Chinese since the attainment of Indonesia's political independence with some reference to the recent period, arguing that economic nationalism in Indonesia is a force to be reckoned with. He acknowledged that:

> although its contemporary manifestations has in general become less aggressive and less strident than in the 1950s, economic nationalism remains a driving force that to a large extent still influences economic policies today.

However, he differentiated the old and new policies: in the 1950s, economic nationalism was directed towards the Dutch and ethnic Chinese business interests, but in the years following the Asian financial crisis in the late 1990s, economic nationalism was mainly directed against the perceived interference of international organizations, particularly the International Monetary Fund (IMF), in the formulation of economic policies.

Focusing on Indonesia's economic policy towards Indonesian Chinese during the Suharto era, he explained the reasons for introducing these policies and their unsatisfactory results. Currently President Yudhyono has adopted a more pragmatic policy despite his vice president's stated preference in promoting affirmative policy favouring indigenous (*pribumi*) businessmen. This is because Indonesia is concerned with economic recovery, and foreign investment is badly needed in order to make Indonesia's economy perform well. Thee Kian Wie did not explicitly argue that economic nationalism against the ethnic Chinese might revive if the present government fails to promote economic development. This cannot be ruled out as economic nationalism is still strong.

There is no doubt that ethnic Chinese (*Tionghoa*) business has been strong in Indonesia. In their joint article, business management scholars Sujoko Efferin and Wiyono Pontjoharyo examined the characteristics and management style of Chinese Indonesian business in the light of globalization and the rise of China as an economic power. Using a limited survey of *Tionghoa* businesses in East Java, they pointed out that although the division between businesses run by *totok* Chinese (defined here in terms of Chinese who still hold traditional Chinese values) and *jiaosen* (*qiaosheng*, local-born and highly Indonesianized Chinese), their business behaviours are getting closer. Both authors disagreed with the conventional Overseas Chinese Business (OCB) models proposed by some writers and noted that ethnic culture "needs to be seen as merely one of the resources available to cope with business problems". Many practices which were linked to "Chinese culture" when they started business were abandoned after they grew bigger. They also noted that Chinese Indonesian businesses are being run in Western/modern style, while "Confucian culture" and business culture have increasingly been separated. Lastly, they argued that it is misleading to equate Indonesian Chinese businesses with small traditional businesses. In fact, many small/medium Chinese Indonesian businesses in the past have now grown to large companies (for example, Maspion Group, Wismilak, Sampoerna and Wings Group, etc.). They also pointed out that Chinese Indonesians who were born after the 1950s were well integrated into Indonesian society and have become part of the local scene rather than that of the "global Chinese community".

Nevertheless, both authors did not discuss the impact of industrialized China on Chinese Indonesian businesses. They did not go into the arguments as to whether globalization and the rise of China as an economic power will harm or benefit Chinese Indonesian businesses.

b) Malaysia

Unlike in Indonesia where the Chinese only constitute about 2 per cent of the Indonesian population, Chinese Malaysians form about 26 per cent of the total population. They are much more conspicuous in Malaysia than in Indonesia and their economic prowess is also strongly felt. In order to restructure the national economy and create a Malay middle class, the Malay-dominated government of Malaysia introduced the New Economic Policy (NEP) in 1970 following the 1969 May Riots. Ho Khai Leong, a political scientist, discussed the Malaysian Government's policy towards the Chinese since the introduction of the NEP. Ho argued that the NEP was a pro-*Bumiputera* policy which was often perceived as a discriminatory policy against the Chinese. It was under this policy that the Malay corporate ownership had grown in twenty years from 2.4 per cent to 20.3 per cent. The Industrial Co-ordination Act was one of the means to increase Malay participation in the economy, giving the bureaucracy the power to control industry. Nevertheless, the Chinese business community responded to the NEP and later the National Development Policy (NDP), by adopting various means and strategies, including initiating a self-help programme and Sino-Malay business alliances. Ho maintained that Malaysian society has now been gradually transformed from an ethnic-based to a class-based society. The Chinese community, in order to survive and develop, has adopted a national rather than ethnic economic approach. The issues raised are national rather than ethnic. In the era of globalization, the quota system, which was introduced during the NEP period, is no longer relevant. In an open economic competition, it is no longer possible to introduce protectionism and the Chinese businesses faced both domestic and external competition. The impact of China as an economic power may not necessarily strengthen the Malaysian Chinese economic position, although many believe that this is going to be the case.

While Ho Khai Leong addressed the Malaysian Government's economic policies towards the ethnic Chinese and the Chinese business responses, political economist Lee Poh Ping and historian Lee Kam Hing in their chapter examined the impact of globalization and the rise of China on Chinese-Malaysian businesses. They argued that China's rise has had both positive and negative impacts on ethnic Chinese business in Malaysia. The impact is particularly noticeable in the areas of investment, trade and services. Using statistical information, they maintained that Malaysian Chinese are unfamiliar with the conditions in China and their investment in China is limited and mainly in the property rather than manufacturing sector. Nevertheless, the greatest impact is still on trade. "Chinese imports into the country threaten the profitability and survival of several industries. These include the footwear and textile industries which have been forced to enhance their competitiveness." However, many were unable to compete. They import mainly all kinds of Chinese products for the Malaysian market. In the area of services, however, China's impact has brought benefits especially to the Malaysian higher educational and tourism sectors, but it is not without its problems. They concluded that

> for many Chinese who earlier saw a rising China as one of unalloyed opportunities, advances made by China is beginning to limit and even compete with Malaysian business particularly Malaysian Chinese.

They also noted that

> ... while resourceful Malaysian Chinese can still maintain a competitive edge, for the majority the response may require a state master plan for future industrialization strategy.

Leong Kai Hin, an economist who specializes in Malaysian Chinese business, recently conducted a survey of a number of Chinese businesses. He studied the impact of globalization on some Malaysian Chinese businesses and the strategies adopted by them to face such challenges. He measured its impact by looking at their financial performance over this period of globalization, discovering that while large business firms benefited from globalization and the rise of China, small and medium firms were not so lucky. Many used outsourcing as a strategy to survive. Most seriously hit were those in shoes and garment manufacturing. Some Malaysian-Chinese businesses which failed to compete closed down their business and became traders.

c) Singapore

The problems posed by globalization and the rise of China to Singapore, an island republic dominated by ethnic Chinese, are not much different. The rise of China also posed both challenges and opportunities to Chinese businesses. Ng Beoy Kui, an economist, maintained that ethnic Chinese businesses in Singapore, despite their structural weaknesses, were able to weather the storm of the Asian financial crisis with government assistance. He further argued that the rise of China with its open-door policy also provides ample opportunities for these businesses to exploit their ethnic advantage in their investment in China, but at the same time, the ventures also brought painful experiences, arising from cultural differences between Singapore and China. Of significance is the stiff competition provided by mainland Chinese businesses in the third country markets, not to mention the issues of the "hollowing-out effect" and "offshore outsourcing".

In the face of globalization and the rise of China, Ng Beoy Kui noted that the focus of the Singapore Government's policy is to enhance ethnic Chinese businesses' capabilities so that they can be effective partners in a tripartite alliance among government-linked corporations (GLCs) and SMEs in their venturing abroad, especially investment in China.

d) Philippines

Globalization and the rise of China as an economic power have also raised concerns in the Philippines. Nevertheless, Teresita Ang See and Go Bon Juan, both keen observers on the Philippine Chinese affairs, maintained that the threat of China to Southeast Asia in general and to the Philippines particularly, has been exaggerated, if not baseless. Nevertheless, they admitted that Chinese cheap manufactured goods have indeed threatened some Philippine SMEs, many of which are owned by ethnic Chinese. However, big Chinese businesses have ample opportunities to do business with China. They argued that the Federation of Filipino-Chinese Chambers of Commerce did not have a concerted effort to deal with the challenge of globalization; in addition, Chinese-Filipino businessmen are not united in organizing themselves in responding to the challenge. Chinese Filipinos need to re-invent themselves and improve their effectiveness in order to cope with globalization and the rise of China.

Ang See and Go also maintained that trade relations between China and the Philippines are in favour of the former, but at one time, the gap was very narrow. The impact of the rise of China as an economic power, they argued, is not always negative. In fact, it would bring benefits to the Philippine economy in general. The spillover effect to the Philippines will also stimulate its economic growth. Chinese Filipinos will be able to serve as facilitators in improving China-Philippine economic ties in order to have a win-win situation.

Ellen H. Palanca, an economist, surveys the Philippine public policy towards ethnic Chinese businesses with some reference to globalization and the rise of China. She maintained that ethnic Chinese in the Philippines

> suffered the effect of the adverse colonial policies aimed at them and the nationalist policies in the post-independence period when the political situation in China did not leave them with much alternative option. They started to enjoy equal economic rights under the law when mass citizenship was granted in mid-1975. More opportunities were made available to them in the 1980s, the Philippine Government adopted economic liberation policies and China opened its economy. Globalization and China's economic boom provided even more investment opportunities. Since then we saw the rise of *nouveau riche* Chinese, most of who(m) rose from practically nothing. They now form part of the elite group that can lobby for government legislation, regulation and policy-making.

Palanca also mentioned the rise of the Chinese-Filipino economic elite *vis-à-vis* the Spanish-Filipino economic elite. While the latter is the traditional elite (oligarchs) who has long controlled the property markets, the former has now broken their monopoly. She presented a vivid case in which the Chinese-Filipino elite combined forces with other Chinese tycoons from Indonesia and Malaysia to win the projects to build malls and golf courses, defeating the Ayalas group. Nevertheless, she interestingly pointed out that the Chinese-Filipino elite is still less powerful in politics compared to the oligarchs, many of whom are Spanish Filipinos. Nevertheless, Chinese Filipinos are part and parcel of the Philippine society and they have been integrated into the political-economic system of the country, and have even become part of the patron-client relationship system.

There is no doubt that globalization and the liberalization of the economic system benefited Chinese-Filipino tycoons.

e) Thailand

Ethnic Chinese business tycoons in Thailand have also benefited from globalization and the rise of China as an economic power. Pavida Pananond, an international business scholar, presented her study on the most well-known, if not the largest, ethnic Chinese business in the country, the Charoen Pokphand (CP) Group, which specializes in agri-business. She maintained that in the past, there was an over-emphasis on the ethnicity of CP's founder, Dhanin Chearavanont. As a result,

> the studies overwhelmingly stressed how CP's characteristics resembled other ethnic Chinese businesses throughout Southeast Asia, rather than unveiled the group's behaviour from an economic or business perspective. The weight given to the group's Chinese ethnicity was further emphasized following the group's extensive expansions in China.

Pavida admitted that the CP Group has the characteristics of an "Overseas Chinese" business group. "With its conglomerate structure, family ownership and control, extensive investments in China, and expertise in cultivating networks with those in power, CP has often been known as the Thai representative of ethnic Chinese business."

However, Pavida contended that this did not sufficiently explain how the CP Group has been able to survive and develop in China and Thailand and beyond. The explanation, she argued, lies in the strategic directions behind the overall development of the group and international activities of the group before and after the 1997 economic crisis. She then offered her detailed analysis of the development strategies of the CP Group, the changing dynamics of the CP Group's international operations, arguing that,

> in the agribusiness and aquaculture sectors, CP's post-crisis adjustments have indeed strengthened its status as an agribusiness multinational company. Through the process of downstream integration into retailing and distribution, value addition to its products, and division of responsibility among overseas production bases, the CP Group emerged as a more globally focused and integrated agribusiness multinational.

Nevertheless, in an era of globalization where China is an open market, the CP Group will face more fierce competition. She noted that while the group's ethnicity and extensive networks in China may have contributed to the group's success earlier, the immediate challenges facing CP have less to do with ethnicity issues but more with business competence.

CONCLUDING REMARKS

Globalization and the rise of China are significant events, which "started" in the last decades of the twentieth century. Globalization has released political, social and economic forces which have had a major impact on various regions, including Southeast Asia. The rise of China as an economic power has been strongly felt in this region. People can no longer ignore China as the "world factory" which is able to attract world investment and offers huge markets. China's cheap products, together with other countries' products, have "flooded" Southeast Asian markets. China has now become both a challenge and opportunity to Southeast Asia.

It is general knowledge that the ethnic Chinese in Southeast Asia have played a significant economic role, leading to a stereotype of the Chinese in Southeast Asia as the "trading minorities". In fact, the ethnic Chinese are not a homogeneous group. There are poor and rich Chinese and their occupations also vary. With regard to Chinese businesses, they can also be divided into large, medium and small businesses. Many Southeast Asian countries which experienced "economic nationalism" or more correctly, "economic indigenism", often considered their ethnic Chinese population as "foreign elements" and introduced various regulations and policies to restrict the economic activities and reduce their economic strength. Despite discriminatory measures against them, ethnic Chinese continued to be able to maintain their economic position.

Other ethnic groups, however, are also emerging, but their economic position has not reached that of the ethnic Chinese.

Nevertheless, the economic crisis in 1997 and economic globalization forced many Southeast Asian governments to review their regulations and policies towards the ethnic Chinese. Eventually a policy of liberalization will strengthen ethnic Chinese economic power, as they will be freer to be active in the economic fields. With capital, skills and regional networks, many Chinese business companies will grow even stronger. Many observers fear that the rise of China would further benefit ethnic Chinese businessmen.

Nevertheless, the fact is not simple. The rise of China as an industrial power does not have only one impact on Southeast Asia as a whole and the Chinese community in particular. While Southeast Asian countries enjoy having cheaper products, some SMEs, mainly those owned by ethnic Chinese, also suffered. Nevertheless, Chinese big businesses, which have a stronger economic position, have been able to cope with the situation. They have also been able to invest in China and elsewhere to benefit from globalization and the opening of China. Facing the challenges of globalization and the rise of China, ethnic Chinese communities in Southeast Asia, especially the business groups, have begun to revamp themselves so that they would become more competitive.

Many ethnic Chinese businesses — especially SMEs — in Southeast Asia, in fact, have been Southeast Asianized. The chapters in this book show that they have formed part of the Southeast Asian scene. Chinese ethnicity plays a lesser role while business logic becomes more important. The fate of the ethnic Chinese in the Southeast Asian region is linked to the local economy rather than to China.

Many Southeast Asian governments have realized that with the rise of China, they need to foster closer economic cooperation so that both China and the ASEAN states will enjoy the benefits of this cooperation. Nevertheless, nationalism in Southeast Asia has not died and economic nationalism will become a challenge to the betterment of Sino-Southeast Asian relations.

1

China's Economic Rise and Its Implications for Southeast Asia: The Big Picture

John Wong*

CHINA IN REGIONAL PERSPECTIVE

Since 1979, China's economy has experienced spectacular growth as a result of its successful economic reform and open-door policy. In the process, China's economy has also become more closely integrated with its neighbouring economies in East Asia (EA). China's sustained dynamic economic growth has produced a profound impact on the EA region, including the Association of the Southeast Asian Nations (ASEAN).

Initially, the more developed Japan and the four East Asian NIEs (newly industrialized economies) of South Korea, Taiwan, Hong Kong and Singapore (which were economically complementary with China) captured most of the benefits of China's open-door policy by actively trading with and investing in China.

As China continued to press ahead with its export-oriented development strategies, it started to cast a large shadow on the less developed ASEAN economies to its south, many of which were competing head-on with China to attract foreign direct investment (FDI) and in exporting manufactured products to the same third-country markets. The rise of China was at one time considered to be a disruptive force to ASEAN's economic growth, which had lost quite a lot of its former dynamism after the 1997 Asian financial crisis. In recent years, however, as China's imports of ASEAN's manufactured products as well as its primary commodities and natural resources have sharply increased, China's economy has also operated as an additional source of economic growth for the ASEAN economies.

Furthermore, to allay ASEAN's growing apprehension of China, Beijing took a bold step to arrange an FTA (free trade agreement) with ASEAN in order to turn competition into complementation. Signed in November 2002, this landmark Sino-ASEAN FTA deal is designed to increase the region's trade and investment to the benefit of both sides. But it has also indirectly exerted a lot of pressures on Japan and Korea to follow suit by intensifying their economic relations with ASEAN under the general regional cooperation umbrella of the ASEAN plus China, Japan and Korea (ASEAN+3) scheme. With its growing regional political and economic clout, China's FTA initiative with ASEAN has thus sparked off a new economic integration momentum towards the East Asian Economic Community.

Over the longer run, the economic rise of China can be seen not only as a new engine of economic growth for the ASEAN region, but also as a powerful catalyst force for integrating the EA economies. In fact, China's economy in recent years has been the major driving force behind EA's growing regional trade inter-dependency, as most EA economies have experienced the largest percentage-point increases in their exports to China.

THE ECONOMIC RISE OF CHINA

The Chinese economy grew at a highly impressive rate of 9.3 per cent for the period of 1978–2004. Whereas the 1997 Asian financial crisis brought down many Asian economies, China's economy was hardly affected by the crisis as it continued to grow at 8.8 per cent in 1997 and 7.8 per cent in 1998. After this crisis, while economic growth in most of Asia had fallen to low or negative rates, China's economy alone was steaming ahead with strong growth. In 2003, despite disruptions caused by SARS and global economic recession, it still chalked up a hefty 9.1 per cent growth (Figure 1.1). Furthermore, high growth was carried over to 2004, with another sizzling 9.5 per cent growth, which continued to the first half of 2005. In fact, the Chinese Government has since been much concerned over problems of economic overheating, having taken a number of vigorous administrative and macro-economic control measures to cool down overheated economic activities in order to achieve a soft landing.

China's economy has so far been much less affected by external economic shocks mainly because over 80 per cent of China's economic growth is generated by domestic demand (that is, domestic consumption and domestic investment). At the same time, China's exports (that is, external demand) have also been growing very rapidly, averaging at 16

FIGURE 1.1
Crisis and Prolonged Recovery of Selected ASEAN Economies, 1996–2004

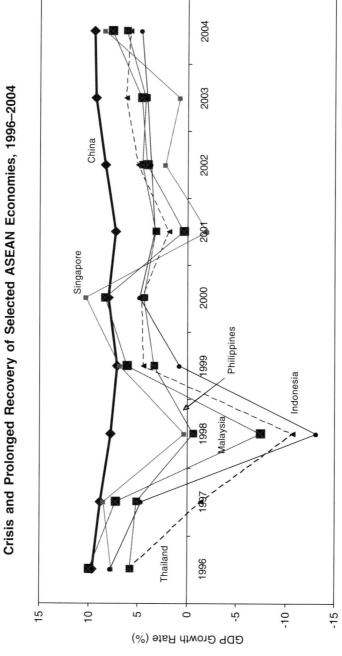

Source: Asian Development Outlook (various issues).

per cent for over the past two decades, rising from US$9.8 billion in 1978 to US$593 billion in 2004. China is now the world's third largest exporter after the United States and Japan.

For FDI, China has since the early 1990s become the world's most favoured destination in comparison with all other developing countries. By early 2005, China had attracted a total of US$580 billion in FDI. In fact, China in recent years has consistently captured more than half of all FDI in Asia. Not surprisingly, over 80 per cent of the world's 500 largest companies and its top 100 information technology firms have set up businesses in China.[1] Above all, on account of its strong external balance, China's total foreign exchange reserves by mid-2005 soared to US$710 billion to become the world's second largest, after Japan. This, in turn, has led to mounting international pressures on China to revalue its *renminbi*. (RMB).[2] And indeed, the much-anticipated revaluation of the RMB took place on 22 July 2005, when the RMB officially went off the US-dollar peg with a 2 per cent appreciation.

In 2004, China's total GDP reached 12.5 trillion yuan (US$1.6 trillion) — or more than twice the combined GDP of Indonesia, Malaysia, the Philippines, Singapore and Thailand. China's per-capita GDP in 2004, at around US$1,200, is about the same as that of Indonesia but higher than that of the Philippines. In nominal total GDP, China is the world's fifth largest economy. In terms of purchasing power parity (PPP), the Chinese economy today is already the world's second largest after the United States — one needs, of course, to be aware of the problem of overstating China's real GDP by the PPP measure[3] (Table 1.1).

Indeed, as a result of its rapid industrialization progress, China is fast becoming the world's foremost manufacturing base. In 2004, China produced 273 million tons of steel, 970 million tons of cement, 73 million sets of colour TV, 66 million air-conditioners, 30 million refrigerators, and 45 million PCs. By 2004, China also became the world's third largest automobile manufacturer, with a total output of 5.1 million units, after the United States and Japan.[4] In 2003, China surpassed the United States as the world's largest telephone market (263 million fixed lines plus 269 million mobile phones (290 million by mid-2004).[5] Also, by mid-2005, China's registered Internet users ("netizens") had surpassed 100 million to form the world's second largest "Web population" after the United States.[6]

When a huge economy like China is industrializing so rapidly, every statistic of its economic activities inevitably turns out to be a jumbo number due to the combined effect of scale and speed. But the economic

TABLE 1.1
East Asian Economies: Performance Indicators

	Population (Million) 2003	Per capita GDP (US$) 2003	PPP Per Capita GDP (US$) 2003	GDP (US$ Billion) 2003	GDP Growth Rate (%)							
					1960–1970	1970–1980	1980–1990	1990–2000	2001	2002	2003	2004
China	**1,292**	**1,120**	**5,220**	**1,445**	**5.2**	**5.5**	**10.3**	**10**	**7.5**	**8.3**	**9.3**	**9.5**
Japan	127	33,751	28,009	4,293	10.9	4.3	4.1	1.3	–0.4	–0.3	2.1	2.7
NIEs												
S.Korea	48	12,620	20,510	605	8.6	10.1	8.9	5.7	3	6.3	2.7	4.8
Taiwan	23	12,690	24,830	286	9.2	9.7	7.9	5.7	–2.2	3.6	3.2	5.9
Hong Kong	7	22,730	27,780	157	10	9.3	6.9	3.8	–0.2	2.3	3	7.6
ASEAN-5												
Indonesia	215	1,100	3,480	243	3.9	7.2	6.1	3.8	3.3	3.7	4.1	4.7
Malaysia	25	4,130	9,850	103	6.5	7.9	5.3	6.5	0.4	4.2	4.7	7.7
Philippines	81	937	4,180	79	5.1	6.0	1	3.3	3.2	4.6	4.3	6.2
Singapore	4	21,790	27,945	91	8.8	8.3	6.7	7.4	–2	2.2	0.8	8.4
Thailand	64	2,234	7,410	143	8.4	7.1	7.6	3.8	1.8	5	6.2	5.8

Sources: World Development Report 1995, 2000/2001, 2002, 2003, 2004; EIU Countrydata, EIU Dataservice; World Investment Report 2004, UNCTAD.

implications of such a large-scale production should not be lightly missed. When a country can produce 70 million units of colour TVs, the economies of scale effect it enjoys is simply tremendous. The average cost (AC) will clearly be very low while the marginal cost (MC) will be near to zero. That explains why many smaller developing countries find it very hard to compete with China.

Accordingly, the meteoric rise of China's economy has become a "hot" topic in international and regional media.[7] Many Asian economies are concerned about the potential displacement effect of China becoming the factory of the world. Others even point fingers at China for their own economic woes, including the accusation of China exporting deflation to them. Even the Japanese were worried by China's recent dynamic industrial expansion. The noted Japanese economist Kenichi Ohmae even used a sensational title "Asia's Next Crisis: 'Made in China'" to talk alarmingly about the rise of China.[8] Not surprisingly, many Asian economies, especially the smaller ASEAN countries, are watching the rise of China with apprehension. Many small and mid-size American manufacturers even saw China as "a company-killer and a job-killer", largely responsible for the disappearance of 2.7 million U.S. factory jobs since 2001.[9]

Whereas in the early 2000s, China was mostly referred to as a rising regional economic power operating a regional economic growth engine, by 2004, China's economy had reached a new turning point whereby its domestic production, consumption and foreign trade had, for the first time, started to exert a significant impact on the world economy. On account of its relentless industrial expansion, China has become the world's top consumer of a wide variety of natural resources and primary commodities from steel, aluminium, to oil and gas, and its rising demand for these products had driven up their world prices. For instance, the recent oil price hike was attributed to China's increased demand for oil as it has now become the world's second largest consumer of oil. For boom or for bust, the movement of China's economy has started to become a disruptive force for the global economy.[10]

Nothing is more indicative of China's growing financial and commercial clout than the rise of the RMB as a hot international financial issue for the world's large capital markets from London to New York, and from Tokyo to Hong Kong. In the business arena, an event of great symbolic significance was the purchase in December 2004 of the PC (personal computer) division of America's most venerable computer firm, IBM, by China's computer giant Lenovo. More recently, China's CNOOC's (China

National Offshore Oil Company) bid to acquire America's Unocal has stirred great controversies or even fears in the United States over the sudden rise of China's economic might.[11]

A crucial question may be posed: Can China's dynamic economic growth be sustained? To begin with, China's high economic growth of the past two decades as reflected in its official GDP statistics, though very impressive, is actually not exceptional in the historical context of many high-performance East Asian economies. As shown in Table 1.1, Japan had near double-digit rates of growth in the 1950s, 1960s and most of the 1970s. The four NIEs (newly industrialized economies) of South Korea, Taiwan, Hong Kong and Singapore had such high growth for more than three decades, the 1960s, the 1970s, and the 1980s, while several ASEAN economies also experienced similarly high growth performance in the 1980s.

China is a much larger country than its East Asian neighbours. China should in theory have much more internal dynamics to sustain an even longer period of high growth, as China has virtually a whole continent to develop for itself. Of course, it is not possible for any economy to repeat a near double-digit rate of growth year after year without getting overheated or running into physical and economic bottlenecks. But considering the historical pattern and structural conditions of China's past economic growth, we can easily be optimistic about its future growth potential, though at the same time we can also see many emerging constraints and obstacles ahead, particularly those related to the social aspects of China's economic growth (for example, increasing regional and income disparities) and the environmental costs of its growth (for example, serious problems of air pollution and water shortages).[12]

CHINA AND ASEAN IN THE DYNAMIC EAST ASIAN GROWTH PROCESS

Put China and the ASEAN-5 in the whole East Asia (EA) region, which is commonly defined as comprising Japan, China, the four Newly Industrialized Economies (NIEs) of South Korea, Taiwan, Hong Kong and Singapore, and the four Association of Southeast Asian Nations (ASEAN) of Indonesia, Malaysia, the Philippines, and Thailand — the original ASEAN members.[13] Situated on the western rim of the Pacific, many of these East Asian economies (EAEs) have displayed dynamic growth for a sustained period until 1997 when they were hit, in varying degrees, by the regional financial crisis. The World Bank in its well-known study referred to this high growth phenomenon as the "East Asian Miracle".[14]

Historically speaking, the EA growth process is marked by three waves. Japan was the first non-Western country to become industrialized. Its high growth dated back to the 1950s after it had achieved its rapid post-war recovery, and carried the growth momentum over to the 1960s and much of the 1970s. Japan's economic growth engine was initially based on the export of labour-intensive manufactured products; but it was soon forced by rising wages and increasing costs to shed its comparative advantage for labour-intensive manufacturing in favour of the four NIEs, which started their industrial take-off in the 1960s. These four NIEs, once dubbed "Asia's Four Little Dragons", were arguably the most dynamic economies in Asia, as they had sustained near double-digit rates of growth for three decades, from the early 1960s to the 1980s. The rise of the NIEs constituted the second wave of the region's growth and integration.

By the early 1980s, high costs and high wages had also caught up with these four NIEs, which had to restructure their economies towards more capital-intensive and higher value-added activities by passing their comparative advantage in labour-intensive products to the late-comers of China and the four ASEAN economies and thereby spreading economic growth to the latter. In this way, China and some ASEAN economies were able to register high growth through the 1980s and the 1990s. Many Japanese scholars like to depict this pattern of development in Asia as the "Flying Geese" model[15] (see Table 1.1).

During the past two decades, as the Chinese economy chalked up near double-digit rates of growth, many East Asian economies, due to a number of institutional and structural constraints, were losing growth dynamism. The rise of China therefore promises to usher in the third wave of growth and integration for the region, with even greater geo-political and geo-economic implications than the previous two waves because of China's vast size and diversity. At the very least, the rise of China will ensure that the EA region as a whole will not lose its economic dynamism.

As the EAEs keep on growing, they also increase their economic interaction with each other. Thus, an important feature of these EAEs is their growing economic inter-dependence. The EAEs, despite their inherent political, social and economic divergences, can actually integrate quite well as an informal and loosely constituted regional economic grouping. This is essentially the underlying meaning of the "flying geese" principle. To start with, Japan is the natural economic leader of the group and has in fact been the prime source of capital and technology for the other EAEs, first the NIEs followed by China and ASEAN. The resource-based ASEAN-4 complement well with the manufacturing-based NIEs while both are also complementary with the more developed Japanese economy. Then the huge potential of China, with its vast resource base and diverse needs, offers additional opportunities for all.

Accordingly, the EA region has already developed a fairly high level of intra-regional trade. As shown in Table 1.2, the EA region in 2003 absorbed 46 per cent of Japan's total exports, 45 per cent of China's total exports; 49 per cent of Korea's, 56 per cent of Taiwan's, 59 per cent of Hong Kong's, 58 per cent of Singapore's, and 57 per cent of the average of the ASEAN-4, though only 39 per cent of Japan's — still unusually high for Japan as a global trading power.

Table 1.2 also describes the process of EA's growing export dependence over the past two decades. It shows Japan's highly remarkable shift in export orientation over the years towards greater regional focus, with its export share to the EA region increasing from 22 per cent in 1980 to 46 per cent in 2003. The four NIEs have similarly made significant shifts in the same period by re-orientating their exports towards the EA region, mainly as a result of the opening up of China: Korea from 24 per cent to 49 per cent, Taiwan from 49 per cent (2000) to 56 per cent, Hong Kong from 52 per cent to 59 per cent, and Singapore from 40 per cent to 58 per cent. Likewise, the ASEAN-4 has also shown a slight reduction of export dependence on the EA region, from 51 per cent in 1980 to 57 per cent in 2003. China, on the other hand, has moved in the opposite direction by reducing its export dependence on the region from 53 per cent to 45 per cent as its exports are increasingly gearing more to the United States and the EU.

Apart from intra-regional trade, intra-regional FDI flows have also operated as a powerful integrating force for the EA region, especially since a great deal of regional FDI is trade-related in nature. The EAEs, as essentially open and outward-looking economies, are highly dependent on foreign trade and foreign investment for their economic growth. Both China and ASEAN have devised various incentive schemes to vie for FDI, which is generally treated not just as an additional source of capital supply but, more importantly, as a means of technology transfer and export market development.

In particular, China in recent years has become the most favoured destination of all developing economies for FDI. As can be seen from Table 1.3, the EA region, especially Hong Kong, Taiwan, Japan, Singapore

TABLE 2(a)
Origins and Destinations of East Asian Intra-Trade, 1997–2003

Origin of Regional Exports	Year	Total Exports (US$ Million)	Share of Regional Exports Destinated For (%)							
			Japan	China	Korea	Taiwan	Hong Kong	Singapore	ASEAN-4*	EA SUM
Japan	1980	130,441		3.9	4.1	–	3.7	3.0	7.0	21.7
	1988	264,856		3.6	5.8	5.4	4.4	3.1	4.9	27.2
	2000	479,249		6.3	6.4	7.5	5.7	4.3	9.5	40.2
	2003	471,817		12.2	7.4	6.6	6.3	3.1	9.2	45.5
China	1980	18,099	22.3		–	–	24.1	2.3	4.3	53.0
	1988	47,540	16.9		–	–	38.4	3.1	2.8	61.2
	2000	249,203	16.7		4.5	2.0	17.9	2.3	3.7	48.1
	2003	437,899	13.6		4.6	2.1	17.4	2.0	4.0	44.7
Korea	1980	17,505	17.4	–		–	–	1.5	4.6	23.5
	1988	60,696	19.8	–		1.6	5.9	2.2	2.8	32.3
	2000	172,268	11.9	10.7		4.7	6.2	3.3	7.2	45.2
	2003	193,817	8.9	18.1		3.6	7.6	2.4	6.5	48.7
Taiwan	1980	–								–
	1988	60,667		3.7						–
	2000	148,321	11.2	16.9	2.6		21.1	3.7	7.4	48.8
	2003	144,174	8.3	14.9	3.2		19.7	3.5	6.6	55.9

TABLE 2(b)
Origins and Destinations of East Asian Intra-Trade, 1997–2003

Origin of Regional Exports	Year	Total Exports (US$ Million)	Share of Regional Exports Destinated For (%)							
			Japan	China	Korea	Taiwan	Hong Kong	Singapore	ASEAN-4*	EA SUM
Hong Kong	1980	19,730	6.1	34.9	1.5	2.5		2.6	0.5	51.6
	1988	63,163	5.2	34.4	1.0	2.5		2.3	0.3	48.8
	2000	201,860	5.5	34.6	1.9	2.5		2.3	0.5	50.6
	2003	95,477	5.4	42.7	2.0	2.4		2.1	0.4	58.6
Singapore	1980	19,375	8.1	1.6	1.5	–	7.7		20.8	39.7
	1988	39,306	8.6	3.0	2.0	2.8	6.2		20.3	42.9
	2000	137,804	7.5	3.9	3.6	6.0	7.9		24.9	56.3
	2003	144,182	6.7	7.0	4.2	4.8	10.0		22.3	57.7
ASEAN-4	1980	47,100	34.5	1.1	1.7	–	1.9	11.8		51.0
	1988	80,080	19.5	2.2	2.8	2.0	2.9	9.0		38.4
	2000	269,099	16.0	3.4	3.7	4.2	4.2	12.6		44.0
	2003	277,975	15.1	6.6	3.7	4.0	5.5	10.9		56.6

Source: Direction of Trade Statistics Yearbook 2004, IMF.
   Taiwan's data is obtained from Bureau of Foreign Trade's Website.
* ASEAN–4 denotes Indonesia, Malaysia, the Philippines and Thailand.

TABLE 1.3
Foreign Direct Investment in China (US$ Million)

	1992		1997		1998		1999		2000		2001		2002		2003	
	Acutual sum of capital	%	Acutual sum of capital	%	Acutual sum of capital	%	Acutual sum of capital	%	Acutual sum of capital	%	Acutual sum of capital	%	Acutual sum of capital	%	Acutual sum of capital	%
Total	11,292	100	45,257	100	45,463	100	40,319	100	40,715	100	45,984	100	51,585	100	51,493	100
Asia Pacific	9,900	88	30,389	84	26,626	59	23,210	57	22,202	55	26,197	57	28,744	56	31,037	60
HK	7,706	68	20,632	63	18,508	41	16,363	41	15,500	38	16,717	36	17,861	35	18,117	35
Taiwan	1,053	9.3	3,289	11	2,915	6.4	2,599	6.4	2,296	5.6	2,980	6.5	3,971	7.7	3,377	6.6
Japan	748	6.6	4,326	4.9	3,400	7.5	2,973	7.3	2,916	7.2	4,348	9.5	4,191	8.1	5,054	9.8
South Korea	120	1.1	2,142	1.4	1,803	4	1,275	3.1	1,490	3.7	2,152	4.7	2,721	5.3	4,489	8.7
ASEAN	271.6	2.4	3,418	3.6	4,197	9.2	3,274	8.2	2,837	7	2,970	6.5	3,201	6.2	2,853	5.5
Indonesia	20.2	0.2	80	0.2	69	0.2	129	0.3	147	0.4	160	0.3	122	0.2	150	0.3
Malaysia	24.7	0.2	382	0.3	340	0.7	238	0.6	203	0.5	263	0.6	368	0.7	251	0.5
Philippines	16.6	0.2	156	0.4	179	0.3	117	0.3	111	0.3	209	0.5	186	0.4	220	0.4
Singapore	125.9	1.1	2,606	1.8	3,404	7.5	2,642	6.6	2,172	5.3	2,144	4.7	2,337	4.5	2,058	4
Thailand	84.3	0.8	194	0.8	205	0.5	148	0.4	204	0.5	194	0.4	188	0.4	174	0.3
USA	519	4.6	3,239	7.4	3,898	8.6	4,216	11	4,384	11	4,433	9.6	5,424	11	4,199	8.2
Others	873	7.7	8,192	8.5	10,729	24	9,619	24	10,218	25	12,062	26	19,642	38	13,404	26

Sources: Statistical Yearbook of China (various issues); China Monthly Statistics.

and South Korea, accounted for an overwhelming share of FDI inflow to China. Such regional predominance has been declining in recent years, as China has made efforts to attract more technology-intensive FDI from North America and the EU. By 2001, the East Asian share of FDI in China declined to 57 per cent, down from 88 per cent in 1992. Suffice it to say that the rise of China has completely altered the FDI landscape of East Asia.

CHINA'S IMPACT ON ASEAN'S GROWTH AND INTEGRATION

It is thus sufficiently clear that China's economic growth fits in quite well with the overall EA growth patterns. Since the EA region absorbs about 50 per cent of China's exports and supplies three-quarters of China's FDI, it is not hard to see that China's rapidly growing economy since 1978 has impacted significantly on many EAEs to each other's advantage. On the one hand, China has been able to harness the region's vast trade and investment opportunities to facilitate its own economic growth. At the same time, China's economic growth and increasing integration with the region also provide new opportunities to enhance the region's overall growth potential and new impetus for regionalism.

Pressures on China's Relations with ASEAN

However, the actual impact of the fast-growing Chinese economy on the EAEs is quite uneven. China's dynamic economic growth has produced both positive and negative effects for the individual EAEs in the region. By and large, Japan and the four NIEs have been able to benefit from China's open-door policy by exporting more high-tech products, and by investing in China, as shown in Table 1.3.

However, the economies of China and ASEAN (minus Singapore) at their present stages of development tend to be more competitive than complementary with each other. In many ways, China's dynamic economic growth has exerted strong competitive pressures on the ASEAN economies, which are vying for FDI with China as well as competing head-on with China's manufactured exports in the developed country markets.[16]

The structure and pattern of China's economic relations with ASEAN have been shaped by many complicated factors. Traditionally, China's relations with "Southeast Asia", referred to as "Nanyang" (or literally "south sea") by the Chinese, have been extensive and deep-rooted on account of history, geography and migration. After the communist revolution in 1949, their relations assumed new dimensions, with complex ideological and political elements coming into play, and this gave rise to a period of "Cold War relations". With the advent of *détente* in the early 1970s, individual Southeast Asian states started to normalize their relations with China.[17]

Initially, China's success in economic reform and development had produced very little impact on the ASEAN countries to its south. Sino-ASEAN trade was very small — in fact, only a small fraction of each other's total trade and with a large part being centred in Singapore (Figure 1.2). Even by the early 1990s, when massive FDI began to flow into China, there was no evidence that China had "sucked" in a lot of capital from the ethnic Chinese in Southeast Asia.[18]

Furthermore, UNCTAD has recently conducted a study, using econometric analysis, to assess if China's growth has adversely affected inflow to other East Asian economies. The findings suggest that once other determinants of FDI are taken into account, China has produced no significant effect on FDI inflows to other East Asian economies. It may be noted that most FDI inflows in the region do not compete with each other as they are the outcome of the rational decisions of individual multinationals. Even for potentially competitive (export-oriented) FDI, China's FDI has actually been encouraging the inflow of FDI to other ASEAN countries as a complement to China's role within the regional production networks. Thus, China "appears to be crowding in rather than crowding out FDI in the region".[19]

Still, many ASEAN economies are watching the recent economic rise of China with apprehension, particularly in the aftermath of the Asian financial crisis. While many ASEAN countries were plagued by persistent economic crises and domestic political instability, China in recent years has been intent on its single-minded pursuit of economic modernization. This has resulted in the further narrowing of development gaps between ASEAN and China. In fact, ASEAN risks being left behind by China's relentless economic growth.

China's Bold FTA Initiative

Mindful of ASEAN's worries over the possible disruptive effects of its rapid economic growth, China in recent years has been under mounting pressures to dispel the "China threat" fears by improving its overall relations with its ASEAN neigbhours. During the 1997 Asian financial crisis, Beijing's steadfast refusal to devalue its *renminbi* was much

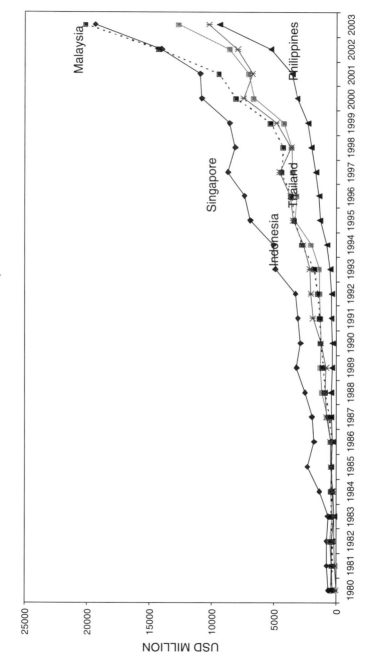

FIGURE 1.2
China's Trade with ASEAN-5, 1980–2003

Sources: United Nations, *Statistical Yearbook for Asia and the Pacific*, 1991 and 2000; *China Statistical Yearbook* (various issues).

appreciated by ASEAN as such a move would have aggravated the region's economic crisis. But the single most important step ever undertaken by China in recent years to upgrade its long-term political and economic relations with the ASEAN region is China's bold FTA scheme.

At the ASEAN-China Summit in November 2001, former Chinese Premier Zhu Rongji proposed the creation of a free trade area between China and ASEAN within ten years. On 4 November 2002, China and the ASEAN countries signed a framework agreement in Cambodia to establish an FTA by 2010.[20] The formation of the China-ASEAN FTA signifies the creation of an economic region of 1.7 billion consumers with a combined GDP of US$2 trillion. It offers an effective means for smaller ASEAN states to overcome its disadvantage of smallness by pooling resources and combining markets. This will in time lead to greater economic integration between China and ASEAN, clearly a win-win situation for both sides.[21] The perceived China's economic threat will then turn into an opportunity for ASEAN.

In the short run, however, ASEAN has to deal with the initial risks of a potential trade diversion effect and related structural adjustment.[22] In general, the FTA scheme will give rise to an uneven distribution of costs and benefit different industries, different sectors, and even different ASEAN countries. After the initial process of adjustment, individual ASEAN economies will then develop their own niches in their economic relations with China.

On 29 November 2004 China and ASEAN formally concluded in Vientiane, Laos, the Agreement on Trade in Goods of the Framework Agreement on Comprehensive Economic Cooperation between the two sides for tariff liberalization under the China-ASEAN Free Trade Area, which would take effect on 1 July 2005. Tariff liberalization would be under a "normal track" and a "sensitive track". Duties on many commodity items under the normal track would be eliminated by 2010.[23]

With China continuing its dynamic economic growth, opportunities will certainly arise for the ASEAN countries to exploit China's growing market. Apart from its primary commodities, ASEAN's resource-based products will be in great demand in China. The recent years have witnessed an upsurge of ASEAN's exports of natural resource products to China to satisfy the voracious demands of its manufacturing sector. China is such a vast and disparate market that East China, South China and Southwest China can individually offer different opportunities to different ASEAN producers. Beyond merchandise trade, FTA also promotes trade in services, including tourism. China may generally have strong comparative advantage in manufacturing because it enjoys the economies of scale, which, however, may not apply to many service activities. In fact, a lot of China's service activities, on account of their socialist legacies, are known to be more backward than those in ASEAN.[24]

As it has happened in recent years, many EAEs have started to experience the positive spillovers of China's economic growth. Apart from the surge in Chinese tourists to other Asian countries, China's imports from Japan, Korea, Taiwan, Singapore, Indonesia, Malaysia, the Philippines, Thailand, India and Australia had for the past two years exceeded its exports to these economies, thereby incurring trade deficits with them, which were offset by China's trade surplus with the United States and the European Union (Figure 1.3). This means that these EA economies are tapping China's vast domestic markets and their growing demand for consumer goods, capital equipment and raw materials. Furthermore, China in recent years has been the major source of export growth of many EA economies. In 2002, China accounted for 59 per cent of Malaysia's export growth in 2002, 57 per cent of Singapore's, 85 per cent of Taiwan's and 73 per cent of Japan's. For 2003, China accounted for 13 per cent of EU's export growth, 22 per cent of the United States', 27 per cent of Australia, 385 per cent of the Philippines' (because its negative trade growth in the previous year), though a lower proportion for Singapore, Hong Kong and Japan (Figure 1.4). Not surprisingly, by the end of 2004, Sino-ASEAN two-way trade had surpassed US$100 billion, with ASEAN becoming China's fifth largest trade partner.[25]

In the years to come, as the China-ASEAN FTA scheme is also gradually phased in, multinationals in the region will gradually restructure their supply chains and rationalize their production networks by taking China and ASEAN together as a single market. This will eventually lead to a reshuffle of regional production networks and hence a redistribution of the regional FDI flows. The new regional production patterns will be based on a bigger and more diverse market. In short, both trade and FDI in the region should continue to grow under the impact of the China-ASEAN FTA. And this will certainly be win-win outcome for both sides.

New Impetus for East Asian Economic Integration

Besides creating a new source of economic growth for the region, China is also seen as a new force for revitalizing the region's economic integration process. China's FTA with ASEAN had exerted tremendous pressures on Japan and Korea to follow suit, prompting similar responses from them.

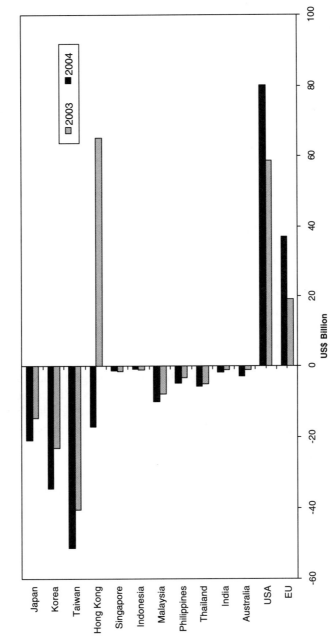

FIGURE 1.3
China's Trade Balance with Selected Countries

Source: China Monthly Customs Statistics; Ministry of Commerce website, www.mofcom.gov.cn.

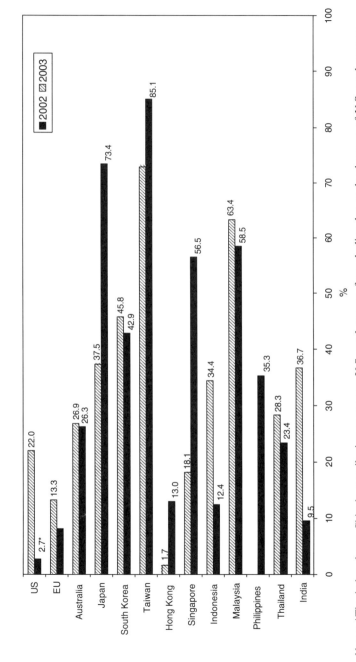

FIGURE 1.4
China's Contribution to the Growth of Selected Countries' Exports

Notes: *The index shows China's contribution to prevent U.S. total exports from decline due to the decrease of U.S. total exports.
Sources: WTO trade statistics 2003, 2002, 2001; Chinese Ministry of Commerce, http://www.mofcom.gov.cn.

Indeed, in the wake of China-ASEAN FTA, Japan had to take action by signing a Framework for Comprehensive Economic Partnership with ASEAN, which is not an FTA but it can comprise Japan's bilateral FTA arrangements with individual ASEAN member countries.

In June 2003, China signed the Closer Economic Partnership Arrangement (CEPA) with Hong Kong (and subsequently with Macau). CEPA is obviously aimed at the eventual integration of these Greater China economies after the inclusion of Taiwan in future.[26] Prior to this, China had agreed to initiate a joint study with Japan and Korea on possible Northeast Asian economic cooperation. In October 2003, Premier Wen Jiabao attended the Ninth ASEAN Summit in Bali, where he signed with the heads of government from Japan and Korea the Joint Declaration on the Promotion of Tripartite Cooperation among these three Northeast Asian countries. This tripartite cooperation is not just for the promotion of economic cooperation and peace dialogue in Northeast Asia, but also aimed at strengthening the process of ASEAN economic integration with other EAEs, that is, a more concrete way of accelerating the realization of the greater East Asian economic integration through the ASEAN+3 process.

Of equal importance, Premier Wen at the summit also signed the Treaty of Amity and Cooperation (TAC) with ASEAN in order to express China's goals of establishing a strategic partnership with ASEAN for "peace and prosperity".[27] China is the first country to accede to ASEAN's TAC, which is a distinctive regional code of conduct governing state-to-state relations within ASEAN. The most important principle in the TAC is the provision that requires all parties involved to renounce the use of force in the settlement of any dispute. In concluding this historic treaty, China has signalled to the ASEAN countries its acceptance of ASEAN's norms and values, and its willingness to play by the rules. In other words, "China wants to be seen as a responsible member of the international community".[28] Since India also followed China by concluding a similar TAC with ASEAN, Japan was once again under tremendous pressures to follow suit.

Viewed in a larger context, China's FTA initiative with ASEAN not only marks the most important first step in the "ASEAN+3" scheme, but in fact also plays a crucial catalytic role in galvanizing what may be called the New Age economic integration process for the East Asian region as a whole. As long as China's economy could sustain its dynamic growth, its regional integration initiatives would carry weight and keep the momentum going. In short, the spate of new cooperation initiatives in recent years has shown that such an economic integration scheme for East Asia is no longer an abstract notion, but something that is achievable once major players like China and Japan are serious about it.

SOME BROADER GEO-POLITICAL IMPLICATIONS

As a rising regional political and economic power, China is destined to play an important role in the growth and development of the ASEAN region. However, there is still a great deal of uncertainty as to: (1) How will China play out its geo-political role in the region? (2) What kind of new security architecture will the region eventually develop? and (3) Will China push for a greater leadership role in the region in order to counter Western (American) influences?

It is commonly assumed that as China grows stronger economically, it will also become politically more assertive in its dealings with neighbouring countries. On the other hand, if China were able to manage its rise as a gradual process of its "peaceful ascendancy" (*heping jueqi*), the total spillover effect on the region would be much less disruptive.[29] On balance, ASEAN should have no problem adjusting to the rise of China particularly when China's economy is operating as another engine of economic growth. China, on its part, is likely to continue its warm relations with ASEAN so long as the latter subscribes to China's core principles like the One-China principle over the Taiwan issue.

Meanwhile, both China and ASEAN still need to step up the process of consensus building and continuing dialogues. On 24 April 2005, Chinese President Hu Jintao and Indonesian President Susilo Bambang Yudhoyono signed a joint declaration for a "strategic partnership" to signal their intention to further improve their relations.[30] On 28 July 2005, the Indonesian President returned a state visit to China and oversaw the signing of five agreements ranging from defence cooperation to Chinese language teaching and a loan from China of US$100 million.[31] To strengthen its relations with the Philippines, China on 28 April 2005 extended loans and investments amounting to US$1.6 billion to the Philippines during a state visit by President Hu Jintao to Manila.[32] More recently, Malaysian Prime Minister Abdullah Ahmad Badawi criticized the U.S.-Japan view of China as a potential military threat and said that China had no hegemonic ambitions.[33]

Thailand's overall relations with China have been among the warmest in ASEAN, on both political and economic fronts. Besides their burgeoning economic relations in terms of trade and FDI, Thailand is the first ASEAN country to sign the "early harvest" agreement with China for zero tariff in fruits and some agricultural products. China has also supported many of Thailand's regional initiatives such as GMS (Greater Mekong Sub-region), ASEAN+1 and ASEAN+3. Their good relations have been extended to the cultural area, with Thai Princess Maha Chakri Sirindhorn (who had made seven visits to China) recently sponsoring a "Two Countries, One Family" concert in Beijing.[34]

Speaking at a forum in Tokyo on 24 May 2005, Singapore's Prime Minister Lee Hsien Loong also warned that it would be "futile to resist China's growing economic clout".[35] Singapore believes that it can continue to play a pivotal role in the growing China-ASEAN economic relations as Singapore accounts for a significant proportion of China-ASEAN trade and their two-way FDI flows. First, Singapore's political relations with China have matured and are ready to move forward, thereby providing potentially useful guideposts for some ASEAN countries over their burgeoning relations with China. Second, Singapore can be China's convenient gateway to ASEAN, providing China with useful Southeast Asian perspectives and helping China to better understand ASEAN.

In the 1980s, on account of the dynamic growth of the EA economies, it was common for commentators to talk about rise of the Pacific Century. But the subsequent economic stagnation of Japan coupled with the increasing economic and technological predominance of the United States had rendered such a notion much less credible, or even unrealistic. The rise of China together with Japan's economic recovery, rekindles new hopes of making the twenty-first century the Pacific Century. To realize this, China will have to sustain its economic growth momentum and develop even closer economic symbiosis with its neighbouring economies so that the EA region as a whole can benefit from China's economic rise. Continuing economic growth and integration is essentially what all these EA economies aim to achieve in the long run, despite their great political and social divergences.

Notes

* The author is grateful to Dr. Liang Ruobing and Dr. Zhang Yang for assistance in the preparation of tables and charts.
[1] "Investors Keep Eyes Peeled on Dragon", *Beijing Review* 48, no. 22 (June 2005).
[2] See Lu Ding, "Why and How China Maintains RMB's Stability", *EAI*

Background Brief no. 178, 16 January 2004. For China's foreign reserves, see *Mingpao* (Hong Kong, 15 July 2005).

3   *World Bank, World Development Report 2004/2005* (New York: Oxford University Press).

4   National Bureau of Statistics, "Statistical Communiqué of the People's Republic of China on National Economic and Social development in 2004" (in Chinese), 28 February 2005.

5   "China Now Second Most Wired Nation on the Globe", *China Daily*, 21 July 2004.

6   "China's Internet Users Top 100 Million", *China Daily*, 29 June 2005.

7   Recently at the World Economic Forum in Davos, "everything is China, China, China", according to one observer. ("The Talk of the Town at Davos: China", *International Herald Tribune*, 26 January 2004. China's emergence as the world's manufacturing powerhouse after two decades of dynamic growth has invited prominent worldwide attention. The international media have recently portrayed China's economic resurgence as an economic threat. David Roche, a famous Wall Street economist, commented on China being a source of current global recession with its mass production of a wide range of low-priced manufactured products for the world market. In early 2003, Japan's *Nikkei Weekly* reported about China setting pace in markets for commodities around the world. The Chinese media and academia have since come out to defend China's position.

8   "Asia's Next Crisis: 'Made in China' ", *The Straits Times*, Singapore, 2 August 2001.

9   Charles Stein, "The Rise of China Inc", *Boston Globe*, 19 August 2003.

10   For further discussion, see John Wong, "China's Economy in 2004: Stability Takes Precedence over Growth", *EAI Background Brief* no. 222, 10 January 2005.

11   See Sarah Schafter and Stephen Glain: "China Buys American", *Newsweek International*, 3 July 2005; and David Francis, "China, the Behemoth? Not so Fast", *Christian Science Monitor*, 20 June 2005.

12   For a more detailed discussion of these issues and problems, see John Wong, "Sustaining China's High Economic Growth: Challenges and Risks for the New Leadership", *Cross-Strait and International Affairs Quarterly* (Taiwan) 1, no. 2 (2004). Also, "China's Growing Pains", *Economist*, London, 21–27 August 2004.

13   Singapore is historically and geographically an integral part of Southeast

Asia, and politically a member of ASEAN. However, economically and socially, Singapore is more akin to the other East Asian NIEs, and hence commonly labelled as one of the four East Asian NIEs.

[14] *The East Asian Miracle* (New York: Oxford University Press, 1994).

[15] The "flying geese" concept of development was coined by a Japanese economist, Kaname Akamatzu. ("A Historical Pattern of Economic Growth in Developing Countries", *Developing Economies*, no. 1 (March/August, 1962).

[16] For further discussion of this topic, see Prakash Loungani, "Comrades or Competitors? Trade Links between China and Other East Asian Economies", *Finance & Development* (June 2000).

[17] For a more detailed discussion, see John Wong, *The Political Economy of China's Changing Relations with Southeast Asia* (London: Macmillan Press, 1984).

[18] See John Wong, *Southeast Asian Ethnic Chinese Investing In China* (EAI Working Paper no. 15, 23 October 1998).

[19] "China is not Crowding out FDI from the Rest of East Asia, Experts Say", *Information Note* (Press Information 2005), UNCTAD/PRESS/IN/2005/007, 7 March 2005).

[20] The framework agreement signed by the eleven nation states sets out a road map for trade liberalization in goods and services for most countries by 2010 and for the less developed ASEAN nations (namely Cambodia, Laos, Myanmar and Vietnam) by 2015.

[21] For further discussion of this topic, see John Wong and Sarah Chan, "China-ASEAN Free Trade Agreement: Shaping Future Economic Relations", *Asian Survey* XLIII, no. 3 (May/June 2003).

[22] Trade diversion occurs when members of a free trade grouping trade more among themselves than with other non-member countries, due to a lowering of tariffs or non-tariff barriers within the FTA. Structural adjustments occur because when intra-regional barriers are dismantled, industries will expand in some countries and contract in others as industries relocate in response to differences in factor endowments. The costs of adjustment resulting from such relocation of economic activity can be asymmetrical since some economies will incur higher costs in the short run than others.

[23] "ASEAN Tariff-cut Steps towards Free Trade", *China Daily*, 30 November 2004.

[24] See John Wong and Ruobing Liang, "China's Service Industry (II): Gearing Up for WTO Challenges", *EAI Background Brief* no. 163, Singapore, 28 July 2003.

[25] "ASEAN-China Trade Better than Expected", *China Daily*, 4 November 2004.

[26] See John Wong and Sarah Chan, "China's Closer Economic Partnership Arrangement (CEPA) with Hong Kong: A Gift from Beijing?" *EAI Background Brief* no. 177, 12 December 2003.

[27] "ASEAN, China Forge Strategic Partnership", <www.chinaview.cn> 2003-10-08:50:33.

[28] See Isagani de Castro, "China Snuggles Up to Southeast Asia", <http://www.atimes.com>.

[29] Yoichi Funabashi, "China is preparing a 'peaceful ascendancy' ", *International Herald Tribune*, 30 December 2003. See also, Bruce Klingner, " 'Peace Rising' seeks to allay 'China threat' ", <www.atimes.com>.

[30] "China and Indonesia Boost Ties", *Asian Wall Street Journal*, 26 April 2005.

[31] "China, Indonesia Sign Five Deals to Deepen Ties", *China Daily*, 29 July 2005.

[32] "Philippines, China sign US$1.62 b deals", *China Daily*, 28 April 2005.

[33] "Badawi Raps U.S.-Japan View of China as Threat", *China Daily*, 2 June 2005.

[34] "Sino-Thai Ties Enhanced", *China Daily*, 1 July 2005.

[35] "Lee: Futile to Resist China's Growing Clout", *China Daily*, 25 May 2005.

2

The Emergence of China's Economic Power and Its Implications for Chinese Businesses in Southeast Asia

Sarasin Viraphol

THE "BIG PICTURE": ENLARGEMENT OF THE CHINESE STAKES

Beijing actively pursues a national strategy which identifies economic development as a top priority. This so-called "economic first" (*jingji jianshe wei zhongxin* 经济建设为中心) approach[1] has important bearings on world trade, investment, finance, and energy and primary materials procurement. China's mercurial rise as a leading global trading nation and manufacturing base creates reverberations on such issues as cost and profit margin, availability and scarcity of traded goods, free and fair trade, and intellectual property rights violation and protection, not to mention systemic shifts in the course of international trade and investment within the contexts of the emergence of Asia and the prospect of North-South cooperation. While China has succeeded with the expansion of international trade, its success has intensified protectionist practices by the industrial nations. The displacement of industries and businesses stokes anti-globalization polemics, and generates negative political responses in the United States. Notwithstanding the call for increased international trade liberalization through bilateral (FTA) as well multilateral (WTO) channels, advanced countries resort to anti-dumping and other technical measures — safety and quality standards of imports including agro-food products — to try to rein in the Chinese charge. As China comes to be regarded as the world's "factory", it acquires the dubious honour of being targetted for unfair trade practices, and for intellectual property infringement. Nevertheless, seen as a huge market of more than 1.4 billion potential customers, China invariably receives the lion's share of foreign investment (FDI) to the developing countries — US$60 billion — annually. At the same time, the recent series of high-profile Chinese purchases of foreign commercial enterprises has conjured images of China as a giant vacuum cleaner sucking up everything in its path. For its economic development requirements, China's "hunger" for primary and strategic commodities including energy, coal, metals (steel), and grains (wheat, rice, soybean, corn) impacts on global production, pricing and logistics.[2] Complementing this development, Chinese publicly-listed and partially government-owned corporations are expanding aggressively overseas in keeping with Beijing's "going-out" (*zouchuqu* 走出去) guideline for corporate investment overseas. Ongoing acquisitions of major international firms in the energy, IT and manufacturing sectors by China's own new breed of multinationals are reminiscent of Japan's corporate "shopping" frenzy during the 1980s. The pace of China's rapid economic advances is also discernable in the global financial realm. Thanks to mounting trade surpluses, China is expected to amass some US$800 billion in foreign reserves by the end of 2005, which would effectively replace Japan as the world's largest foreign reserve holder. The Chinese currency, the *renminbi,* is facing mounting revaluation pressure by the West, with the Chinese side countering that Beijing would decide on the issue in its own time, and that no sustainable global trading balance is possible with the unilateral adjustment of the *renminbi's* worth. Finally, the ideological manifestation of the "economic first" policy, as seen in the official adoption of the alternative "socialist market" model to signify the inclusion of market forces in the national command economy, is a testimony of the power of the state-sanctioned economic change on China's societal and ideological directions.

Beijing's economic achievement has further lent weight to its efforts aimed at shaping the conduct of inter-state relations. The essence of China's foreign policy, as articulated on more than one occasion by the top Chinese leadership, appears benign yet proactive and pragmatic. First, Beijing is to pursue South-South as well North-South cooperation. Second, Beijing is for fostering mutually beneficial interests, focusing on commonality and management of differences. Third, Beijing advocates the "good neighbourliness" (*mu lin* 睦邻) approach to underline relationships with neighbouring states which are based on mutual respect and benefit. Pertaining to Southeast Asia, one manifestation of such "goodwill" is China's tax exemption for imports from the developing countries with common borders. Another important "gesture" is the Chinese-proposed free trade agreement with the ten Southeast Asian states of ASEAN which includes an "early harvest" provision for the expeditious elimination of tariffs on fruits and vegetables.[3]

EVOLUTION OF THE "ECONOMIC FIRST" STRATEGY: A SOUTHEAST ASIAN INPUT

The success of the "economic first" strategy follows the implementation of various pragmatic measures undertaken since Deng Xiaoping announced his landmark "reform and opening" policy in 1978. One involves the participation by entrepreneurs of Chinese origin from outside of the Chinese mainland, primarily those from Hong Kong/Macao, Taiwan and Southeast Asia, who generated over seventy per cent of China's external trade and investment during the first twenty years. This formative period saw the set up of overseas Chinese-financed small and medium enterprises particularly in the Pearl River Delta in Guangdong. With the improvement of cross-strait relations in the early 1990s, Taiwanese businessmen stepped up their presence in China to cater to the exploding demands for basic consumer products, while filling China's rising demands for managerial skills and meeting its new export-oriented strategy.

From the start overseas Chinese businessmen had enthusiastically pursued trade and investment opportunities in China in short-term, one-off deals, mainly in small-scale, value-added and labour-intensive manufacturing — such as garment — in places with ancestral and clan links. Thailand's Charoen Pokphand (CP) group was perhaps an exception to the rule when the company set up the first international joint venture in agri-business in the newly-established special economic zone of Shenzhen in 1979. This Thai multinational subsequently proved itself to be a major driving force behind China's agricultural reform. Beijing's reiteration of its commitment to economic liberalization as symbolized by the Deng Xiaoping's "southern visit" in 1992 rekindled the hopes of Southeast Asian overseas Chinese investors, who joined the growing ranks of their Taiwanese and Hong Kong counterparts in venturing beyond the Pearl River Delta to the Northeast, and to the new Pudong development zone in Shanghai as well as the Yangtze River Delta. Singapore since the 1980s had effectively paved the way in the development of industrial parks in China with its investment in the Suzhou Industrial Park project. Malaysian, Singaporean, Indonesian and

Thai entrepreneurs started investing in hotel and residential projects (notably the Shangri-la group of Malaysian tycoon Robert Kwok). The post-Cold War optimism saw the diversification of Southeast Asian investments into agriculture and aquaculture, telecommunication, and property development (port facilities, commercial complexes), and manufacturing (food processing, sugar refining, wood processing, textile construction materials). The flow of Southeast Asian capital into China suffered a serious but short-termed disruption in the wake of the Asian financial meltdown in 1997.

The start of the twenty-first century turned out to favour China's fortunes in more than one way. The heady technological advances spurred by the IT revolution had boosted global expectations in the inevitability — and the challenge — of globalization, and, following its entry into WTO in 2000, China was capturing the West's attention as humanity's biggest marketplace for trade and investment. Emerging from the shadows of the 1997 crisis, Southeast Asian firms cannot but note the urgency in answering to China's "global engagement" strategy. More than anything else, the surge in China's newly emergent middle class ranks of more than one hundred million concentrated in the country's Beijing-Hebei, Shanghai/Lower Yangtze, and Canton/Pearl River Delta areas represents a ready market for various consumer manufactures and services, while Beijing's grand blueprints for the development of China's western region are a renewed testimony of a China filled with trade and investment opportunities. In increasing numbers, Southeast Asian enterprises are joining others from around the world seeking a foothold in large-scale retailing and distribution (modern trade), agro-foods, food service (restaurant business), finance and banking, automotive, independent power generation and provision, energy and minerals, tourism, and international education.

The ongoing effort to realize the China-ASEAN FTA by 2010 is a major impetus for economic integration by both sides. The size of the Chinese-ASEAN trade has quadrupled in a decade as Southeast Asia becomes an important source for commodities such as rubber, timber, palm oil, minerals and energy for China's expansive manufacturing. To date, ASEAN-China trade has topped US$100 billion, with China as ASEAN's fourth largest trading partner and ASEAN as China's fifth largest.[4] Trade-related activities, notably tourism, have also become significant, as Southeast Asia and China are now important tourism destinations for millions of tourists from both ends, boosted by officially-sanctioned incentives such as long holidays in an effort to encourage Chinese to embrace a more consumption-based lifestyle.

Physically adjacent to China's western region is the Greater Mekong Sub-region (GMS) — comprising the Mekong riparian states of China (Yunnan), Myanmar, Thailand, Laos, Cambodia and Vietnam — which is currently seen as providing for increased connectivity between China and Southeast Asia. Efforts are under way among the GMS states to forge cooperation in agriculture, industry, communications and transportation, energy, health, and human resource development. Apart from public sector inputs, the GMS private sector is expected to take an increasingly proactive role. This should substantially enhance ASEAN's modest investment in China of US$30 billion, and China's miniscule investment in ASEAN of US$500 million. Meanwhile potential new opportunities for investment respective to China and ASEAN encompass service trade, edu-business (international language and management schools), entertainment and wellness business, "creative" tourism (eco-tourism, cultural tourism), "creative" business (fashion, industrial design, software), outsourcing (manufacturing), food and drinks processing, distribution, logistics and supply chain management, medical services (dentistry, plastic surgery, nursing care) and independent power provision. With aggregated and complementary markets of close to two billion people, China and ASEAN face a common challenge of an increasingly borderless and seamless global economy in the management of their economic relations.

IMPLICATIONS FOR SOUTHEAST ASIAN CHINESE BUSINESSES

Notwithstanding the positive acknowledgement of China's economic influence and the urgency to tap the China market, Southeast Asian entrepreneurs are at the same time concerned about "hollowing out" effects from losses of competitiveness for market share. Nevertheless, most share a sense of optimism for the long term that the globalization process, despite its unrelenting competitiveness, will also create expanded "space" for trade and investment.[5]

Historically, the Chinese official dealings with Southeast Asia had taken the form of political and cultural ties which were collectively assumed as tributary relations. The states of Southeast Asia maintained their normal relations with Imperial China under tributary rituals designed not merely to acknowledge the primacy of the Chinese rule, but also to symbolize China's "magnanimity" towards lesser states within the "Sinic world order". The regulated system of relationships was also meant to underpin the self-sufficiency nature of the Chinese state, and hence, the official disdain regarding commercial pursuits. One of the most illustrative episodes in the Chinese historical annals which reflects such an official stance is the famous voyages by Grand Eunuch Zheng He (郑和) of the Ming court some 600 years ago. His maritime visits to Southeast Asia and the Indian Ocean are cast as the Chinese imperial court's "indiscriminate" treatment (*yi shi tong ren* 一视同仁) of neighbouring states in all spheres including commerce. It is also supposed to demonstrate the time-honoured rationale that imperial China had no real need for material exchange with the outside world, but was in a position to give rather than take from others (*hou wang bo lai* 厚往薄来). Nevertheless, through the ensuing centuries, and in spite of official Chinese sanction against overseas commercial activities, regular maritime commerce between China and Southeast Asian conducted by private Chinese merchants ensured the continued development of close bilateral relations as well as the subsequent large-scale migrations of overseas Chinese to Southeast Asia.

In the contemporary periods, the preoccupation of China and most Southeast Asian states with their respective internal situations, along with the external factors as conditioned by Western colonialism and the Cold War, was distracting to closer economic ties. In the absence of political ties, whatever commerce conducted was by the overseas Chinese businessmen working within relatively confined perimeters.

ASEAN is a central piece in China's "win-win" (*gong ying* 共赢) strategy, given its traditional amicable contacts, its geographical proximity and strategic location, as well as its resources and market. In this "soft approach", one cannot overlook the role of Southeast Asian businessmen of Chinese origin (*huaren* 华人), given their resources and resourcefulness as well as ethnicity, in the continuing evolution of China's economic ascendancy.[6]

Just as they have previously performed the crucial role to implement Deng Xiaoping's reform and opening programme, the new generation of overseas Chinese entrepreneurs are serving as "connectors" in the mobilization of global resources of capital, market, know-how and talent. At the same time, Beijing maintains the traditional approaches to the Chinese business communities in Southeast Asia — the so-called united front strategy — in mobilizing support among Chinese business associations on issues which are related to China's interaction with the international community.

RESPONSE BY CHINESE BUSINESSES IN THAILAND

Certain characteristics and settings have helped Thailand forge a uniquely amicable and cooperative bilateral relationship with China. Geographical location, natural abundance relative to manageable demographic density, cultural diversity, political openness and religious tolerance are factors which facilitate the development and appreciation of Chinese business skills and industrious nature. Traditionally, Chinese entrepreneurial resources were leveraged in agriculture (gardening, rice milling, rubber plantation, livestock), industrial manufacturing (saw milling, sugar refinery, food processing), and services (banking, insurance, pawnshop, warehousing, transport, trading and retailing). As various instruments for capital mobilization through the stock market and other foreign monetized facilities (FDI, other offshore banking and financial facilities) became available in more recent times, other forms of business under Chinese ownership and management have sprung up: modern trade (chain retail stores), agri-business (livestock integration, shrimp and fish cultivation), food processing, and industrial manufacturing (automotive, electrical appliances, metals, petrochemicals). Chinese enterprises have gone from the traditional business environment to assume a new paradigm in seeking out new globalizing commercial opportunities. The "Chinese-ness" in such Thai-Chinese enterprises is being abated, and with it, the declining influence of traditional trade associations and the characteristic exclusivity in the Chinese-dominated business orientation that has prevailed as a result of the decades-long Chinese commercial preeminence. Hence, with the emergence of the Chinese economic power, Sino-Thai enterprises and entrepreneurs face the challenge — and the "irony" — of having to seriously rethink, and relearn about China and the Chinese way — in understanding business, language, culture, politics and society.[7]

In keeping with the newly-found global "China Fever", a new wave of enthusiasm for doing business with China is rising in Thailand, notably among publicly-listed Thai companies. These Thai enterprises which have sufficiently recovered from the Asian financial crisis of 1997 are increasingly active on the China market scene, in line with the rationale of increased global connectivity. The Thai automotive company Thai Roong has made a major investment in truck body stamping manufacture in Shenyang, northeast China. The Siam Cement Group, Thailand's blue-chip construction materials manufacturer, is re-positioning itself in China to take advantage of the physical urban expansion across China. Thai banks, particularly the Bangkok Bank and Thai Farmers' Bank, are moving vigorously into China in step with the increased financial liberalization and growing presence of Thai companies — as exemplified by Bangkok Bank's recent addition of its Beijing Branch. The Thai minerals giant Banpu has bought into Chinese coal mines in light of China's increased use of coal for energy. Similarly, a long-time Thai investor in China Saha Union is expanding its investment in independent power provision as China's requirement for electricity continuously soars. Saha Union is seizing a business opportunity by filling a niche in the growing need for international education by growing numbers of foreign expatriates' offsprings in China, through the opening of franchised international schools. The Thai energy-drink company the Red Bull Group has diversified into property businesses including golf and recreational facilities development in the Beijing area. Other Thai companies seeking rising investment opportunities in China range from such sectors as furniture, processed foods and beverages, jewellery, Thai fruits distribution, and tourism. As facilitators of investment credits and opportunities, the Thai banks' increased presence in China should further boost the entry of more Thai enterprises.

After twenty-seven years in China, the CP Group, the pioneer Thai company in China, has launched new expansion programmes in agri-foods and retailing, across the country in keeping with the continuing revamp of the Chinese rural sector and the growing connectivity between the rural and urban sectors. As demands for meat proteins rise, CP is employing its vertical integration ("farm-to-fork") model to ramp up its production of food supply — for both animals and humans. The company utilizes its resources (available in its farms, mills, processing plants, together with a workforce of over 50,000) in feed, livestock, technology, management, etc. in manufacturing agri-foods. On the service side, CP with its retail operations from cities, towns and counties, down to villages (with a network of some seventy hypermarkets and tens of thousands of local sales agents) is contributing to the nascent development of the rural/urban connectivity through the establishment of distribution and logistics networks. The outcome of all such business expansion is that CP is able to contribute to the commercialization of the rural economy, facilitate the exchange and flow of goods and services throughout the country, and contribute to trade with the international community. (For instance, the company has been instrumental in promoting the export of poultry products to neighbouring Japan and South Korea.) In meeting the new challenge of its business expansion in the coming years, the company is obliged to engage in an ambitious undertaking of developing qualified human resources in response to the emergence of Chinese entrepreneurship with the entry of growing numbers of young Chinese entrepreneurs into the marketplace amidst the diminution of governmental control of business.

A NEW MISSION FOR SOUTHEAST ASIAN BUSINESSES?

The rise of China's economic influence should galvanize governments and businesses of the ASEAN states to devise collective approaches and trade and investment strategies. Governments are more conscious of the attraction of developing business partnerships with China based on the latter's "win-win" and "mutuality of interests" rationalization. Through the eventual conclusion of their free trade agreement, China and ASEAN expect to enhance their economic complementarities and forge a commonality of purpose and in the connective, highly competitive global market. Meanwhile both sides need to jointly consider short-term and long-term business issues affecting their interests, such as the hollowing out threat, spiralling costs of fuel oil and commodities due to China's insatiable energy demand, the cost and profit margin question, the veritable level of currency exchange rates, free and fair trade, developmental imbalances among nations, poverty and prosperity, environmental degradation, and other economic-related matters. Chinese and ASEAN multinationals are already meeting these challenges with their own limited resources. In order to create the world's largest trade and investment area, ASEAN and China can vigorously pursue opportunities in such business areas as finance and banking, electronics, metals, petrochemicals, power generation, biotechnology, agri-business and agri-food, textile and garment, shipbuilding, modern trade, tourism, fashion and design, education, and the automotive industry. To this end, both China and ASEAN should agree to establish services and facilities for assisting prospective entrepreneurs interested in investing in China and ASEAN. The availability of such a service, to be officially supported and professionally run, would certainly bode well for risk management — which is vital to business — and boost commercial interaction.

For Southeast Asian businessmen, they realize the necessity in meeting the challenge of a rising China for their own ultimate survival, which calls for working realistically and creatively to boost their interaction with China in trade and investment. It would seem that the need for developing and deploying such a "win-win" strategy in trade and investment for entrepreneurs from both China and ASEAN is never more apparent, especially for those who appreciate the significance of globalization for all Asian countries.[8]

Notes

[1]   This strategy has been in effect officially since the end of the 1970s. See Hu Angang 胡鞍钢 et al., *Di e'ci zhuanxing guojia zhidu jianshe* 第二次转型国家制度建设 (Second Transformation in the National Institutional Structuring), Beijing, Qinghua University Press, 2003, pp. 1–2.

[2]   *Shijie Ribao* 世界日报 [*Universal Daily*], Bangkok, 16 January 2005, p. 8. China has replaced the United States as the world's biggest consumer of wheat, rice, meats, coal and steel, and places behind the United States in fuel consumption.

[3]   For an overview of China's pragmatic foreign policy, see Guo Shurong 郭树永, "Zhongguo maixiang shijie daguo de waijiao zhexue shiwei" 中国迈向世界大国的外交哲学思维 [China's Going the Way of the World's Major Powers: Philosophical Considerations in Diplomacy], in *Zhongguo Pinglun* 中国评论 [*China Review*], Hong Kong, November 2001, pp. 27–28.

[4]   Information obtained from Thailand's Ministry of Foreign Affairs.

[5]   Interview with Ling Nan University Professor Rao Meijiao 饶美蛟, in *Zhongguo Ping Lun* 中国评论 [*China Review*, Hong Kong, 11 (2001): 29–32.

[6]   Bruce Vaughn, *China-Southeast Asia Relations* (Washington, D.C., Congressional Research Service, 2005), p. 5.

[7]   Yun Guanping 云冠平 et al., *Dongnan Ya huaren qiye* 东南亚华人企业 [*Southeast Asia's Chinese Enterprises*], Bejing: Jingji Guanli Shubanshe 经济管理出版社, 2000), pp. 43–71.

[8]   "Zhongguo jingzhengli 中国竞争力 " [*China's Competitiveness*], in *Xin Caifu* 新财富 [*New Fortune*], November 2003, pp. 79–82.

References

Books

Yun Guanping 云冠平, Chen Qiaozhi 陈乔之. *Dongnan Ya huaren qiye* 东南亚华人企业 [*Southeast Asia's Chinese Enterprises*] (Beijing: Jingji Guanli Shubanshe 经济管理出版社, 2000).

Hu Angang 胡鞍钢. *Zhongguo da zhanlue* 中国大战略 [China's Grand Strategy] (Zhejiang: Zhejiang Renmin Shubanshe 浙江人民出版社, 2002).

Hu Angang 胡鞍钢, Wang Shaoguang 王绍光, et al. *Di e'ci zhuanxing guojia zhidu jianshe* 第二次转型国家制度建设 (Beijing: Qinghua Daxue Shubanshe [北京清华大学出版社], 2003).

Bruce Vaughn. *China-Southeast Asia Relations* (Washington, D.C., Congressional Research Service, 2005).

Magazines and Newsprint

"Inside the New China". *Fortune*, 4 October 2004.

"Zhongguo jingzhengli" 中国竞争力. *Xincaifu* 新财富 [*New Fortune*], 11 November 2003.

Zhongguo Pinglun 中国评论 [*China Commentary*]. Hong Kong, November 2001.

Shijie Ribao 世界日报 [*Universal Daily News*].

3

Flattening Impact of a Reawakening China on Ethnic Imbalance in Indonesian Business

Djisman S. Simandjuntak

INTRODUCTION

Given the transitional nature of development in which both China and Indonesia are currently faced, any conclusion on how the rise of China is going to affect Indonesians is provisional by necessity. While miraculous growth performance gives China a more attractive look to a world which is obsessed with wealth accumulation, the litmus test of sustainability still lies ahead for China when the time comes to address political rights of more than one-fifth of world population. One should not overlook the fact that back in the fifteenth century, China was on the threshold of being industrialized, but it is in faraway England that mechanization became for the first time commercialized, harnessing together technological ingenuities from around the globe. The post-crisis economic performance of Indonesia undoubtedly pales against that of China. However, Indonesia has at least dared to step into the long road to political democratization, though it, too, is yet to pass the litmus test of effective delivery of goods and services that people expect from a democratic government.

The impact of the rapid rise of China on Southeast Asia in general and Chinese Indonesians in particular as explored in this chapter are highly complex. While China can be seen as the masterpiece of globalization of the last quarter of the twentieth century, it is faced with a number of downside risks emanating from domestic, regional and global developments. How Indonesians look at a rapidly progressing China depends, among other things, on how they perform economically in comparison with the Chinese. A rapidly progressing economy is much more likely to result in a positive perception of China than one that stagnates. Chinese Indonesians would be less inhibited in exploiting the opportunities that emerge in the wake of China's rise under a strong performance of the Indonesian economy. Even at the cost of being repetitive, discussion in this chapter covers first of all, the sustainability of the rise of China; secondly, the global and regional environment; thirdly, outlook for a strong growth in Indonesia; and lastly, the impact of China's remarkable transformation on Chinese Indonesians who for a long time have served as the backbone of Indonesia's commercial sector.

THE RISE OF CHINA: ISSUES OF SUSTAINABILITY

The rapid economic transformation of China is perhaps one of the most important changes in the twenty-first century seen from the material well-being of the human race. China's per capita gross domestic product (GDP) in constant 2000 US dollar rose from a mere US$173 in 1980 to US$1,067 in 2003. China is exceptional in terms of investment activities. It spends consistently over 30 per cent of its GDP on gross capital formation. The fraction went up to as high as 44 per cent in 2003, fuelling in turn another round of high economic growth. In the developing world, China towers exceptionally high as host for foreign direct investment (FDI). Back in 1980, inflow of FDI to China was as small as US$57 millions. It went up to US$1,659 millions in 1985 and US$53,505 millions in 2003, of which by far the greatest part originated from East Asia, notably Hong Kong, China and Taiwan, Province of China. Countless analyses have been published about the extraordinary economic performance. Projecting China as an economic superpower of a not too distant future has also become a very popular exercise.

The statistics reveal only part of the story of how complex it must have been to decide and follow through the reopening of a nation of 1.2 billion people after a prolonged closure under different political systems. For almost half a millennium China was pushed to the periphery of world commerce, to put it mildly. The footprints of isolation under the Ching dynasty and its immediate predecessor seem to have been erased and the damages inflicted under the Great Leap Forward and Cultural Revolution cured as far as the economy is concerned, though one can certainly wonder where China would have been, had it stuck to the open policy of the early fifteenth century all along. China might have been home of the first industrial revolution and the first in many other areas that the human race finds worthwhile to pursue. The recent experience of China with hyper growth suggests that humans are capable of accomplishing extreme growth, if they are given the opportunity to do so. The recent rise of India reinforces the hypothesis that human beings are capable of attaining a world which is far better than the one they made before the end of the Cold War. Writing in the context of the Millennium Development Goals and profiting from long and extensive experiences with development advisory around the globe, Jeffrey Sachs shares a similar opinion that freeing humans from poverty within a relatively short period is a real possibility provided that governments stick to good policies and that they are willing to share a minimum amount of resources that is needed to catapult poor countries into the orbit of development (Sachs 2005). Under the circumstance where China, India and Indonesia can sustain their respective current rates of growth, the door to a world that is free of extreme poverty is open, considering that the three countries are home to 2,628 million of the 6,457 million world population in 2005. It is hard to find news that is as pleasant as a sustainable high growth in these three densely populated developing countries. The benefits would be felt far and wide beyond national borders through a variety of transmission mechanisms.

Generally speaking, people are upbeat about the prospect for a sustaining high growth in China. Some even go as far as to suggest that China will soon make it to join the club of developed economies. It is hard to argue against success. The fact that China has sustained high economic growth for as long as two decades provides a strong reason to believe that the encouraging experience will last another two decades. The Government of China has also demonstrated the ability to deal with the political crisis of 1989 without jeopardizing the rapid economic growth. Between the risen China and the rest of the world, there has developed a wide network of inter-dependence, which is unlikely to do away with at low cost. Consumers, retailers and manufacturers around the globe alike have grown used to China's mastery of efficient production and distribution as a source of greater value. They enjoy the lower prices that China offers for quality products. Under the current circumstances there is no perfect substitute for China. Nevertheless, growth is probabilistic as many East Asians experienced it in the late 1990s.

First of all high growth is prone to bubbling. Most people are positive-feedback traders when it comes to assets, buying when the price is rising and selling when it declines. Following a high economic growth, the prices of financial and real estate assets tend to rise far above reproduction costs. Demand for assets rises as a consequence, fuelling another round of asset price increases. Informed traders can accelerate or even trigger in fact the process, buying today at a slightly raised price in order to sell tomorrow at an even higher price. Such cycles have afflicted the world repeatedly. Yet it is hard to tell when an economy has entered the stage of bubbling and when the bubble will burst in spite of countless of studies on fragility indicators and other instruments of early warning system. At the current stage of development, few people are worried about a meltdown in China. As indicated earlier the world has become dependent on China's mastery of efficient production and distribution and is, therefore, unlikely to uncouple from China even in cases of strained relations. Even Japan has discovered the necessity of being present in China. The friction that arises from unresolved issues relating to Japan's past as a colonialist of China does not prevent trade and investment relations from strengthening. Considering the eagerness of foreign investors to continue to play a role in China's growth and the relatively firm government control of the financial services industry, a soft landing is highly probable for China. Undoubtedly, there are pitfalls in a state-dominated financial system (Boyreau-Debray and Wei 2005). However, China is said to have dealt with the problems in time.

Disturbances to global trade can destabilize China's growth. The rapid pace at which China's export has been growing has already instigated unpleasant comments from different corners of the world. China in the first decade of the 2000s has some similarities with Japan of the 1980s. Some Americans have set forth a China-bashing tendency in a similar way that some Americans were bashing Japan in the 1980s (Bown and McCulloh 2005). Many analysts suggest that the *renminbi* is undervalued at a high margin and should, therefore, be revalued substantially (Shane and Gale 2004). At the core of such bashing is the accusation of mercantilist policy of enriching oneself at the cost of trading partners. Such accusation is difficult to substantiate. China's export expansion is accompanied by a similarly strong increase of import, leaving a modest overall trade balance, though bilateral balances differ greatly across economies. When East Asian currencies were devalued deeply in the late 1990s, China did not join the bandwagon in spite of the obvious risk that the decision not to devalue put Chinese products at an exchange rate disadvantage *vis-à-vis* the products of their East Asian neighbours in the same strategic group (Prasad and Wei 2005). The rapid rise of China's foreign exchange reserve is only partly attributable to trade success. A great deal of it originates from a positive capital account, thanks largely to FDI inflows. What is more, China has so far managed to persuade the rest of the world of the benign nature of its economic rise (Starr 1997). China's rise has not destabilized the world in general and East Asia in particular. China has demonstrated its normalcy as a rapidly growing economy in that in invests in the rest of the world with a view to securing access to needed raw materials. On this score, China does not differ much from earlier East Asian industrializers: Japan, Singapore, South Korea. Be as it may, the rest of the world may still find the rapid rise of China's trade objectionable and find ways and means of forcing China to change its policy stance. Yet, China-bashing is not likely to be disruptive to China's trade and economic growth.

Commitment around the world to open trade is now much stronger than it was before World War II. The probability of protectionism going wild has greatly diminished in the course of the last sixty years. The fruits of open trade have been reaped almost everywhere, giving proponents of open trade a strong moral support. Even the most severe imbalance is not likely to open the gates wide to the return of wholesale protectionism. A failed Doha Development Round is certainly saddening, but is likely to give a push to other initiatives, notably regional liberalization initiatives. Sector-wise, China does not need to worry much. Should China's advantages in unskilled labour manufactures get eroded, alternative advantages have been sown in knowledge-intensive industries. (Schaaper 2004). New entrants into the trade-led development are unlikely to pose insurmountable challenges to China. In short, there is no acute threat to China's trade-led development. While world trade continues to fluctuate, the amplitude is not likely to increase to a level that is lethal to world trade expansion. China with its layered advantages can expect to continue to see world trade expansion serving as a tailwind to its rapid economic transformation.

Some other possible threats to the sustainability of China's rise lie outside the economic realm. One of them relates to a very fundamental issue of policy direction. So far China has managed to benefit masterfully from the pragmatic economic reform while avoiding taking a firm stance on the issues of ownership. Only history can tell how long the pragmatic strategy can prevail. On the one hand, there is no compelling reason to believe that private state ownership cannot co-exist with state ownership.

There is more than one economy in the world where the co-existence delivers what people expect to get from a good economy: Employment, rising income and rising wealth. Lacking major crises that would bring in the IMF's conditional crisis management, governments can argue convincingly in favour of retaining state ownership. Exposing firms to deep reform is a real possibility even under state ownership (McGoldrick and Walsh 2004). On the other hand, opening a window to private ownership necessarily creates a demand for opening the gate. There is in other words, an inherent escalation in the demand for opening. At the current stage of development China is still searching for the right path to private sector development (Kanamori and Zhao 2005). Chinese business people may find the governance challenges of the modern firm too cumbersome and rediscover instead *guanxi* as the dominant pattern of relationship within the firm. Guanxi is rooted very deeply in Chinese tradition (Kipnis 1996). It must have had positive impacts on fitness. Otherwise it would have been selected out in the course of evolution. After all Chinese are said to be averse to laws. They associate laws with unpleasant things (Braendle, Gasser and Noll 2005). As alternative an informal network of protection is said to have been cultivated along kinship lines. Such governance mode may turn inadequate in a world that is increasingly information-driven. Transparency appears to have become conditional to successful governance in the twenty-first century. However, even under traditional mode of governance, China's private sector is going to grow bigger and bigger. In time it may even reduce state-owned enterprises into irrelevance in a growing number of sectors. In other words, the issues of ownership reform cannot be postponed indefinitely. This brings us to the issues of an even more fundamental nature — those of political reform.

So far Chinese leaders have navigated China skilfully along a course that combines market competition in the economic realm and communist monopoly in the political realm. Both market competition and communist monopoly of political power have been challenged more than once. The challenges were overwhelmed. Yet, they are bound to reincarnate. The questions related to the mixture between market competition and political participation will have to be addressed sooner or later (Mitter 2004). Apparently the likely direction is toward greater participation. The Chinese Government has also demonstrated a willingness to be more forthcoming to wider participation, even though it refuses to compromise on the one-party system. Opponents of democratization can cite some examples where a rapid transition to a political democracy is associated with deteriorating economic performance. On the other hand, proponents of democratization can also point to a number of disappointing experiments with the combination of economic freedom and political dictatorship. China will have to find its own path, loosening in stages politically, as circumstances get more conducive in the wake of an improved economic security assuming more wealthy people are more resilient to political changes than poorer one (Fewsmith 2001). Risks of destabilization can be reduced through diverse networks of cooperation with the rest of the world, notably East Asia.

The optimistic message about a sustaining high growth of China does not take into account the probability of natural disasters, which can range from floods to drought. They may strike unexpectedly. Nevertheless, governments around the globe are now better equipped with disaster management. While a disaster may still turn out to be very costly, the probability of it halting the entire economic development is small.

THE WORLD'S NEW GEOGRAPHY AND DEMASSIFICATION OF GOVERNANCE

Interactions between Chinese and Indonesians cannot be delinked from the larger context of globalization. Given their accomplishments in science and technology, arts and politics in the course of a millennia, Chinese have been a major force of globalization notwithstanding intermittent periods of aberrations. China has demonstrated the ability to survive behind a closed door for almost six centuries. Deteriorating economic conditions forced it, however, to reopen in a dramatic way. Indonesians have contributed less to globalization but they, too, have participated actively in it. Of the strange attractors that led to the age of commerce in the fifteenth and sixteenth centuries, Moluccas and its spices were very important. Some of the important episodes of the history of circumnavigation were staged in the Indonesian archipelago, though the main actors were Europeans (Bergreen 2003). Given its geographic condition Indonesia is destined to be an open economy. Isolation has no chance to succeed in a country that consists of countless islands. Attempts at insulating Indonesia from the rest of the world have repeatedly failed and were abandoned after a short while. The two examples suggest that highly restrictive policies, not to speak of isolation, represent only a brief interruption in globalization. Sooner or later they are abandoned following the increasingly unbearable costs that are associated with a closed-door policy.

There is no need to dwell on globalization at great length in this chapter, considering the enormous number of works written on globalization in the last two decades. Nevertheless, some remarks are in order.

The last three decades in world history have truly been an amazing episode. At the end of the 1970s, China decided to do away with Stalinist central planning having suffered greatly from the system of "dining from the same rise bowl". A little later USSR showed clear signs of decline, heralding the dawn of a new era of political freedom. West Europe and North America returned to conservative rule, paving the way to the dismantling of many of the edifices of socialist experimentation, which was given a major boost with the Great Depression of the 1930s. The East Asian NIEs emerged more unmistakably as cases of successful capitalist transformation, enlarging the dots of prosperity on the East Asian map. Slowly the pejorative views on Asian ways development attenuated. The *dependencia* paradigm, which left clear footprints in the UN system, started to lose its lustre. The inferior economic performance of Latin America relative to that of developing East Asia further disadvantaged the proponents of *dependencia*. Some of them indeed became champions of integration as the path to development. International institutions underwent major changes at roughly the same time. The massive architecture of global order began to crumble. The Bretton Wood System fell apart. IMF mutated into a debt-crisis management institution, feared in deeply troubled economies but unnoticed in healthy economies. The General Agreements on Tariff and Trade (GATT) also diminished in importance as protection rate fell asymptotically following unilateral, regional and multilateral liberalizations. Its transformation into the World Trade Organization (WTO) coincided with its extension to new issues, which it handles with great difficulty so far. The "Three Worlds System" increasingly proved to be too simple to be of use to deal with world affairs. Notwithstanding policy convergence, the world of many countries can no longer be divided in a simplified way into just three blocks. Within the "Third World" alone, there struggle many economies with extreme poverty on the one hand and a number of other economies on the graduation to higher stages on the development ladder on the other. Protectionist interpretations of nationalism stumbled on their limits. Massive intervention of governments through cross-border and domestic measures failed to deliver the promised progress and was, therefore, brought under thorough scrutiny and eventual redesign in favour of greater openness. Admittedly, the new punctuated equilibrium is less than universal in coverage. A few countries have kept to an authoritarian regime behind a tight wall *vis-à-vis* the rest of the world. Some others refuse to even bother about reconsidering the monarchy and have to rely on external alliances to defend the system. Nevertheless, changes as far reaching as the ones the world was going through in the last two decades of the twentieth century are a rarity in human history.

The world has witnessed many more episodes of punctuated equilibria as regards the ease at which goods, services, capital, information and people can move across national borders or any other man-made borders. The probability is more 0.5 that similar dramatic changes occur again in the future. Globalization is inherent in human evolution. Once it emerged out of the womb of evolution the homo sapiens did not wait too long before it spread to all corners of the globe. As they move around, modern humans bring their cultures along: Languages, writings, religions, ideologies, taboos, epics, plays, laws, technologies and many other man-made things and ideas. Best practices of all kinds spread worldwide irresistibly. Barriers may be erected against the inflow of such best practices but they fall apart again and again. People who stick to those barriers for too long suffer from a widening gap with the rest of the world. Both Chinese and Indonesians understand very well how a closed-door policy deprives an economy of the necessary renewal of growth pulses. Without diffusion of foreign ideas and technologies the speed of development is hard to accelerate in the developing world. The underlying forces of globalization are simply too strong to be resisted durably by humans. They seem to have been wired in nature since the beginning of life.

The nature of globalization does change from one era to another. In the beginning it was diasporic in nature. Humans dispersed from one origin to different corners of the world. In the process their cultures speciated or became unique. Even, biologically, human developed different features as a result of adjustment to different physical environments. Those who toil in the sun of the tropics developed dark skin colour. The temperate climate selects for fair skin colour, however. The diasporic globalization is creative and innovative. As a group of people separate durably from others they invented unique cultures, including technologies. This led in time to a great diversity, though commonality of origin is unmistakable among elements of the diversity. Diasporic globalization is less vulnerable to conflict. The dominant strategy in diasporic globalization is that of avoidance. Trade was perhaps invented during the diasporic globalization. As migrants returned to their original home for reunion, they must have brought things that are unique to the new homes, quickening the dispersion of plants and animals beyond their original habitats. The diasporic globalization was largely completed when Polynesians settled in even the most remote islands of the vast Pacific Ocean.

With a long overlap "implosive globalization" followed. More powerful chiefdoms conquered others to mutate into city states. A superior city state conquered other city states and mutated into state. A powerful state conquered others to form empire. People from villages streamed to cities, which in turn allowed division of labour that later served as the elixir of wealth. People flock to places where progressive ways of doing things or revolutionary ideas are being adopted rapidly. They can be religious practices, martial art practices, movie-making practices or education practices, war practices or even crime practices. They draw people from the eight winds. In parallel, best practices also find their way out of points of origination to the rest of the world. They may stumble on resistance in the beginning but prevail sooner or later. As best practices move out of the points of their origination, they do so not with a perfect symmetry. Instead, they agglomerate in urban centres where they serve as attractor of implosion of people. As more and more people squeeze together in urban centres, reasons for conflicts are bred. The struggle for existence is staged in its toughest form at megacities.

Headmen were adequate in times of diasporic globalization when life was organized along the lines of kinship. The pinnacle of the kinship governance is the Westphalian system of sovereign nation states. The system is being strained to the utmost. Absolute sovereignty has been eroded seriously in relevance. Independent states can no longer insulate their people from the rest of the world. The greenhouse gases that human communities emit at greatly different intensities affect life almost indiscriminately. A virus can now spread very quickly, hitch-hiking with humans who in turn can travel around the world in less than a day. Many issues that are of critical importance to life require international cooperation, if not supranational authority. The leap-frogging of the European communities into the European Union with a single currency is perhaps an early sign of what is likely to come as regards national sovereignty. To be effective in dealing with contemporary issues, national sovereignty will have to be pooled to one of a larger geographical scope. In dealing with some issues, a global pooling is indeed necessary. In response to the new realities, networks of government develop (Slaughter

1999, 2004; Anderson 2005; Cuellar 2004; Bievre 2004). Through the networks, mutual understanding of issues is facilitated and convergence of interests crafted.

China and Indonesia have also accepted the fact of relative sovereignty. The two countries share membership in many international organizations. They also play active roles in giving birth to and nurturing cooperation in a myriad of regional forums. These include the Association of Southeast Asian Nations (ASEAN) and cooperation networks related to it, Asia-Pacific Economic Cooperation (APEC) and Asia Regional Forum (ARF). Non-governmental organizations from the two countries also meet one another increasingly frequently, both bilaterally and regionally. Admittedly, East Asians have been helpless in debating the East Asian community. They talk about regional community while showing inflexibility in the pooling of national sovereignty in favour of a regional one, at least in dealing with issues that are regional in nature. Perhaps it is part of the irony that the Westphalian system of sovereignty is redesigned first in its place of origin while it is still guarded almost uncompromisingly in many other parts of the world, including China and Indonesia.

History is not perfectly irreversible. Despite disappointing outcomes of earlier attempts at bringing globalization to a halt, some future leaders may repeat the same mistakes and revive isolationism in one way or another. Yet, the future is going to differ fundamentally in respect of the pulses of globalization. Attempts to silence them are doomed to be ephemeral. Human quest for gene-culture immortality is unbreakable in spite of the illusory nature of such dreams. Humans will do everything to lengthen the survival of their genes. They toil incessantly to leave footprints in human accomplishments. The search for ubiquity continues. Humans hunt for new uniqueness, faster speed, lower costs and combinations thereof for the sake of better fitness. While searching, humans recognize that the known world is smaller than the unknown one, though some may argue that with quantum physics and the double helix there is little left to be explored. However, humans of the early twenty-first century have yet to find answers to countless important questions such as the ones related to the perfection of the human body, alternatives to cheap oil and how to fix the ozone. More than one billion people still struggle with extreme poverty and threatened existence. Many more are swaying between poverty and modest prosperity. The unsolved issues offer opportunities for growth. In a similar way that China rises to economic prominence and that India and

Vietnam join the small club of hyper-growth economies and that Indonesia proves able to grow moderately in spite of seemingly tangled problems, many other economies will pleasantly surprise the world sooner or later. Globalization will spread prosperity to the poor of the world, assuming that innovations and adaptations are made in governance. China's rise and Indonesia's moderate growth are products of globalization. Their sustainability requires that globalization is well internalized in development policies.

LEARNING TO LIVE WITH POLYMORPHIC DIVERSITY

Domestic developments in Indonesia co-determine to an important degree how the rise of China is going to affect Indonesian businesses, including businesses of Chinese Indonesians. Generally speaking, a prosperous China is a better neighbour to other countries in East Asia than an impoverished one. Many will feel enthusiastic about China serving as a new centre of growth. However, the rise of China can also bring about losses to some people. Higher market penetration can awaken protectionist sentiment among domestic producers, politicians and workers. I argue that the attitude of Indonesians toward richer China is a highly complex one. Two of the important factors that are critical to the attitude will be discussed more deeply: Ability of Indonesians to do justice to its own polymorphic diversity and the extent to which the economy can quickly return to a high growth path.

Indonesia is destined to be home to a complex diversity. Physically the archipelago may look homogeneous as a greenish-blue belt on the equator. In reality Indonesia is not much different from many other countries. West and East of the Wallace Line the archipelago is endowed with different floral and faunal systems. The differences affect how people live in each of the two halves of the archipelago. Lowland areas sustain a different lifestyle from highland areas. Peasants in lowland areas cultivate mainly rice. Highlanders usually engage in tree crops agriculture and are net importers of rice. Coastal areas and interior areas differ greatly in terms of the dominant cultures bred. "Sea-locked" small islands and land-locked small villages that are scattered throughout the archipelago certainly subscribe to different styles of living. Thus a remote Indonesian villager shares much less in common with an Indonesian dweller of a major city than the latter shares with a dweller of another major city outside Indonesia. The differences have hardly been given attention. Indonesians are told from early on that their motherland is one. It is said to be a very richly endowed motherland in spite of the fact that many parts of the archipelago are poorly endowed. Some Indonesians must have sung the song about a very rich Indonesia amidst the trap of poverty. Uncovering the different fortunes of the different parts of the archipelago is an important part of the missing component of Indonesian civic education.

Diversity of religions constitutes another element of Indonesia's diversity. This dimension of diversity is important considering the centrality of religion in the value system adhered to by most Indonesians. In fact belief in God is written in the preamble of the republic's constitution. Modern-day Indonesia is a hot-pot of religions. Prior to the arrival of Islam, Hinduism and Buddhism had already found significant followers among the inhabitants of the archipelago. Islam came in the first half of the second millennium and became the religion of the majority of Indonesians. Christianity arrived later. Its followers remain a relatively small minority. Nevertheless, there are some areas where the population is overwhelmingly Christian. They include the area surrounding Lake Toba in North Sumatra, Manado in North Sulawesi, Toraja in South Sulawesi, East Sunda Islands and the Indonesian part of Papua. Competing ideologies also arrived in Indonesia at different points of time. Even communism was at one time a major stream in Indonesian politics, notwithstanding its atheistic flavour. Remnants of local systems of belief survive to this day. Even in the practices of Islam and Christianity the remnants of indigenous religions are observable. In other words, Indonesia can be counted as a case of religious pluralism. Yet under the harmonious appearance there lay hidden and persistent threats of intolerance. For a long time conflicts pertaining to religions were defused along with ethnic and racial issues. They were made taboo under Suharto's government. In spite of the post-crisis reform, debates on religious issues are muted, partly because of the strong habit of self-censorship among the people occupying leadership positions. Obtaining permit for the construction of a place of worship is made conditional on the approval of people living in the neighbourhood and is notoriously difficult. Occasionally the conflicts do erupt. Places of worship have repeatedly fallen victim to destructive acts. The issues of religion are not completely uncoupled from ethnicity. Indonesian Non-Muslims are usually multiple minorities: ethnic minority confessing religion of minority. There are less Muslim Chinese Indonesians for instance than there are Chinese Indonesians confessing Christianity and Buddhism.

Ethnically Indonesia is also a complex reality of diversity. Indonesia is home to the largest number of Melanesians who were perhaps pushed eastward by the ethnic groups, which are now lumped together as Malay. The Melanesians and neighbouring ethnic groups are the most indigenous among all Indonesians, if indigenousness is derived from the dates of arrival. However, by far the largest number of Indonesians are Javanese. Their descendants account for an insignificant share in population in other parts of the archipelago following the routes of commerce. The rest of Indonesians are fragmented in hundreds of tribes. They speak dialects that are mutually unintelligible. The tribal and linguistic diversities arose because of the relative isolation in which migrants live in their respective new homes. As a political issue ethnicity has undergone a discouraging simplistic polarization. The two poles are called indigenous and non-indigenous Indonesians respectively. Non-indigenous Indonesians consist of different ethnicities but the word non-indigenous usually is meant to refer to Chinese Indonesians.

A great deal has been written about Chinese Indonesians. The anti-Chinese sentiment is certainly a complex issue. Disentangling it is difficult. Nevertheless, economic disparity is among its root causes. Little is scientifically known about the disparity. The fact that ethnicity is considered a taboo has had negative consequences. Studies on the economic gap that separates indigenous Indonesians from Chinese Indonesians are rare. While debating the gap, people usually rely on impressions based on casual observations. By necessity they are imprecise. In the absence of a thorough scientific study, people will have to continue to rely on impressions based on casual observations. Bearing in mind that such observations require empirical validation, the income and wealth gaps are obviously very wide. Ownership of business establishments is highly skewed in favour of Chinese Indonesians. Most major shops in Indonesians cities and towns are owned by Chinese Indonesians. Private domestic banks are also owned by Chinese Indonesians, though some of them have recently been sold to alien owners from outside Indonesia. The same applies to manufacturing establishments. More recently, Chinese Indonesians have also ventured into plantation and mineral sectors, which in the past were exclusive sanctuaries for state-owned and foreign-owned enterprises. Prior to the stock market liberalization in the late 1980s, people could only guess who owns what. Thereafter owners are revealed in the cases of listed companies in accordance with the requirements of the stock exchange. The very high concentration of ownership in favour of Chinese Indonesians in general and in favour of a few families among the Chinese Indonesians in particular is made public information. At one time in the 1980s and 1990s, compilation of business ownership was a popular business, though little investigative work was done to track the origin of the concentration.

It really sounds enigmatic that, exposed to the same policy environment, Chinese Indonesians perform much better in business than indigenous Indonesians. Where does the success of Chinese Indonesians in wealth accumulation come from? Why have indigenous Indonesians lagged so far behind Chinese Indonesians in terms of accumulated business wealth? While waiting for a thorough scientific study, the following discussion can serve as a road map to future research.

The success of Chinese Indonesians is perhaps less enigmatic than the weak performance in business of indigenous Indonesians. Chinese Indonesians represent the latest wave of migrants to Indonesia. Migrants are said to be self-selected (Chiswick 2000). People who dared to sail away from the southern coastal areas of China must have had certain advantages over the ones who preferred to stay back. The first migrants had at least a daring spirit. Those who followed had someone to look up to as role model in the new home. Migrants have no luxury of being choosy in terms of profession. They are hyper pragmatists, accepting whatever is available as employment for survival, usually under the guidance of the earlier migrants. There is something that can be seen as the privilege of being the latest migrants to Indonesia. It stems from the fact that a migrant is landless and is, therefore, deprived of access to agriculture, at least in the beginning period. A migrant is also less welcome in rural areas than he or she is in urban centres. As a result migrants are forced from the outset to struggle in non-agricultural activities.

In the case of Chinese migrants to Southeast Asia, they arrived when the commercial sectors were in the making under European influence. The non-agricultural sectors had a better prospect for growth. Chinese Indonesians were, therefore, in a fortunate position relative to indigenous Indonesians who were stuck with food agriculture with its constraining Engel's Law. What is more, at their early stage of development, non-agricultural sectors endowed players with monopolistic power. In a backward economy, secrets are among the basic features of commerce and industry. Incumbents enjoy an enormous opportunity to exploit such secrets. Property rights in the emerging sectors of commerce and industry were also better defined and, thereby, better protected. Admittedly property rights in agriculture can also be defined and protected better through land reform as earlier East Asian industrializers of Japan, Taiwan and South

Korea demonstrated. However, such reform failed to materialize in the case of Indonesia in spite of repeated attempts. Traditional communal ownership of land and water remains in widespread use to the present day. It lacks a clear definition of rights and is commercially of inferior quality. In short, a dynamic business environment favours migrant more than indigenous citizens in a variety of ways. On this issue Indonesia is in no way unique.

Whether or not and the extent to which Chinese values were of relevance to the success of Chinese migrants and their descendants in Southeast Asia is hard to ascertain. Parsimony certainly contributes to better fitness in an environment where capital accumulation is among the important features. Chinese migrants are famous for parsimony. Thanks to thriftiness, Chinese migrants are better positioned to renew business capital and to send children to the best available education. Respect for parents may also have prevented limited capital from being fragmented into meaningless sums, though on this matter Chinese Indonesians have yet to prove the ability to prevent wealth from being fragmented in the hands of the second generation following the demise of founders. In cases where savings fall short of investments, Chinese migrants are said to be able to tap onto *guangxi* even across national borders. Few may have benefited from access to regional centres of capital market such as Hong Kong and Singapore, but such access is not available to the majority of Chinese Indonesians. Attributing many of the old virtues to specific ethnicity is highly fallacious. Parsimony, hard work, strong demand for education and informal network of mutual help are shared widely among migrants irrespective of origins. Wherever one goes, one finds recent migrants flocking to the same sanctuaries, sharing values that are very similar to the Asian values.

The apparent failure of indigenous Indonesians in business is much more enigmatic than the success of Chinese Indonesians. Business start-ups are numerous by indigenous Indonesians. Walking along the streets of urban centres, one would encounter countless stalls offering all kinds of products and services. In the sea of "nano enterprises" one finds indigenous Indonesians in a much greater number than they are in larger businesses. Ascent to medium size among businesses under indigenous ownership is still encouragingly high in frequency, though it differs among ethnic groups. The migrants of Bugis from South Sulawesi, Minang from West Sumatra and Batak of North Sumatra are said to have been more successful in business than many other ethnic groups, though one has to caution against exaggeration hidden in such a statement. The rise of indigenous Indonesians to prominent positions in large businesses is truly rare, however. Large-scale firms owned by indigenous Indonesians are very small in number. They belong to a rare breed in the world of large businesses in Indonesia.

Different hypotheses have also been put forward in connection with the failure of indigenous Indonesians to catch up with fellow Chinese Indonesians in business. It is said that among many indigenous Indonesians, business is shunned, though a clear change of attitude is observable among young indigenous Indonesians. On the other hand, people tend to associate clerics, teachers, politicians, attorneys, judges, lawyers, medical doctors, and bureaucrats with altruistic behaviour, however cautious one has to be in interpreting such association. In stark contrast, a capitalist is considered a disreputable profession, at least up until recently. Having settled as farmers for a very long time, many indigenous Indonesians may have unlearned the way of living with risks. It also means settling in a sector of weak prospect for growth as compared with commerce and industry. Considering the importance of scientific discovery and technological changes to productivity improvement, the disadvantages of the traditional sectors relative to the modern sectors of commerce and industry from the viewpoint of growth are obvious. Weak representation in business may also have something to do with the rural legacy. The city is the womb of wealth. The history of wealth coincides in fact with the history of cities (Mumford 1961). By far the greatest part of human wealth is located in a few major cities. Struggling in a city is more likely to lead to greater wealth than struggling in a village. Herein lies another advantage of migrants who usually flock to major cities rather than to rural villages. Migrants flock to where the wealth accumulation is the most vibrant, thereby improving the chance of getting to at least the debris of wealth.

Deciphering the forces behind the puzzlingly weak presence of indigenous Indonesians in medium and large businesses is an act of groping in the dark. A lot more work needs to be done to disentangle them. However, the more relevant question to be asked at this juncture is whether or not the weak presence can somehow be attributed to government policies. The core issue involved is anything but crystal clear. Is ethnic balancing of business ownership of any relevance to politics, which is supposed to deal with affairs that concern all citizens? If the answer is affirmative, can agreement be reached on a fair division of wealth along ethnic lines? Answers to these questions are doomed to be very controversial. Consumers do not seem to care much about who owns the factory that produces the cloths offered in the market. What they care about more is availability, affordability and many other issues that deal with consumption decision. Workers judge employers not on the basis of ethnicity. What they expect the most from employment relations is life-long income, social insurance, and continuous human development, though a mistake committed by people of the minorities is often wrongly considered a worse evil than one committed by people of the majorities. Government should also judge business people on the basis of their contribution to economic development rather than on their ethnic origin. Nevertheless, a better balance of ownership is desirable, all else being equal.

The imbalance in ownership of business is partially a policy failure. Part of the obstacles to a successful business is political in nature. Weak propensity to take risk is partly the consequence of a "dirigisme" in which the government economic presence is very extensive. Under such an environment, entrepreneurship is muted to some extent. Avoidance of business may also result from confusing signals. Important information about prospective businesses may be withheld or hidden in chaotic noise. Transmission can be manipulated in such a way so that unwanted recipients get confused rather than enlightened by receiving a message. Even if one assumes good encoding and transmission, the same signal can mean different thing to different people due to differences in cognition. Starting up a new business in a high-entropy environment can be very frustrating indeed. One has to go through and endure a complex web of bureaucratic processes before the first unit of product is sold. The processes are costly and are penalizing by default new businesses more heavily. Government may also fail to safeguard fair competition and make life, thereby, increasingly difficult for newcomers in a labyrinthine world of competition. Earlier entrants enjoy a wide range of advantages *vis-à-vis* late entrants. Challenging incumbents becomes a hopeless undertaking, if they engage in anti-competitive practices unpunished. The latter may include collusion among incumbents to pre-empt entry. Incumbents can even bribe government officials to make entry very difficult or even prohibitive. They can ask the government to declare the closure of a business to new entrants or to make new entry conditional on expensive requirements. In short, there are many ways in which policies penalize new entrants to business. Indigenous Indonesians have also suffered from some policy practices that make entry to business a scary undertaking. Not that they are victims of reverse discrimination. Non-indigenous Indonesians seem to have mastered the art of dealing with bureaucratic red tape much better than their fellow indigenous business people.

While seeking to reduce ethnic imbalance in the ownership of business, people are very quick to ask for affirmative actions. Many governments around the world have experimented with such policy. Indonesian governments, too, have also deployed affirmative actions repeatedly with meagre results. In spite of the unconvincing result, demand for affirmative action persists. However, time does not make affirmative action more promising. Designing an affirmative action in favour of the majority of a population like the indigenous Indonesians is a Herculean task, to put it mildly. Formulas that have proved a failure cannot turn a miracle just because of a change in political leadership. Rather than repeating the same mistakes, the Indonesian Government is well advised to consider going the indirect way of promoting successful entry to business. Such policy is bound to meet with sceptical reactions. However entrepreneurship facilitation is perhaps the only realistic way for the Indonesian Government to go, considering the disappointments of direct measures in the past and the very tight human and financial resource constraints facing the government in the period after the financial crisis of 1997–98.

Learning to live with a multi-dimensional diversity is necessarily an evolutionary process. In the case of Indonesia, a deeply entrenched "segregation of a kind" where politics is *de facto* reserved for indigenous Indonesians on the one hand, and business is overwhelmingly owned by Chinese Indonesians, on the other, stands in the way of a shared and functioning diversity. Under such segregation, mutual mistrust will be very hard to overcome. Given their leading position in business, Chinese Indonesians have more to benefit from the rise of China than indigenous Indonesians do. Nothing is mysterious in such a fact. Chinese-ness is not essential to such an equation even if some Chinese Indonesians feel somehow proud to witness the rise of China as one of the distinctive features of the early third millennium. Unfortunately the wide gap in business ownership is a fertile soil for criticism or even suspicion that the rise of China is unfairly exploited by Chinese Indonesians.

RETURN TO SUSTAINABLE HIGH GROWTH

By and large, Indonesia has been a success seen from its share in world population. Without competitive advantages such increase in share is unattainable. At the very least, such a share indicates the ability to feed a growing population. The experiment with the route of assimilation to nationhood has yet to demonstrate success, but it too, is still alive. However, history has witnessed Indonesia as a case of Sisyphean development. It repeatedly kicked off episodes of high growth, but each of them ended up in a deep fall. Political fragmentation remains a challenge as can be seen in the number of political parties represented in the parliament without a majority. The recent crisis threw Indonesia back into a very difficult new starting condition.

Like China, Indonesia is searching for the right design or architecture. What Indonesians find in the search process is bound to affect the extent to which Chinese Indonesians can continue to enjoy the benefits that stem from the rise of China. Sukarno experimented with soft socialism, but brought the Indonesian economy to a disappointing episode of scarcity. Suharto walked the pragmatic way. He combined foreign entrepreneurship, Chinese Indonesian entrepreneurship, and military-anchored stability in a thriving region as crucible to high growth. It is under Suharto's New Order that Indonesians enjoyed the most durable increases in per-capita income. It is also during Suharto's term that Indonesia came closest to a market economy, allowing Indonesia to be included in the group of high-performing economies. Unfortunately, the Sisyphean growth persists. At the later stages of his rule, Suharto committed the mistake of allowing nepotism to disorient the economy. Under his long rule Indonesia drifted to "premanisme" or "criminal state" (Lindsey 2001). The cancerous nepotism and collusion turned growth-phobic. A new direction is needed somewhat reminiscent to China's New Culture, which predated the economic miracle by decades. Some call the new architecture "open social market economy", which should constitute an important element in a new Indonesia. Open means as exposed to the rest of the world as those economies immediately ahead of Indonesia in the relentless human journey to sustainable prosperity. Market signifies decisions and actions that are based on individual interests that in turn interact in a way that unleash ingenuities and *de-facto* leads to the least objectionable imbalance in a long-term perspective. The design also includes a social state where citizens agree to support each other at life's pre-competitive stages, particularly in the accumulation of human capital. Social connotes adequate protection that ensures the sense of ownership of the development process among the largest possible segment of the population.

Generally speaking Indonesian politicians have voted for swimming with the current of globalization. After all Indonesians are a product of globalization whether one talks about them as people, their religions, their technologies or even their genes. However, there is going to be a number of local flavourings to globalization as adhered to among Indonesians.

First of all, by far the largest majority of Indonesians profess to Islam. Any variant of globalization is bound to fail in Indonesia unless it succeeds to emancipate Muslims economically. Sustainable prosperity amidst poor Muslims is a contradiction in terms in the context of Indonesia. It is not likely that the main stream of globalization bends to please locals, including Indonesians. It is the Indonesians who should complement globalization with local empowerment. Attempts are being made to enrich globalization with Islam-philic elements or, indeed, more friendly to the poor at large (Lubis 2004). Yet, more seems to be needed. Indonesians of all persuasions will have to embrace the deepest forces of globalization, namely science and technologies and equality of opportunities in order to make it through to a lasting growth. The world economy has always belonged to open economies, though openness alone is insufficient to produce success.

The second local flavouring relates perhaps to the facts of diversity in Indonesia. East and west of the Wallace Line, Indonesians' home is an Eden of diversity. Among East Asians, Indonesia is home to the largest pool of descendants of Melanesians. Being followers of Abrahamic religions, Indonesians are somehow unique in East Asia, however ephemeral such uniqueness may be in evolutionary terms. In the Asian world of strong central government, Indonesia appears to be badly in need of a wide-ranging decentralization. Indeed, Indonesians may never cease to demand decentralization before they arrive at a federal structure. Short of federalism, decentralization constitutes a major element in post-Suharto reform. Indonesia is being de-massified into smaller and smaller units of local government to the extent that it threatens to fall into the perennial trap of fragmentation.

It is hard to judge whether or not Indonesia is unique when it comes to the issues of overseas Chinese. Some say it almost made it to craft such uniqueness through the *peranakan,* but failed to pull through. (Wang 2001). Be as it may, the fact remains that Chinese Indonesians are the backbone of the post-colonial economy of Indonesia. Politicians have come and gone in Indonesia, but little has changed in the ethnic balance of business ownership. Such imbalance may look disturbing politically. Yet the resilience of Chinese Indonesians to repeated blows, including some pogroms, suggests that Indonesia is equipped with a core class of entrepreneurs who would not run away from their business even under a heightening threat of discrimination. This core group of entrepreneurs can be expected to accomplish greater things, if relieved of unnecessary burdens. Unchained they may catapult Indonesia into the orbit of hyper growth. Indigenous Indonesians can learn a great deal from the core group of Chinese Indonesian business people. To be productive such learning requires, however, the unlearning of a great deal of business-phobic deeply rooted habits. Such unlearning is a painstaking process. Malays, including those making up the majority of Indonesians, are yet to prove their ability to go through such unlearning and endure the process thoroughly. The experiences of China show that the unlearning of business-phobic habits is an evolutionary process. It took China's New Culture decades to get to the Four Modernizations Policy. However, the unlearning and subsequent learning of new habits have endowed China with unimaginably great success.

Some people tend to belittle the accomplishments of Chinese Indonesians by suggesting that the success is linked with collusion with ruling political elites. Reference is also made to the extractive nature of businesses under Chinese Indonesian ownership in contrast to innovation-based businesses that one finds in countries like South Korea. Yoshihara Kunio coined the term "*erstatz* capitalists" when referring to Chinese business people of Southeast Asia in a pejorative way. Yet, life is a matter of adaptations and mutations as response to incremental changes and dramatic changes in living environment. When the legal environment fails to provide adequate protection, players cultivate informal networks of ersatz-protection including tribalism, *guangxi* and collusion with ruling elites. Nothing is particularly Indonesian or Chinese in such development.

TOWARDS NORMAL RELATIONS

To avoid misunderstanding it is appropriate at this juncture to float the question of who we are before giving the impression that some Indonesians would benefit from the rise of China just because they descend from Chinese ancestors and parents. Indigenous Indonesians and Chinese Indonesians are children of migrants. Long time ago people living along the Yang-tse Kiang were sinicized under the Chou and Han dynasties. Some fled southward to the fringes of the Asian continent. Some others arrived in the archipelago through Taiwan (Diamond 1999). Peter Bellwood tells us about the commonalities of roots among Southern Chinese and Southeast Asians as compared with Sino-Tibetans (Bellwood 1997). If one cares to look further back to the distant past, East Asians stemmed most probably from the same ancestor (Olson 2002). Modern humans are in fact related to one another, having descended from the same genetic ancestor who emerged somewhere in Africa hundreds of millennia ago.

It may sound naïve to judge the relationship between people of different republics on the basis of deeply shared genetic and cultural inheritances. Yet, the time when people were moving away from each other and speciating in the process in what is referred to earlier as "diasporic globalization", came to an end when Polynesians reached the most remote places in the vast Pacific Ocean. Since then humans have engaged in "implosive globalization", flocking to the most glittering centres of wealth accumulation and prosperity. Under the implosive globalization, "races" get recombined both genetically and culturally. Much suffering would have been avoided or at least ameliorated and more wealth created, had humans known earlier the oneness of their gene-culture or gene-memetic heritage. Steps would have been taken to reduce pogrom amok, of which Southeast Asia in general and Indonesia in particular is notorious.

Undoubtedly, time-bound differences exist between migrants that rode different waves of migration to the same destination or transits. In a similar way that a Batak Indonesian observes Batak traditions, cares to share the fruits of his sweat with relatives who chose to stay back home around the great Lake Toba, enjoys visiting his village of birth during festive seasons, or even has his dead commensurate with the latter's deeds flown back to be buried on one of the hills of the Toba Highland, Chinese Indonesians are entitled to observe traditions of their own. There is a risk of fragmentation in such pluralism. Where ethnicity is overstretched as to intrude into politics, it not only turns into obstacle to progress in nationhood, but it also serves as a fertile soil for zero-sum interactions of a nepotistic nature. Corruption, for example, is found to correlate positively with the number of spoken dialects in a country. However, the risk is worth taking. Exposure to the same or similar education, professions, religions, work and challenges of having to prevail in tough global competition has served and will continue to serve as buoyant sources of glue between different ethnic groups of the same nationality. To an important degree Indonesians of all ethnic origins have undergone the process of "de-tribalization", which is a necessary step in nation-building. The attainment has been short of assimilation as pointed out again and again by students of Southeast Asian Chinese, but time is always in favour of "assimilationists" whenever people of different ethnic origins share the same habitats.

Some students of Southeast Asian Chinese convey the impression that a special relationship exists between Southeast Asian Chinese and China based on a shared gene-culture pool (Wilson 1996). Testing such special relationship is difficult, however. Individual Southeast Asian Chinese have different perceptions of China as pointed out in countless analyses (Ananta and Arifin 2004). The existence of local organizations or associations bearing Chinese names does not necessarily prove ties with China. A Chinese Indonesian importer of motorbikes may continue to prefer Japanese brands for practical commercial reasons. The fact that a competitor decides to import Chinese substitute bikes has to do largely with commercial interests rather than ethnic ties. Likewise Chinese Indonesian exporters of rubber are not going to jeopardize their relationship with buyers around the globe just for the sake of ethnic relations with importers in China. That they venture to the Chinese market is a logical commercial consequence of the rise of China. All traders and investors are well advised to build bridges to China irrespective of ethnicities. Just to get closer to the Chinese market is a commercial imperative of the day.

China on its side has repeatedly told all ethnic Chinese outside China to comply with the laws of the countries of their respective citizenship rather than to let themselves be trapped between two lines. After all, a bigger number of citizens is perhaps the last thing that China wishes to have. China's interest in returning Chinese is perhaps confined to a small circle of great minds in science and technologies, which are mostly educated and trained in North America and a few other centres of excellence. China is not alone in seeking to attract such great minds. That China is interested in good relations with Southeast Asian Chinese is also self-explanatory. The whole world is interested in getting connected with them attracted by the engine of wealth accumulation under their command. Governments competing to woo great capitalists, scientists and engineers are among the salient features of "implosive globalization".

China's rise or re-awakening is undoubtedly a lucrative opportunity for those who aspire to accelerate their journey to prosperity by tapping the tailwind of global trade and investment. At first glance, Southeast Asian Chinese may look privileged while seeking to benefit from the great opportunities. When one scrutinizes deeper, the world of trade and investment does not offer much room for such privileged relationship. Globalization carries flattening forces (Friedman 2005). Such flattening applies also to primordial ties, including racial discrimination and its reverse form in which minorities discriminate against majorities. A faster growth in China and Indonesia is bound to make ethnicity less and less contentious in the world of commerce.

References

Ananta, Aris and Evi Nurvidya Arifin, eds. 2004. *International Migration in Southeast Asia* (Singapore: ISEAS).

Anderson, Kenneth. 2005. "Squaring the Circle? Reconciling Sovereignty and Global Governance Through Global Government Networks". Book Review in *Harvard Law Review* 118 (January): 1255–312.

Bellwood, Peter. 1997. *Prehistory of the Indo-Malaysian Archipelago*. Revised Edition (Honolulu: University of Hawai'i Press).

Bergreen, Laurence. 2003. *Over the Edge of The World* (New York: Harper-Collins Publishers Inc.).

Bown, Chad P; McCulloch, Rachel. 2005. "US Trade Policy Toward China: Discrimination and Its Implications". Brandeis University Department of Economics and International Business School Working Paper Series. July.

Boyreau-Debray, Genevieve and Wei, Shang-jin. 2005. "Pitfalls of a State-Dominated Financial System: The Case of China". NBER Working Paper no. 11214. March.

Braendle, Udo C.; Gasser, Tanja; Noll, Juergenn. 2005. "Corporate Governance in China. Is Economic Growth Potential Hindered by Guangxi?" University of Vienna Department of Business Studies Working Paper Series, July.

Chiswick, Barry R. 2000. 'Are Immigrants Favorably Self-Selected?' In Caroline B. Brettel and James F. Hollifield, editors, *Migration Theory. Taking Across Disciplines* (New York: Routledge).

Chiswick, Barry S; Hatton, Timothy J. 2002. "Interntional Migration and the Integration of the Labor Markets". IZA Discussion Paper no. 559.

Cuellar, Mariano-Florention. 2004. "Reflections on Sovereignty and Collective Security" in *Stanford Law School Research Paper* no. 95. July.

De Bievre, Dirk. 2004. "Governance in International Trade: Judicilisation and Positive Integration in the WTO". In *Preprints of the Max Planck Institute for Research on Collective Goods*, no. 7.

Diamond, Jared. 1999. *Guns, Germs and Steel* (New York: W.W. Norton and Company).

Diamond, Jared. 2005. Collapse. *How Societies Choose to Fail or Survive* (London: Penguin Books).

Fewsmith, Joseph. 2001. *China Since Tianianmen. The Politics of Transition* (Cambridge: Cambridge University Press).

Frieman, Thomas. 2005. *The World is Flat. A Brief History of the Twenty-first Century* (New York: Farrar, Strauss, and Giroux).

Kanamori, Toshiki; Zhao Zhijun. 2005. "Modelling Private Sector Development in the People's Republic of China". *ADBI Research Paper Series*. No. 62. June.

Kipnis, Andrew B. 1996. "The Language of Gifts. Managing Guanxi in a North China Village". In *Modern China* 22, no. 3 (July) (Saga Publications, Inc.).

Lindsey, Tim. 2001. "The Criminal State: Premanisme and the New Indonesia". In *Indonesia Today. Challenges of History*, edited by Grayson Lloyd and Shannon Smith (Singapore: Institute of Southeast Asian Studies), pp. 283–97.

Lubis, Nur A.P. 2004. "Financial Activism among Indonesian Muslims". In *Islamic Perspectives on the New Millennium*, edited by Virginia Hooker and Amin Saikal (Singapore: Institute of Southeast Asian Studies), pp. 91–112.

McGoldrick, Peter and Patrick Paul Walsh. "Reforms and Productivity Dynamics in Chinese State-Owned Enterprises". *IZA Discussion Paper* no. 1201 (Bonn: Institute for the Study of Labour).

Menzies, Gavin. 2003. *1421. The Year China Discovered the World* (London and New York: Bantam Books).

Mitter, Rana. 2004. A *Bitter Revolution. China's Struggle With the Modern World* (Oxord: Oxford University Press).

Mumford, Lewis. 1961. *The City in History* (San Diego: Harcourt Inc.).

Murray, Charles. 2003. *Human Accomplishments* (New York: Perennial).

Olson, Steve. 2003. *Mapping Human History* (Boston: Houghton Mifflin Company).

Prasad, Eswar and Wei Shang-jin. 2005. "The Chinese Approach to Capital Inflows: Patterns and Possible Explanations". NBER Working Paper no. 11306, April.

Sachs, Jeffrey. 2005. *The End of Poverty. How We Can Make It Happen in Our Life Time* (London: Penguin Books).

Schaaper, Martin. 2004. "An Emerging Knowledge-Based Economy in China? Indicators from OECD Data Bases". OECD STI Working Paper no. 4.

Shane, Matthew and Fred Gale. 2004. "China: A Study of Dynamic Growth". USDA Economic Research Service Working Paper Series. October.

Shiue, Carol H. and Wolfgang Keller. 2004. "Markets in China and Europe on the Eve of the Industrial Revolution". NBER Working Paper Series no. 10778, September.

Slaughter, Anne-Marie. 1999. "Agencies on the Loose. Holding Government Networks Accountable". In Harvard Law School Public Law and Legal Theory Working Paper Series no. 006.

Slaughter, Anne-Marie. 2004. "Global Government Networks, Global Information Agencies, and Disaggregated Democracy". In Harvard Law School Public Law Working Paper no. 018.

Starr, John Bryan. 2001. *Understanding China. A Guide to China's Economy, History and Political Culture.* Revised edition (New York: Hill and Wang).

van der Eng, Pierre. 2001. "Indonesia's Economy and Standard of Living in the 20th Century" in Grayson Lloyd and Shannon Smith. Indonesia *Today. Challenges of History* (Singapore: Institute of Southeast Asian Studies).

Wang, Gungwu. 2001. *Only Connect. Sino-Malay Encounters.* Singapore: Times Academic Press.

Wei, Yinggi; Liu, Xiaming. 2004. "Impacts of R&D, Exports and FDI on Productivity in Chinese Manufacturing Firms". Lancaster Uinversity Management School Working Paper, no. 3.

Wilson, Dick. 1996. *China the Big Tiger. A Nation Awakes* (London: Little, Brown and Company).

Wu, Yuan-li and Wu, Chun-his. 1980. *Economic Development in Southeast Asia. The Chinese Dimension* (Stanford: Hoover Institution Press).

Yoffee, Norman. 2005. *Evolution of the Earliest Cities, States and Civilizations* (Cambridge: Cambridge University Press).

4

The Indonesian Government's Economic Policies Towards the Ethnic Chinese: Beyond Economic Nationalism?

Thee Kian Wie

THE ROLE OF ECONOMIC NATIONALISM

To a much greater degree than has been the case in the other newly-independent countries in Southeast Asia, economic nationalism in Indonesia has remained a potent force until the present. Although its contemporary manifestations has in general become less aggressive and less strident than in the 1950s, it remains a driving force that to a large extent still influences economic policies today. Whereas economic nationalism during the early years of independence in the 1950s was mainly directed at the economic dominance of the Dutch and ethnic Chinese business interests, in the years following the Asian economic crisis in the late 1990s, it was mainly aimed at the perceived interference of international organizations, particularly the IMF, in the formulation of Indonesia's economic policies.

Despite the strong economic nationalism, pragmatic considerations have often overruled ill-considered economic nationalism. In this way, pragmatic policies have often been able to mitigate the adverse economic and political effects of emotional economic nationalism. This was already evident when the Indonesian Government in the second half of the 1950s terminated the unsuccessful *"Benteng"* (Fortress) Programme, which was the Indonesian Government's first affirmative policy to promote indigenous Indonesian businessmen (*pengusaha asli Indonesia*).[1]

THE 'CHINESE PROBLEM'

Unlike the Malaysian Government, which since 1970 has pursued an explicit affirmative policy, the New Economic Policy (NEP), to advance the economic position and intensify the political hegemony of the Malay *bumiputera* population (Jesudason 1997, p. 124), the Indonesian Government since the early years of independence up to the present has never formulated a comprehensive economic policy relating to the Chinese minority. Although laws and decrees were issued which regulated the life and activities of the Chinese minority, such as its economic activities, these laws and regulations had an *ad hoc* character, which were not part of a comprehensive policy towards the Chinese (Coppel 1983, p. 29).

This absence of a comprehensive policy was not caused because the Chinese were not seen as a "problem", but because the Indonesian Government in the early 1950s tended to be fragmented, which made coordinated policy-making, including policy formulation towards the Chinese difficult (Coppel 1983, p. 29). In fact, anti-Chinese feelings were virulent in the early independence years, when Indonesian citizens of Chinese descent were still viewed with great distrust and not accepted as full-fledged citizens. Even then, however, no explicit anti-Chinese economic policies were introduced, but rather affirmative policies, such as the *"Benteng"* (Fortress) programme, to promote indigenous Indonesian entrepreneurs.

However, during the early years of independence, it was continued Dutch economic control of the economy which posed the major political and economic problem for the Indonesian Government. If economic nationalism in newly-independent countries is defined as "the national aspiration to have nationals own and control the productive assets owned by foreigners or residents considered as aliens and perform the important economic functions hitherto performed by foreigners or resident aliens" (Johnson 1972, p. 26), the primary target of Indonesia's economic nationalism during the early 1950s was the elimination of Dutch economic dominance, particularly over the modern sectors of the economy, rather than dealing with Chinese economic dominance.

Under the terms of the Financial-Economic Agreement (Finec), reached at the Round Table Conference (RTC) in The Hague in late 1949, the Indonesian Government guaranteed that Dutch business could continue to operate in Indonesia without any hindrance. Nationalization of Dutch enterprises would only be permitted if it was considered to be in

Indonesia's national interest, and only when it was mutually agreed by both parties. The amount of compensation for the nationalization of the enterprise would be decided by a judge on the basis of the real value of the nationalized enterprise (Meier 1994, pp. 46–47).

The success of the Dutch delegation at the RTC in persuading the Indonesian delegation to agree with most of the items contained in Finec, including the guarantees, concessions, and rights accorded to Dutch business in independent Indonesia, could be attributed to the determination of the Dutch Government to secure the maximum possible economic benefits from Finec (Meier 1994, p. 46). In return, the Dutch were prepared to make political concessions to the Indonesians.

On its part, the Indonesian delegation, led by Vice President Hatta, was prepared, though reluctantly, to yield to the Dutch demands because it realized that for the foreseeable future Indonesia would, whether it liked it or not, still need Dutch capital and enterprise for the reconstruction of its war-ravaged economy and generate the export revenues needed to import foodstuffs, raw materials and capital equipment for its manufacturing industries. As a pragmatic nationalist, Vice President Hatta realized that no matter how unpalatable the continuing Dutch economic dominance would be to the Indonesian people, there was in the short run no viable alternative.

Having achieved political independence without meaningful economic independence, the Indonesian Government took several steps to counter Dutch economic dominance insofar as this was possible within the constraints of Finec. One of the most important early measures was the nationalization of the Java Bank (*Javasche Bank*), the former bank of circulation in the Netherlands Indies, through the purchase of shares from both domestic and overseas shareholders. The purchase of shares proceeded smoothly, and on 6 December 1951 law no. 24 of 1951 on the nationalization of the Java Bank was officially enacted (Saubari 2003, p. 72). In 1953 the Java Bank was renamed Bank Indonesia, which became the central bank of Indonesia. Sjafruddin Prawiranegara, former Minister of Finance in the Hatta and Natsir cabinets, was appointed as the first Governor of Bank Indonesia.

Throughout the first half of the 1950s, heated political debates raged about the pace at which the vestiges of Western (that is, Dutch) capitalism should be eliminated in order to build up a national economy which, most nationalist leaders agreed, would not be built along capitalist lines. A vocal group of radical nationalists advocated the establishment of state-owned enterprises (SOEs) occupying the "commanding heights of the economy" and cooperatives for the "economically weak groups in society" to replace the foreign-owned capitalist enterprises. Arrayed against them was a smaller, less cohesive group of pragmatic nationalists, who argued that the pace of eliminating capitalist enterprises, particularly the foreign-owned ones, would have to be gradual to prevent serious economic disruption (Paauw 1983, p. 207).

While these political debates proceeded, political relations with the Netherlands deteriorated rapidly after the mid-1950s as a result of the unresolved political conflict over the status of West Irian (West New Guinea, now called Papua province). When in the autumn of 1957 the Indonesian Government failed to persuade the United Nations General Assembly to force the Netherlands to negotiate with Indonesia about the future status of West Irian, militant trade unions took over several Dutch enterprises. To re-establish order and wrest control from the communist-oriented trade unions, General Nasution, the army chief of staff, ordered the seized enterprises to be placed under the supervision of local army commanders (Dick 2002, p. 164). In February 1959 all the seized Dutch enterprises were formally nationalized, and transformed into state-owned enterprises (SOEs) which were mostly run by military officers. With this one sweeping measure, the powerful Dutch business presence in Indonesia, which had operated in Indonesia since the early 1870s, was eliminated.

GOVERNMENT ECONOMIC POLICIES TOWARD THE CHINESE

The nationalization of Dutch enterprises went a long way towards satisfying the national aspiration "to convert the colonial economy into a national economy". However, this conversion was not felt as complete, as the large indigenous population was still facing the economic dominance of ethnic Chinese businessmen, including Indonesian citizens and resident aliens, which dominated important sectors of the economy, particularly the intermediate trade and money lending.

Building a "national economy" (*ekonomi nasional*) gave expression to the national aspiration for an economy which would be controlled by indigenous Indonesians (*Indonesia asli*) rather than by "foreign" groups, like the ethnic Chinese, regardless of whether they were citizens or not (Coppel 1983, p. 3).

In view of the historically weak position of Indonesian businessmen since the Dutch colonial period, Indonesian policymakers since the early 1950s put a high priority on promoting the development of indigenous Indonesian entrepreneurs. Aside from the above-mentioned measures to counter Dutch economic dominance, the Indonesian Government also considered steps to reduce the economic role of the ethnic Chinese.

However, in view of the above factors, taking measures to curtail Chinese economic activities proved to be more difficult than eliminating Dutch economic interests. For one thing, the number of ethnic Chinese was much greater than the Dutch, and their economic activities in the rural areas were much more intertwined with the economic activities of the indigenous population than the Dutch activities had ever been. Moreover, the large ethnic Chinese group included Indonesian citizens as well as citizens of the People's Republic of China and a small group of pro-Taiwan "stateless" citizens.[2] It was therefore quite difficult for the Indonesian Government to take measures directed at all ethnic Chinese, as this group also contained the relatively large group of Indonesian citizens. Having fought against Dutch colonialism and its implied racism, many Indonesian leaders found that overly discriminatory policies against its citizens of Chinese descent did not accord well with the ideals of the Indonesian revolution.

The 'Benteng' (Fortress) Programme

Since the early 1950s pressures for preferential treatment of indigenous Indonesian businessmen had grown stronger. In general the only fields in which indigenous Indonesians operated was in small-scale agriculture, a few medium-sized modern retail stores, and small-scale industries, such as batik and clove cigarettes. To promote the faster development of indigenous entrepreneurs, Djuanda, the minister of welfare, in April 1950 issued a regulation which gave priority to indigenous businessmen to import goods from abroad. To facilitate this import trade, indigenous businessmen were given easy access to cheap credit. This programme was called the "Benteng" (Fortress) programme (Siahaan 1996, p. 168).

Besides building up a class of indigenous businessmen, the Benteng programme was also aimed as yet another measure to counter Dutch economic dominance (Sumitro 2000, p. 144), particularly the power of the Dutch trading houses. Although Sumitro himself was responsible for the implementation of the Benteng programme when he was minister of trade and industry in the Natsir cabinet (1950–51), as an academically trained economist, he basically considered market forces as the best way to ending the import monopolies of the Dutch general trading companies. By liberalizing the import trade, the market power of the Dutch companies could be eroded by import competition. However, most other economic nationalists viewed the Western-trained Sumitro with great suspicion, and wanted to continue the pre-war system of import controls which had been introduced during the early years of the Great Depression in the early 1930s. This time the import controls, however, had to benefit indigenous rather than the Dutch import companies (Booth 1998, p. 222).

Protection to the indigenous importers was to be provided by reserving the import of certain categories of goods (which were referred to as "*benteng*" goods) solely for indigenous importers and by channelling credits to these importers by the state-owned bank BNI (Bank Negara Indonesia) (Sutter 1959, pp. 1017–18). The required qualifications for receiving preferential treatment through the Benteng programme were, at least on paper, quite stringent. To qualify for this preferential treatment, an indigenous businessman had to be "a new Indonesian importer" and a legal entity, such as a corporation, silent partnership or partnership, and possess a minimum amount of working capital of 100,000 *rupiah*, an office large enough for "several full-time employees", and officers with previous business experience. Another qualification was that at least 70 per cent of the capital had to be provided by indigenous Indonesians (*bangsa Indonesia asli*). However, among these provisions there was no specific reference to non-indigenous Indonesians, including Sino-Indonesians (Sutter 1959, p. 1018).

Choosing the import trade as the first major economic activity, on which policies to promote indigenous entrepreneurship would be focused, was understandable, as at the time almost all the export and import trade were in the hands of the Dutch and the Chinese (Suhadi 1967, p. 218). Focusing on the import trade to secure indigenous Indonesian dominance appeared to be the most feasible, as this trade seemed to be most responsive to state direction through controls over the allocation of import licenses (Robison 1986, p. 44). The import trade also appeared the most accessible to indigenous businessmen, as they could easily set up their business with a minimum of overhead investment, could concentrate on products sufficiently standardized which only required a minimum of business experience, and could deal in goods that enjoyed a seller's market because of import restrictions (Anspach 1969, p. 168).

Prospective indigenous importers could also learn from the example of the "Big Five" Dutch general trading companies (Borsumij, Jacobsen van den Berg, Geo Wehry, Internatio and Lindeteves), which had used their activities in the import trade as a springboard to diversify into plantation agriculture, internal distribution, insurance and the manufacture of various import-competing goods (Anspach 1969, p. 168). Learning from the experience of these Dutch general trading companies, several indigenous importers, including Dasaad Musin, Djohan Djohar and Rahman Tamin had diversified their economic activities into other fields (Anspach 1969, p. 168). The government hoped that like these indigenous business pioneers, the "Benteng" importers could use their activities in the import trade as a base for capital accumulation which would sustain the expansion of indigenous capital into other sectors (Robison 1986, p. 44).

To assist the indigenous importers, the government selected certain kinds of goods which could only be imported by the Benteng importers. Most of these goods were simple consumer goods which could be easily sold, such as yarn, textiles, paper, stationery, matches and sundries (Suhadi 1967, p. 218).

Implementing the Benteng Programme

The Benteng programme attracted a lot of interest. While in 1951 some 250 businessmen had registered with this programme, in 1952 this number had increased to 741, and to 1,500 in 1953 and to 2,211 in 1954 (Siahaan 1996, p. 168). As a result, the percentage of total government foreign exchange credit allocated to the Benteng importers increased from 37 per cent in 1952–53 to 76.2 per cent in late 1954 (Robison 1986, p. 45).

This great interest was not surprising, since the government, making ample use of the existing system of import control, allocated scarce foreign exchange to the favoured indigenous importers who, as a result, could earn windfall profits from importing various goods. Lobbying to obtain an adequate share of the foreign exchange, the indigenous importers formed a group which, after the Benteng programme, was called the "Benteng Group" (Suhadi 1967, p. 218). As a result of this programme, by the early 1950s around 70 per cent of the import trade was conducted by indigenous businessmen (Burger 1975, p. 171).

Another group which attempted to obtain a share in the rents created by the foreign exchange control system of the Benteng programme was the relatively small group of indigenous industrialists who realized that their prospects for making good profits depended very much on the opportunity of purchasing imported raw materials and capital goods at official prices. As the Indonesian Government since the early years of independence had been anxious to promote industrialization, it had put important industrial raw materials in the category of essential goods in its approved list of imports. Imported raw materials were therefore charged with low tariffs or sometimes could be imported duty free. However, as it were the indigenous importers who were free to sell their imported goods, it was they who benefited most from the rents created by the foreign exchange control system and not the industrialists (Suhadi 1967, pp. 219–20).

From the time that the new indigenous importers had started receiving preferential treatment under the Benteng programme, with several of them lacking capital or business experience or both, engaged in certain business practices which, although not in violation of the letter of the law, did offend ethical standards. There were of course several other new indigenous importers which had established a *bona fide* cooperation between their indigenous companies and non-indigenous or foreign companies. However, there were many more cases which could hardly be named *bona fide* enterprises, in which indigenous importers and ethnic Chinese businessmen (whether Indonesian citizen or foreign national) had set up so-called "Ali-Baba" concerns. In fact, "shotgun wedding" between new indigenous importing companies and the older importing companies owned by ethnic Chinese businessmen proliferated under various forms, such as fronts and straw men and the selling of import licences to genuine, mostly ethnic Chinese, importers (Sutter 1959, p. 1027).

Several of the new indigenous importers also turned out to be individuals associated with powerful officials in the government bureaucracy or in the political parties, who controlled the allocation of import licences and credit.

These bogus importers also often failed to repay the credits they had received from the state-owned BNI bank (Robison 1986, p. 45). Hence, the Benteng programme did not foster a strong, self-reliant indigenous merchant class, but a group of licensed brokers and political fixers, in short what are now called unproductive "rent-seekers" or "rent-harvesters". Not surprisingly, these importers were often referred to as "briefcase importers" (*importir aktentas*), whose only qualification as an importer was that they carried a briefcase (Siahaan 1998, p. 168).

As the Benteng programme progressed, it became increasingly apparent to the government that the programme was not successful in achieving its stated aims. In 1953 the government started screening the officially registered indigenous importers, and as a result was able to reduce the number of registered importers by more than half from about 4,300 to about 2,000 (Burger 1975, p. 171).

This measure, however, turned out to be ineffective, as in August 1954 the Central Office of Imports estimated that about 90 per cent of the registered national importers were not *bona fide*. This estimate was confirmed by another screening in 1955 ordered by Roosseno, the new Minister of Economic Affairs, who had replaced Iskaq. Even Iskaq, former Minister of Economic Affairs who had been a strong supporter of the Benteng programme, acknowledged that import licences were being sold at 200 to 250 per cent of their nominal value (Anspach 1969, p. 174).

To eliminate the abuses of the Benteng programme, Roosseno introduced a foreign exchange auction system in the textile sector. He also banned discrimination on ethnic grounds, and thus allowed Sino-Indonesian businessmen to openly participate in the import trade. The auction system, however, turned out to be unsuccessful, as it did not allow indigenous importers with inadequate financial resources with access to the auctioned foreign exchange quota. Hence, indigenous importers with inadequate financial resources continued to serve as agents for ethnic Chinese businessmen (Anspach 1969, pp. 174–75). Thus Indonesia's experience with its first affirmative programme to promote a strong and self-reliant indigenous business class proved to be a failure and in the second half of the 1950s came to an inglorious end, even though this programme was never officially abolished.

THE BAN ON OWNERSHIP OF ENTERPRISES BY ALIENS

Like during the Dutch colonial period, Chinese businessmen continued to own and control most of the rice mills in Indonesia. For instance, in 1952 not less than 138 out of 154 rice mills in East Java were mostly owned by ethnic Chinese (Anspach 1969, p. 182). In view of the important economic role played by these rice mills, the Indonesian Government issued a regulation in 1954 aimed at transferring the ownership of rice mills from the Chinese to indigenous Indonesians by March 1955. The regulation decreed that no new licences for running rice mills would be issued to aliens, while the existing rice mills were to be transferred to indigenous Indonesians, specifically those persons having sole Indonesian citizenship. Since the Indonesian citizens of Chinese descent still had, at the time of the regulation, dual citizenships, the 1954 regulation also affected them (Suryadinata 1992, p. 132).

Since in early 1956 only six medium- and large-scale mills were owned by indigenous Indonesians, while the remaining 269 were still owned by Chinese, the deadline for compliance with the decree was postponed to March 1957 (Anspach 1969, p. 184). Moreover, because of the difficulties in implementing this regulation, the government reportedly still granted licences to Chinese aliens on an annual basis (Suryadinata 1992, p. 32).

Since stevedoring, harbour transport and wharfage enterprises were also mostly owned and controlled by Chinese, the government in 1954 also issued a decree that all these enterprises had to be transferred to indigenous Indonesian ownership by 1956. However, this date had to be continually extended, with the last extension set for June 1959 (Anspach 1969, p. 184).

THE ASSAAT MOVEMENT

Although the strongly anti-Chinese Assaat movement, which was quite powerful in 1956–57, did not directly lead to an explicit anti-Chinese economic policy, it is necessary to mention this movement as it was symptomatic of the anti-Chinese atmosphere in the second half of the 1950s. In the tumultuous years of the mid-1950s when anti-Chinese sentiments were quite strong, the emergence of the strongly anti-Chinese Assaat movement in 1956 found wide resonance among many indigenous businessmen and the wider public in general. This movement, initiated by Assaat, a businessman and former Minister of the Interior in the Natsir cabinet (1950–51), called for the government to discriminate in economic affairs against the Chinese (including those who were Indonesian citizens) and in favour of the indigenous Indonesians (Coppel 1983, p. 37). At a convention of the All-Indonesian Congress of National Importers in Surabaya in March 1956, Assaat called for a specifically discriminatory policy in government regulations of the economy which should favour indigenous Indonesians in their economic competition with other businessmen, particularly the ethnic Chinese. In his speech Assaat accused the Chinese of responsibility for the many difficulties faced by the Indonesian economy. He also called them opportunists, who had helped the Dutch during the Dutch colonial period and Chiang Kai-shek in China during Kuomintang rule and now supported the communist government of Mao Tse-tung (Feith 1964, pp. 481–82).

Assaat's speech expressed with great directness the anti-Chinese feelings which many Indonesians had long had, but hesitated to express in public. Once a man with the authority of Assaat had defied the prevailing restraints on public expression of racist feelings, these restraints quickly lost their power. Within a few weeks committees in support of Assaat's ideas were established in various parts of the country. In the following year the

Assaat movement grew in strength and organizational cohesion. Although this movement drew sympathetic responses from many Indonesians, active participation in this movement was largely confined to businessmen (Feith 1964, p. 482).

Baperki (*Badan Permusyarawatan Kewarganegaraan Indonesia*, Consultative Body for Indonesian Citizenship), a political organization established to defend the interests of Indonesian citizens of Chinese descent, strongly reacted to the challenge posed by the Assaat movement. Baperki argued that protection of the economically weak groups was eminently desirable. However, the determination of just who was economically weak should be on a class basis band and not according to race (Somers 1964, pp. 11, 37). In this effort to oppose discriminatory policies advocated by the Assaat movement, Baperki was supported by the Indonesian Communist Party (PKI).

However, the Assaat movement did not quite succeed in achieving its stated objective of achieving official discrimination against the ethnic Chinese. In fact, the Assaat movement withered away in 1958, not so much because of the strong opposition of Baperki and the PKI, but because Assaat had compromised himself by joining the PRRI rebellion in West Sumatra (Somers 1964, pp. 17–18).

MEASURES AGAINST THE PRO-TAIWAN LOCAL CHINESE

Angry about the support of the Taiwan Government and the "stateless" Taiwan-oriented local Chinese to the PRRI and Permesta rebellions, the Indonesian Government in 1958 closed down all organizations, schools, newspapers and enterprises connected in any way to Taiwan. In addition, Chinese community leaders who were pro-Kuomintang were arrested (Suryadinata 1992, p. 175).

In quantitative terms, however, the closure or nationalization of the enterprises of the pro-Taiwan "foreign" Chinese did not appreciably reduce the economic activities of the ethnic Chinese. The reason was that the number of pro Taiwan Chinese was relatively small, certainly much smaller than the foreign Chinese who were nationals of the People's Republic.

The Chinese Government hailed these measures, as they were aimed at its political opponents. However, its satisfaction about the measures aimed at the pro-Taiwan Chinese did not last long, as the following year the Indonesian Government took a much more drastic measure to curb the economic activities of the "foreign" Chinese.

THE BAN ON RETAIL TRADE BY ALIENS IN RURAL AREAS

With the nationalization of all Dutch enterprises in 1958, the Chinese community emerged as the strongest element in the economy, aside from the government itself. In the rural areas the Chinese since the Dutch colonial period had built a position of dominance in retail trade, in rice milling and in rural finance (Mackie 1971, p. 9). Given this position of economic dominance of the Chinese, the deteriorating economic conditions and the general distrust of the political loyalty of the ethnic Chinese, it was only a matter of time before the Chinese, particularly the large number of "foreign" Chinese who were nationals of the People's Republic, would be the next target of government policy.

One of the first steps was an attempt in 1959 to break the Chinese hold on intermediate trade throughout the country by eliminating all "foreign" Chinese from retail trade in the rural areas (Somers Heidhues 2003, p. 238). In May 1959 Rachmat Muljomiseno, the then Minister of Trade and a strong supporter of the Assaat movement, issued a regulation banning foreign nationals from engaging in rural trade, and requiring them to transfer their business to Indonesian citizens by 30 September 1959 (Suryadinata 1992, p. 135). However, before the minister could implement this regulation, a new cabinet headed by President Sukarno himself was installed.

President Sukarno's dissolution of the Constituent Assembly on 5 July 1959 heralded the introduction of Guided Democracy and Guided Economy in Indonesia. Despite the official fanfare surrounding Guided Democracy and Guided Economy, economic chaos set in as sound economic policies were increasingly disregarded in favour of revolutionary slogans. The support of the army for Sukarno's Guided Democracy also meant that the interference of the army in the economy and administration was increasing (Rickleffs 1993, p. 267).

On 16 November 1959 Government Decree no. 10 of 1959 was issued which decreed that as from 1 January 1960, foreign nationals would be banned from rural trade and would have to transfer their business to Indonesian nationals (Suryadinata 1992, p. 135). Although Indonesian nationals benefiting from this Decree could also include Indonesian citizens of Chinese descent, the government hoped that much of the rural trade run by the "foreign" Chinese would be taken over by cooperatives and businesses owned and run by indigenous Indonesians.

This decree in effect strengthened the regulation on the ban on foreign nationals to engage in rural trade issued a few months earlier by Rachmat

Muljomiseno. Although Decree no. 10 of 1959 applied to all foreign nationals, it was mainly an army-instigated move to hurt the foreign Chinese (who, the anti-communist army suspected, could be a fifth column for China), weaken Jakarta's (that is, Sukarno's) growing friendship with China, and embarrass the PKI. Although the Chinese Government put heavy pressure on the Indonesian Government not to carry out, if not rescind, this decree, the army in 1959 began forcibly moving the "foreign" Chinese from the rural areas to the cities. As a result of this expulsion, in the course of 1960–61 about 119,000 Chinese nationals were repatriated to China (Rickleffs 1993, p. 267). The ban also caused a serious rupture in the political relations between Indonesia and China.

Since neither cooperatives nor indigenous businessmen were fully equipped to replace the Chinese traders, or to engage in rural trade with equal efficiency, the ban caused considerable economic disruption. At least in the short run, the ban caused more hardship to the villagers it was supposed to help (Somers 1964, p. 28). In order not to weaken the position of Sukarno, who was viewed as a strong anti-communist ally of China, and since it had difficulty accommodating the large number of repatriated Chinese, China toned down its anti-Indonesia rhetoric. Sukarno himself, realizing the danger to both the country's economy and his own power of continuing the anti-Chinese campaign, succeeded in curbing anti-Chinese measures. Although Government Decree no. 10 was never lifted, its further implementation was temporarily suspended. (Suryadinata 1992, p. 137).

As economic conditions continued to deteriorate in the early 1960s and Sukarno's and the army's attention were increasingly focused on reclaiming Irian Barat from the Dutch, a resumption of the implementation of Government Decree no. 10 did not take place. Moreover, with the emphasis on "Indonesian-style socialism" the introduction of new affirmative programmes to promote indigenous private businessmen was never considered.

ECONOMIC POLICIES AGAINST THE ETHNIC CHINESE UNDER THE 'NEW ORDER'

Despite the strong anti-Chinese sentiments among several senior officers of the army and hostile policies towards China and the ethnic Chinese, including the Sino-Indonesians, and the outbreak of virulent anti-Chinese riots in various places at the beginning of the "New Order", pragmatic considerations again gained the upper hand. With the New Order regime's key policy objective of pushing economic growth (Booth 1998, p. 325), it was realized that the Chinese were an essential element to achieve this goal. To achieve this goal, it was necessary to lift various restrictions on the economic activities of the Chinese which had been introduced during the Sukarno era. While the Chinese were thus given wide opportunity to be active in the economic field, in other fields, such as politics and culture, their activities were severely restricted, if not outright banned. Baperki was banned because of its close association with PKI, as were also all Chinese schools and newspapers and magazines in Chinese. Celebrating Chinese New Year in public was prohibited, as was the use of Chinese characters. To erase their ethnic identity, the Cabinet Presidium of the emerging New Order regime issued a decision (Decision no. 127 of 1966) urging, in some instances even forcing Sino-Indonesians, to change their Chinese names into indigenous Indonesian names. The official rationale for the decree was "to accelerate the process of assimilation of Indonesians of 'foreign descent' into the body of the Indonesian nation", and that "replacing the names of Indonesians of foreign descent with names which conform to indigenous Indonesian names will assist in assimilation" (Coppel 2002a, p. 33).[3] This policy reflected the need to minimize social differences, which in the past had often erupted in anti-Chinese riots, and strive for social harmony (Elson 2001, p. 161), an important policy objective for the fledgling New Order government.

Despite the gloomy outlook for the Chinese, including the Sino-Indonesians, at the beginning of the New Order, the regime's emphasis on economic development opened new economic opportunities to the Chinese. With their long commercial experience, greater business acumen, better access to capital, managerial and technical skills, international business contacts (particularly their contacts with the Chinese business networks in Southeast and East Asia) and, in some instances, their mutually profitable contacts with powerful power holders, the Chinese were in general able to move into a wide range of economic activities on a large scale, including large estate agriculture, manufacturing, construction, banking, real estate, and services, and to prosper to a much greater degree than during the Dutch colonial period, the Japanese Occupation, and the early period of Indonesian independence. This did not only apply to the regime's Chinese business cronies, who in cahoots with the political power holders established large conglomerates, but also to the medium-sized and smaller enterprises, the majority of which, however, unlike the

Chinese conglomerates, had to survive by their own wits. In general, one can state without too much exaggeration that the ethnic Chinese during the New Order had never had it so good.

In the following pages, the major economic policies and measures of the New Order government affecting the ethnic Chinese directly or indirectly will be discussed.

The Whitewash Policy

The coming to power of the New Order government heralded a new phase in economic policy-making in which private enterprise, both domestic and foreign, was, unlike during Sukarno's Guided Economy period, encouraged again to foster economic growth and employment. In line with the new favourable attitude towards foreign direct investment, a new Foreign Investment Law was enacted in 1967 and a new Domestic Investment Law in 1967. The Foreign Investment Law of 1967 contained various incentives and guarantees to prospective foreign investors (Sadli 1972, p. 204). Any incentives granted to the foreign investors were also granted to the domestic investors.

In fact, domestic investors received more incentives than the foreign investors. For instance, no questions were asked about the legitimacy of the origin of the funds to be invested in Indonesia. This meant that back taxes would not be imposed on these funds (Sadli 1997, pp. 244–45).

Offering strong encouragement and incentives to domestic capital owners, who were potential investors and were mostly ethnic Chinese was politically risky given the political and nationalistic policies of the Sukarno government, which had introduced various anti-Chinese policies, such as the ban on rural trade by foreigners. However, this "whitewash" policy turned out to be quite successful as new domestic investment, along with foreign direct investment, increased rapidly during the first years after these more liberal investment policies were enacted.

Despite the government's determination to boost economic growth by encouraging direct investment by "domestic foreign capital", that is, domestic capital which had been "parked" abroad by many ethnic Chinese during the final tumultuous years of the Sukarno government, explicit and implicit discrimination in various forms against the ethnic Chinese continued. As a result, many ethnic Chinese businessmen were forced to collaborate with indigenous businessmen, who held the required business licenses (Suryadinata 1999, pp. 140–41). In this sense not much had changed from the Sukarno era. In fact, over time the Ali Baba system of the Sukarno era was "improved" and grew into the hated, well-connected conglomerates of the late New Order era, which gave rise to renewed anti-Chinese sentiments and riots during this period.

THE EXPULSION OF THE CHINESE FROM
WEST KALIMANTAN'S INTERIOR

During the military confrontation against Malaysia, the Indonesian military recruited Chinese youth from Sarawak, local Chinese and local sympathizers of the Indonesian Communist Party to support the Indonesian military in its attacks on Sarawak, which in 1963 had joined the Malaysian federation. The change in government after the failed coup of 30 September 1965 and the subsequent peace with Malaysia, however, rendered this group dispensable.

In late 1966 through early 1967, the Indonesian military attempted to wipe out the stranded anti-Malaysia and pro-communist guerilas, but were unsuccessful in this effort. Although these guerilas also consisted of local indigenous Indonesians sympathetic to the communist cause, the Indonesian military blamed the Chinese and were determined to "drain the ethnic Chinese waters in which the guerila fish were swimming". This meant that the ethnic Chinese had to be removed from the interior of northwest Kalimantan, where most of the Chinese had been living for generations (Somers Heidhues 2003, pp. 244–45).

To this end the military incited the Dayaks to drive out all the Chinese from West Kalimantan's interior. Although the Chinese and Dayaks had lived together in relative harmony for many generations and in their economic activities had what could be called a "symbiotic" relationship, the Dayaks were receptive to the military's attempt to drive a wedge between them and the Chinese when several Dayaks were killed during an attack on a village, which was blamed on the Chinese guerillas. In late October 1967 the Dayaks turned against the Chinese, initially only looting Chinese shops and vandalizing their rubber gardens and farms, but later killing many Chinese (Somers Heidhues 2003, pp. 245–49).

As a result of the Dayak raids, hundreds of Chinese were killed and more than 50,000 Chinese refugees fled from the interior to the coastal regions (Coppel 1983, p. 145). As tens of thousands of Chinese refugees fled to the coastal areas, the local government was faced with the problem of providing them with adequate food, medical care, housing and employment, which took years to solve. Concerned that the anti-Chinese violence would spread to other parts of the country, the Indonesian

Government attempted to ensure that the anti-Chinese campaigns remained localized in that province (Coppel 1983, pp. 148–49).

THE GOVERNMENT RESPONSE TO THE MALARI AFFAIR

While private, and particularly foreign direct investment, was encouraged during the relatively liberal period of the late 1960s, by the early 1970s the government began to shift to more interventionist policies in favour of national, private entrepreneurs and state-owned enterprises (SOEs). Two factors accounted for this return to more interventionist and nationalist policies (Thee 1995, pp. 17–18). For one thing, since the early 1970s economic nationalism began to rear its head again in response to the perceived "sell-out" of the national economy to foreign capital, particularly Japanese capital, and the perceived preferential treatment accorded to non-indigenous (that is, ethnic Chinese) entrepreneurs. The public resentment against the perceived "over-presence" of Japanese investment projects culminated in anti-Japanese riots in January 1974 (referred to as the "Malari Affair").

The second factor which led to more interventionist policies was the two oil booms of the 1970s which enabled the government to obtain vastly increased revenues and export earnings, which removed the most important constraint on the government's development plans. Having overcome the economic difficulties left by the Sukarno government, the government now felt able and confident to revise its erstwhile liberal, free market policies in favour of more interventionist policies (Mackie and MacIntyre 1994, p. 35) in the field of foreign investment and industrial strategy.

The government responded to the "Malari Affair" by introducing more restrictive measures against foreign investment and more promotional policies in favour of indigenous Indonesian businessmen. For instance, as from 1974 new foreign direct investment could only enter Indonesia in the form of joint ventures with national businessmen or companies in which *pribumi* Indonesian businessmen, rather than *non-pribumi* Chinese businessmen, held majority equity ownership and/or majority control (Thee 1995, p. 18).

Over time Chinese businessmen, like in the past, found ways to circumvent these rules. However, the restrictive foreign investment policies were only fully lifted in June 1994 when the government found it necessary to deregulate (that is, liberalize) the economy in order to sustain productive investment (particularly in export-oriented investment) and economic growth.

THE TWO PRESIDENTIAL DECREES ON GOVERNMENT CONTRACTS

When the government was still awash with revenues from the oil boom in the late 1970s and early 1980s, it decided to pursue another affirmative policy to give indigenous Indonesian businessmen a head start. To this effect it issued two Presidential Decrees in 1979 and 1980 (*Keputusan Presiden no. 14/1979* and *Keputusan Presiden no. 14a/.1980*), which stipulated that government contracts of up to 20 million *rupiah* were solely reserved for entrepreneurs from the "economically weak groups in society" (*golongan ekonomi lemah*).[4] While for contracts up to 100 million *rupiah*, bids had to be awarded by tender, preferential treatment would still be given to entrepreneurs from the "economically weak groups in society", if their tenders were up to 10 per cent higher than the others (Daroesman 1981, p. 15).

To qualify as an entrepreneur from the "economically weak groups", at least 50 per cent of his/her enterprise would have to be owned by *pribumi* entrepreneurs, while more than half of the board of management would have to be *pribumi*. In addition, the amount of capital and net assets of the enterprise would have to be less than 25 million *rupiah* in the case of trade and related activities, or 100 million *rupiah* in the case of manufacturing and construction. Moreover, local cooperatives would also qualify as economic activities owned by the "economically weak groups" (Daroesman 1981, pp. 15–16). Over time, these regulations turned out to be more successful than the *Benteng* programme in that it was able to nurture a larger group of successful *pribumi* entrepreneurs (the Kodel group) than had been the case with the ill-fated *Benteng* programme.

THE APPEAL TO HELP COOPERATIVES

Increasingly aware that there was much discontent about the perceived widening economic gap between rich and poor and between the Sino-Indonesian minority and the *pribumi* majority, Suharto in March 1990 convened a meeting at his large Tapos ranch with the heads of the leading business conglomerates, the large majority of them Sino-Indonesians. Many of these conglomerates had grown rapidly during the New Order, thanks to the preferential treatment, for instance in the allocation of large, subsidized credits, which these conglomerates were able to obtain because of the personal relationships which the heads of these conglomerates were able to establish with powerful "*pribumi*" power holders, including the president. The size of these conglomerates had only become evident, when they or their subsidiaries had gone public after the stock exchange boom in 1989.

Suharto used this meeting to reduce sensitivity about the visible role and influence of the "Chinese" conglomerates, and to portray himself as the "little people" (*wong cilik*) (Elson 2001, p. 268). On national television Suharto used this meeting to appeal to the assembled businessmen to assist in the development of cooperatives (owned mostly by the "economically weak groups in society") by transferring a quarter of their vast assets to cooperatives and to allow the cooperatives to buy shares in the private companies as a means of closing the gap between rich and poor. This equal sharing of the nation's wealth would emerge as a constant theme in Suharto's speeches through the 1990s (Elson 2001, p. 268).

However, beyond some token steps on the part of the conglomerates to heed Suharto's appeal, however, this appeal was, as was to be expected, quite unsuccessful in reducing the economic power of the conglomerates in any way and in increasing the role and strength of cooperatives. It could also be argued that this Tapos meeting was a way to deflect public attention from the growing role of the conglomerates owned and controlled by the president's own children.

THE POST-SUHARTO PERIOD

The rise of powerful Chinese conglomerates under the patronage of a corrupt president and other corrupt senior military officers and government officials created social tensions and gave rise to the strong public perception in the late Suharto era about the widening gap between rich and poor, and between the *non-pribumi* (non-indigenous) and *pribumi* (indigenous) citizens. These social tensions led to various anti-Chinese riots in several cities and towns, particularly in Java, in the final years of the Suharto era.

When the Indonesian Government, specifically President Suharto, proved to be unable or unwilling to take the necessary measures to deal decisively with the Asian economic crisis of 1997–98, as agreed upon in its Letter of Intent (LoI) to the IMF, the economic crisis eventually led to a full-blown political crisis, which led to the inglorious fall of President Suharto in May 1998. The unsettled political conditions were utilized by contending political and military factions to create even greater unrest by inciting violent anti-Chinese riots in Solo and Jakarta on the eve of Suharto's fall in May 1998.

Acutely aware of the country's economic meltdown as a result of the Asian financial and economic crisis, and of the need to attract foreign direct investment (FDI) into Indonesia to support Indonesia's economic recovery, President Habibie's government took several measures to attract new FDI into the country. Anxious to persuade many Sino-Indonesian businessmen to repatriate the capital they had transferred overseas after the anti-Chinese riots, President Habibie took some steps to reassure the Sino-Indonesians that there was still a place for them in Indonesia. These steps included the ratification of the United Nations Conventions on the Elimination of All Forms of Racial Discrimination and the instruction to end the practice of specially marking the identity cards of Sino-Indonesians (Anwar 1999, p. 42).

These measures to reassure the ethnic Chinese was also considered important, as prospective foreign investors would be persuaded to also invest in Indonesia if the Sino-Indonesian businessmen, who would know their country better than foreigners, would repatriate their capital back to Indonesia (Thee 2002, p. 38).

Despite the efforts of the Habibie administration and the successor governments of Presidents Abdurrachman Wahid, Megawati Sukarnoputri, and Susilo Bambang Yudhoyono to encourage new FDI into the country, these efforts have as yet not been successful in attracting large FDI inflows into the country. Although some domestic capital of the ethnic Chinese businessmen have been repatriated back to Indonesia, it is also doubtful that all the Chinese capital has returned in view of the Indonesian Government's continuing inability to greatly improve Indonesia's poor investment climate.

In several aspects Indonesia's business landscape has changed a great deal after the collapse of the Suharto regime. The big conglomerates, owned and controlled by the leading ethnic Chinese tycoons, notably Sudono Salim, Eka Cipta Wijaya, Prajogo Pangestu, and Sjamsul Nursalim, and the leading *pribumi* businessmen, including President Suharto's children and relatives, were severely battered by the Asian economic crisis. The private banking sector, which before the Asian crisis was largely owned and controlled by the ethnic Chinese conglomerates, has largely been taken over by the Indonesian Government and by foreign investors (Dhume 2004, p. 65). The increase of state ownership in this banking sector was the result of large capital injections by the Indonesian Government to forestall the collapse of several private banks and the nationalization of leading private banks (Sato 2004, p. 163), including Bank Central Asia (BCA), Indonesia's largest private bank largely owned by the Salim group.

Despite the battering which the conglomerates of the ethnic Chinese businessmen have suffered as a result of the Asian economic crisis, large parts of Indonesia's private economy are still dominated by ethnic Chinese businessmen, including small and medium entrepreneurs (Dhume 2004, p. 61). Smaller and less visible ethnic Chinese corporations, such as the leading pharmaceutical firms Kalbe Farma, Dexa Medica, which did not rely on government patronage as did the large conglomerates, while also adversely affected by the crisis, have largely been able to restructure their business successfully and pay off their foreign debts, and as a result have been able to resume their rapid growth. A number of manufacturing industries, including the important export-oriented garment industry and the supporting (supplier) industries making parts and components for the automotive and other engineering goods industries continue to be populated by a significant number of small and medium-scale enterprises (SMEs) owned and operated by ethnic Chinese businessmen. The service industries, including auto repair shops and shops selling electronic products (TV sets, audio and video equipment, and personal computers) and white goods (refrigerators, washing machines), also continue to be owned and run by ethnic Chinese businessmen.

CONCLUSION

At present anti-Chinese sentiments have abated, at least for the time being, as other social conflicts, sometimes religious and sometimes ethnic in nature, have arisen following the collapse of the strong authoritarian state under Suharto. To a certain degree public animosity towards the Chinese has abated because of the collapse of many debt-ridden Chinese conglomerates as a result of the Asian economic crisis. Nevertheless, there is still concern that these conglomerates, after having undergone restructuring, will in an unobtrusive way be able to buy back many companies which had been taken over by the now liquidated Indonesian Banking Restructuring Agency (IBRA) as collateral in return for Bank Indonesia's liquidity credits to bail out the banks they owned.

To replace the conglomerates, at present small- and medium-scale enterprises (SMEs), many of them owned by *pribumi* entrepreneurs, are now given high priority, as reflected by various schemes to provide lavish credit to these SMEs. This focus on SMEs has been strengthened by the widely held perception that many of these SMEs, unlike the conglomerates, were not only able to survive the Asian economic crisis, but also to prosper. As explicit affirmative policies to promote *pribumi* enterprises are now frowned upon, the emphasis on the promotion of SMEs serve as a code word for the promotion of *pribumi* businessmen.

However, with a growing awareness that to achieve strong economic recovery, restore rapid economic growth and raise the international competitiveness of Indonesian companies, ethnic cleavages between *pribumi* and *non-pribumi* entrepreneurs are now seen as unproductive and futile by several members of Indonesia's political elite. There is thus some hope that with the emergence of a new generation of political leaders and and a more competent and confident class of *pribumi* entrepreneurs, opportunities for a more fruitful and mutually profitable business cooperation between *pribumi* and *non-pribumi* businessmen will open up.

Despite controversial statements by Jusuf Kalla, the current vice-president, before the inauguration of President Susilo Bambang Yudhoyono (SBY) and Vice President Jusuf Kalla, that affirmative policies to promote *pribumi* businessmen were necessary, thus far no discriminatory policies against the ethnic Chinese have been introduced. As things stand at present, it appears unlikely that discriminatory affirmative policies will ever be introduced given the pragmatic bent of the SBY administration, particularly the economics ministers, and the lack of racist sentiments on the part of President SBY.

In this respect, there is a similarity between the pragmatism of the post-Suharto governments and the Suharto government in that both governments realized the economic importance of mobilizing the ethnic Chinese to support the economic recovery of Indonesia. One crucial difference between the Suharto government and the post-Suharto governments is that while the former gave the ethnic Chinese wide opportunities in the economic field, it severely limited their activities in other fields, notably in politics. In the much more open political atmosphere after the fall of Suharto, the ethnic Chinese can not only continue their economic activities, but since the Abdurrachman Wahid presidency, are now given wide opportunity to be active in other fields as well, including in politics.

Although the continuing perceived ethnic Chinese domination of the Indonesian economy still render them politically vulnerable, there is now a growing tendency on the part of many, though not all *pribumi* Indonesians, to accept the ethnic Chinese as fellow Indonesians. This attitude contrasts sharply with the early independence period under President Sukarno period when, in the aftermath of the bitter armed struggle against the Dutch, anti-Chinese sentiments were virulent and anti-Chinese measures to limit or even ban their economic activities in wide circles were viewed as "politically correct" and economically desirable. These measures were popular, as ethnic Chinese, including those having Indonesian citizenship, were still considered foreigners in the Indonesian body politic.

Despite the fact that pragmatic economic considerations have often prevailed in Indonesia, even at times during the Sukarno period, and thus shielded the ethnic Chinese from harsher measures considered against them, the long-term security of the Sino-Indonesians in their country of birth will only be assured if the economic gap between the Sino-Indonesian minority and the *pribumi* majority will gradually but steadily be narrowed within a reasonable period of time. To a large extent, this will depend on sound economic policies, which can successfully combine rapid economic growth with equity, including rapid social development.

Notes

[1]   During the early independence period, the term "*Indonesia asli*" was used to denote indigenous Indonesians, while during the Soeharto era the term "*Indonesia pribumi*" was used.

[2]   As Indonesia only recognized the People's Republic of China as the only legitimate government of China, pro-Taiwan Chinese were treated as stateless citizens.

[3]   See Appendix C in Coppel's article (Coppel 2002*a*, p. 33) for an English translation of Decision of the Cabinet Presidium no. 127 of 1966, dated 27 December 1966.

[4]   Since overly racist references to the ethnic Chinese were, just like during the Sukarno era, still frowned upon, the government and the public, including the press, the euphemistic term "economically weak groups in society" were used. However, this term not quite correctly assumed that the "economically weak groups in society" were identical to the indigenous Indonesian majority.

References

Anspach, Ralph. 1969. "Indonesia", in Golay, et al., 1969, pp. 111–201.
Anwar, Dewi Fortuna. 1999. *The Habibie Presidency*. In Forrester (ed.), 1999, pp. 33–47.

Arsyad Anwar, M; Aris Ananta and Ari Kuncoro (eds.) 1997. *Widjojo Nitisastro 70 Tahun — Pembangunan Nasional: Teori, Kebijakan, dan Pelaksanaan* [Widjojo Nitisastro 70 Years — National Development: Theory, Policy, and Implementation], Fakultas Ekonomi Universitas Indonesia (FEUI), Jakarta.

Basri, M. Chatib and Pierre van der Eng (eds.) 2004. *Business in Indonesia — New Challenges, Old Problems* (Singapore: Institute of Southeast Asian Studies).

Booth, Anne. 1998. *The Indonesian Economy in the Nineteenth and Twentieth Centuries — A History of Missed Opportunities* (London: Macmillan Press).

Burger, D.H. 1975. *Sociologisch-Economische Geschiedenis van Indonesie — deel II: Indonesia in de 20e Eeuw* [Sociological-Economic History of Indonesia — Volume II: Indonesia in the 20th Century].

Coppel, Charles. 1983. *Indonesian Chinese in Crisis* (Singapore: Oxford University Press).

———. 2002*a*. "Chinese Indonesians in Crisis, 1960s and 1990s". In Coppel, 2002*b*, pp. 124–47.

———. 2002*b*. *Studying Ethnic Chinese in Indonesia* (Singapore: Singapore Society of Asian Studies).

Daroesman, Ruth. 1981. "Survey of Recent Developments". In *Bulletin of Indonesian Economic Studies* 27, no. 2 (August): 1–41.

Dhume, Sadanand. 2004. "A New Political Economy? Politics, Ethnicity and Business in Indonesia". In Basri and van der Eng (eds.), 2004, pp. 61–71.

Dick, H.W. 2002. Formation of the Nation State, 1930s–1966. In Dick, et al., 2002, pp. 153–93.

Dick, Howard, Vincent Houben, Thomas Lindblad and Thee Kian Wie. 2002. *The Emergence of a National Economy — An Economic History of Indonesia, 1800–2000* (Sydney: Allen & Unwin).

Drysdale, Peter (ed.) 1972. *Direct Foreign Investment in Asia and the Pacific* (Canberra: The Australian National University Press).

Elson, Robert. 2001. *Soeharto — A Political Biography* (Cambridge: Cambridge University Press).

Feith, Herbert. 1964. *The Decline of Constitutional Democracy in Indonesia*, Second printing (Ithaca, N.Y.: Cornell University).

Forrester, Geoff (ed.) 1999. *Post-Soeharto Indonesia — Renewal or Chaos?* (Singapore: Institute of Southeast Asian Studies).

Glassburner, Bruce (ed.) 1971. *The Economy of Indonesia — Selected Readings* (Ithaca, N.Y. and London: Cornell University Press).

Golay, Frank, Ralph Anspach, M. Ruth Pfanner and Eliezer B. Ayal. 1969. *Underdevelopment and Economic Nationalism in Southeast Asia* (Ithaca, N.Y. and London: Cornell University Press).

Hill, Hal (ed.) 1994. *Indonesia's New Order — The Dynamics of Socio-Economic Transformation* (Sydney: Allen & Unwin).

Jesudason, James V. 1997. Chinese Business and Ethnic Equilibrium in Malaysia. In *Development and Change* 28, no. 1 (January): 119–41.

Johnson, Harry. 1972. "The Ideology of Economic Policy in New States", in Wall (ed.), 1972.

Lindblad, J. Thomas (ed.) 2002. *Asian Growth and Foreign Capital — Case Studies from Eastern Asia* (Amsterdam: Aksant Academic Publishers).

Mackie, J.A.C. 1971. "The Indonesian Economy, 1950–63", in Glassburner (ed.), 1971, pp. 16–69.

Mackie, Jamie and Andrew MacIntyre. 1994. in: Hill (ed.), 1994, pp. 1–53.

Meier, Hans. 1994. *Den Haag-Djakarta — De Nederlands-Indonesische betrekkingen, 1950–1962* [The Hague-Djakarta — Dutch-Indonesian Relations, 1950–1962] (Utrecht: Uitgeverij Het Spectrum, B.V.).

Paauw, Douglas S. 1983. *The Economic Legacy of Dutch Colonialism to Independent Indonesia.* Paper presented at the Conference on Indonesian Economic History During the Dutch Colonial Period, Research School of Pacific Studies, The Australian National University, Canberra, 12–13 December.

Rickleffs, M.C. 1993. *A History of Modern Indonesia Since c. 1300.* Second edition. London: Macmillan.

Robison, Richard. 1986. *Indonesia — The Rise of Capital* (Sydney: Allen & Unwin).

Sadli, Mohamad. 1972. "Indonesia", in Drysdale (ed.), 1972, pp. 201–25.

———. 1997. Technocratic Decision Making in Economic Policy, in Arsyad Anwar, et al. (eds.), pp. 241–52.

Sato, Yuri. 2004. Corporate Ownership and Management in Indonesia: Does It Change? In Basri and van der Eng (eds.), 2004, pp. 156–77.

Saubari, Mohammad. 2003. "Recollections", in Thee (ed.), 2003, pp. 69–73.

Siahaan, Bisuk. 1996. *Industrialisasi di Indonesia — Sejak Hutang Kehormatan sampai Bintang Stir* [Industrialization in Indonesia — Since the Debt of Honour until the Turn-Around] (Jakarta: Pustaka Data).

Somers, Mary F. 1964. *Peranakan Chinese Politics in Indonesia*, Interim Report Series, Modern Indonesia Project, Cornell University, Ithaca, New York.

Somers Heidhues, Mary. 2003. *Golddiggers, Farmers, and Traders in the 'Chinese Districts' of West Kalimantan, Indonesia* (Ithaca, New York: Southeast Asia Program Publications, Cornell University).

Suhadi Mangkusuwondo. 1967. *Industrialisation Efforts in Indonesia: The Role of Agriculture and Foreign Trade in the Development of the Industrial Sector*. Ph.D. Thesis, University of California, Berkeley.

Suryadinata, Leo. 1992. *Pribumi Indonesians, The Chinese Minority and China*. Third edition (Singapore: Heinemann Asia).

Sutter, John O. 1959. *Indonesianisasi: A Historical Survey of the Role of Politics in the Institutions of a Changing Economy, from the Second World War to the End of the General; Elections (1940–1955)*. Ph.D. Thesis, Cornell University, June.

Thee, Kian Wie. 1995. *Government- Business Relations in Indonesia in Historical Perspective*. Unpublished manuscript, Jakarta, December.

———. 2002. "The Impact of the Asian Economic Crisis on the Prospects for Foreign Direct Investment in Indonesia", in Lindblad (ed.), 2002, pp. 37–58.

———. (ed.) 2003. *Recollections — The Indonesian Economy, 1950s–1990s* (Singapore: Institute of Southeast Asian Studies).

Wall, David (ed.) 1972. *Chicago Essays in Economic Development* (Chicago: University of Chicago Press).

5

Chinese Indonesian Business in the Era of Globalization: Ethnicity, Culture and the Rise of China[1]

Sujoko Efferin
Wiyono Pontjoharyo

INTRODUCTION

Chinese Indonesians[2] (also known as *Tionghoa*) have been acknowledged as one of the major engines in Indonesia's economic development. Although they are the minority, it is estimated that their share of total private domestic capital far exceeds that of any other ethnic group in the country. There are controversies regarding the share of Chinese capital in the Indonesian economy (for example, see Kwik 1978; Amir 1978; Hadiz 1997; and Ning 1987). Until now it has been difficult to get data about the precise composition of capital ownership. However, it has been widely accepted that the state has the largest share of domestic capital in Indonesia followed by Chinese capital.

In the year 2000, some of the major ethnic groups in Indonesia are the Javanese (41.71 per cent), the Sundanese (15.41 per cent), and the much smaller groups such as the Melayu (3.45 per cent), the Madura (3.37 per cent), and the Batak (3.02 per cent) (Suryadinata et al. 2003). The Chinese are estimated to make up 1.40 per cent to 1.99 per cent. Other ethnic groups of foreign origin also exist albeit in very small numbers (for example, Arab, Indian, Indo-European). It is estimated that there are more than 400 ethnic groups in Indonesia (Brown 1994). However, until recently there is a dichotomy between the Chinese and other ethnic groups (the so-called *pribumi*).[3] In the New Order era (1966–98), the classification of *non-pribumi* was often applied solely to the ethnic Chinese. They were distinguished exclusively from other ethnic groups and regarded as the only alien one in Indonesia being discriminated against politically, socially, and economically during the New Order Era (see Heryanto 1997, 1998).

The ethnic group's economic roles and significance has grown significantly during the New Order era. Interestingly, in this era, they were discriminated against most extensively in the social, cultural, and political spheres. The rise of the New Order regime (1966–98) marked the peak of extensive and gross practices of racism against the Chinese involving both state discriminations, and frequent and violent mass attacks on Chinese property and life (Heryanto 1997, 1998; Ning 1987; Coppel 1983). Consequently, their ethnicity has become a dominant issue and institutionalized in various social, cultural, political, and economic activities.

Studies about business practices in the context of Chinese business and the Southeast Asian region are considered increasingly important in today's business environment because Chinese business is one of most powerful economic forces in the world today (Redding 1993; Yeung 1999). The rise of China as a major economic force in the world may have significant impact upon the business/investment decisions of the Southeast Asian Chinese due to their possible cultural/emotional ties and the investment incentives offered by the Chinese Government (Wang 2004). Unfortunately, studies of ethnic Chinese business in Southeast Asia (Indonesia included) tend to be restricted to cultural issues, that is, how Confucianism influences the business practices and gives rise to their success (Mackie 2000; Chan 2000). A small body of literature examining Chinese Indonesian business from a purely political economy perspective is also available (see for example, Robison 1986). These different strands of studies can be reconciled by using a more holistic perspective viewing how culture and socio-cultural environment are intertwined in shaping business practices. In fact, culture itself is dynamic and has been shaped and reproduced by the socio-political environments of the ethnic group (Ong 1999). A case study of Efferin (2002) has also revealed how Confucian culture has been modified by local cultures and the ethnicity of the Chinese Indonesians in shaping their managerial practices. Nevertheless, studies that use empirical investigation from the perspectives of Chinese Indonesian businessmen are still limited. Hence, more studies are needed in this area.

This study is aimed at gaining an understanding of Chinese Indonesian business in the era of globalization and the rise of China from the perspective of the business actors. As a sample, this study will focus on

Chinese businessmen in Surabaya. There are several reasons for this. Firstly, Surabaya is the second city of Indonesia in terms of economic and political importance. Business activities including export and import activities have been well developed since hundreds of years ago. In fact, many large, influential Indonesian companies are owned by Chinese from Surabaya. Secondly, the reason is access. The researchers already know many influential Chinese Indonesian businessmen in Surabaya who have local and international businesses and are willing to cooperate and support this study. Their support is imperative for the success of this study. More specifically, this study attempts to answer the following research questions:

1. What are the characteristics of the Chinese Indonesians business behaviours in terms of managerial ideology, organizational structure, managerial functioning, inter-firm relations and business development?
2. To what extent does ethnicity and culture *vis-à-vis* business scale influence their business behaviours in the light of globalization and the rise of China?

THE ETHNICITY OF CHINESE INDONESIAN

Perspective of Ethnicity

Ethnicity is about social classifications emerging within relationships in which people distinguish themselves from others — the distinction between "us" and "them" (Fenton 1999). The classification gives rise to so-called ethnic groups where people possessing certain similar social identities are grouped together. In this sense, the boundaries of ethnic groups may be both symbolic (language, ancestry, religion, kinship, or more generally, culture) and material, that is, constituted within structures of power and wealth in a broader society. Ethnicity functions as a dimension in social actions and organizations in various fields. Social, political and economic relations among groups of people may be characterized by this dimension, and this can be activated or suppressed in a wide variety of contexts. According to Brown (1994), the state may influence the distribution of power, status and wealth in society, and, hence, the type of situational insecurities and threats with which individuals and groups are faced. In many post-colonial societies, there has been a high correlation between ethnic identity and class membership (Eriksen 1993).

The above perspective provides the basis for explaining the ethnicity of Chinese Indonesians. Virtually all the Chinese in Indonesia are either themselves China-born immigrants or descendants of earlier immigrants through the male line who have intermarried with local women. Indeed, the term Chinese does not refer to simple racial/biological criteria. There are, for example, many persons in Java who are uniformly considered as Chinese but are by ancestry less than one-quarter Chinese, while other persons who by ancestry are more than one-quarter Chinese consider themselves and are considered by others as indigenous/*pribumi* (Skinner 1963). Therefore, the definition of who is and who is not Chinese is, to some extent, about social identification when he/she functions as a member of, and identifies with, Chinese society.

It is argued that the ethnicity of Chinese Indonesians cannot be separated from, if it is not totally the creation of, the roles played by various states governing the country including the Dutch colonial rulers (pre-independence era), the Sukarno regime and the New Order state (Efferin 2002). Created for the first time by the colonial rulers, the ethnicity was shaped and reified further by their successors, especially the New Order state. The consequence of this situation is a social division between the ethnic Chinese and *pribumi* giving rise to a sense of ethnic prejudice and insecurity. Thus ethnicity may influence every aspect of life including the business behaviours of the Chinese Indonesian.

Categorization of the Ethnic Chinese: Totok and Jiaosen

Conventional categorization of Chinese Indonesian (*Tionghoa*) between *totok* and *peranakan* (see for examples, Suryadinata 1974, 1978) and its meaning have gradually changed. The socio-cultural diversity of the ethnic Chinese is no more in terms of political orientation (with loyalty to mainland China or Indonesia). In his later paper, Suryadinata (2002) argues that there is a wide spectrum of the group referring to various cultural degrees of Chineseness. He proposes four categories of Chinese Indonesian: *Peranakan* and new-style *peranakan*, *totok* and new-style *totok*. The new-style *peranakan* and *totok* are a result of the assimilation policies and strong Indonesian nationalism after the independence of the country. The new-style *peranakan* are still unable to speak Mandarin and the new-style *totok* do not have a good command of the Chinese language anymore. However, both of them are highly proficient in the Indonesian language or local dialects where they live.

Parallel findings are also mentioned by Efferin (2002). Based upon his observation, the most common categorization in popular vernacular among the ethnic group is *totok* and *jiaosen*. *Totok*, in this sense, means those who still practise traditional Chinese/Confucian values in their daily life, speak Mandarin/other Chinese dialects albeit to various extent, educate their children based upon those Chinese/Confucian values, and celebrate Chinese traditional events (for example, Chinese New Year, the Moon Cake Festival, and the Remembering Ancestors Day/*Cing Bing*). Becoming Chinese for them is a matter of preserving their cultural heritage. Most of them embrace Buddhism or Khong Hu Chu as their religion. On the other hand, the *jiaosen* do not practise Chinese traditions in their daily life and speak little or no Chinese of any kind. So, their culture is a mixture of Western, local and Chinese/Confucian cultures and customs. For them, becoming Chinese is merely an ethnic identity. The majority of *jiaosen* embrace Christianity/Catholicism and few embrace Islam. Albeit small in number, deviance from the above general characteristics of Chinese Indonesian exists. For example, a small Chinese community in Tangerang, West Java — the so-called Cina Benteng, show an interesting phenomenon. They largely practise Betawi (one of the local ethnic groups in West Java) culture and cannot speak Mandarin but they still embrace Khong Hu Chu as their religion.

In fact, the different categorizations demonstrate the dynamics of the transformation processes of the cultural identities of the Chinese Indonesians. The above findings have revealed that culture is a direct result of the political treatment of the Indonesian state which is a part of its nation-building strategies. Furthermore, the findings have agreed upon there being a tendency for the majority of younger Chinese Indonesian generations to become increasingly "peranakanized". This does not mean that the ethnic group has lost all Confucian values. To some extent, Chinese parents continue to teach their cultural values to their children. There is a separation between religion and culture for the younger generation. The parents give family education that, to some extent, contains Confucian values regarding proper conduct in interactions with family members, older people and society, whereas Christianity and Catholicism focuses on faith and relationships with God.

Unfortunately, there is no study specifically examining how Chinese they are and what kind of business culture emerges from the above combination. Moreover, simple all-inclusive categorization, either *totok*–new-style *totok* and *peranakan*–new-style *peranakan* or *totok* and *jiaosen* may not be adequate to fully capture the complexity of the cultural identities of the group. The identities are actually a continuum in which any category can be divided into more sub-categories and sub sub-categories. Since the terms *totok* and *jiaosen* and their new meanings are widely known and more popular in the daily interactions of the ethnic group, they will be used throughout the rest of the study. The terms are important since during the data collection of this study, the respondents were asked to identify themselves whether they perceive to be *totok*, *jiaosen* or unsure. The term "unsure" is also important to check whether the terms *totok* and *jiaosen* make sense to them.

Post New Order Era (After 1998)

The fall of Suharto in 1998 dramatically changed the situation in Indonesia including the social environment of Chinese Indonesians. Many newspapers and magazines began to expose the political strategy of the New Order state in scapegoating the ethnic Chinese for almost every national problem. With the revocation of Presidential Instruction 14/1967, which prohibited the cultural activities of the ethnic Chinese, by Presidential Decree 6/2000, the ethnic group is now free to celebrate its cultural activities. The word *WNI Keturunan* (literally means "Indonesian citizen with foreign origin") used to describe their nationality is now gradually being replaced by simply "Indonesian citizen", while Chinese is recognized as one of various Indonesian ethnic groups instead of as a foreign-origin ethnic group (Piliang 2001). The word *Tionghoa* has been used by many mass media to replace the controversial word *Cina*, which is considered derogatory by many people.

There has been an interesting phenomenon in the post New Order era. Mandarin courses have been widespread and followed by many Indonesians regardless of their ethnicity. Many *jiaosen*, *totok* and non-Chinese take the courses for business purposes. They consider that in the era of globalization, a good command of Mandarin is necessary for the success of their business negotiations. However, there is another side effect. The definition of *totok* and *jiaosen* can no longer be made based upon proficiency in Mandarin language since the *jiaosen* and non-Chinese still maintain and practise their own "culture". Thus, the best way of differentiating *totok* and *jiaosen* nowadays is by self-acknowledgement, whether they perceive that they still practise traditional Chinese values in their daily life or not. The cultural practices now become the most reliable criterion in differentiating *totok* and *jiaosen*.

However, it is too early to say that there is no longer an ethnic/racial problem in Indonesia. The whole aspect of Indonesian life is undergoing dramatic changes, from an authoritarian to a democratic state, from strong military political roles to civil rule, and from political prejudice to tolerance and pluralism. In this uncertain period, it is more appropriate to say that most of the Chinese Indonesian businessmen prefer to take cautious action and to wait and see the dramatic changes in the Indonesian social and political situation rather than say that they have forgotten their bad experiences.

Ethnicity and Globalization

Wang (2004) compares ethnicity with the nation-state. Ethnicity is described as a long-standing, historical and evolutionary process involving a sense of cultural identification whereas the nation-state is a modern phenomenon, can be built afresh and is shaped and controlled by institutions such as the bureaucracy and political and legal systems. Wang argues that nation-building processes in Singapore, Malaysia and Indonesia have not finished yet and these may be made more complicated by the fact that most Chinese have inherited a deep-rooted, demanding and distinctive culture, something that is recognized as their civilization. To move from a culture-based people to a state-based people, needs a mental process that is not easy and takes time. While the process is still going on, there is another development, that is, globalization.

According to Wang, globalization makes the Southeast Asian Chinese look beyond national borders and even return to cultural identification. The Chinese may try to take advantage of the globalization by using it as part of the tactics of survival, of dealing with discrimination or injustices that they feel within the nation-building processes. A mechanism is now available to avoid some parts of nation-building that they do not like. One interesting issue is raised by Wang here: How will the Chinese in the Southeast Asia respond to global and transnational opportunities if opened to them?

Tan (2004) gives a rather different perspective. According to her, the Chinese Indonesian has had a long involvement in the nation-building process since before the independence of Indonesia. The reformation in Indonesia that has given Chinese Indonesians more space for public participation should be the opportunity to improve their image in the eyes of the other ethnic groups in Indonesia. Winarta (2004) and Dahana (2004) also suggest that Chinese Indonesians enter non-economic fields as a way to eliminate ethnic tensions and discriminations. Tan also mentions that there is now increasing awareness of the Chinese Indonesian to become involved in politics and other public areas to fight against discrimination.

Anything can happen in this era where there are so many political, social and cultural changes both at national and global levels. Another important fact in the globalization era is the rise of China as one of the major economic powers. This could raise another interesting issue: How do Chinese Indonesian businessmen respond to the rise of China? Hence, empirical studies about this matter are needed to gain a deeper understanding about the way Chinese Indonesian businessmen think and act.

CONFUCIANISM

Confucianism is a philosophy concerned with social, moral and governmental problems (Suryadinata 1974). According to Suryadinata (1974), *tao* is based upon human heartedness (*jen*) consisting of *chung* (sincerity and honesty) and *shu* (altruism). Some other major values also include frugality, asceticism, diligence and prudence (Xu 2000; Cleary 1992).

Confucianism can also be divided into two inter-related concepts: Vertical and horizontal order. The concept of vertical order represents the relationships between those from higher and lower levels of the social hierarchy, such as parents and children, family members (for example, husband and wife, parents and children, and elder and younger brothers), masters and servants, rulers and people, and so on (Suryadinata 1974). Every social position contains ascriptive responsibilities and duties. Hence, individuals bearing these names have ascriptive roles that must be fulfilled accordingly (known as *li*).

The horizontal order refers to the relationship between people from the same hierarchy. The person "invests" in a group, and the investment, which he cannot afford to lose, becomes his "face" (Redding 1993). This results in limited and bounded trust among particular groups called *guanxi*. People trust their families, friends and acquaintances to build mutual dependence and invest face on them. Family is seen as the basic survival unit and the very foundation of society and the nation. The welfare of individuals is seen as the family's responsibility rather than the state's.

Confucianism penetrates overseas Chinese society *via* a combination of formal school education (for example, for countries like Singapore, Taiwan and Hong Kong that adopt Confucian values in their education system) and the family teaching of overseas Chinese throughout the world (Redding 1993). Parents are constantly instilling notions of discipline, order, and above all, identity within the family.

THE OVERSEAS CHINESE BUSINESS (OCB) MODEL

Chinese overseas business practices have been regarded as unique and different from Western and even the other East Asian (Japanese and South Korean) business practices (Tam 1990; Redding 1993; Whitley 1991). Despite some variations due to the local socio-political and cultural context of particular countries (societal effects), it is commonly argued that Confucianism, to some extent, characterizes their business. The characteristics of OCB behaviours can be elaborated into five dimensions: Managerial ideology, organizational structure, managerial functioning, inter-firm relations and business domain/development (Redding 1993; Whitley 1991; Tam 1990).

Managerial Ideology

Managerial ideology is the fundamental ideas and beliefs possessed by the Overseas Chinese when conducting their businesses. According to Redding (1993, pp. 155–66), at the organizational level, there are three concepts of the ideology: Patrimonialism, personalistic relations of patronage and obligation and limited/bounded trust.

Patrimonialism is the idea/belief that power cannot exist and be legitimate unless connected to the ownership. The inseparability of ownership and management within Chinese companies is closely related to the value of the family as a basic survival unit. Power is derived from ownership and, in turn, is vested in the family rather than the individual. Furthermore, Chinese organizations duplicate family structure; the head of the household is the head of the organization, family members are the core of the employees, and sons are the ones who will inherit the firm (Hamilton and Biggart 1988). If the firm prospers, the family will reinvest the profit in branch establishments or more likely, in an unrelated but commercially promising business venture. Different family members run different enterprises and, at the death of the head of the family, assets are divided by allocating separate enterprises to the surviving sons.

It is then followed by autocratic-paternalistic leadership, that is, centralizing authority in decision-making where the responsibilities of the subordinates is not to make decisions but to do what their superior has told them to do. Such a relationship reflects the assumption of the superiority of the leaders where they have the didactive roles in organizations. Finally, this idea/belief requires reciprocal vertical obligation between superiors and subordinates. A superior/employer has the responsibility of taking care of the welfare of the subordinates/employees, fitting them into the right slots, the stewardship of resources, helping the inefficient and being understanding. On the other hand, the employees/subordinates should have strong, unquestioning obedience to their employers and show the character of diligence in performing their jobs.

Personalistic relationship means that personal relationships and feelings about other people come before more objectively defined concerns such as organizational efficiency or neutral assessment of abilities. According to Redding (1993, p. 165), who you know is more important than, or at least as important as, what you know. Friendship is important in building work relations. Authority is based upon the exchange of balancing obligations through interpersonal and highly personal processes. The upward flow of loyalty and conformity is exchanged for the downward flow of protection, and this serves to stabilize the structure and dampen the resentment of subordination, which is otherwise institutionalized in industrial relations structures (for example, trade unions) (Redding and Whitley 1990).

Limited and bounded trust refers to the use of family members/trustworthy persons to run the critical functions of the organization to enhance organizational efficiency in terms of identification with goals, motivation, and confidentiality of information. Suspicion of professionals may exist since they are seen as having potentials to undermine the paternalistic/patronage relationships built by the owners/employers. Hence, trust-based personal relationship is preferred as opposed to neutral relations. Nepotism is often used as a means of counteracting the problem of limited trust that reinforces, as well as is a result of, the family business form. In the Indonesian context, ethnic suspicion and antagonism between Chinese Indonesians and *pribumi* that was shaped and reinforced by the New Order regime has also caused some Chinese businessmen to trust Chinese employees more than *pribumi* employees (Efferin 2002).

Organizational Structure

This study adopts the Aston organizational studies' approach in describing organizational structure (Redding 1993, p. 154). There are five major dimensions, namely: Centralization, specialization, standardization, formalization and configuration.

Centralization refers to a sense of where hierarchically in the organization the majority of decisions are taken. It is argued that OCBs tend to have higher level of centralization compared to Western organizations (Redding 1993; Harrison et al. 1994; Birnbaum and Wong 1985).

Specialization reflects the extent to which employees is divided. This includes dividing an organization into specialized units and allocating defined roles to the employees which is manifested into organizational charts, titles on employees' positions and job descriptions to make clear what they do, whom they report to and whom they are responsible for. It is argued that OCBs tend to have lower specialization compared to Western organizations (Redding 1993; Harrison et al. 1994). The allocation of roles is shifting and kept open to change and reinterpretation by the owners/superiors as the holder of legitimate authority.

Standardization reflects the extent to which rules and definitions are used to regularize procedures and roles. This can be used to indicate the difference in the balance achieved in each case between the use of a neutral bureaucratic system and the reliance upon a more personalistic override. It is argued that OCBs tend to have low standardization (Redding 1993).

Formalization refers to the extent to which activities are formalized through paperwork systems. It is argued that OCBs tend to have a similar pattern to their Western counterparts (Redding 1993). The OCBs are particularly strong on the use of paperwork to control the workflow process of their organizations such as production scheduling, detailed records related to the work process in order to maintain efficiency.

Configuration conveys the balance of line *versus* staff personnel. It is argued that OCBs tend to have low configuration (Redding 1993). This may be due to the pragmatism of OCBs which refuse to spend money unless it is highly necessary. Supporting functions are seen as frills since they do not directly produce profit.

Managerial Functions

There are five main managerial functions: Planning and control, financial management, human resource management, production/operation management and marketing management.

Planning and Control

Redding (1993, p. 168) reveals that in Indonesia and Hong Kong, the OCB puts more emphasis on controlling people and production activities compared to other managerial functions. The fact that planning and control are directed primarily towards the production activities reflect the extent to which the core activity of the organization is a matter of intense management concentration where the power of ownership is a stimulant to taking care of the use of assets.

Merchant (1998) has revealed another perspective on the OCB especially in Southeast Asia. He categorizes management control into result control, action control and personnel/cultural control. The first two are more related to the use of bureaucratic, formal control whereas the third is control that is exercised through a group's norms/values which produce social pressures on the deviants in the group. The OCB is said to emphasize more on cultural, informal control rather than highly sophisticated, bureaucratic control due to the high degree of collectivism/emotional ties in the community which stems from Confucianism. A case study of Chinese Indonesian management control by Efferin (2002) has also revealed that a cultural approach is often used by Chinese Indonesian superiors to control their subordinates and cope with possible ethnic antagonisms in the company.

Finance

In financial functions, Redding (1993, p. 170) has also argued that OCBs have strategies based upon some principles:

1) Low margin and high volume as a means of penetrating markets and of generating steady flow of profit;
2) Rigorous control of inventory to achieve low capital investment and high rates of inventory turnover;
3) The reduction of transaction costs by using the Chinese community networking;
4) Maximizing the use of capital from sources outside the firm to improve gearing potential.

According to Redding, those principles are accumulated as folk wisdom passed on from parents to children over generations rather than taken from any Chinese literature.

Human Resource Management

Redding (1993, p. 171) argues that OCBs in Hong Kong tend to accord high importance and extensive attention to performance appraisal, reward/punishment and recruitment. Personnel development is given lower priority.

He claims that this is due to Chinese pragmatism: Refusing to spend money unless absolutely necessary, the impact of paternalism and the relatively low emphasis on using professionals.

Production/Operation Management

Production/operation management is an area where OCBs pay a lot of attention compared with other functions. Redding argues that there is no significant difference in the degree of organizing between the OCBs (in Hong Kong and Indonesia) and the Western organizations regarding this matter. The production management covers the following areas: Quality maintenance, time control, work study, planning and structure and control by process. These are seen as reflecting the main concerns of the owner-managers towards their capital/assets.

Marketing Management

Redding also argues that OCBs in Hong Kong and Indonesia do not pay too much attention to marketing management. It has the following characteristics:

1) Standard trade marks are less used in Hong Kong but highly used in Indonesia.
2) Displays are less standardized.
3) Catalogues are little used.
4) There is almost no standard sales policy.
5) There is little market research.
6) There is less organizing of distribution.

These characteristics are said to be caused by the existence of trust-based networks (*guanxi*) in the inter-firm relations which have simplified the marketing processes. The inter-firm relations are described further in the next section.

Inter-Firm Relations

In the area of inter-firm relations, the OCB tend to manage buying and selling relationships with a degree of less formality and sub-contracting based upon personal/familial trust bonds (Redding 1993, pp. 150–51; Whitley 1991). Chan (2000, p. 9) mentions that the Chinese trust-based network (*guanxi*) can be formed based upon many attributes such as kinship, schoolmates, colleagues and common interests. *Guanxi* places considerable emphasis upon unwritten codes of conduct to guard against opportunistic behaviour of its members.

The fundamental principles are reciprocity, obligation, maintenance of reputation and face (Chan 2000; Redding 1993). Before someone is admitted into a network, his track record and reliability is inquired into. Efferin's case study (2002) has also shown that *guanxi* has been used as a defensive and solidarity mechanism to cope with the ethnicity of Chinese Indonesians (hostile environment). The network also serves as a source of vital business information such as business partners, credit sources, trustable employees and so on.

The application of *guanxi* can produce low transaction costs in economic exchanges since many transactions, which in other societies require contracts, lawyers, guarantees, investigations, and delays, are dealt with reliably and quickly among the overseas Chinese by telephone, handshake, or over a cup of tea (Low 1995; Yeung 1999). This does not necessarily mean that legal properties are entirely missing but they are not prerequisites to agreement and, for the majority of transactions, they can be ignored.

Business Development

Whitley (1991) provides some characteristics of the OCB. The OCB tends to restrict their business to a particular area in which their specialized skills and knowledge provide distinctive capabilities. In addition, their development is primarily evolutionary within a given sector. Redding (1993) also states that the person running it is most likely the majority stakeholder and is deeply committed to the generation of a return for the risk he feels personally responsible for. Borrowing money from banks is commonly an area for inhibition since there is an anxiety of being over-stretched. This reflects the conservative, cautious way of doing business to conserve the family's wealth that can be traced back to the old Confucian principle of asceticism.

RESEARCH METHOD

This is a grounded decriptive-interpretive study performed from November 2004 to March 2005. The data collection methods used were interviews and questionnaires. Interviews were conducted with ten *Tionghoa* businessmen for about twenty hours to get in-depth understanding of their perceptions, understandings, opinions, thoughts and experiences related to the ways they do business.

Questionnaires are used to obtain general characteristics of ethnic Chinese business practices. Because the Chinese usually tend to guard the confidentiality of their business practices and company's internal information, this study uses convenient sampling for the questionnaires. Convenient sampling is the collection of data from members of the population who are available to provide data (Efferin et al. 2004). Hence, the data are collected from those who are willing to cooperate in this study. The sample size is 113 *Tionghoa* businessmen/senior managers in Surabaya. In terms of educational background, 64 respondents (56.64 per cent) have university degrees and 49 respondents (43.36 per cent) have high school/primary school/Chinese school degrees. Their characteristics can be seen in Table 5.1.

The classification of *totok* and *jiaosen* is based on self-acknowledgement. The respondents were explained about the terms *totok* and *jiaosen*. Then, they were asked whether they considered themselves as *totok*, *jiaosen* or unsure. Most of the respondents (104 people, 92.04 per cent) were certain when categorizing themselves and only 9 repondents were unsure. This reveals that for them such terminologies are well-known.

Two dimensions were used to categorize the sample: Business scale and cultural orientation. In terms of business scale, the questionnaire respondents were classified into Small/Medium Enterprises/SMEs (69 people) and Large Enterprises or LEs (44 people). The interview respondents consisted of 2 SMEs and 8 LEs. In terms of cultural orientation, the questionnaire respondents were classified into *totok* (52), *jiaosen* (52) and those who are unsure (9). The interview respondents are 7 *totok* and 3 *jiaosen*. The reason for this is to ensure the representativeness of different components among Chinese businessmen which may have different impacts upon the way they do business and to examine whether there are different patterns among them.

There are many versions of the definition of SMEs in Indonesia. This study adopts Bank Indonesia's (Indonesian Central Bank) definition as follows:

Types of enterprises	Sales value per annum
Small and Medium (SMEs)	<= 3,000,000,000 rupiah
Large (LEs)	> 3,000,000,000 rupiah

TABLE 5.1
Characteristics of the Respondents Based upon Business Scale and Cultural Orientation

Characteristics		Business Scale		Cultural Orientation		
		SMEs	LEs	Totok	Jiaosen	Unsure
Fields of Business	Trading/Service	52 (75%)	25 (57%)	37 (71%)	34 (65%)	6 (67%)
	Manufacturing	11 (16%)	10 (23%)	8 (15%)	13 (25%)	0 (0%)
	Plantation	2 (3%)	1 (2%)	3 (6%)	0 (0%)	0 (0%)
	Construction	1 (1%)	4 (9%)	1 (2%)	3 (6%)	1 (11%)
	Real estate	0 (0%)	1 (2%)	1 (2%)	0 (0%)	0 (0%)
	Combination of above	1 (1%)	3 (7%)	2 (4%)	1 (2%)	1 (11%)
	Others	2 (3%)	0 (0%)	0 (0%)	1 (2%)	1 (11%)
		69 (100%)	44 (100%)	52 (100%)	52 (100%)	9 (100%)
Main Customers	End user	36 (52%)	11 (25%)	21 (40%)	21 (40%)	5 (56%)
	Other industries	6 (9%)	14 (32%)	10 (19%)	9 (17%)	1 (11%)
	Combination of above	27 (39%)	19 (43%)	21 (40%)	22 (42%)	3 (33%)
		69 (100%)	44 (100%)	52 (100%)	52 (100%)	9 (100%)
Market	Mostly overseas	4 (6%)	3 (7%)	5 (10%)	2 (4%)	0 (0%)
	Mostly local	15 (22%)	14 (32%)	17 (33%)	12 (23%)	0 (0%)
	Overseas only	2 (3%)	1 (2%)	1 (2%)	2 (4%)	0 (0%)
	Local only	48 (70%)	26 (59%)	29 (56%)	36 (69%)	9 (100%)
		69 (100%)	44 (100%)	52 (100%)	52 (100%)	9 (100%)
Role in the Business	Owner and senior executive	42 (61%)	25 (57%)	33 (63%)	29 (56%)	5 (56%)
	Owner	21 (30%)	7 (16%)	14 (27%)	11 (21%)	3 (33%)
	Senior executive	6 (9%)	12 (27%)	5 (10%)	12 (23%)	1 (11%)
		69 (100%)	44 (100%)	52 (100%)	52 (100%)	9 (100%)

Some other definitions from various institutions are based upon asset value and number of employees (see for example, the definition of Indonesian Statistical Bureau-BPS and the Ministry of Cooperation and Small/Medium Enterprises). Definitions based upon asset value may be biased because of the different types of industries (manufacturing, trading and services). Definitions based upon number of employees may also be biased because of the different characteristics of technologies employed (labour intensive *versus* capital intensive or low technology *versus* high technology). Hence, definitions based upon sales value are chosen because they are relatively free from such biases.

EMPIRICAL ANALYSIS

All analysis will be based upon the results from questionnaires and interviews. Answers in the questionnaires include options representing the so-called "OCB model" as prescribed in the above sections, Western model as prescribed by many conventional literatures and other alternatives (respondents were required to specify). This is to give respondents freedom when choosing answers that fit for them.

Managerial Ideology

Patrimonialism

The results are described in Table 5.2. The majority of Chinese Indonesian/ *Tionghoa* respondents (69.03 per cent, 78 out of 113) assumed that the highest source of authority is the owner of the company. The majority of the SMEs (81 per cent) chose owner instead of formal top management, whereas only 50 per cent of LEs chose the option. Apparently, business scale matters more than cultural orientation since the differences are smaller between *totok*, *jiaosen* and "Unsure". Hence, the *Tionghoa* generally regard that power cannot be separated from ownership.

Similar responses also arose in viewing company's objectives, ownership of assets and successors. The majority of *Tionghoa* regarded the company's objectives as the owner's objectives (66 respondents: 58.41 per cent), company's assets as owner's private property (75 respondents: 66.37 per cent), and that leadership successors must come from the family circle (73 respondents: 64.60 per cent). Those thoughts are much more widespread in the SMEs rather than in LEs whereas there are smaller

TABLE 5.2
Patrimonialism Based upon Business Scale and Cultural Orientation

Questions		Q#	Business Scale		Cultural Orientation		
			SMEs	LEs	Totok	Jiaosen	Unsure
The highest source of authority	Owner	5.A	56 (81%)	22 (50%)	38 (73%)	33 (63%)	7 (78%)
	Formal top management	5.B	13 (19%)	21 (48%)	14 (27%)	18 (35%)	2 (22%)
	Others	5.C	0 (0%)	1 (2%)	0 (0%)	1 (2%)	0 (0%)
			69 (100%)	44 (100%)	52 (100%)	52 (100%)	9 (100%)
Company's objectives	Based on owner's objectives	6.A	46 (67%)	20 (45%)	26 (50%)	35 (67%)	5 (56%)
	Based on stakeholder's interests	6.B	23 (33%)	23 (52%)	26 (50%)	16 (31%)	4 (44%)
	Others	6.C	0 (0%)	1 (2%)	0 (0%)	1 (2%)	0 (0%)
			69 (100%)	44 (100%)	52 (100%)	52 (100%)	9 (100%)
Ownership of assets/ investments	Owner's property	7.A	51 (74%)	24 (55%)	33 (63%)	35 (67%)	7 (78%)
	Organization's property	7.B	17 (25%)	19 (43%)	18 (35%)	16 (31%)	2 (22%)
	Others	7.C	1 (1%)	1 (2%)	1 (2%)	1 (2%)	0 (0%)
			69 (100%)	44 (100%)	52 (100%)	52 (100%)	9 (100%)
Leadership successors	Family members	8.A	49 (71%)	24 (55%)	35 (67%)	33 (63%)	5 (56%)
	Capable employees	8.B	6 (9%)	9 (20%)	7 (13%)	7 (13%)	1 (11%)
	Recruit professionals	8.C	13 (19%)	10 (23%)	8 (15%)	12 (23%)	3 (33%)
	Others	8.D	1 (1%)	1 (2%)	2 (4%)	0 (0%)	0 (0%)
			69 (100%)	44 (100%)	52 (100%)	52 (100%)	9 (100%)
Ideal roles of employer	Teaching employees	9.A	36 (52%)	14 (32%)	25 (48%)	23 (44%)	2 (22%)
	Empowering employees	9.B	26 (38%)	29 (66%)	22 (42%)	26 (50%)	7 (78%)
	Others	9.C	7 (10%)	1 (2%)	5 (10%)	3 (6%)	0 (0%)
			69 (100%)	44 (100%)	52 (100%)	52 (100%)	9 (100%)

continued on next page

TABLE 5.2 – continued

Questions		Q#	Business Scale		Cultural Orientation		
			SMEs	LEs	Totok	Jiaosen	Unsure
Responsibility of employer	Taking care of and helping employees	10.A	28 (41%)	21 (48%)	28 (54%)	19 (37%)	2 (22%)
	Fulfilling his/her formal obligations	10.B	33 (48%)	21 (48%)	20 (38%)	28 (54%)	6 (67%)
	Others	10.C	8 (12%)	2 (5%)	4 (8%)	5 (10%)	1 (11%)
			69 (100%)	44 (100%)	52 (100%)	52 (100%)	9 (100%)
Ideal roles of employee	Doing what is told by employer	11.A	41 (59%)	18 (41%)	24 (46%)	30 (58%)	5 (56%)
	Giving advice/being critical	11.B	16 (23%)	18 (41%)	21(40%)	10 (19%)	3 (33%)
	Making policy	11.C	8 (12%)	8 (18%)	4 (8%)	11 (21%)	1 (11%)
	Others	11.D	4 (6%)	0 (0%)	3 (6%)	1 (2%)	0 (0%)
			69 (100%)	44 (100%)	52 (100%)	52 (100%)	9 (100%)
Responsibility of employees	Obeying the employer	12.A	27 (39%)	9 (20%)	14 (27%)	20 (38%)	2 (22%)
	Fulfilling his/her job descriptions	12.B	36 (52%)	35 (80%)	34 (65%)	30 (58%)	7 (78%)
	Others	12.C	6 (9%)	0 (0%)	4 (8%)	2 (4%)	0 (0%)
			69 (100%)	44 (100%)	52 (100%)	52 (100%)	9 (100%)

differences among the *totok*, *jiaosen* and "unsure". Hence, business scale also matters more than cultural orientation.

Interesting results emerge when viewing the ideal roles and responsibilities of the employer (questions 9 and 10). Common description that OCBs favour autocratic-paternalistic leadership is not supported. Only 50 respondents (44.25 per cent) chose the didactive role of the employer (teaching employees), whereas empowering and other roles were chosen by 55 (48.67 per cent) and eight respondents (7.08 per cent) respectively. In this sense, business scale matters more than cultural orientation. The majority of SMEs (52 per cent) chose the didactive role, whereas only 32 per cent of LEs chose the answer. By contrast, the majority of large businesses (66 per cent) chose the empowering role and only 38 per cent of SMEs chose such a role.

The deviation from the conventional OCB leadership style is further supported in the results of question 10. Only 49 respondents (43.36 per cent) chose paternalistic responsibility of employer (taking care of and helping employees in work and personal life), whereas fulfilling formal obligation and other kinds of responsibility were chosen by 54 (47.79 per cent) and 10 respondents (8.85 per cent) respectively. However, the *totok* tend to share the paternalistic role much more than the *jiaosen*. Fifty-four per cent of *totok* chose the employer's paternalistic responsibility compared with only 37 per cent of *jiaosen*. By contrast, fulfilling formal obligation and other kinds of responsibility were chosen by 64 per cent of *jiaosen* and only 46 per cent of *totok*. Thus, cultural orientation seems to matter in this issue.

The results of the questions 11 and 12 (ideal roles and responsibilities of employee) have also questioned the strength of the autocratic-paternalistic leadership as a main characteristic of OCB. In question 11, 59 respondents (52.21 per cent) preferred employees to merely do what is told by the employer whereas the other 54 (47.79 per cent) chose more participative roles such as giving advice/critiques to employer and making policies. Fifty-nine per cent of SMEs agreed on the submissive role of employees compared with only 41 per cent of LEs. By contrast, more participative roles were chosen by only 35 per cent SMEs but 59 per cent LEs. Interestingly, the *jiaosen* tend to support the employee's submissive role more than *totok* (58 per cent and 46 per cent respectively). The image that the employer demands unquestioning obedience of employees in OCBs is also challenged further in the results of question 12. Only 36 out of 113 (31.86 per cent) *Tionghoa* businessmen regarded unquestioning obedience as the main responsibility of employees. The others (77 persons: 68.14 per cent) preferred fulfilling formal job description as the employees' main responsibility. All categories of respondents showed rather consistent responses. However, the view of employee's formal responsibility tended to be more widespread in LEs than in SMEs.

Hence, patrimonialism in the *Tionghoa* businessmen appears only in the aspects of the source of authority (all categories), company's objectives (much higher in SMEs), the ownership of company's assets (much higher in SMEs) and leadership successors (all categories). The four aspects can be seen as the legacies of the so-called Confucian managerial ideology that are still common among *Tionghoa* businessmen. However, they tend to have participative-empowering managerial thoughts in viewing employer's roles (mainly LEs) and responsibilities (mainly *jiaosen*), and employees' roles (mainly LEs) and responsibilities (all categories). Interesting statements were made by three businessmen:

> Confucius never taught people to have unquestioning obedience to their master. Critical attitudes are even sought as long as the manners are polite. Politeness is important in all kinds of relationship. A master owes to his servants if they can remind him when he is doing something wrong. Confucius taught that you should not to rebel against your master. (Mr. Sing, LE, *Totok*)

> I prefer a smart and critical person as my employee rather than obedient and loyal but foolish one. What is the good? (Mr. Sul, LE, *Totok*)

> An employee should obey his superior only if his order is right. If it's not right, the employee should argue and give alternative solution. (Mr. Sam, LE, *Jiaosen*)

The interview respondents argue that Confucianism does not necessarily require absolute obedience and blind loyalty. It is more about good manners that can be interpreted in various ways. The manners are important since they will make the interaction between employers and employees smooth. Nevertheless, manners are merely means and they do not replace the end which is, in this context, organizational effectiveness. The respondents quite understand that their organizations can only grow and survive if they empower their employees. Hence, for the *Tionghoa* businessmen,

Confucianism is more about ways of communication rather than managerial ideology.

Furthermore, business scale seems to matter more than cultural orientation in determining the degree of patrimonialism. For the *Tionghoa*, the roles and responsibilities of employers and employees may be more related to organizational complexity than culture where simple organizations (for example, SMEs) do not need too much participative management and empowerment than complex organization (LEs). Consequently, LEs tend to have lesser degree of patrimonialism than SMEs.

Personalistic Relationship

The results are described in Table 5.3. Question 13 is about what employers would do when distributing work to employees for the first time. Only 37 *Tionghoa* respondents (32.74 per cent) considered that knowing the employee's personal characters was the first step in building work relationships. The rest chose more objective measures including educational background (36 respondents: 31.86 per cent) and past achievements (32 respondents: 28.32 per cent). Other alternatives were chosen by 8 respondents (7.10 per cent). In terms of business scale, personal character was the most popular alternative for SMEs (38 per cent) and the least popular one for LEs (25 per cent). By contrast, past achievements was the most popular alternative for LEs (41 per cent) and the least popular one for SMEs (20 per cent). From the perspective of cultural orientation, the *totok* placed employee's educational background as the most popular alternative (44 per cent). This option was the least popular alternative for the *jiaosen* (23 per cent). By contrast, the employee's past achievements was the most popular alternative for the *jiaosen* and the least one for the *totok*.

Question 14 is about expectations of the employer towards his/her employee. Loyalty towards the employer personally was the option representing the OCB model whereas loyalty towards formal duties represented the Western/bureaucratic model. Only 34 respondents (30.09 per cent) preferred loyalty towards the employer. Meanwhile, the rest choose loyalty towards formal duties (71 respondents: 62.83 per cent) and other alternatives (8 respondents: 7.10 per cent). Strong support for loyalty towards duties is also evident in all categories of respondents. The following interesting statements are made when asked about loyalty towards employer *versus* loyalty towards duties:

TABLE 5.3
Personalistic Relationship Based upon Business Scale and Cultural Orientation

Questions	Q#	Business Scale		Cultural Orientation		
		SMEs	LEs	Totok	Jiaosen	Unsure
First step in building work relationships						
Knowing employees personal characters	13.A	26 (38%)	11 (25%)	17 (33%)	16 (31%)	4 (44%)
Knowing employees educational background	13.B	22 (32%)	14 (32%)	23 (44%)	12 (23%)	1 (11%)
Knowing employees past achievements	13.C	14 (20%)	18 (41%)	8 (15%)	20 (38%)	4 (44%)
Others	13.D	7 (10%)	1 (2%)	4 (8%)	4 (8%)	0 (0%)
		69 (100%)	44 (100%)	52 (100%)	52 (100%)	9 (100%)
Expected loyalty						
Loyalty towards employer	14.A	24 (35%)	10 (23%)	17 (33%)	15 (29%)	2 (22%)
Loyalty towards formal duties	14.B	37 (54%)	34 (77%)	31 (60%)	34 (65%)	6 (67%)
Others	14.C	8 (12%)	0 (0%)	4 (8%)	3 (6%)	1 (11%)
		69 (100%)	44 (100%)	52 (100%)	52 (100%)	9 (100%)
Most important criterion in assigning vital jobs/duties						
Loyalty	15.A	30 (43%)	23 (52%)	25 (48%)	23 (44%)	5 (56%)
Experiences	15.B	15 (22%)	10 (23%)	11 (21%)	12 (23%)	2 (22%)
Intelligence	15.C	17 (25%)	8 (18%)	11 (21%)	12 (23%)	2 (22%)
Others	15.D	7 (10%)	3 (7%)	5 (10%)	5 (10%)	0 (0%)
		69 (100%)	44 (100%)	52 (100%)	52 (100%)	9 (100%)

Surely, loyalty towards duties. I often practise this in my company. When I need a person, I always ask him first 'I need you to do something but have you finished your main duties?' The question must be asked since it is useless if he finishes my order but neglects his regular duties. (Mr. Welly, LE, *Jiaosen*)

Loyalty depends on both the employer and employees. The employer must understand the needs of the employees. Thus, there is no one-side loyalty. Everything must be based upon "give and take" principle. (Mr. Sam, LE, *Jiaosen*)

Fifty-three respondents (46.90 per cent) regarded loyalty as the most important criterion to consider when assigning vital jobs (for example, accounting, finance, purchasing) to individual employee (question 15). Experiences, intelligence and other criteria were chosen by 25 (22.12 per cent), 25 (22.12 per cent) and 10 (8.85 per cent) respondents respectively. A rather similar picture occurred in all categories of respondents. This does not mean that experiences, intelligence and other criteria are not important. Many interviews reveal that personal character is crucial for higher level positions yet the persons occupying those positions must already have minimum/certain standard of skills and abilities. Loyalty must be built among those who already have certain skills/standards before they can be promoted. In other words, it is not enough for a person with very good personal character and loyalty to hold responsibilities in strategic positions.

According to the conventional OCB model, personal relationships and feelings about employees come before more objective assessment of their abilities and the upward flow of employees' loyalty and conformity is vital to stabilize the structure and dampen the resentment of subordination. However, the results do not support this since the majority of respondents in all categories preferred to use more measurable criteria (for example, educational background and past achievements) rather than personal character in building work relationships. Most of them also preferred employees' loyalty towards their duties rather than towards employers personally. Personal character and loyalty are important considerations for fulfilling strategic positions when the other criteria have been satisfied. Thus, for the *Tionghoa* businessmen in general, more objective performance criteria of employees precede personalistic relationship.

Limited and Bounded Trust

In question 16, only 39 (34.51 per cent) and 10 (8.85 per cent) of respondents respectively considered family circle and close friends as the most trustable persons for doing business.

The majority felt that they could be anyone depending on the individual character (64 respondents: 56.64 per cent). This reveals that the assumption of limited and bounded trust among the ethnic Chinese is questionable. This belief is shared by all categories of respondents except the *totok* where 54 per cent still believed that family circle and close friends were the most trustable ones. As mentioned by three *Tionghoa* businessmen:

> I have had many bad experiences of doing business with my relatives. They stabbed me from behind... I don't want to hire them anymore. It is also difficult to fire them or demand them to be professional if they work here. (Mr. Ming, LE, *Totok*)

> Business is risky. If you do business with your relatives, there is a danger that we tend to tolerate many things just because he/she is your brother or sister. This can be a disaster in the future. (Mr. Fu, SME, *Totok*)

> In my company, even my relatives who don't perform well will be punished. I demoted one and fired another one. Family relationship is not known and we only know formal superior-subordinate relationship. (Mr. Sam, LE, *Jiaosen*)

However, where there is no person who can ideally fulfil all criteria in recruitment, the majority of the respondents (92 persons: 81.42 per cent) preferred to recruit those they had already known (question 17). These responses are consistent in all categories of respondents.

The limited and bounded trust among the Chinese is often considered as ethnic based-trust. Surprisingly, the result of question 18 reveals a different picture. Only 46 respondents (40.71 per cent) thought that ethnic Chinese were generally more trustable. Two respondents (1.77 per cent) considered ethnic Chinese less trustable and 29 respondents (25.66 per cent) placed the ethnic Chinese in extreme positions (they were always either "much better" or "much worse" than other ethnic groups. The rest (36 respondents: 31.86 per cent) were more objective believing that ethnicity did not have any relation to trustworthiness. A relatively similar pattern could be found in all categories of respondents. The following statements are noteworthy:

TABLE 5.4

Limited and Bounded Trust Based upon Business Scale and Cultural Orientation

Questions		Q#	Business Scale		Cultural Orientation		
			SMEs	LEs	Totok	Jiaosen	Unsure
Most trustable persons	Family members	16.A	27 (39%)	12 (27%)	25 (48%)	13 (25%)	1 (11%)
	Close persons	16.B	5 (7%)	5 (11%)	3 (6%)	6 (12%)	1 (11%)
	Can be anyone	16.C	37 (54%)	27 (61%)	24 (46%)	33 (63%)	7 (78%)
			69 (100%)	44 (100%)	52 (100%)	52 (100%)	9 (100%)
In case of no ideal persons, you will recruit those who are/have	Personally known	17.A	60 (87%)	32 (73%)	42 (81%)	42 (81%)	8 (89%)
	Highest academic achievement	17.B	3 (4%)	4 (9%)	5 (10%)	2 (4%)	0 (0%)
	Most experienced	17.C	2 (3%)	3 (7%)	2 (4%)	3 (6%)	0 (0%)
	Best psychotest result	17.D	4 (6%)	5 (11%)	3 (6%)	5 (10%)	1 (11%)
			69 (100%)	44 (100%)	52 (100%)	52 (100%)	9 (100%)
General perception of ethnic Chinese	More trustable	18.A	28 (41%)	18 (41%)	26 (50%)	17 (33%)	3 (33%)
	Less trustable	18.B	1 (1%)	1 (2%)	1 (2%)	1 (2%)	0 (0%)
	Either highly better or worse	18.C	16 (23%)	13 (30%)	13 (25%)	13 (25%)	3 (33%)
	Ethnicity doesn't matter	18.D	24 (35%)	12 (27%)	12 (23%)	21 (40%)	3 (33%)
			69 (100%)	44 (100%)	52 (100%)	52 (100%)	9 (100%)

Many of them (non-Chinese) can (be reliable) at the moment. Some Chinese employees sometimes demand too much and they treat their *pribumi* colleagues like their own employees. You know Lena (disguised name, non-Chinese)? She works excellently. I also have an employee who always wears *jilbab*. Although she is not intelligent she is very loyal. (Mr. Ming, LE, *Totok*)

It is difficult to say whether Chinese are more trustable or not. It is just a coincidence that the majority of my partners are Chinese because most of the players here are Chinese. But I think we cannot just believe other people's words even though they are Chinese. (Mr. San, SME, *Jiaosen*)

Actually, I don't think Chinese employees are more trustable. We can understand them more easily, that's all. Maybe because we speak in the 'same frequency' due to our similar family education and background. Sometimes I prefer a Chinese employee merely for communication purposes. (Mr. Welly, LE, *Jiaosen*)

Chinese are more trustable as employees because they need the jobs. State-owned enterprises such as Garuda and Petrokimia will not admit them, they only accept *pribumi*. So Chinese need to cooperate to survive. (Mr. Sul, LE, *Totok*)

Hence, limited and bounded trust only applies to emergency conditions such as in the recruitment and selection of business partners provided that there is no ideal candidate or enough information to make decisions. In such cases, the only certain variables are previous personal relationship or personal background. Those variables then become the starting point to make decisions.

Although respondents who agree that Chinese are more trustable are the largest compared with the other options, their percentage is less than 50 per cent (except the *totok* where it reaches 50 per cent). The state's ethnic discrimination in the past and a sense of solidarity are among the reasons for the trust. The solidarity has been created due to their common experiences in facing the state's past discriminatory measures towards them rather than ancestral ties. The measures drew boundaries and identities in their daily lives including their business activities. Thus, psychologically, they feel safer to do business with people around them who have similar social advantages and disadvantages. As a cause of solidarity, ancestral ties is weaker than shared experiences since many of them also have negative stereotypes of Chinese from certain areas in Indonesia with whom they avoid doing business.

A substantial percentage of respondents even believe that Chinese have much more potential to be either much better or much worse than other ethnic groups. The view of the ethnic Chinese' extreme potentials indicates that ethnic-based trust is actually problematic for many Chinese Indonesians. The Chinese are perceived to be more intelligent than other ethnic groups. Consequently, they are more cautious when dealing with Chinese employees/business partners. But once they are convinced about the trustworthiness of a Chinese, they will rely very much on him/her.

A larger percentage of respondents also believe that individual character is more relevant than ethnicity. Ethnicity, for them, is not a dominant dimension in doing business. This view is a signal that many of the Chinese have been able to separate their political/social trauma from their business activities. The percentage of the *jiaosen* possessing this view is much more than the *totok* as they usually have more interactions with people from different ethnic groups since their childhood (for example, schools and religious communities). It has been mentioned that *jiaosen* are usually Christians, Catholics or Muslims. Hence, those interactions give them opportunities to learn about the different personal characteristics of other people from different ethnic groups.

Organizational Structure

Answers for questions 19–24 were in interval scale (1–5) whereby respondents were asked to circle a number that best describes the extent of their preferences for a dimension of organizational structure (see Table 5.5). Number 1 indicates that a respondent's extent of preference of the dimension is the least whereas number 5 shows that the extent of preference is the most.

Question 19 is about where hierarchically the majority of decisions/policies in their organizations are made. Score 1 is for top level management only and score 5 is for lower level management only. The results of all categories reveal that, generally, *Tionghoa* businessmen tend to favour centralization rather than decentralization in decision-making. More specifically, SMEs tend to favour centralization slightly more than LEs and, surprisingly, *totok* tend to favour decentralization slightly more than *jiaosen*. The following statements are noteworthy:

TABLE 5.5
Organizational Structure Based upon Business Scale
and Cultural Orientation

Questions	Q#	Business Scale		Cultural Orientation		
		SMEs	LEs	*Totok*	*Jiaosen*	Unsure
Decentralization	19	1.4	1.7	1.7	1.4	1.2
Specialization	20	3.9	4	3.9	4.1	3.4
Formalization: Job Description	21	3	3.1	2.9	3.2	3.2
Standardization	22	2.8	3.2	3	2.9	3.3
Formalization: Written Records	23	3.9	3.7	3.8	3.9	3.2
Configuration	24	2.6	3	2.7	2.9	2.1

> As an owner and director, I have been building this company for a long time.... So I know all the problems. I am on the top of a mountain and I can see all sides of the mountain with complete view. My employees are at the bottom so they only have partial view. That's why all strategic decisions and policies are made by myself. (Mr. Ali, LE, *Totok*)

> Like a car, you can either drive by yourself or use a driver. Which one is better? It is situational. But if you want to be safe you must drive by yourself because you can control the steering wheel. (Mr. Welly, LE, *Jiaosen*)

Question 20 is about how to assign daily duties to employees. Score 1 is for allocation based upon the availability of employees with no specialization and score 5 is for allocation strictly based upon predefined roles in specialized units. The results challenge the theoretical OCB model since, generally, *Tionghoa* businessmen tend to favour specialization. Although all categories show similar tendencies, LEs tend to favour specialization slightly more than SMEs and the *jiaosen* tend to favour specialization slightly more than the *totok*.

Questions 21 and 23 refer to formalization: The importance of written job description and records of activities/transactions. Score 1 is for using no formal job description (#21) and no written records (#23). Score 5 is for using formal job description in all positions (#21) and highly detailed written records (#23). The results of the two questions reveal that, generally, *Tionghoa* businessmen tend to favour formalization. However, written records of activities/transactions are given more emphasis than formal job description. Furthermore, the use of formal job description tend to be more common among the *jiaosen* than *totok*.

Question 22 is about standardization: The extent to which rules and definitions are used to regularized procedures in their organizations. Score 1 is for using flexible procedures extensively in all activities and number 5 is for using strictly rigid, standardized procedures in all activities. The results reveal that, generally, *Tionghoa* businessmen tend to favour rather intermediate, pragmatic pattern of standardization. This is different from the theoretical OCB model which proposes that Chinese businesses have low standardization. Furthermore, business scale has more influence than cultural orientation in which LEs favour standardization more than SMEs. Interestingly, the *totok* has a slightly greater score than the *jiaosen*.

Question 24 is about configuration: The respondents' perception of the relative importance of the roles played by line *versus* staff personnel in creating efficiency and generating profit for their organizations. Score 1 is for placing importance highly on line personnel and score 5 is for placing importance highly on staff personnel. The averages in all categories reveal that, generally, *Tionghoa* businessmen tend to favour low configuration. Furthermore, LEs and *jiaosen* tend to favour higher configuration than SMEs and *totok*.

Thus, there are some differences between the *Tionghoa*'s organizational structures and the theoretical OCB model. Their structures are consistent with the model in terms of high centralization, high formalization and rather low configuration (especially SMEs and *totok*). However, formalization is an aspect in which there is no substantial difference between OCB and Western organizational structures. Furthermore, the structures are inconsistent in terms of specialization and standardization. The *Tionghoa* have relatively high level of specialization and moderate standardization which make them relatively similar to Western model. Therefore, high centralization is the only salient characteristic which can distinguish them from Western organizational structure.

Managerial Functions

Management control

It has been stated above that the OCB put more emphasis upon controlling people and production activities than other managerial functions, reflecting that production (operation) is considered as the core activity of the OCB organizations. However, the findings from question 25 reveal that the respondents' first priority for controlling managerial area was spread almost evenly (see Table 5.6). The most popular choice was finance (39 respondents: 34.51 per cent) followed by human resource management (38: 33.63 per cent), marketing (19: 16.81 per cent) and production (17: 15.04 per cent). Interestingly, LEs put much more emphasis upon human resource management (50 per cent) than other areas whereas SMEs tend to give greater priority upon finance (38 per cent). By contrast, the *totok* and *jiaosen* do not show a substantial different pattern of their priority. It seems that technical environments (for example, scale, market and types of industries) matter here. Different technical environments require different strategies and priorities of control.

Culture is important in determining the perception of control effectiveness (#26). Chinese values of vertical order (*li* and *hsiao*) emphasizing family-like relationships, reciprocal obligations and personal trust are seen as increasing employee cohesiveness and identification with the organization. Seventy respondents (61.95 per cent) regarded informal control as the most important control to use, emphasizing the creation of mutual understanding based on collectively shared cultural values (that is, personal/cultural control). This is followed by more bureaucratic control such as result and action controls, that were chosen by only 22 (19.47 per cent) and 21 (18.58 per cent) of respondents respectively. As mentioned in the following interviews:

> We cannot watch them (employees) all the time. We need to educate them that self-responsibility is crucial both for themselves and for the company.... The use of target is only effective after they have that kind of attitude. (Mr. Ali, LE, *Totok*)

> Do you know why many of my employees have been working here for more than twenty years? Because I give them challenges and opportunities. They even get some portion of the company's profit.... Employee's sense of belonging to company is very important since it will create self-control. This is my priority. (Mr. Sam, LE, *Jiaosen*)

However, it must be stressed that this does not mean companies only use one of them. The three controls are used simultaneously and the findings are merely to describe the respondents' perception of their effectiveness. A rather similar picture also takes place in all categories of respondents where personal/cultural control is the most popular option.

TABLE 5.6
Management Control Based upon Business Scale and Cultural Orientation

Questions		Q#	Business Scale		Cultural Orientation		
			SMEs	LEs	Totok	Jiaosen	Unsure
Most important area to control	Production	25.A	11 (16%)	6 (14%)	8 (15%)	8 (15%)	1 (11%)
	Finance	25.B	26 (38%)	13 (30%)	20 (38%)	18 (35%)	1 (11%)
	HRM	25.C	16 (23%)	22 (50%)	15 (29%)	18 (35%)	5 (56%)
	Marketing	25.D	16 (23%)	3 (7%)	9 (17%)	8 (15%)	2 (22%)
			69 (100%)	44 (100%)	52 (100%)	52 (100%)	9 (100%)
Most important control type	Personal/cultural control	26.A	48 (70%)	22 (50%)	34 (65%)	30 (58%)	6 (67%)
	Action control	26.B	10 (14%)	11 (25%)	10 (19%)	10 (19%)	1 (11%)
	Result control	26.C	11 (16%)	11 (25%)	8 (15%)	12 (23%)	2 (22%)
			69 (100%)	44 (100%)	52 (100%)	52 (100%)	9 (100%)

However, a substantial difference appear between SMEs and LEs in which the respondents who chose that option were 70 per cent and 50 per cent respectively. The *totok* also tend to rely upon personal/cultural control more than the *jiaosen*.

Hence, type of control emphasized (personnel/cultural control) can be seen as a typical characteristic of the *Tionghoa* businessmen since a salient pattern of preference has been shown by the respondents. This finding is consistent with the thesis of Merchant (1998) about the importance of cultural, informal control rather than highly sophisticated, bureaucratic control for Southeast Asian Chinese business. By contrast, there is no salient pattern in the priority for the areas of control (production/operation, marketing, finance and HRM) that can be regarded as another typical characteristic of *Tionghoa* businessmen' MCS.

Finance

The findings are described in Table 5.7. Results from question 27 show that the respondents' main strategy to penetrate market and generate profit is to emphasize on product quality (58 respondents: 51.33 per cent) followed by differentiation/uniqueness (33: 29.20 per cent) and low margin-high volume (22: 19.47 per cent). Product quality is also chosen as the most popular strategy in all categories of the respondents. Hence, the conventional model of OCB as mentioned above has been challenged since low margin and high volume is, in fact, the least popular option among the *Tionghoa* businessmen. As mentioned in the following interviews:

> High profit margin is important... I have no problem if I must lose my volume due to the high selling price. I am not the kind of businessman who pursues high sales volume by cutting price. The most important is our product quality. If the quality is bad, no matter how hard we try, (like) cutting (our) price to 20 per cent or even breaking our back, everything will be useless. (Mr. Budi, LE, *Totok*)

> High margin low volume is suitable for business in Indonesia. Our currency is unstable so it is important for us to have enough financial reserve. I apply this principle strictly. Maybe in the U.S., for example, we can pursue volume more than margin. (Mr. Welly, LE, *Jiaosen*)

TABLE 5.7
Finance Based upon Business Scale and Cultural Orientation

Questions	Q#	Business Scale		Cultural Orientation		
		SMEs	LEs	Totok	Jiaosen	Unsure
Strategy to penetrate market and of generating steady flow of Profit						
Low margin & high volume	27.A	18 (26%)	4 (9%)	13 (25%)	6 (12%)	3 (33%)
Quality	27.B	34 (49%)	24 (55%)	20 (38%)	33 (63%)	5 (56%)
Differentiation/ uniqueness	27.C	17 (25%)	16 (36%)	19 (37%)	13 (25%)	1 (11%)
		69 (100%)	44 (100%)	52 (100%)	52 (100%)	9 (100%)
Main source of Financing						
Family sources	28.A	27 (39%)	8 (18%)	20 (38%)	13 (25%)	2 (22%)
Business colleagues	28.B	3 (4%)	6 (14%)	6 (12%)	2 (4%)	1 (11%)
Banks	28.C	29 (42%)	28 (64%)	21 (40%)	32 (62%)	4 (44%)
Others	28.D	10 (14%)	2 (5%)	5 (10%)	5 (10%)	2 (22%)
		69 (100%)	44 (100%)	52 (100%)	52 (100%)	9 (100%)

The most popular source of financing is bank (57: 50.44 per cent), followed by family sources (35: 30.97 per cent), others (12: 10.62 per cent) and business colleagues (9: 7.96 per cent). Bank is also the most popular choice in all categories of respondents. However, there are differences between SMEs and LEs and between *totok* and *jiaosen*. The percentage of SMEs choosing bank is much less than that of LEs whereas the percentage of SMEs that prefer family source is much more that of LEs. In terms of cultural orientation, the percentage of *totok* choosing bank is much less than that of *jiaosen*. In contrast, the percentage of *totok* choosing family sources is much more than that of *jiaosen*. This reveals that the role of banks as financial intermediary for *Tionghoa* businessmen is crucial. In the case of SMEs and the *totok*, the role of family sources is almost as crucial as the bank. The following statements are noteworthy:

> The bank is my favourite place as a financial source.... Using family sources for financing our business involves personal feelings. This makes the business inflexible. If we want to revise the rate due to (macro) economic changes, we may feel embarrassed or afraid to offend them. (Mr. Ming, LE, *Totok*)

> At first, we used loans for tax purposes only. It was just to show to the taxation agencies that we did not generate much profit. We relied upon ourselves (for financing). But time has changed. It is important for us to have bank loan in order to protect our own money given the situation in Indonesia. For me, security is everything. (Mr. Welly, LE, *Jiaosen*)

The results challenge the conventional view that borrowing money from banks is commonly an area of inhibition for OCBs due to the anxiety of being over-stretched. Family relationship is often considered as a potential source of conflict. Given the importance of family as a basic survival institution, many *Tionghoa* attempt to avoid conflict by using banks for financing. Moreover, many *Tionghoa* still have trauma due to the state's repression and discrimination towards them in the past. They are afraid for the security of their personal assets and investments in the future. Hence, the bank is seen as a way of minimizing conflicts among relatives and, simultaneously, protecting family assets from Indonesia's unstable political situations.

Human Resource Management (HRM)

The results are described in Table 5.8. The respondents tend to accord highest importance and most extensive attention upon selection and recruitment (57 respondents: 50.44 per cent). This is, then, followed by performance appraisal (29: 25.66 per cent), training and development (20: 17.70 per cent) and reward/punishment (7: 6.19 per cent). The same pattern also happen in all categories.

The theoretical OCB model is only supported in the sense that selection and recruitment was the most popular answer. However, different from the model, reward and punishment was the least popular choice, way below training and development. Hence, the statements of Chinese pragmatism (refusing to spend money unless absolutely necessary) and low emphasis on using professionals in HRM are questionable in the context of Chinese Indonesian businesses. The following statements are noteworthy:

> We need professionals.... Even my father told me that if his children were stupid, our companies would be better to be handled by professional employees. Our real estate company is now 100 per cent managed by employees. I am concentrating on the commodity trading company. If I were capable of developing it, I would hand it over to my employees. (Mr. Ming, LE, *Totok*)

> It's true that this company is a family company but it is also a professionally-managed company. Personally, I can feel the changes in the last twenty-two years.... From the internal perspective, we feel the complexity is so high that we must recruit more professionals. From the external perspective, globalization has produced more intense competition and change of regulations. We need many professionals to support us with their ideas. (Mr. Li, LE, *Totok*)

Many of the *Tionghoa* believe that selection and recruitment is fundamental to everything. Recruiting the right people who already possess certain cultural values, knowledge and skills simplifies the task of the employers to train them and provide necessary resources. This, in turn, increases the probability that a job will be done properly. This is quite common in any culture. Much of Western human resource management

TABLE 5.8
HRM Based upon Business Scale and Cultural Orientation

Questions		Q#	Business Scale		Cultural Orientation		
			SMEs	LEs	Totok	Jiaosen	Unsure
Most important activity in HRM	Performance appraisal	29.A	19 (28%)	10 (23%)	13 (25%)	14 (27%)	2 (22%)
	Reward & punishment	29.B	4 (6%)	3 (7%)	3 (6%)	4 (8%)	0 (0%)
	Selection and recruitment	29.C	33 (48%)	24 (55%)	27 (52%)	24 (46%)	6 (67%)
	Training and development	29.D	13 (19%)	7 (16%)	9 (17%)	10 (19%)	1 (11%)
			69 (100%)	44 (100%)	52 (100%)	52 (100%)	9 (100%)

literature also have similar thinking. The difference is in the cultural values required from applicants. Some *Tionghoa* businessmen prefer those who already possess certain Confucian values such as asceticism, diligence and altruism. However, this also depends upon the extent to which the employers share such values. The more *totok* an employer is, the more he/she requires such values from an applicant.

Operation Management

The results are described in Table 5.9. Answers from question 30 show that the majority of respondents performed quality control (68: 60.18 per cent) regularly, whereas 36 respondents (31.86 per cent) reported that they did it occasionally. Only 9 respondents (7.96 per cent) did not perform any quality control at all. This also happened in production/operation scheduling (#31) where 60 respondents (53.10 per cent) acknowledge that they did it regularly and 25 (22.12 per cent) only occasionally. Twenty eight respondents (24.78 per cent) claimed that they never did it at all. Obviously, these areas were serious concerns of the *Tionghoa* businessmen. The same pattern happened in all categories of the respondents. Hence, the results support the theoretical description of the OCB model.

The situation is rather different in R&D activities (question 32). There were only 28 respondents (24.78 per cent) who performed R&D regularly yet 52 respondents (46.02 per cent) did it occasionally. The rest (33 respondents: 29.20 per cent) reported that they never did any R&D. However, regular R&D in LEs tend to be more common than that in SMEs. The SMEs' relatively lower priority for R&D is possibly due to their shortage of research resources (money, knowledge and skills) and positioning strategy (market followers). Thus, technical reasons are at play here rather than cultural reasons.

Marketing

The results are described in Table 5.10. In the marketing function, standard displays, standard sales policies and using own distribution channels are the most common activities for the *Tionghoa* businessmen (see results from questions 34, 36 and 38). Sixty respondents (53.10 per cent) admitted that they had standard displays for all their products whereas 21 respondents (18.58 per cent) reported that standard displays were only used for some of their products. Only 32 respondents (28.32 per cent) did

TABLE 5.9

Operation Management Based upon Business Scale and Cultural Orientation

Questions		Q#	Business Scale		Cultural Orientation		
			SMEs	LEs	Totok	Jiaosen	Unsure
Quality control	Always	30.A	42 (61%)	26 (59%)	27 (52%)	36 (69%)	5 (56%)
	None	30.B	4 (6%)	5 (11%)	7 (13%)	0 (0%)	2 (22%)
	Sometimes	30.C	23 (33%)	13 (30%)	18 (35%)	16 (31%)	2 (22%)
			69 (100%)	44 (100%)	52 (100%)	52 (100%)	9 (100%)
Production/operation scheduling	Always	31.A	38 (55%)	22 (50%)	28 (54%)	29 (56%)	3 (33%)
	None	31.B	17 (25%)	11 (25%)	13 (25%)	11 (21%)	4 (44%)
	Sometimes	31.C	14 (20%)	11 (25%)	11 (21%)	12 (23%)	2 (22%)
			69 (100%)	44 (100%)	52 (100%)	52 (100%)	9 (100%)
Research & development	Always	32.A	14 (20%)	14 (32%)	13 (25%)	15 (29%)	0 (0%)
	None	32.B	21 (30%)	12 (27%)	16 (31%)	14 (27%)	3 (33%)
	Sometimes	32.C	34 (49%)	18 (41%)	23 (44%)	23 (44%)	6 (67%)
			69 (100%)	44 (100%)	52 (100%)	52 (100%)	9 (100%)

TABLE 5.10
Marketing Management Based upon Business Scale and Cultural Orientation

Questions	Q#		Business Scale		Cultural Orientation		
			SMEs	LEs	Totok	Jiaosen	Unsure
The use of standard trade marks	33.A	Always	26 (38%)	21 (48%)	22 (42%)	23 (44%)	2 (22%)
	33.B	None	30 (43%)	14 (32%)	19 (37%)	20 (38%)	5 (56%)
	33.C	Sometimes	13 (19%)	9 (20%)	11 (21%)	9 (17%)	2 (22%)
			69 (100%)	44 (100%)	52 (100%)	52 (100%)	9 (100%)
The use of standardized display	34.A	Always	36 (52%)	24 (55%)	29 (56%)	28 (54%)	3 (33%)
	34.B	None	24 (35%)	8 (18%)	14 (27%)	15 (29%)	3 (33%)
	34.C	Sometimes	9 (13%)	12 (27%)	9 (17%)	9 (17%)	3 (33%)
			69 (100%)	44 (100%)	52 (100%)	52 (100%)	9 (100%)
The use of product catalogue	35.A	Always	17 (25%)	17 (39%)	17 (33%)	13 (25%)	3 (33%)
	35.B	None	35 (51%)	16 (36%)	21 (40%)	27 (52%)	4 (44%)
	35.C	Sometimes	17 (25%)	11 (25%)	14 (27%)	12 (23%)	2 (22%)
			69 (100%)	44 (100%)	52 (100%)	52 (100%)	9 (100%)

not have standard displays at all. The majority of the respondents also claimed that they always used standard sales policies (60: 53.10 per cent) and their own distribution channels (64: 56.64 per cent). Partial use of standard sales policies and their own distribution channels were performed by 32 (28.32 per cent) and 31 (27.43 per cent) respondents correspondingly. Thus, only a few respondents did not use them at all. These patterns are relatively consistent in all categories of respondents which means that business scale and cultural orientation do not matter here. Hence, the results are substantially different from Redding's theoretical model of OCB which tends to underestimate the importance of those activities in the Chinese business context.

Market research (question 37) was also quite popular yet only 45 respondents (39.82 per cent) performed it constantly as a tool for making strategic decisions whereas 42 respondents (37.17 per cent) performed it occasionally. Those who never use market research are relatively small in percentage (26 respondents; 23.01 per cent). Relatively similar patterns can be found in all categories of respondents. Again, the results provide a different picture from the conventional OCB model which proposes that market research is of little importance for the Chinese.

Standard trade marks and product catalogues were the least popular features in the marketing functions of the respondents (questions 33 and 35). Only 47 respondents (41.59 per cent) admitted that they always used standard trade marks for all their products whereas 22 respondents (19.47 per cent) reported that standard trade marks were used for only some of their products. A substantial number of respondents (44: 38.94 per cent) did not have standard trade marks at all. This was more apparent in the use of product catalogues. Only 34 respondents (30.09 per cent) claimed that they had product catalogues for all their products whereas 28 respondents (24.78 per cent) reported that product catalogues were used for only some of their products. A substantial number of respondents (51: 45.13 per cent) did not have product catalogues at all. However, constant use of standard trade marks and product catalogues was considerably more common in LEs than in SMEs. The percentage of LEs that did not use the two features at all was also much less than that of SMEs. A substantially different pattern was not found between the *totok* and *jiaosen*. Technical reasons are possibly behind this finding rather than cultural reasons. Most of the LEs have been in their businesses for a long time and hence, the brand images of their products have been well established. By contrast, many of the SMEs do not have, if any, their own strong trade marks and some still focus on getting orders through subcontracts.

Inter-Firm Relations

The results are described in Table 5.11. It is previously stated that the OCBs rely very much upon personal/familial bonds called *guanxi* since trust must be built beforehand. However, the findings from question 39 provide a different picture. The number of respondents who relied upon personal/familial bonds was only 39 (34.51 per cent). Thirty-seven respondents (32.74 per cent) reported that the majority of their main partners were previously unknown with best proposals whereas 37 respondents (32.74 per cent) had main partners almost equally between previously known and unknown persons. Of those who had partners who were mostly or almost equally previously known persons (76 respondents), only 28 (36.84 per cent) had business partners originating from the family circle (question 40). There were many more LEs with partners from outside personal/familial bonds than had SMEs. Interestingly, the percentage of the *totok* having partners mostly from personal/familial bonds was much less than the *jiaosen*. By contrast, there were far more *totok* having partners outside personal/familial bonds than the *jiaosen*. Apparently, personal/familial bonds are no longer the main source of business partners. Once their companies grow to be large enterprises, the *Tionghoa* need better/more reliable vendors and buyers. Consequently, they must look beyond their existing friends/relatives to ensure the growth of their businesses.

Furthermore, there are only 41 respondents (36.28 per cent) agreed that trustable business partners are generally ethnic Chinese (question 44). Fifty-two respondents (46.02 per cent) disagreed with such a statement and 20 respondents were unsure (17.70 per cent). Apparently, ethnic identity is not an imperative consideration in choosing main business partners. These are also strengthened by the findings from question 45. Only 60 respondents (53.10 per cent) reported that their main partners were mostly or entirely from ethnic Chinese. Forty-seven respondents (41.59 per cent) had Chinese and non-Chinese almost evenly as main business partners whereas 6 respondents (5.31 per cent) admitted that their main partners were mostly non-Chinese. Similar patterns can be found in all categories of respondents.

The findings from questions 44 and 45 reveal that business is about rational calculation rather than mere ethnic solidarity. The *Tionghoa* have learned that ethnic identity is not a guarantee for trustworthiness. They cannot rely solely upon the Chinese community if they want to develop their businesses. Some *totok* businessmen of very large businesses develop

TABLE 5.11

Inter-Firm Relations Based upon Business Scale and Cultural Orientation

Questions		Q#	Business Scale			Cultural Orientation			
			SMEs	LEs	Totok	Jiaosen	Unsure
The majority of main business partners	Previously known persons	39.A	25 (36%)	14 (32%)	16 (31%)	21 (40%)	2 (22%)
	Previously unknown persons with best proposals	39.B	20 (29%)	17 (39%)	19 (37%)	14 (27%)	4 (44%)
	Almost even	39.C	24 (35%)	13 (30%)	17 (33%)	17 (33%)	3 (33%)
			69 (100%)	44 (100%)	52 (100%)	52 (100%)	9 (100%)
Main origin of business network	Family members	40.A	21 (41%)	7 (28%)	15 (43%)	12 (32%)	1 (20%)
	Religious environment	40.B	1 (2%)	0 (0%)	0 (0%)	1 (3%)	0 (0%)
	Schoolmates	40.C	0 (0%)	2 (8%)	0 (0%)	2 (5%)	0 (0%)
	Others	40.D	29 (57%)	16 (64%)	18 (51%)	23 (61%)	4 (80%)
			51 (100%)	25 (100%)	33 (94%)	38 (100%)	5 (100%)
Most important criterion to assess business proposals	Direct financial advantages	41.A	24 (35%)	12 (27%)	19 (37%)	15 (29%)	2 (22%)
	Future long-term relations	41.B	38 (55%)	30 (68%)	29 (56%)	33 (63%)	7 (78%)
	Others	41.C	7 (10%)	2 (5%)	4 (8%)	4 (8%)	0 (0%)
			69 (100%)	44 (100%)	52 (100%)	52 (100%)	9 (100%)
Main business information sources	Friends/personal networks	42.A	43 (62%)	31 (70%)	33 (63%)	36 (69%)	5 (56%)
	Newspapers/magazines/TV	42.B	15 (22%)	9 (20%)	9 (17%)	11 (21%)	4 (44%)
	Private agencies	42.C	2 (3%)	1 (2%)	2 (4%)	1 (2%)	0 (0%)
	Governmental agencies	42.D	1 (1%)	2 (5%)	2 (4%)	1 (2%)	0 (0%)
	Others	42.E	8 (12%)	1 (2%)	6 (12%)	3 (6%)	0 (0%)
			69 (100%)	44 (100%)	52 (100%)	52 (100%)	9 (100%)

TABLE 5.11 – continued

Questions	Q#	Business Scale		Cultural Orientation		
		SMEs	LEs	Totok	Jiaosen	Unsure
The majority of business deals	43.A	28 (41%)	11 (25%)	17 (33%)	18 (35%)	4 (44%)
Mutual trust only, minimum legal written contracts						
Legal written-contracts	43.B	10 (14%)	14 (32%)	12 (23%)	12 (23%)	0 (0%)
Almost even	43.C	31 (45%)	19 (43%)	23 (44%)	22 (42%)	5 (56%)
		69 (100%)	44 (100%)	52 (100%)	52 (100%)	9 (100%)
Trustable business partners are generally ethnic Chinese						
Agree	44.A	26 (38%)	15 (34%)	25 (48%)	13 (25%)	3 (33%)
Disagree	44.B	31 (45%)	21 (48%)	18 (35%)	29 (56%)	5 (56%)
Unsure	44.C	12 (17%)	8 (18%)	9 (17%)	10 (19%)	1 (11%)
		69 (100%)	44 (100%)	52 (100%)	52 (100%)	9 (100%)
Main business partners based upon ethnicity						
All ethnic Chinese	45.A	3 (4%)	1 (2%)	2 (4%)	2 (4%)	0 (0%)
Mostly ethnic Chinese	45.B	34 (49%)	22 (50%)	28 (54%)	24 (46%)	4 (44%)
Almost even	45.C	29 (42%)	18 (41%)	19 (37%)	24 (46%)	4 (44%)
Mostly non-ethnic Chinese	45.D	3 (4%)	3 (7%)	3 (6%)	2 (4%)	1 (11%)
All non-ethnic Chinese	45.E	0 (0%)	0 (0%)	0 (0%)	0 (0%)	0 (0%)
		69 (100%)	44 (100%)	52 (100%)	52 (100%)	9 (100%)

their *guanxi* through formal socio-cultural associations based upon surnames or places of origin in China. They include for examples: Sie Ho Se (for surname Liem), Sien Cik Kong Hwee (for surname Po), Senopati Foundation and some funeral associations (for example, for the Cantonese, Hokkien and Teochew). In such organizations, a sense of solidarity and mutual trust based upon kinship/ancestry are still strong. But the majority of *Tionghoa* businessmen do not belong to any formal ethnic association and their networks are developed through informal/daily interactions.

Nevertheless, this does not mean that trust-based network is not important anymore for the *Tionghoa*. Sixty-eight respondents (60.18 per cent) admitted that the possibility of future long-term relations was the most important criterion in assessing business proposals (question 41). Looking for long term business relations is often seen as a way of reducing the risk of being cheated by dishonest businessmen. Furthermore, the networks are also considered a vital source of information (question 42). There were 74 respondents (65.49 per cent) admitting that their main sources of information were informal/personal networks (friends and acquaintances). A similar pattern applied to all categories of respondents. The information exchanged among the members of the networks is about some critical issues such as business opportunities, credibility of certain businessmen, political issues and so on.

Apparently, emotional ties based upon kinship and ancestry have been decreasing and, in most cases, no longer serve as the means for conducting social and business activities. Their current ethnic identity is largely constructed by the New Order's discriminatory policies that led to their concentration in economic activities, mixing them together regardless of their kinship and other sub-ethnic characteristics. As a whole, the *Tionghoa* received the same treatment and faced the same consequences of being ethnic Chinese in their daily lives. Thus, kinship, ancestry and places of origin is no longer a dominant dimension for the majority of them. Their networks are commonly established through rational business calculation and track records. This may be a signal that there has been a shift in the *Tionghoa*'s paradigm of business networking. The following interviews reveal the shift:

> I always assess the personal qualities of a main partner. It is not important whether he is my relative or not. In my business, personal trustworthiness is very important. My suppliers can mix high quality tobaccos with low quality ones. I may not realise that. (Mr. Welly, LE, *Jiaosen*)

My father told me that a trustable partner has certain characteristics such as physical appearances or places of origin. However, I have had some experiences in this (matter). A person recommended by my father finally deceived me… He might have been honest when my father was active but time has changed him… Another person was recommended by my relative. Finally, I lost 800 million rupiah because of him. So I prefer to talk to someone face to face to read his trustworthiness… In my father's time, (a) verbal gentleman's agreement was enough. But I always ask (for) written legal contract now… Guanxi is still important to help us. But we cannot rely solely upon personal recommendation. (Mr. Ming, LE, *Totok*)

I didn't know my main suppliers previously. My business is very specific; we only sell lingeries and female underwear. Salesmen from the factories come and give some proposals to us and we choose the best offers. Because they are reliable and (there are) no complaints from our customers, we order from them repeatedly. (Mr. Fu, SME, *Totok*)

Another interesting finding relates to the use of formal legal contracts. The conventional OCB model mentions that for the majority of business transactions, legal properties (for example, written contracts) are ignored due to the mutual trust among the Chinese. However, results from question 43 give a different picture. Only 39 respondents (34.51 per cent) relied upon mutual trust and used no or minimum legal written contracts. Twenty-four respondents (21.24 per cent) reported that they used legal contracts for the majority of their business deals whereas 50 respondents (44.25 per cent) used legal contracts in about half of their business deals. Those who relied upon mutual trust only were much more common in SMEs than LEs whereas there was no substantial difference between the *totok* and *jiaosen*. However, a balanced combination of mutual verbal trust and legal contracts was the most popular choice in all categories of respondents.

Therefore, business scale matters more than culture in determining the *Tionghoa*'s pattern of business interaction and making decisions. The larger their businesses, the less they rely upon upon familial/personal circle/Chinese community in most cases. They have learned that such a view will only restrict their business development. In this sense, personal trustworthiness can be from anywhere (either inside or outside personal/familial bonds, Chinese or non-Chinese). Although trust-based networks are still important, these do not necessarily replace the use of formal legal written contracts as a form of protection. The *Tionghoa* businessmen build long-term relationships based upon track records rather than ethnicity and their *guanxi* serves as a source of information to minimize potential risks.

Business Development

The results are described in Table 5.12. The respondents' most popular fields for developing businesses (question 46) are fields related to their current businesses (47 respondents: 41.59 per cent). This is followed by any field with good prospects (32: 28.32 per cent), current business field(s)/ intensification (24: 21.24 per cent) and no specific strategy/other choices (10: 8.85 per cent). Different patterns between the *totok* and *jiaosen* appear. The *totok* tended to develop their business in related fields and any field with good prospects. The *jiaosen* preferred to develop fields related to their current businesses followed by current business field(s)/ intensification and any field with good prospects. Thus, Whitley's proposition (1991) that the OCB tend to restrict their businesses to a particular area in which their specialized skills and knowledge provide distinctive capabilities is not supported. Intensification was only preferred by a relatively small percentage of respondents. Interestingly, the *totok* tend to be less conservative than the *jioasen* where the choice of businesses development in any field with good prospects was one of the most popular.

With regard to daily personal involvement in managing new businesses, 65 respondents (57.52 per cent) regarded their personal involvement as absolutely necessary. This was followed by necessary/moderate to high personal involvement (36 respondents: 31.86 per cent), only when problems arise/minimum involvement (10: 8.85 per cent) and unnecessary (2: 1.77 per cent). Interestingly, business scale mattered very much whereas there was almost no difference between the *totok* and the *jiaosen*. The majority of SMEs believed that their personal involvement was absolutely necessary whereas only 36 per cent of LE respondents did so. Moderate to high personal involvement in new businesses were preferred by 48 per cent of LEs and 22 per cent of SMEs respondents. The results reveal that personal involvement in the daily management of new businesses is still considered as important. However, the degree is much higher in SMEs than in LEs. This is possibly because the LEs have had much more experiences in handling multiple strategic business units. Such experiences provide them with knowledge about the technical difficulties in involving

TABLE 5.12
Business Development Based upon Business Scale and Cultural Orientation

Questions		Q#	Business Scale		Cultural Orientation		
			SMEs	LEs	Totok	Jiaosen	Unsure
Field(s) to focus upon when developing business	Current business field(s)	46.A	15 (22%)	9 (20%)	7 (13%)	14 (27%)	3 (33%)
	Related business field(s)	46.B	28 (41%)	19 (43%)	21 (40%)	23 (44%)	4 (44%)
	Any fields with good prospect	46.C	19 (28%)	13 (30%)	21 (40%)	11 (21%)	0 (0%)
	No specific strategy	46.D	5 (7%)	3 (7%)	2 (4%)	3 (6%)	2 (22%)
	Others	46.E	2 (3%)	0 (0%)	1 (2%)	1 (2%)	0 (0%)
			69 (100%)	44 (100%)	52 (100%)	52 (100%)	9 (100%)
Intensive personal involvement when developing new business	Absolutely necessary	47.A	49 (71%)	16 (36%)	30 (58%)	30 (58%)	5 (56%)
	Necessary	47.B	15 (22%)	21 (48%)	16 (31%)	16 (31%)	4 (44%)
	Only when problems arise	47.C	4 (6%)	6 (14%)	5 (10%)	5 (10%)	0 (0%)
	Unnecessary	47.D	1 (1%)	1 (2%)	1 (2%)	1 (2%)	0 (0%)
			69 (100%)	44 (100%)	52 (100%)	52 (100%)	9 (100%)
Most wanted country to invest	Indonesia	48.A	32 (46%)	17 (39%)	19 (37%)	24 (46%)	6 (67%)
	China	48.B	17 (25%)	15 (34%)	20 (38%)	10 (19%)	2 (22%)
	Other Southeast Asian countries	48.C	16 (23%)	12 (27%)	11 (21%)	16 (31%)	1 (11%)
	The rest of the world	48.D	4 (6%)	0 (0%)	2 (4%)	2 (4%)	0 (0%)
			69 (100%)	44 (100%)	52 (100%)	52 (100%)	9 (100%)
Perceived impact of the rise of China	Positive	49.A	47 (68%)	29 (66%)	37 (71%)	34 (65%)	5 (56%)
	Negative	49.B	8 (12%)	5 (11%)	7 (13%)	6 (12%)	0 (0%)
	Unsure	49.C	14 (20%)	10 (23%)	8 (15%)	12 (23%)	4 (44%)
			69 (100%)	44 (100%)	52 (100%)	52 (100%)	9 (100%)

themselves personally in every business area. Hence, their views in this matter have become rather pragmatic.

The implication of globalization and the rise of China for the *Tionghoa* businessmen is explored in questions 48 and 49. For the *Tionghoa*, Indonesia was still regarded as the most attractive country to invest (49 respondents: 43.36 per cent), followed by China (32: 28.32 per cent), other Southeast Asian countries (28: 24.78 per cent) and the rest of the world (4: 3.54 per cent). No substantial difference was found in the dimension of business scale yet it appeared in the dimension of cultural orientation. For the *totok*, China and Indonesia were the most attractive countries to invest (38 per cent and 37 per cent) followed by Southeast Asian countries (21 per cent). For the *jiaosen*, Indonesia was ranked number one followed by other Southeast Asian countries and China. The attractiveness of China as a place for investment is related to how well the *Tionghoa* businessmen know the country. As stated by the following businessmen:

> Indonesia is my first priority to invest since I know its culture, advantages and disadvantages. Probably, many people say that other countries are more promising. But I don't know exactly the conditions...My consideration is purely business, no emotional ties involved.... (Mr. San, SME, *Jiaosen*)

> If I want to expand my business, I prefer to invest in Indonesia.... We are here so we have more capacity to control our business in Indonesia than in China. In my business, the availability of raw materials (rattan) is crucial and Indonesia has abundant resources. (Mr. Budi, LE, *Totok*)

> Although Indonesia is not an ideal place to invest, we know the environment very well. When we invest in a country, it's not only about the money but also about human resources. You have to learn about the characters... I believe the *Tionghoa* are basically comfortable about Indonesia but in some cases they have no choice other than to invest in other countries. (Mr. Welly, LE, *Jiaosen*)

The *totok* respondents generally have more knowledge than the *jiaosen* about China due to their cultural orientation. The *jiaosen* usually have little knowledge about China. Some *totok* still have contacts with their relatives in China. Thus, as a place for investment, China tend to be more popular in their eyes. Nevertheless, many *totok* still consider Indonesia as the first country to invest in due to their better knowledge of business potentials, opportunities and challenges in Indonesia. Hence, considerations based upon technical business matters and the anxiety of entering a new environment are dominant in viewing this matter.

Furthermore, the above findings are supported by the results from question 49. Generally, the respondents regard that the rise of China will have a good impact on them (76 respondents: 67.26 per cent). Twenty-four (21.24 per cent) were unsure and only 13 respondents (11.50 per cent) thought that the rise of China would have a negative impact on them. Relatively similar patterns could be found in all categories of respondents. Many of the businessmen view this matter from a purely business perspective. As mentioned in the following interviews:

> They have much more knowledge than us in some fields such as traditional medicine. We need to worry about that. They have reached the stage where they can mix herbs with parts of animals. In Indonesia, we only know about how to use herbs in much earlier stages. (Mr. Welly, LE, *Jiaosen*)

> For me, the rise of China is positive. They have a very large market. We can export many things to China.... But we must be very careful. There are many tricky persons there. My father almost lost a large amount of money because they cheated him. Fortunately, one of my relatives has many connections there so he could help us. (Mr. Ming, LE, *Totok*)

> Actually, many of our products are also produced by China manufacturers. We have head-to-head competition with them in most cases. But this is good since we are forced to be watchful and creative all the time. (Mr. Li, LE, *Totok*)

However, political perspectives based upon the fear for the future of ethnic Chinese in Indonesia also appear. As mentioned in the following comments:

> I am very happy with the rise of China. Why? Because we are *Zhongguoren*.... If the industries of China are strong, at least, this gives *hoaqiao* like us more bargaining power... Many investors suspect that the vice president is anti-Chinese... But I am also unhappy since we may not be ready to compete with them such as in the shoe and garment industries. This is the negative side. (Mr. Sul, LE, *Totok*)

Wang (2004) argues that most Chinese in Singapore, Malaysia and Indonesia have inherited a deep-rooted, demanding and distinctive culture that makes them not ready to move from a culture-based people to a state-based people. It is believed that globalization, especially the rise of China, will make this issue more complicated. However, Tan (2004) argues that the Chinese Indonesian has had a long involvement in the nation-building process since before the independence of Indonesia, which means that there is no dichotomy between cultural orientation and state orientation. The above findings reveal that reasons based upon technical business considerations are more dominant than reasons based upon cultural identification or loyalty towards ethnic group/mainland China in viewing the rise of China. Thus, the findings tend to support Tan's argument. For the *Tionghoa*, business/investment decisions have no relationship with cultural/emotional ties. The rise of China is seen as the rise of a competitor with positive and negative consequences rather than the awakening of a state of which they are a part. Being a *Tionghoa* means being a Chinese Indonesian rather than an Indonesian Chinese. To some extent, emotional ties exist among the *Tionghoa* but not between *Tionghoa* and mainland Chinese or other overseas Chinese.

However, some of the findings are also consistent with Wang's statement that the Southeast Asian Chinese may try to take advantage of globalization by using it as part of the tactics of survival, of dealing with discrimination or injustices that they feel in their country. Fear of possible continuing state discrimination as happened during the New Order era have been among the reasons for some respondents to respond positively to the rise of China. It is a very practical reason; the rise of China as a global economic player will force the Indonesian Government to maintain good relationship with the country. As a result, the government will have to abolish state discrimination completely towards them. Many respondents have stated that they were more familiar with, and identified themselves as part of the Indonesian environment. Thus, such a practical reason expresses a pragmatic outlook rather than an ideological view stemming from their denial to be state-based people.

CONCLUSION: THE OCB MODEL REVISITED

This chapter attempts to gain a more specific understanding of Chinese Indonesian (*Tionghoa*) business from five dimensions: Managerial ideology, organizational structure, managerial functions (MCS, finance, HRM, operation, and marketing), inter-firm relations and business development. The extent to which ethnicity and culture *vis-à-vis* business scale influence their business behaviours in the light of globalization and the rise of China is also explored.

In terms of managerial ideology, patrimonialism among the *Tionghoa* businessmen appears only in the aspects of the legitimate source of authority, company's objectives, the view ownership of company's assets and leadership successors. However, they tend to have participative-empowering managerial thoughts in viewing the roles and responsibilities of employer and employee. Furthermore, measurable and objective performance criteria (for example, educational background and past achievements) generally precede personalistic relationship when building work relationships in their organizations. Trust-based personal relationships are only used in emergency conditions such as in recruitment where there is no ideal candidate. Finally, the percentage of respondents who view Chinese employees as more trustable is less than fifty per cent. The state's ethnic discrimination in the past and a sense of solidarity are among the reasons for the trust. Those aspects of managerial ideology, to various extent, are influenced by both business scale and cultural orientation. However, business scale seems to be more influential. Conventional OCB model generally tend to be more visible in SMEs than in LEs.

In terms of organizational structure, *Tionghoa* businesses tend to have high centralization, high formalization and rather low configuration. Those aspects are consistent with the OCB model prescribed by many literatures. Nevertheless, the *Tionghoa* have relatively high level of specialization and moderate standardization which make them relatively similar to the so-called Western model. Thus, high centralization is the only salient characteristic which can distinguish them from Western organizational structure.

In management control function, the *Tionghoa* tend to emphasize personnel/cultural control rather than bureaucratic control. The Confucian cultural dimension of collectivism is at play here. However, there is no special pattern in the emphasis of the area to control (production/operation, marketing, finance and HRM) that can be regarded as another typical characteristic of *Tionghoa* businessmen's MCS.

In finance, another interesting finding emerges. Different from the conventional OCB model, the *Tionghoa* tend to use market penetrating strategy based upon quality and differentiation rather than low margin and high volume. Banks are also regarded as the most important financial source. Family relationship is often considered as a potential source of conflict and banks are seen as a way of protecting family assets from Indonesia's unstable political situations.

In HRM, the conventional view that the Chinese put low emphasis on using professionals is not supported. Recruitment/selection to get professionals is considered as crucial for the *Tionghoa*. They have realized that, in today's business environment, the growth and survival of a company depend very much upon the availability of professionals. Thus, generally, there is no dichotomy between the concepts of family business and professional business for them in viewing the roles of professionals.

In operation/production management, there is no indication that Confucianism leads to some typical characteristics. Operation/production is a matter of technicalities. Most *Tionghoa*, to various extents, are familiar with and have used quality control, production/operation scheduling and research and development. The latest is less common and this may be due to limitation of resources rather than cultural reasons.

The marketing activities of the *Tionghoa* are considerably different from the conventional OCB model. Standard display, standard sales policy, distribution channels, market research, standard trade marks and product catalogue are quite common for them. However, constant use of standard trade marks and product catalogues are much more common in LEs than SMEs. LEs generally have products with stronger brand positioning in market whereas many of the SMEs do not use their own brands for their products. Building brand image, for the SMEs, has not been a first priority yet since they still focus on getting orders. Thus, the characteristics of their marketing function have more relationship with pure business problems than ethnicity.

In terms of inter-firm relations, the roles of family circles and ethnicity are not very dominant. Business scale has more influence than culture in determining *Tionghoa*'s pattern of business interaction and decision-making. In most cases, verbal contracts based on mutual trust have been replaced by written legal contracts especially for LEs. Furthermore, LEs tend to be more open in developing their networks than SMEs. Interestingly, some very large *totok* businesses utilize formal ethnic-based associations for their business networking but the majority of the *Tionghoa* develop their networks through informal/daily interactions. Hence, for the majority of the *Tionghoa*, their main business partners generally consist of people from various backgrounds (either previously known/ recommended or unknown, Chinese and non-Chinese).

In terms of business development, the majority of the *Tionghoa* do not focus/plan to focus their businesses upon a particular area. Different from what is prescribed by the conventional OCB model, they are willing to enter new area although they have to learn new knowledge/skills. However, personal involvement in the daily management of new businesses is still considered as crucial. Regarding the rise of China, rational business considerations are commonly used in viewing it. China is seen as one of places available for business rather than a place to which they have strong emotional ties. The popularity of China as a place for investment is not very high since most of the *Tionghoa* have little knowledge of the country. Indonesia is still the most popular choice since they know the country well.

Furthermore, the rise of China is seen by the *Tionghoa* as the rise of a competitor with positive and negative impacts. Those who view it positively argue that a new market is now available to sell products there. Those who respond negatively argue that many of Indonesian industries are not ready to compete with China. However, for some *Tionghoa*, the rise is responded to positively due to pragmatic political reasons. As a new global player, China has irresistable economic and political potentials which make the Indonesian Government keen to maintain good relationship with the country. Consequently, the government will have to abolish state discrimination completely towards the *Tionghoa*. This view expresses a pragmatic thought rather than an ideology of loyalty towards China. To some extent, emotional ties exist among the *Tionghoa* but not between *Tionghoa* and mainland Chinese or other Overseas Chinese. The *Tionghoa* tend to identify themselves as Chinese Indonesian rather than Indonesian Chinese.

The above findings reveal how Chinese Indonesian (*Tionghoa*) business characteristics are different from the conventional OCB model. In this sense, Confucianism cannot be used directly to explain all business practices. To various extents, the philosophy has been transformed into the *Tionghoa*'s societal values together with various local values but it does not become the ultimate business culture of the community. Obviously, culture solely cannot explained comprehensiveley the *Tionghoa* business practices. Their business culture is also shaped by various factors such as Indonesia's formal education, the past state's discrimination and erasures of all the cultural identities of the society, their ethnicity, and simply business technical environments. They all need to be taken into account to gain a deeper understanding of the *Tionghoa* business practices.

The influence of business technical environments are highlighted by categorizing the respondents into two groups based upon business scale: Small/medium business enterprise (SME) and large business enterprise

(LE). The influence of Confucianism is demonstrated by categorizing the respondents as *totok* or *jiaosen*. It is apparent that business scale matters much more than cultural orientation. The question is why? There may be, at least, three reasons for this phenomenon.

Firstly, culture needs to be seen as merely one of the resources available to cope with business problems. Confucianism is a general philosophy rather than a specific business philosophy. Hence, culture is referred to when other resources (such as management knowledge/techniques) cannot provide adequate answers to solve problems such as the lack of ideal persons to fill strategic positions, information to make rational calculation and guidance of successful methods in certain situations. Many of the *Tionghoa* have had formal management training or employed many graduates of business schools. The knowledge acquired have provided them with many specific techniques to help them solve business problems when their companies grow. Consequently, many of their traditional practices that were used when starting up their organizations for the first time are left behind.

Secondly, culture is not static but dynamic and, thus, subject to modifications from its environment. The state's cultural repressions in the past have Westernized the *Tionghoa*'s ways of thinking and behaviour in various spheres (business included). Anything related to the expression of a Chinese identity was confronted and discouraged by the state. Confucian values were only passed on to younger generations through parental education and often taught as merely proper conduct in family/ private affairs. Hence, the Westernization process has transformed many core Confucian values into peripheral values (or even abandoned) which then lose their legitimacy and are easily diminished in daily interactions in the public sphere. Thus, Confucian culture and business culture become increasingly separated.

Thirdly, there has been a seemingly premature deduction of equating Chinese business with small traditional family business in many conventional literatures. Many aspects of the conventional OCB are relatively similar to those of small/medium *Tionghoa* companies. Such companies are family businesses but once they grow to be large companies, their management philosophies and techniques will develop in response to the demands of their technical environments. There are many examples in Indonesia of how previously small/medium family businesses developed to become the largest Indonesian companies and showed fundamental transformation of their management practices, such as the Maspion Group,

Wismilak, Sampoerna (which has become a public company and just sold to Philip Morris), Wings Group, and so on.[4]

Furthermore, globalization and the rise of China do not imply that the *Tionghoa* identify themselves as belonging to the global Chinese community. *Tionghoa* generations born after the 1950s have received an Indonesian education and have been familiar with their identity as Chinese Indonesian rather than Indonesian Chinese. They tend to see the two phenomena as economic phenomena and, hence, their responses are more towards business calculations. Although the reformation era (post 1998) in Indonesia has given the *Tionghoa* freedom to learn and practise Chinese culture openly, it is difficult to expect that they will have strong emotional ties towards any global Chinese entity. Business is always about rational calculations and the *Tionghoa* community is no exception.

It is hoped that this study demonstrates how combining data collection based on surveys with in-depth interviews can provide more insights into the relationships among culture, ethnicity and Chinese Indonesian business. The aim is to complement conventional literatures — not to discount it. Studies of ethnic Chinese business in Southeast Asia are important due to their significant roles in the economy of the region. However, there has been a tendency to make simple stereotypes about their business characteristics. Such stereotypes are described in this study as the conventional Overseas Chinese Business (OCB) model. Chinese communities are actually plural and there is no simple one-to-one relationship between Confucianism and business practices. Local context, to some extent, determines the way they do business and this may distinguish *Tionghoa* business behaviours from the Chinese of Malaysia, Singapore or other Southeast Asian countries.

Nevertheless, this study also has its limitations. Firstly, the results of this study may not be fully applied to such countries. This study does not claim that it can explain and predict the behaviours of all *Tionghoa*. Individual differences in their business philosophies and attitudes exist due to their different degrees of internalization of Confucianism and the perceived senses of ethnic insecurities. Hence, more in-depth case studies are needed to enrich our understanding of the Chinese Indonesian business. In this sense, it is hoped that the results of this study could be useful in providing an initial understanding of how their technical and institutional environments have been intertwined and manifested in their businesses.

Secondly, the method of self-acknowledgement used in this study may be a source of another limitation. It is possible that their self-identification contains some biases in categorizing themselves as *totok* or *jiaosen*. However, such possible biases have been minimized by explaining to them the differences between those two categories. Furthermore, almost all of the respondents were very sure in identifying themselves even before the explanations were given, showing that the terms make sense to them. Nevertheless, defining categories of ethnic Chinese in Indonesia is always problematic. Suryadinata (2002) has offered several possible ways of doing so, including objectively-defined, society-defined and self-defined approaches. Whilst self-definition has been chosen in this study, future studies in this area needs to consider this matter and its implications carefully.

Thirdly, the sample size of this study is rather limited. Thus, problems of representativeness may exist. However, this is the first study aimed at gaining the actual thoughts of Chinese Indonesian businessmen in viewing their businesses in relation to their culture and ethnicity. The findings, at least, have provided a rather different picture from the so-called OCB model, that could inspire further, more focused studies in Chinese Indonesian businesses and opened up more critical enquiries into the relevance of the conventional OCB model in explaining overseas Chinese businesses. Thus, the results need to be followed up by a series of further research and should not be used as a sole, conclusive source of understanding Chinese Indonesian businesses.

Notes

[1]   The authors are grateful to Leo Suryadinata, Aris Ananta, Evi N. Arifin and Andi Irawan for advice and comments. We are also thankful for the assistance provided by various companies and businessmen whose ideas and thoughts are described in this study. We also note with gratitude the invaluable transcription and administrative support provided by Dinny Arianti and the teaching assistants of the Faculty of Economics, Universitas Surabaya.

[2]   The term Chinese Indonesian rather than Indonesian Chinese is used to stress the social affiliation of the ethnic group, which identifies itself as Indonesian people who have Chinese origin rather than as a part of Chinese overseas society. However, they still, to various extent, maintain and practise Confucian values.

[3]   The term *pribumi* was politically created in the era of Dutch colonialization. It refers to ethnic groups that are said not to have

foreign origins (pure local origins/indigenous). The term ignores the fact that what are presently known as indigenous groups are, at least partially, the descendants of the intermarriage between various ethnic groups, including the early Chinese immigrants. The use of the term *pribumi* in this study is merely for the sake of practicality.

[4] Two of them are among the interviewees of this study.

References

Amir, M.S. 1978. "The Non-pribumi and Social Justice", in *The Politics of Economic Development in Indonesia: Contending Perspectives*, edited by Ian Chalmers and Vedi R. Hadiz (London: Routledge), pp. 211–13.

Birnbaum, P.H., and G.Y.Y. Wong. 1985. Organizational Structure of Multinational Banks in Hongkong from A Culture-Free Perspective. *Administrative Science Quarterly* 30: 262–77.

Brown, D. 1994. *The State and Ethnic Politics in Southeast Asia* (London, U.K.: Routledge).

Chan, K.B. 2000. State, Economy and Culture: Reflections on the Chinese Business Networks, in *Chinese Business Networks: State, Economy and Culture*, edited by Chan Kwok Bun (Singapore: Prentice Hall-Nordic Institute of Asian Studies).

Cleary, T. 1992. *The Essential Confucius* (San Fransisco: Harper Collins Publishers).

Coppel, C.A. 1983. *Indonesian Chinese in Crisis* (Oxford University Press: Singapore).

Dahana, A. 2004. "Pri and Non-Pri Relations in the Reform Era: A Pribumi Perspective", in *Ethnic Relations and Nation Building in Southeast Asia*, edited by Leo Suryadinata (Singapore: Institute of Southeast Asian Studies (ISEAS) Publications), pp. 45–65.

Efferin, S. 2002. *Management Control System, Culture, and Ethnicity: A Case of Chinese Indonesian Company*. Ph.D. Thesis, University of Manchester, U.K.

————. 2004. "Towards A Theoretical Framework of Management Control System in Chinese Overseas Companies". Keynote paper at the International Call for Paper and Seminar *Building Competitive Advantage through Effective Cross-Cultural Management*. Fakultas Ekonomi Universitas Surabaya, 17–18 March 2004.

Eriksen, T.H. 1993. *Ethnicity and Nationalism: Anthropological Perspectives* (London, U.K.: Pluto Press).

Fenton, S. 1999. *Ethnicity: Racism, Class, and Culture* (London, U.K.: Macmillan).

Hadiz, Vedi R. 1997. "Pribumi-Chinese Relations: Introduction", in *The Politics of Economic Development in Indonesia: Contending Perspectives*, edited by Ian Chalmers and Vedi R. Hadiz (London: Routledge), pp. 204–08.

Hamilton, G.G., and N.W. Biggart. 1988. "Market, Culture and Authority: A Comparative Analysis of Management and Organization in Japan, Taiwan and South Korea". *American Journal of Sociology* 94: 52–94.

Harrison, G.L., J.L. McKinnon, S. Panchapakesan, and M. Leung. 1994. The Influence of Culture on Organizational Design and Planning and Control in Australia and the United States Compared with Singapore and Hong Kong. *Journal of International Financial Management & Accounting* 5, no. 3: 242–62.

Heryanto, A. 1997. "Silence in Indonesian Literary Discourse: The Case of the Indonesian Chinese". *SOJOURN* 12, no. 1: 26–45.

_____. 1998. "Ethnic Identities and Erasure: Chinese Indonesians in Public Culture". In *Southeast Asian Identities: Culture and the Politics of Representation in Indonesia, Malaysia, Singapore, and Thailand* (Singapore: Institute of Southeast Asian Studies), pp. 95–114.

Kwik, Kian Gie. 1977. "The Myth of Chinese Economic Dominance", in Chalmers and Hadiz (eds.), 1997, pp. 208–11.

Low, L. 1995. "The Overseas Chinese Connection: An ASEAN Perspective". *Southeast Asian Journal of Social Science* 23, no. 2: 89–117.

Mackie, J. 2000. "The Economic Roles of the Southeast Asian Chinese: Information Gaps and Research Needs". In Chan (ed.), 2000.

Merchant, K.A. 1998. *Modern Management Control System* (Upper Saddle River, NJ: Prentice-Hall).

Ning, H. 1987. "The Struggles of A Pribumi Entrepreneur". In Chalmers and Hadiz (eds.), 1997, pp. 218–22.

Ong, A. 1999. *Flexible Citizenship: The Cultural Logics of Transnationality* (London, UK: Duke University Press).

Piliang, I.J. 2001. "Dari Politik Aliran ke Politik Etnik". Paper presented at *Seminar Indonesian Nationhood Revisited*. CSIS Thirtieth Anniversary, 5 September 2001, Jakarta, Indonesia.

Redding, S.G. 1993. *The Spirit of Chinese Capitalism* (New York: Walter de Gruyter).

Redding, S.G., and R.D. Whitley. 1990. "Beyond Bureaucracy: Towards A Comparative Analysis of Forms of Economic Resource Coordination and Control". In *Capitalism in Contrasting Cultures*, edited by S.R. Clegg and S.G. Redding (New York: Walter de Gruyter), pp. 79–104.

Robison, R. 1986. *Indonesia: The Rise of Capital* (North Sydney, Australia: Allen and Unwin).

Skinner, G.W. 1963. "The Chinese Minority", in *Indonesia*, edited by R.T. McVey (New Haven: Southeast Asia Studies, Yale University).

Suryadinata, L. 1974. Confucianism in Indonesia: Past and Present, in *The Chinese Minority in Indonesia: Seven Papers*, edited by Leo Suryadinata (Singapore: Chopmen Enterprises), pp. 33–62.

––––––. 1978. *Pribumi Indonesians, the Chinese Minority and China: A Study of Perceptions and Policies* (Singapore: Heinemann Educational Books).

––––––. 2002. "Ethnic and National Identities of the Chinese in Indonesia: A Reexamination". *Asian Culture* 26 (June): 12–25.

Suryadinata, Leo, E.N. Arifin and A. Ananta. 2003. "Penduduk Indonesia: Etnis dan Agama dalam Era Perubahan Politik". Jakarta, Indonesia: LP3ES.

Tam, S. 1990. "Centrifugal versus Centripetal Growth Processes: Contrasting Ideal Types for Conceptualizing the Developmental Patterns of Chinese and Japanese Firms", in Clegg and Redding (eds.), 1990, pp. 153–183.

Tan, Mely G. 2004. "Unity in Diversity: Ethnic Chinese and Nation-Building in Indonesia", in *Ethnic Relations and Nation Building in Southeast Asia*, edited by Leo Suryadinata (Singapore: Institute of Southeast Asian Studies (ISEAS) Publications), pp. 20–44.

Wang, Gungwu. 2004. "Chinese Ethnicity in New Southeast Asian Nations", in Suryadinata (ed.), ibid., pp. 1–19.

Winarta, Frans H. 2004. "Racial Discrimination in the Indonesian Legal System: Ethnic Chinese and Nation-Building", in Suryadinata (ed.), ibid., pp. 66–81.

Xu, Zhi Gang. 2000. *The Analects of Confucius* [*Lun Yu Tong Yi*] (Beijing: People's Literatures Publisher) [*Ren Ming Wen Xue Chu Ban She*].

Yeung, H.W.C. 1999. "Internationalisation of Ethnic Chinese Business Firms from Southeast Asia". *International Journal of Urban and Regional Research* 23, no. 1: 103–27.

6

China's Economic Rise and Its Impact on Malaysian Chinese Business

Lee Poh Ping
Lee Kam Hing

INTRODUCTION

The impact of a rising China on Malaysia has been in evidence over the last ten years or so. On the positive side the opening of China offers opportunities to Malaysian investors, in particular, Malaysian Chinese investors. There are those who see possible high returns from investments in a country where many fields of business have yet to fully develop. Furthermore there is expectation that Malaysia would benefit from a growing market as China further opens up her economy. Indeed China has long been one of the largest buyers of Malaysian commodities such as rubber and palm oil.

On the negative side, China is, firstly, attracting a huge proportion of foreign direct investment (FDI). Since 1997–98 there has been a decline of FDI to the ASEAN region including Malaysia. There are those who argue that the FDI that went to China might have gone to the ASEAN states. However, the FDI decline in ASEAN was due also to reasons exposed by the Asian financial crisis — weak accountability, non-transparency and cronyism — and the region has not entirely recovered from that.[1]

Secondly, the rise of China has led to competition for export markets, with Malaysian producers losing out to cheaper goods from China. In addition, cheaper costs of production in China have also encouraged a relocation of factories from Malaysia and this has led to job loss and the multiplier consequence to the general economy in a particular region when factories close down. There is also the loss of technology transfer when a foreign-owned factory leaves.

This chapter looks at the impact of the rise of China on the Malaysian Chinese economy. At the outset, it has to be stated that the economy of the Malaysian Chinese, being part of and integrated into the general Malaysian economy, cannot easily be separated and analyzed in isolation. However, there is an economy which is recognizably Chinese in ownership and management, both in the general perception as well is in governmental policy. The chapter will focus on this economy though it needs to be pointed out that the impact of the rise of China on the Malaysian Chinese economy must be understood within the impact on the broader Malaysian framework.

There have, so far, been very few systematic studies on the impact of the rise of China on the Malaysian Chinese economy.[2] To address this lacuna to some extent, this chapter will offer some research data on the impact of the economic rise of China on Malaysia in the areas of investment, trade and services.[3] Two problems arise with such an approach. Firstly, given that the impact of the rise of China on the three areas varies, being greatest in the area of trade, on which area should the emphasis be given? Related to this is the question of what sub-sectors within each of these three areas should the focus be? Secondly, Malaysian Chinese business is not a homogeneous grouping. We have elsewhere discussed in some detail the diverse groupings of Malaysian Chinese business.[4] How are the various levels of this business to be distinguished and again on which level should the focus be?

In answering these questions, the chapter is guided by two considerations. The first of this concerns the availability of data.[5] The chapter relies on a variety of published sources and interviews. The most important of the publications are reports of Malaysian governmental bodies such as Bank Negara and the relevant ministries. Newspapers and magazines are also consulted extensively. A particularly useful magazine is the *Malaysia-China Business Magazine* published by the Malaysia-China Chamber of Commerce. The articles are mainly in Chinese, although there are some in English and Malay. Another importance source are information and reports released by the Chinese Embassy in Kuala Lumpur. These are mostly in Chinese.

In addition, information is obtained through a series of interviews with Malaysians who have been involved in the China business. Those interviewed come from big business, small and medium enterprises, the education sector as well as those close to Malaysian policy makers. The interviews are valuable not only for the data the interviewees provide but also for the informed opinions they give on the China business they are involved in and for a sense of what is happening in particular sectors of the Malaysia-China business.

The second consideration is that of focus — on where the impact on the Malaysian Chinese business is most evident. Three levels are identified. The first level consists of the big Malaysian Chinese groupings. These groupings are largely those of the publicly listed companies in Malaysia as well as large enterprises that remain privately owned.[6] The second level comprises those from the small and medium enterprises (SMEs), 80–90 per cent of which are Malaysian Chinese owned. But because the definition of SMEs changes every now and then, particularly in relation to capitalization and to the number of people employed, the chapter will not go into any precise definition of the SMEs.[7] The third level consists of very small scale Malaysian Chinese business that employ ten or less than ten workers.

BRIEF HISTORY OF MALAYSIA-CHINA ECONOMIC RELATIONS

It was only in 1974 that diplomatic relations between China and Malaysia were established. But the move did not immediately boost economic exchanges between the two countries. China had yet to move towards a market economy and towards integrating itself to the world economy. Furthermore, a large Malaysian Chinese population and a still surviving communist insurgency in Malaysia constrained the Malaysian Government from developing a policy that would fully open up business with China. Nevertheless some trade was conducted as part of what was called a controlled relationship. Under this, imports from China to Malaysia had to go through Pernas, the National Trading Corporation, which imposed a 0.5 per cent commission on every consignment of goods imported. Malaysian importers were also required to apply for approved permits (APs) from the Malaysian Government before they were allowed to import from China. Also, Malaysian delegations to trade fairs in China had to obtain permission from the Ministry of Home Affairs. All trade delegations were led by Pernas or some governmental agency.[8]

A turning point in bilateral economic relations came in November 1985 when the then Prime Minister, Dr. Mahathir Mohammad, because of a desire to take advantage of China's economic rise and a growing belief that China was not a threat, decided to accelerate economic ties with China despite a still continuing communist insurgency in Malaysia. In that year, Dr. Mahathir led a Malaysian delegation to visit China.

This visit later led to the signing of several bilateral economic agreements. One of the most important of these, as far as the Malaysian Chinese were concerned, was the Bilateral Trade Agreement of 31 March 1988 which removed all restrictions that impeded direct economic relations between both countries. These included the removal of the AP requirement and the 0.5 per cent commission on Chinese products to Malaysia imposed by Pernas. Subsequently, the Malaysian government also permitted the free travel of Malaysians to China. Such steps led to the full normalization of bilateral economic relations, resulting in much increased trade, investment, and services between both countries. Thus, trade has so developed that by 2002, Malaysia was China's largest trading partner in ASEAN.

The mid-1980s was also a time when large Malaysian Chinese business groups began to look to overseas to invest. This was a period of economic recession in Malaysia. Furthermore, the effects of the New Economic Policy which sought to restructure the Malaysian economy and to create a Malay corporate class, had begun to affect adversely on Malaysian Chinese business. Malaysian Chinese business had not only to give up equity share to Malay business groups, but were restricted in their participation in many sectors. These included infrastructure, transport, telecommunications and increasingly in the financial services. Given the reduced investment opportunities in Malaysia, many Malaysian Chinese companies began to look to overseas such as Hong Kong and Australia to invest.

Therefore with China opening up, Malaysian Chinese saw China as a new and additional place for investment. The size of the market and the stage of economic development there encouraged Malaysian Chinese to see China as offering great potential. Yet it was not until about the early 1990s that the more established Malaysian Chinese companies entered the China market. Today there are more than a hundred Malaysian companies investing in China, the majority being Malaysian Chinese-owned.

MALAYSIAN INVESTMENT IN CHINA

Value of Investment

Below are two sets of figures on the value of Malaysian investments in China. Table 6.1 consists of Malaysian investment overseas in selected countries including China for the decade of the 1990s compiled by

TABLE 6.1
Gross Malaysian Investment Overseas in
Selected Countries, 1992–1999 (RM Million)

Year	Singapore	United States	United Kingdom	Hong Kong	China	Total	% of investment in China Total Investment
1992	258.6	93.9	63	336.7	20.1	1,313	1.5
1993	686.1	627.6	372.2	733.9	112.2	3,412	3.3
1994	995	624	444	1,892	217	6,799	3.2
1995	2,185	544	793	816	331	7,936	4.2
1996	1,806	1,416	1,308	769	514	10,715	4.8
1997	1,783	1,334	1,716	936	331	10,463	3.2
1998	2,096	1,654	822	169	79	11,620	0.7
1999	1,635	513	553	435	201	13,391	1.5

Source: Bank Negara Malaysia.

Rogayah Mat Zin[9] from Bank Negara reports and Table 6.2 consists of Malaysian investment in China from 1996–2002 issued by the Chinese embassy in Kuala Lumpur. While there is no breakdown according to ethnic background, the information from the Chinese embassy states that about 90 per cent of the investments originated from Malaysian Chinese investors.[10]

The figures between the two sets (amounts invested in China in the Bank Negara reports and the actual amounts invested found in the Chinese embassy figures), for the years 1996 to 1999, vary widely. A likely reason for this is the different methods of data compilation. According to the Chinese embassy in Kuala Lumpur, the Chinese figures are derived from the amount Malaysian investors deposited in a special account in China designated for investment purposes. How and where the amount is spent is not indicated in the data. The Bank Negara figures refer specifically to direct equity investment, purchase of real estate and extension of loans to non-residents abroad, including capital invested or loans extended by its foreign-owned companies to their parent companies abroad.

TABLE 6.2
Malaysian Investment in China, 1996–2002

Year	Total Item	Changes (%)	Amounts listed in contract (US$100m)	Changes (%)	Actual amounts (US$100m)	Changes (%)
1996	206		7.57		4.6	
1997	192	–6.79	4.90	–35.27	3.8	–16.98
1998	144	–26.56	3.37	–32.24	3.4	–12.56
1999	131	–7.10	2.65	–20.30	2.27	–32.1
2000	115	–12.20	3.89	46.90	1.9	–16.6
2001	188	63.48	5.03	29.31	2.55	34.5
2002	319	69.68	7.93	57.65	3.68	44.31

Source: The Economic and Commercial Counsellor's Office of the Embassy of the People's Republic of China in Malaysia.

Note: There are errors in the calculation of the changes as given. The figures on the actual amounts, however, tally broadly with figures from other Chinese sources.

While the figures vary, a pattern can be discerned. The Bank Negara figures show a big increase of investments from 1992 (20.1 million ringgit) to 1993 (112.2 million ringgit) onwards. There were two main reasons for this. There was, firstly, the lifting in 1992 of restrictions on Malaysians visiting China. Secondly, following the Tiananmen incident of 1989, Deng Xiaoping made a renewed call for reforms in China. Both sets of figures then show a decline of Malaysian investments in the aftermath of the Asian financial crisis of 1997 and of the investment picking up again after that (as the Chinese figures show) with the Chinese entry into the World Trade Organization (WTO) in 2001.

Nevertheless, while investments may be set to increase in future, the figures as shown on the Malaysian side are not very impressive in both absolute amount and as percentages of total Malaysian investment overseas. Thus for the yearly figures from 1992 to 1999, the percentage for any one year range from 0.7 per cent in 1998 to 4.8 in 1996. They are all below 5 per cent of total Malaysian investment abroad. Data from the Chinese embassy show a much higher figure of Malaysian investments.

It is quite likely that the Malaysian data does not include investments in China by Malaysian Chinese not based in Malaysia. The Robert Kuok controlled business groups are a good example. Many of these are unlikely to be considered as Malaysian.[11] Furthermore, there are Malaysians who have set up companies in Hong Kong. These companies take advantage of benefits enjoyed by Hong Kong-based companies doing business in the mainland. An example is Salcon Bhd, a publicly listed company which has formed a company Salcon Yunnan (HK) Pte. Ltd. in Hong Kong. The Hong Kong company recently entered into a joint venture with Chenggon County Water Supply Company in China to undertake the construction of a water treatment plant to meet the immediate demand for modern New Kunming.[12] Investments of these Malaysian-owned companies are again unlikely to be found in the Malaysian figures. The Chinese figures probably represent a truer picture of the extent of Malaysia investments in China.

Nature of Investments

Malaysian Chinese investments are primarily directed to the provinces of Guangdong, Fujian and the coastal areas of China. Most of these are, according to the Chinese sources, small-scale industries and these are mainly associated with rubber products, food, cosmetics, furniture and animal feed.[13]

There are, however, also big Malaysian Chinese business groupings investing in China. Two of the biggest and best known are businesses controlled by William Cheng (the Lion Grouping) and Robert Kuok (Shangri-La Hotel Chain, Kerry Properties, and Perlis Plantation Bhd).[14] Some of the other big groupings are the Genting Group (oil and gas exploration), Khoo Kay Peng of the MUI Group and an associate of Robert Kuok, Datuk Lau Hui Kang of the Sarawak KTS, Hong Leong Group (property development) Kuala Lumpur-Kepong Bhd (edible oil), the Rimbinan Hijau group controlled by Tiong Hiew King,[15] IOI Berhad, and the Tan Chin Nam-controlled group (hotel and property development).[16]

It is perhaps too early to assess the performance of Malaysian Chinese business in China and the impact of their investments. One interviewee commented that generally, the successful investors are less inclined to publicize their success for fear of attracting competition while the less successful ones will not hesitate to voice their complaints about business conditions in China.

But for two Malaysian Chinese groups at least, the William Cheng (Lion) group and the Robert Kuok group, China constitutes a major part of their business operations. The two groups are always referred to in discussions of Malaysian investments in China. For the Lion group, the importance of China is shown in the geographical distribution of its businesses. The figures, as of August 2004, show that of the total number of employees in their group (40,576), 24,691 are in China.[17] This comes to 60.9 per cent! The comparable figures for employees in Malaysia are 13,458 or 32.9 per cent of the total employees. Another indicator is in the number of retail outlets the Lion group has in China. Out of a total of forty-one Parkson stores, as its outlets are known, fifteen are in China. This is quite a significant percentage.

The Lion Group also has motorcycle assembly plants and breweries in China. The assembly plants are in Zhejiang, Nanjing, and Changchun. In 2004, 860,000 units of motorcycles were produced in Zhejiang, 400,000 in Nanjing, and 80,000 in Changchun. The motor assembly plants come under two listed companies in China and these are the Zhejiang Qianking Motorcyle Co. Ltd. listed on the Shenzhen Stock Exchange and the Anhui Jianghua Automotive Chassis Co. Ltd. which is on the Shanghai Stock Exchange. Lion Group has twelve breweries in five provinces producing 1.6 million tonnes a year.[18]

As for the Robert Kuok group, the figures are not so easily obtained. Robert Kuok has many businesses in China. The most famous is the hotel chain associated with the Shangri-La group. As of 23 March 2005 there are twenty-one such Shangri-La Hotels in China, (not including two in Hong Kong) which is a sizeable percentage of their worldwide total of fifty-five Shangri-La Hotels! The Shangri-La Chain has eight hotels in Malaysia by contrast. So at least in the hotel business, a very core business of the Robert Kuok group, much of that is in China.

For other Malaysian-based companies, China, though less crucial as compared to the Lion and Kuok groups, is also a destination of growing importance for their overseas investments. One example, Top Glove Berhad, a listed company and the world's largest producer of gloves, has one plant in China and is planning to set up another there. (It has, however, eight plants in Malaysia and has set up others in Vietnam.) Top Glove sees opportunity of growth in China as it has technology and market access which producers in China have yet to match.[19] In the field of educational investment, INTI college, a Malaysian Chinese-owned institution, continues to run the INTI Management College in China which it started in 1993. But it no longer has ties with Wu Jie International school in Kunming, Yunnan and the Guangdong Polytechnic Normal University in Guangzhou in Guangdong, China, which it once developed. It is now focusing on franchising to local operators by offering the INTI brand name.

How do the big Malaysian corporations fare in China. The long established like the Robert Kuok group and those involved in property, infrastructure, and resource-based businesses are doing well. But other large companies face serious competition. Some of these competition come from other foreign companies, In the case of William Cheng's Lion Group its Parkson stores have to contend with Western retailers such as Tesco and Carrefour. And William Cheng's brewery, although one of the largest, has slipped in ranking from number two to number four while his motorcycle business in China faces serious local Chinese competitors.

Many of the early problems faced by Malaysian Chinese investors arose from the lack of preparation and understanding of business conditions in China. Malaysian Chinese saw China as an open "frontier" like country where money could be made easily and quickly. They saw China as one huge market waiting to be exploited and the local Chinese as lacking understanding in market economics.[20] Many found to their cost that the Chinese there were often equally sharp businessmen and were able very quickly to set up rival business establishments or replicate products and services once they picked up the know-how from their Malaysian business partner or counterpart.[21] Furthermore, some Malaysian Chinese were not quite prepared for the rigours of doing business in China, be it in adapting to the Chinese style of doing things or to the different geographical environment.

Nevertheless, the Malaysian Chinese are not alone in facing problems. Many of the difficulties they encountered are similar to those experienced by other foreign investors in China. Other major complaints made by Malaysians include the lack of transparency in the way business is conducted in China, the frequent amending of local laws that catch the investor off-guard, the difficulties experienced in finding the right Chinese partners, and the need to deal with a powerful and arbitrary bureaucracy. But as China becomes more exposed to international norms of doing business, it is likely that doing business will become more transparent for Malaysian Chinese than what they had experienced in the early 1990s. Indeed, one of the most successful Malaysian Chinese investor, Robert Kuok who, in anticipating a trend towards transparency, advised Malaysian Chinese investors not to rely too much on *guanxi* but to be open in their dealings with the Chinese. In particular, he warned against putting children of politically connected Chinese in their business as it would be very difficult to remove them if they did not pull their weight![22]

Trends in Investment

As China becomes more integrated into the international economy, and no longer avoided by Western and Japanese investors as it was in the immediate aftermath of the Tiananmen incident in 1989, it will look more to investors with large capital as well as expertise in technology and marketing, particularly if such investors are planning to penetrate the Chinese market.[23] In this regard, Malaysian Chinese investors will be at a disadvantageous position, given their deficiency in all these three assets as compared to Japanese and Western multinationals. It is unlikely that Malaysian Chinese investors will attempt or succeed in large-scale manufacturing investments that produce finished products for the Chinese market.

From what can be gathered, Malaysian Chinese investment in China is likely to fall into the following categories. One will be the continuation of investment by small-scale businesses which are, as stated earlier, mainly involved in food, cosmetics, textiles, and rubber products. A second category is the kind of investment that takes advantage of being a first mover and of a niche or boutique business. An example of the former is William Cheng's Parkson Stores. Despite facing recently-arrived competition from big Western departmental chains, the Parkson chain in China might be able to survive because it has already established a reputation in Beijing, and is making its presence felt in many of the smaller cities in China ahead of the big department chains that might move in.

An example of the latter niche investment, is that undertaken by the Tan Chin Nam group. This group once seized on the idea that there were many Russians doing trading business in Beijing and hence needed suitable facilities and accommodation. Thus, the Tan Chin Nam group constructed a building in Beijing with the lower floors being used by Russian traders and the upper floors being run as a hotel for them.[24]

A third category is investment in the manufacturing of component parts for companies operating in China and for Malaysian manufacturers in Malaysia. And finally, there are the investments in property and the retail business. Property investment will range from hotel development of the highest value, such as that of the Shangri-La chain, to the building of a few apartment blocks. The most famous example of the retail business is of course the Parkson chain.

This last category of investment is likely to last for sometime for two reasons. One is that there is an increasing demand for property and retail business as, according to one interviewee, there is a demand for such facilities from a growing Chinese middle class. Second, property development and the retail business have traditionally been the key strengths of Malaysian Chinese business in Malaysia. With proven experience and expertise, the Malaysian Chinese are in a better position to compete with ethnic Chinese from elsewhere involved in business in China than in sectors where they have not traditionally excelled in or have no comparative advantage. Thus Malaysian Chinese cannot compete with the Taiwanese in manufacturing given the Taiwanese strength in this sector and the impressive success they have so far achieved in China. And for big entrepreneurial and trading deals involving China and the Western world, the Hong Kong Chinese have a far greater ability to do so than the Malaysian Chinese. And finally, Malaysian Chinese will find it difficult to undertake big state-sponsored projects as Singapore did with the China-Singapore-Suzhou Industrial Park project. It is unlikely that Malaysian Chinese would be able to enlist Malaysian Government support for any such projects.

CHINESE INVESTMENT IN MALAYSIA

Chinese investment in Malaysia is very small. There is some Chinese investment in the manufacturing sector and this involve joint-ventures with a few Malaysian Chinese businessmen. If one looks at Chinese investment for the decade of the 1990s it is unimpressive and nowhere compared to that of the Japanese.

But Chinese investment in Malaysia could, in the coming years, expand as the Chinese economy develops. This can be seen in the Chinese search worldwide for energy sources such as oil and gas. China could in future look to Southeast Asia not only for natural gas but for other raw materials such as wood. In fact, the Chinese had planned a big investment project in Sabah in wood and pulp processing that was to cost 4.56 billion ringgit. It is interesting to note that a Malaysian Chinese company controlled by William Cheng originally had a twenty per cent stake in it.[25] In the event, this Sabah project did not materialize. The reason given was that it might damage the environment. An intriguing question arises as to whether or not the presence of Malaysian Chinese intermediaries

TABLE 6.3
Investment from China (paid-up) in
Companies in Production in Malaysia
(RM Million)

Year	Amount
1990	1.4
1991	3.8
1992	6.4
1993	7
1994	8.7
1995	23.0
1996	21.5
1997	32.5
1998	22.5

Source: Figures compiled from Statistics of Malaysian Industrial Development Authority (MIDI) by Tham Siew Yean in her article "Can Malaysian Manufacturing compete with China in the WTO?" In *Asia-Pacific Development Journal* 8, no. 2, December 2001, pp. 19–20.

between Chinese investors and local Malaysian concerns might develop into a pattern for Chinese investment in big resource exploitation projects.

Malaysian Exports to China

The trading component is the most impressive aspect of bilateral Sino-Malaysian economic relations. One needs only to look at the data for the past decade or so. In the years from 1992–2002, total bilateral trade has gone up almost ten times (from 4.44 billion ringgit in 1992 to 43.44 billion ringgit in 2002 (see Table 6.4).

The task is in extracting from the figures the extent of Malaysian Chinese involvement in this trade. Matrade figures for the major Malaysian exports to China for the years 1995, 2000 and 2002 include palm oil, wood and electrical and electronic products.[26] Significantly, these are sectors where there is extensive Malaysian Chinese participation.[27]

While China offers an expanding market to Malaysian products, its exports to Malaysia is also growing. Indeed the Malaysian figures in Table 6.4 show Malaysia experiencing a slight deficit in the balance of trade between the two countries for the year 2002.[28] As far as Malaysian Chinese business is concerned, imports from China can cut both ways. On one hand, Chinese imports threaten the Malaysian Chinese SMEs especially in footwear and garments. On the other hand, the imports greatly increase trading opportunities for Malaysian Chinese business

TABLE 6.4
Malaysian Trade With China 1992–2002
(Value in RM Billion)

Year	Total Exports	Total Imports	Total Trade	Balance of Trade
1992	1.96	2.48	4.44	−0.52
1993	3.09	2.82	5.92	0.27
1994	5.06	3.58	8.64	1.49
1995	4.90	4.30	9.20	0.61
1996	4.80	4.72	9.52	0.08
1997	5.26	6.27	11.53	−1.02
1998	7.77	7.26	15.03	0.51
1999	8.80	8.15	16.96	0.62
2000	11.51	12.32	23.83	−0.81
2001	14.68	14.47	29.16	0.21
2002	19.97	23.47	43.44	−3.51

Source: Malaysia External Trade Corporation.

groups. Such groups include big business, SMEs, and very small-scale businesses. We will now focus on the last two groups.

Impact of Imports from China on SMEs

It is among the Chinese in Malaysia particularly those in manufacturing, that the impact of a rising China is most felt. Malaysian Chinese, both in large companies and in SMEs, are involved in manufacturing. Manufacturing especially of the SMEs contributed some 82.9 per cent of Malaysian exports, 34.4 per cent of Malaysian GDP and 27 per cent of Malaysian employment. During the 1997–98 financial crisis, export from manufacturing drove the country's recovery.

But not long after the 1997–98 financial crisis, manufacturing especially by the SMEs began to face difficulties. The pegging of the ringgit to the U.S. dollar had helped the sector in the first years or so but for many manufacturers, with having to replenish inventories, found that the import of materials has become expensive. And at this point their predicament increased with strong competition from Chinese products. Today, Malaysian manufacturers face major problems competing against imports from China. These are firstly the lower prices due to cheaper labour costs. Secondly, there is the large China market which allows economies of scale for Chinese manufacturers. Thirdly, many SMEs in Malaysia are component part producers. Many come under the Original Equipment Manufacture category. In many cases, the main manufacturer relocates from Malaysia to China because of the attractive conditions there. Thus OEM producers in Malaysia supplying to the principal producer have either to relocate or to close down.

Two industries in particular have been hardest hit by the China competition. These are garments and footwear. Both were two thriving industries with export markets in the United States and Europe. However, both are in decline with serious loss of overseas market share. Many are no longer viable. The surviving ones are those that have established brand name in the up-market range such as for example, Padini in garments. Data from the furniture and the plastic industry show a similar impact of competition from China. The furniture industry, which performed strongly in export during the financial crisis, is now suffering from the China competition. In 2004 export of Malaysian furniture showed a decline for the first time.

The important electrical and electronics industry also deserves attention. The trends are similar to what is happening in garment and in shoe-making. According to Matrade figures, the electronics sector forms some 75 per cent of manufacturing exports in Malaysia, many of them under OEM. There are more than 900 companies in operation employing over 335,000 workers. In 2004, Malaysia exported more than 200 billion ringgit of electronics goods. In Penang, several semiconductor producers have moved out, in no small part due to the China attraction, and there has been loss of jobs.

Options for Malaysian Chinese Business

So how are Malaysian Chinese business responding or what options do they have in facing the competition from China. There are three likely options. The first is to appeal for state support. Affected SMEs, particularly those in the textile industry, lobbied the Malaysian Government not so much for protection but for the removal of certain taxes which they believe reduce their competitiveness. For example, the textile manufacturers would like the government to remove the import duty of ten per cent on raw materials from non-ASEAN countries and the sales tax of ten per cent, all of which have added to costs of production.[29] However, the Malaysian Government has so far not acceded to such appeals.

The second option is to relocate. Many are moving to China — to take advantage of lower costs in labour and even in land and to produce parts or the complete product according to Malaysian designs. This is especially the case with the footwear industry where the final products are sold to Malaysian, European, Australian and Southeast Asian markets. According to a spokesman for the footwear industry, Malaysian shoes are still preferred for their quality in the above mentioned markets.[30]

Pensonic, a Penang-based company, which is the largest electrical and electronics manufacturer in Malaysia is shifting some of its production units to China to take advantage of the lower costs there to stay in the market.[31] But it may not necessarily be only to China because Vietnam and Thailand offer similar advantages of costs, and China may not be as attractive in the future. Relocation also becomes necessary when the principal manufacturer has moved, so as to remain in the supply chain of production. This migration of contract and OEM manufacturers would further reduce contract manufacturing opportunities for smaller SMEs that are left behind.

The third option is to be more competitive, to advance into high-value areas such as digital electronics and thereby stay ahead of China's competition. To move up the value chain or to relocate is not an easy option and only the larger ones have the resources to invest in research and development (R&D) to stay competitive or to be able to relocate. The primary problem here for SMEs is on enhancing their competitiveness. Even if the government were to remove taxes, the garment and footwear industries as with many other SMEs affected by imports from China, will have great difficulties staying ahead of the Chinese. This is because the Chinese are able also to catch up, if not move ahead in quality and innovation. If that happens, as indeed it may be happening already, Malaysian Chinese SMEs may no longer be able to rely on claims of the superior quality of their products. According to Mimos Berhad, a government-funded technology company, expenditure on R&D in Malaysia is 0.4 per cent of GDP compared with 0.8 per cent in China. For many middle size and smaller SMEs, given the loss of markets, the choice is to close down. It is anticipated that the present 40,000 OEM manufacturers of SME scale will decline to some 10,000 in the next ten years. Some SMEs would survive through this process of consolidation.

The relocation of Malaysian Chinese business particularly manufacturers could lead not only to shifting out or extending production lines overseas but would see an increase in the number of Malaysian Chinese working, for instance, in China. It is estimated that there are some 30,000 to 40,000 Malaysian Chinese working in China today. Many are in the financial services, in banks, accounting firms but others are plant managers of factories. In a sense this is a reflection of the globalization process where Malaysians seek work not only in China but also in other parts of the world.

There is, for many small manufacturers another option, and that is to turn from being manufacturers of textile and shoe making, for instance, to become traders. It has been noted that it is more viable and profitable to buy products from China which are cheaper than what could be produced locally and to distribute these in the region and markets they have long been familiar with. These and other Malaysian Chinese manufacturers have become intermediaries for China's export and this intermediary role can remain until such time as manufacturers in China acquire the contacts themselves to take over.

There are, nevertheless, some cases of largely Malaysian Chinese-owned companies in manufacturing, both listed or unlisted in the KLSE, that have fared well in face of the China challenge. Of the listed companies, Khind Holdings has a complete range of electrical and electronic products under its twin brands of Khind and Mistral. It does contract manufacturing in China, Korea and Thailand.[32] Then there is an unlisted company Thong Fook Corporation Sdn Berhad in Ipoh, Perak which does contract manufacturing that includes the Sony Erickson blue tooth technology for handphones. Starting off as a family groundnut factory, and still maintaining that product, it now has a thousand workers and its technology development centre has more than a dozen engineers.

Very Small-Scale Malaysian Chinese Business

As China produces a very wide variety of products at very reasonable prices, many Malaysian Chinese business groups are taking to importing such products from China for resale in Malaysia and in the region. Many of these products come through Malaysian Chinese companies that have established links with China. But there is an increasing group of very small-scale businesses employing anywhere from one to ten employee, which are trying to benefit from imports from China. There is a lot of anecdotal evidence of the presence of this group of very small-scale business.[33] The former Malaysian ambassador to China, Datuk Majid Khan in a recent speech to a reception given in his honour by some Malaysian Chinese business groups, spoke of the innumerable occasions when many individual Malaysian Chinese businessmen, in addition to the big Malaysian Chinese business, turned up at the Malaysian embassy door to complain or seek for help from the Malaysian Government over their business difficulties in China.[34] Anecdotal evidence of the presence of this group is not a totally satisfactory way of proving its existence, efforts were made to look for documentation that will give us some idea of the size of this group as compared to the bigger groups involved in the China trade. The Chinese Ministry of Finance sources provide a list of Malaysian companies involved in the China trade as importers. There were 5,655 such Malaysian companies or foreign companies based in Malaysia listed. These companies were then broken down according to the number of employees in each company. Some 3,763 companies had employee figures that allow analysis. Out of these 3,763 companies, there were 919 companies with ten or less than ten employees, giving such companies a sizeable twenty-four per cent of the total number of importers.

In talking to a number of such small enterprises doing business in China, we found that many importers first developed business contacts through attending Chinese trade fairs as part of delegations led by the Malaysian Chinese Chamber of Commerce.[35] Some also make contacts by themselves. Most of these Malaysian Chinese businessmen know some Mandarin. And the Chinese trading business is increasingly made easier by their Chinese counterparts, some of whom require payment only after the products have been delivered to Malaysian Chinese businessmen.[36] This reflects the competition among producers in China and as such could open new opportunities to Malaysian Chinese businessmen.

An interesting note is that a number of small Malay enterprises are also trying to get involved in the China trade. They send agents to China to buy up goods from the factories and these are then sold to wholesalers and retailers in largely Malay areas.

THE EXPANDING SERVICE SECTOR IN MALAYSIA-CHINA BUSINESS

The increase in bilateral economic relations has led to an increase in many types of services performed by Malaysians such as those in education and tourism as well as in insurance and shipping. The latter two services facilitate trade between the two countries. However data for Malaysian Chinese involvement in the insurance and shipping services is difficult to obtain. Instead this section of the chapter will focus on education and tourism for the following reasons. One is that the Malaysian Chinese involvement in these sub-sectors is identifiable. For example, the private twinning colleges which play a very important role in accepting Chinese students are mostly Malaysian Chinese controlled and managed. Second, the "export" of students and tourists is quite a salient aspect, especially in recent times, of the economic rise of China. Malaysia, for its part is keen to host such students and tourists for the revenue they bring. They also enhance the image of Malaysia as a regional educational hub and a place for tourists to visit. And third, data is more accessible in these two areas.

Students from China in Malaysia

The liberalization of higher education by the Malaysian government began with the decision to allow twinning colleges and private universities to be established. This was partly because the government was keen to stem the huge outflow of foreign exchange which occurred from the eighties onwards as a result of British and Commonwealth universities charging full fees for Malaysian students. Until then, fees had been subsidized by the British Government. As a result of the success of this educational liberalization, a policy of making Malaysia a regional hub of education developed. And increasingly, Malaysia is targetting students from China who are responding for the following reasons.[37] Almost all of these students from China desire a Western degree. They, however, find it difficult in many cases to get visas to enter universities in the West. Malaysia, on its part, has a fairly liberal visa policy for these students. Second, the twinning colleges and private universities offer degrees from Western universities, thus enhancing their attractiveness to these Chinese students. Third, the cost in Malaysia is less than in the West. And finally, Chinese students find the Malaysian environment easy to adapt to because of the presence of a large Malaysian Chinese population. Thus, from figures obtained from the Higher Education Ministry, the percentage of students from China of total foreign students in private tertiary institutions is quite high. For the year 2003 it was as high as forty per cent (see Table 6.5).

Also, in many of the more reputable twinning colleges, the students from China constitute a sizeable percentage of not only the foreign student population but also of the entire student population. One twinning college in Kuala Lumpur known as the Higher Education Learning Programme or HELP has about 600 students from China as of early 2005 out of a total student population of 8,000.[38] This is about 8 per cent. In another college, Nilai College in Negeri Sembilan, it is, as of early 2005, as high as 35 per cent![39]

It is thus clear that the profitability and indeed the survival of many of these colleges depend on students from China. Yet Malaysia faces problems in its ability to further attract, and indeed retain, students from China. For example, INTI, one of the largest Malaysian Chinese owned college, which in the past has a very large number of students from China, has since last year been experiencing a decline of some 10 per

TABLE 6.5
Number of International Students in Public and Private Higher Education Institutions (2003–04)

(1) Year	(2) No. of Students Public & Private	(3) No. of Students in Private	(4) No. of Students from China	% of (4)/(3)
2003	31,288	25,158	10,230	41
2004	32,254	25,939	9,075	35

Source: Higher Education Ministry, as published in *Star* Newspaper, 20 February, 2005, Kuala Lumpur, p. 7.

cent of these students. Increasingly there is competition from other countries which are also keen on attracting students from China. Singapore is one example. Second, many Western universities are going direct to China to set up branches. Students from China can study for a Western degree in their own country rather than go to a country like Malaysia to get one. Thus, similar to the challenge of retaining investment from multinationals which are increasingly being diverted to China, Malaysia will have to "upgrade" its private higher education. This may require some private institutions to link up with more prestigious Western universities. Another alternative is to focus on boutique or niche courses. These courses may include accountancy as it is estimated that China needs a large number of accountants which it is presently very short of. Chinese students may be attracted to Malaysia as there are Malaysian linkages with Western professional accountancy bodies that the Chinese have yet to establish.[40]

Arrival of Chinese Tourists

Tourism is another service sub-sector that has much Malaysian Chinese involvement. Many of the travel agents, hotels, and restaurants that service tourists to Malaysia are owned and controlled by Malaysian Chinese businessmen. What then is the impact of tourism from China on the Malaysian economy, including Malaysian Chinese business? From the data for the past decade and half, (Table 6.6) Chinese tourists came in great numbers from 2000 onwards. The number increased almost twofold in 2000 from the year 1999. There was a drop in 2003 and this was probably due to the SARS outbreak which dampened travel in the Asia-Pacific region.

The Chinese tourist, increasingly, is also not a small spender. Even though Chinese tourists are not the number one spender in per diem terms, they rank among the top ten, bested primarily by those from the Middle East (Table 6.7).

But because the Chinese tourists come in such numbers, the financial impact of their tourism is very great. The table (Table 6.8) below shows the gross tourist receipts from the Chinese tourists which in the year 2002 came to about 1.5 billion Malaysian ringgit! It is no wonder that Malaysia, as with many other countries, are keen to tap this Chinese tourist market in addition to the Chinese education market.

It should also be mentioned that tourism also works the other way around. And it is significant, according to figures from China National

TABLE 6.6
Number of China Tourists Arrived in Malaysia

Year	Tourists arrivals	Growth
1989	9,928	–
1990*	6,895	–30.5
1991	12,800	85.6
1992	46,811	265.7
1993	81,874	74.9
1994	95,789	17.0
1995	103,130	7.7
1996	135,743	31.6
1997	158,679	16.9
1998	159,852	0.7
1999	190,851	19.4
2000	425,246	122.8
2001	453,246	6.6
2002	557,647	23.0
2003	350,597	–37.1

Note: *Drop due to Tiananmen Square incidence (4 June 1989).
Source: Departing Visitor Survey Unit, Planning & Research Division of Tourism Malaysia.

TABLE 6.7
Top Ten per Diem Expenditure (RM)

Country of Residence	2003	2002
Syria	618.1	N/A
UAE	614.2	N/A
South Africa	539.2	524.3
Saudi Arabia	528.6	N/A
Portugal	527.1	N/A
Hong Kong	487.4	451.3
Turkey	486.3	N/A
China	477.4	459.9
Brunei	434.8	482.0
Singapore	434.0	412.9

Source: Departing Visitor Survey Unit, Planning & Research Division of Tourism Malaysia.
Note: According to Ministry of Tourism criteria, those tourists who come as part of tour groups, those who stay in expensive hotels and those who come to do shopping rather than for rest and recreation score high in this computation of *per diem* expenditure. As such, those from Western countries, many of whom are backpackers and who prefer rest and recreation, do not score high.

TABLE 6.8
Performance of China Tourist Arrival

Year	Tourist Arrivals	Tourist receipts (RM mil)	Average per Capita (RM)	Average per Diem (RM)	Average length of stay (night)
1993	81,874	170.9	2,090.0	321.5	6.5
1994	95,789	180.7	1,912.0	261.9	7.3
1995	103,130	171.9	1,666.7	276.1	6.0
1996	135,743	305.0	2,247.0	387.4	5.8
1997	158,679	294.1	1,863.7	300.5	6.1
1998	159,852	363.8	2,276.0	490.6	4.6
1999	190,851	531.2	2,783.5	568.1	4.9
2000	425,246	1,226.4	2,884.0	565.5	5.1
2001	453,246	1,270.0	2,802.2	438.5	6.4
2002	557,647	1,487.5	2,667.5	459.9	5.8
2003	350,597	903.8	2,578.0	477.4	5.4

Source: Departing Visitor Survey Unit, Planning & Research Division of Tourism Malaysia.

Tourism Association, that there were about 440,000 Malaysian visitors to China for the year 2000. Malaysian visitors are the fifth largest among countries sending tourists to China.

Network

The literature on doing business in China refers to the part played by networking and traditional ties.[41] It is not the purpose here to engage in this debate except to argue that based on findings so far business involvement of Malaysian in China is primarily guided by the profit motive. There may have been a time in the early years of the twentieth century when some investments by Malaysian Chinese were inspired by sentiments to help modernize China. The question today is whether or not this search for profit in China by Malaysian Chinese businessmen involves networking with other overseas ethnic Chinese businessmen, particularly those of their own clan and dialect groups? Also in doing business in China, do Malaysian Chinese businessmen focus mainly in the provinces their ancestors came from?

Research carried out so far suggests that Malaysian Chinese businessmen from the SMEs and the very small-scale businessmen in the main do not rely on partners from Southeast Asia in their China business.

There is no evidence of an extensive Chinese network in Southeast Asia which can be used to do business in China. It is, however, the case that small Malaysian Chinese businessmen generally proceed to do business in Guangdong, Fujian, and Hainan, the provinces from where their ancestors came, as they can at least speak the dialects of these provinces. But there is also the fact that there are more business opportunities in these regions. In the last century some businessmen were willing to invest in their ancestral homeland to help develop the region without profit as the main motivation. This is not the case today.

Among the big Malaysian Chinese business groups, there is a greater likelihood of their collaboration with ethnic Chinese from elsewhere. But this is because these Malaysian Chinese grouping have regional offices or connections, and not because of reasons of clan or dialect group affinity. An example will be the Hong Leong group, involved in construction in China, that have offices in Singapore and Hong Kong from where expertise can be tapped for the China business. It is also possible that a big businessman like Robert Kuok could collaborate with a Hong Kong tycoon like Li Ka Shing to do business in China. But their collaboration is more a result of previous successful cooperation rather than of any ethnic or sub-ethnic affinity. Li Ka-Shing after all is a Teochew and Robert Kuok is a Fuzhou whose ancestors came from northern Fukien. Interestingly, much of Robert Kuok's business in China, like his Shangri-La Hotels, are not in northen Fukien.

This does not mean that Malaysian Chinese businessmen do not use places outside of Malaysia to do business in the Chinese mainland. Many had used Hong Kong as a base before the Malaysian Government lifted restrictions on travel to China and many still do because of the proximity of Hong Kong to the Chinese mainland. And there are also many Malaysian Chinese who use Singapore as a base for China business because of the comprehensive agreements Singapore has with China that make business dealings more transparent. But again, these are done primarily for pragmatic reasons rather than from clan or dialect group solidarity.

Related to the issue of the network is the question of whether or not knowledge of Mandarin is an advantage for Malaysian Chinese doing business in China. Everyone interviewed believes that this is an advantage particularly if a knowledge of Mandarin is accompanied by a good knowledge of Chinese conditions. This is particularly so in small-scale trading where Malaysian Chinese, without much capital or established business networks, will have to rely on Mandarin and a sensitivity to local Chinese conditions to effect contacts in China. But the interviewees also believe that knowledge of Mandarin has only a limited advantage. What is more important are assets associated with starting, maintaining and making a success of a business. And these are capital, technology, marketing connections, and business skills. The Chinese will prefer doing business with people in possession of such assets even if they do not know Mandarin.

The Political Dimension

Given that the overwhelming number of Malaysians investing in China are of Chinese origin, why has public criticism not persisted after Tengku Razaleigh, a former UMNO leader and finance minister, some years ago contended that such investment should be redirected back to Malaysia. There was an implied allegation of a lack of patriotism in such China investment. But Razaleigh's criticisms were not taken up by government or other Malay political leaders. The reasons for this are many. One is the policy of the Malaysian Government to encourage business and investment abroad, particular following the recession of the 1985.[42] This being the case, there is little reason for criticizing Malaysian Chinese investment in China particularly when the latter's economy has been growing impressively. Second, there are also government-linked corporations (GLCs) investing or planning to invest in China. These corporations include Sime Darby, Proton the Malaysian car manufacturer, and the top Malaysian bank, Maybank. Thus, if it makes business sense for Malaysian GLCs to invest in China, it should also make business sense for other Malaysians to do so. And third, Malaysian Chinese business groupings, particularly the publicly listed ones, are not totally Malaysian Chinese-owned. They all have Malay participation in ownership and some Malay participation in management. What profits made from investment in China go back to these Malays in dividends and share value appreciation.

Still, there have been advice from both the official Chinese and Malaysian sides to encourage more non-Chinese, particularly Malay, participation in the China business. The Chinese embassy in Kuala Lumpur noted this lack of Malay participation in Malaysian investment in China. It urged Malaysian Chinese businessmen to partner Malay businessmen and through this, to gain access to capital from the Malaysian Government. It even went on to suggest that Malaysia should have a China-Singapore Suzhou-type project! Similarly, the Malaysian envoy to China, Syed Norulzaman is also keen to see more non-Chinese businessmen and government linked enterprise doing business in China.[43]

CONCLUSION

The rise of China is having its impact on Malaysian Chinese business in the areas of investment, trade, and services. Malaysian Chinese investment in China was stepped up from 1992 onwards though such investment does not constitute a very large percentage of total Malaysian investment overseas. Investment in China has, moreover, not been without some difficulties. The problems that arose resulted from the lack of Malaysian preparation and unfamiliarity to conditions in China. Malaysian businessmen complained about the lack of transparency, bureaucratic delays, and cumbersome laws that add up to costs and difficulties in doing business. For the moment Malaysian Chinese investment will concentrate on property and retail, the traditional strength of Malaysian Chinese business. As far as manufacturing is concerned, the focus of investment will be on component parts rather than on complete products for the China market.

The trade impact of China on Malaysian Chinese business is also of concern. Chinese imports into the country threaten the profitability and survival of several industries. These include the footwear and garment industries which have been forced to enhance their competitiveness to survive. Some have turned to being producers of components in China. Others become importers of goods they once produced, thus becoming traders rather than manufacturers. However the expected trade opportunities China offers have led to the growth of many very small scale Malaysian Chinese enterprises which are involved primarily in importing all kinds of Chinese products.

In the area of services, the China impact has brought benefits especially in the Malaysian higher educational and tourism sectors. Malaysia has been reasonably successful in attracting Chinese students and tourists in the past few years. But it faces difficulties in the educational sector in maintaining the high number of Chinese students because of competition from other countries and from Western universities setting up campuses in China.

For many Malaysian Chinese who earlier saw a rising China as one of providing unalloyed opportunities, advances made by China are beginning to make China a competitor with Malaysian Chinese business. And while resourceful Malaysian Chinese can still maintain a competitive edge, for the majority, the response may require state aid involving a more supportive government role for the SMEs such as funding, research and development, efficient development of resource-based industries, and the removing of regulations and restrictions that have hindered development. Others see the need for Malaysian investors to work more smoothly with their Chinese partners and this requires knowledge by Malaysians of China and the conditions there.

Notes

[1]   Khoo Kay Peng, "A Critical Analysis of FDI in ASEAN: Balancing Business in International System", Department of Public Administration and International Studies, University of Warwick, February 2004.

[2]   For Southeast Asian Chinese business and the Chinese impact on Asia, see Henry Wai-chung Yeung, "Under Siege? Economic Globalisation and Chinese Business in Southeast Asia". *Economy and Society* 28, no. 1 (February 1999): 1–29. See also Shaun Breslin, "China in the Asian Economy", in *Does China Matter: A Reassessment: Essays in Memory of Gerald Segal*, edited by Barry Buzan and Rosemary Foot (London and New York: Routledge, 2004); Orville Schell, "Enigma of China's Economic Miracle", *The Edge Malaysia* (Kuala Lumpur), 10–17 November 2003.

[3]   Persons interviewed by writers and Tan Miau Ing, a research aide: Dr. Paul Chan, Executive Director, HELP College, a leading twinning college; Dr. TanYew Sing, President, INTI College, Nilai; Dr. Mahani Zainal Abidin, Head, Globalization Unit, National Economic Action Council, Prime Minister's Department, Malaysia; Tan Sri Ngan Ching Wen, Advisor, UNICO-Desa Plantation Berhad; Mr. Ong Kim Seng ACCCIM (Association of Chinese Chambers of Commerce and Industry) Secretariat; Dato Tan Chin Nam and daughter, Ms. Tan Lei Cheng; Tan and Tan Group, developer of the Mid Valley Megamall in Kuala Lumpur one of the biggest malls in Malaysia; Mr. Tan Kai Hee, President, Malaysia-China Chamber of Commerce, and Managing Director, Hai-O Group; Mr. Yew Chin Liong, Yew Trading Sdn. Bhd. President, Textiles and General Goods Importers and Exporters Association of Federal Territory and Selangor.

[4]   See Lee Kam Hing and Lee Poh Ping, "Malaysian Chinese Business: Who Survived the Crisis?" *Kyoto Review* (online journal), Center for Southeast Asian Studies, Kyoto, Issue 4, October 2003.

[5]   Concerning data from interviews, most of those interviewed were done face to face, though one or two were conducted through the telephone.

[6]   Data on these come from magazines like *Malaysian Business* (Kuala

Lumpur) which every year lists the richest Malaysians, and the American magazines, *Forbes* and *Fortune* which have their annual lists of the richest people by country including Malaysia.

[7] See Rogayah Mat Zin, "Small and Medium Industries: A Renewed Source of Growth?" Paper presented at MIER National Outlook Conference, Kuala Lumpur, 2000.

[8] See Ong Kim Seng, "Development of Malaysia-China Economic Cooperation", ACCCIM Secretariat, Kuala Lumpur (unpublished paper with no date).

[9] Taken from Tham Siew Yean, "Can Malaysian Manufacturing Compete with China in the WTO?", in *Asia-Pacific Development Journal* 8, no. 2 (December 2001).

[10] "The Present Situation of Malaysian Investment in China and suggestions to encourage such investment" (in Chinese) by The Economic and Commercial Counsellors Office of the Chinese embassy in Kuala Lumpur <http://my.mofcom.gov.cn/article/200311/250311/00131939_1.xm> (access date: 1 March 2005), p. 3.

[11] For example, "Present Situation" mentions that Robert Kuok's group of Shangri-La Hotels and other investment in China are based in Hong Kong, op. cit., p. 3.

[12] Salcon Unit Takes Over China Water Operations", *The Star* (Kuala Lumpur), 7 September 2005.

[13] "Present Situation", op. cit., p. 3.

[14] The Lion Group controlled by William Cheng is mentioned as the largest Malaysian investor in China. "Present Situation", ibid., p. 3.

[15] *The Star* (Kuala Lumpur), 31 July 2000.

[16] Compiled from the website of the Kuala Lumpur Stock Exchange <http://www.bursamalaysia.com/website/listing/lcwebsites.htm> (access date: 1 March 2005).

[17] Taken from Corporate Information of the Lion Group under "Our Business" <http://www.lion.com.my> (access date: 1 March 2005).

[18] *The Star* (Kuala Lumpur), 26 May 2004.

[19] "Top Glove: On the World Map", *Malaysian Business*, 16 January 2005, pp. 48–50.

[20] It was mentioned frequently by those interviewed that many Malaysian Chinese tend in the early years of their investment in China to consider their Chinese counterparts as stupid. See also Robert Kuok, "Western China full of business opportunities", in *Malaysia-China Business Magazine* (publication of Malaysian-China Chamber of Commerce) Vol. 12 (April 2004): 91.

[21] One interviewee mentioned his experience of having his business very quickly emulated by his Chinese counterpart. This interviewee subsequently lost out to his emulator.

[22] See Robert Kuok, op. cit., p. 81.

[23] One interviewee told of his experience with a powerful Chinese official who told him that the Chinese authorities would only listen to complaints from Malaysian Chinese investors if they were very large investors.

[24] Information supplied by Dato Tan Chin Nam.

[25] See "Stop All Work at Kalabakan Forest Project Site, Govt Urged". In *The Star* (Kuala Lumpur), 5 April 2002. A Chinese company was supposed to contribute 40 per cent. The rest are contributed by Malaysians.

[26] Matrade is Malaysia External Trade Corporation.

[27] Two of the largest Malaysian Chinese-owned plantations, Industrial Oxygen Incorporated (101) and Kuala Lumpur — Kepong (KL-K) have substantial palm oil output. The owner of 101 is listed in *Malaysian Business* (Kuala Lumpur),12–28 February 2005 as the sixth richest man in Malaysia. Though we have no exact figures, it is likely both export a very substantial amount of their palm oil output to China. KL-K also has investment in China.

[28] Chinese figures show the balance of trade in Malaysia's favour. Again, this discrepancy arises because of different statistical methods used to compile figures. The Chinese figures however also show a great increase in bilateral trade for the same years.

[29] See "Malaysian Garment Makers Unscathed by China's WTO Entry" by Ho Wah Foon in *Malaysia–China Business Magazine*, op. cit., pp. 43–45.

[30] See "The Shoe Industry is not a Sunset Industry", an interview with the Chairman of the Association of Malaysian Shoe Manufacturers, Fang Li Siang (in Chinese) in *Malaysia–China Business Magazine* (Kuala Lumpur), April 2003, pp. 33–35.

[31] "Low-Intensity Export War", *The Star*, 28 August 2003; "Pensonic to Tap China for Electrical Goods", *The Star*, 18 June 2004.

[32] "Worldwide Reach: Khind Holdings is Expanding a Home-Grown Brand Globally", *Malaysian Business*, 1 December 2004, pp. 48–49.

[33] The *Washington Post* in a recent article on the impact of China wrote of a Malaysian Chinese who gave up academic life to go into importing strawberries from China. *Washington Post* (online), 26 February 2005, p. A01.

34 Speech given on 11 March 2005, at a function organized by the ACCCIM in Kuala Lumpur.

35 Information supplied by Mr. Ong Kim Seng, ACCCIM Secretariat.

36 Trustful relations between Malaysian Chinese businessmen and their Chinese counterparts are not always the case, as there are also many stories of misunderstanding in trade between both parties.

37 Based on discussion with Dr. Paul Chan, executive director of Higher Education Learning Programme College (HELP), which is one of the top twinning colleges in Malaysia. See also Tan Yew Sing "Partnering China in Education" *Malaysia-China Business Magazine* 13, July 2004.

38 Data supplied by HELP College.

39 See *New Straits Times* (Kuala Lumpur), 20 February 2005.

40 *The Star* (Kuala Lumpur), 6 July 1997.

41 Edmund Terence Gomez, *Chinese Business in Southeast Asia: Contesting Cultural Explanation, Researching Entrepreneurship* (London: Routledge Curzon, 2004); Kris Old and Henry Wai-chung Yeung, "(Re)shaping 'Chinese' Business Networks in a Globalising Era", *Environment and Planning D: Society and Space 1999*, vol. 17; Michael Backman, *Overseas Chinese Network in Asia* (Canberra: East Asian Analytical Unit, Department of Foreign Affairs and Trade,1995).

42 See Tham Siew Yean, op. cit., p. 18.

43 See "Present Situation", op. cit., p. 7 and "Embrace China, Envoy Tells Businesses" in *The Star* (Kuala Lumpur), 22 March 2005.

7

Competition, (Ir)relevance and Market Determinants: Government Economic Policies and Ethnic Chinese Responses in West Malaysia

Ho Khai Leong

INTRODUCTION

Since Malaysia's independence in 1957, the nation's economy has been doing reasonably well with economic growth averaging 8.7 per cent annually. This trend continued until 1997, when the Asian financial crisis hit almost all the countries in the Asia-Pacific region. It is widely recognized that Malaysia's strong economic performance in the 1980s and most of the 1990s had been built on effective economic planning and a relatively efficent civil service (Ho 2002). The country had also enjoyed strong inflows of foreign direct investment in the decade before the Asian financial crisis. In retrospect after the crisis, Malaysian state policies have undergone a number of phases of adjustment — from state expansion to divestment to privatization, from the New Economic Policy to the National Development Policy to the New Vision Policy, from manufacturing to industrialization to the K-economy. These changes were by no means trivial or insignificant, and they have transformed the country's economy to what it is today.

The economic fate of the Malaysian Chinese is invariably linked to external environments (such as the forces of globalization, emergence of China, Taiwan's "Look South Policy" etc.), as well as internal factors, such as pro-*Bumiputera* (pro-Malay) policies and regulations, aimed at wealth redistribution in the country. With various restrictions and constraints imposed by the United Malays National Organization (UMNO)-led Barisan Nasional [National Front] government, Malaysian Chinese businesses have gone through various periods of adaptation and adjustment, submitting memoranda through business associations and political parties, building alliances with Malay bureaucrats and businesses, and lately, responding to the emergence of China as a destination for business expansion.

This chapter will examine the patterns of government economic policies and their impact on Malaysian Chinese business development over the past thirty years. While the government's pro-*Bumiputera* policies were restrictive toward Chinese economic development, the ethnic Chinese business community responded to these governmental discriminatory actions by making itself more competitive through organizational restructuring, political alliance and patronage, and discerning outsourcing. The Chinese economic resilience is proven through their entrepreneurial attitudes *vis-à-vis* discriminatory state policies, which seemed at times to have been irrelevant as far as some of the top Chinese businesses are concerned.

THE FEDERAL CONSTITUTION AND THE
NEW ECONOMIC POLICY (NEP)

To understand Malaysia's state policies regarding ethnic groups, one has to begin with the federal constitution. The federal constitution grants the Malays certain rights. Clause 1 of Article 153 states: "It shall be the responsibility of the *Yang di-pertuan Agong* (the King) to safeguard the special position of the Malays and the legitimate interests of other communities in accordance with the provision of this Article." Clause 2 states that the *Yang di-pertuan Agong* shall safeguard the special position of the Malays by reserving positions "of such proportion as he may deem reasonable" for public service, educational facilities, and business licences.

Strictly speaking, there are no government policies specifically targetted toward the ethnic Chinese. Malaysian state economic policies do not specifically address the question of an ethnic Chinese (or non-Malay) economy. The official stance on this policy is often broadly given, thus: "No ethnic communities should feel deprived." The benevolent objective of national unity is constantly stressed. These economic policies were formulated to bring about supposedly "greater equity and balance among Malaysia's social and ethnic groups in their participation in the development of the country and the sharing of the benefits from modernization and economic growth". (Malaysia, *Second Malaysia Plan*, pp. 3–4).

However, behind this objective is the Malay political leadership's firm belief that racial imbalance in the socio-economic arena stands in the way of "national unity"; for this purpose, "nation unity" is dependent on the elimination of such socio-economic imbalance. How did the Malay-dominated government convince those who are better off in their society, a majority of which are non-Malays, that addressing these socio-economic imbalances would be fair and just? To reduce the fears of the latter group, state strategies based on the principle described as "irrespective of race" are pursued. In that spirit, Malaysia's economic policies were openly pro-*Bumiputera* and were never officially acknowledged as discriminatory toward the Chinese. However, there are two sides of the same coin.

While pursuing a win-win situation is an ideal, in practice, something that may be beneficial to Mr. Ahmad may be detrimental to Mr. Tan. It is for this reason that Jomo (1997, pp. 252–53) argued that "Malaysia is generally considered to have had the most hostile policies toward Chinese business of any country in Southeast Asia." In any case, it was clear that a strategy of diffusing racial tensions by satisfying the socio-economic dreams of the Malays came at the expense of the non-Malay communities.

In this chapter, I will regard Malaysia's state economic policies as independent variables and Malaysian Chinese business as a dependent variable. In other words, Malaysian Chinese business operations are not the focus of this chapter, as the determinants of their capital formations have been detailed elsewhere (Gomez 1999; Heng 1992, 1997; Jesudason 1989). The bulk of the discussion, therefore, will rest on government policies rather than Chinese businesses.

Malaysian economic policies were a function of the country's multi-ethnic political system. From independence until the late 1960s, the economy was dominated by foreign investment and ethnic Chinese capital. The agricultural based economy relied principally on primary products, such as rubber, tin, and oil palm. The Malays who had political power were dissatisfied with the distribution of wealth, which then was disproportionately in Chinese hands. Formulated after the racial riots in 1969, the New Economic Policy (NEP) was a set of grand policies designed by the Malay ruling stratum to address their own perceived "basic economic problems in the country". It had the benevolent "over-riding objective of national unity", with a two-pronged strategy — "to reduce and eventually eradicate poverty, by raising income levels and increasing employment opportunities for all Malaysians, irrespective of race", and "to correct economic imbalance, so as to reduce and eventually eliminate the identification of race with economic functions". (Malaysia, *Second Malaysia Plan*, pp. 3–4).

There are three aspects of the NEP which have impacted the Chinese business community.

Structural Transformation of Capital

The motivating factor for the NEP policy planner which has had the most impact on the Chinese business community was the target for transferring 30 per cent of the national wealth to the *Bumiputera* within a twenty-year time frame. The NEP's initial intent was to move the ratio of economic ownership from a 2.4:33:63 ratio of *Bumiputera*, other Malaysian, and foreign ownership to a 30:40:30 ratio. Reaching this 30 per cent objective within the planned time-frame required more than merely developing state-owned enterprises and cultivating individual entrepreneurship. It called for the extensive participation of the private sector and the increased role of private investment as well as the large-scale acquisition of big companies by state-owned enterprises. Such a redistributive process could only be hastened, however, by state actions through legalization and procedural facilitation (Ho 1999).

In contrast to state actions assisting the *Bumiputera* business community, no official assistance was offered to non-*Bumiputera* to achieve the 40 per cent goal in an actual implementation of the NEP. The NEP resulted in the Bumiputera's equity increasing from 4 per cent in 1970 to about 20 per cent in 1997. By 2004, official figures showed that *Bumiputera* equity was 18.7 per cent, which was far short of the 30 per cent target. In 2005, some Malay politicians used this statistics as a pretext to advocate for a revival of the NEP, which then in 1990 was replaced by the National Development Policy (NDP).

Regulatory Agencies as Implementers

It was apparent that the *Bumiputera* political class was determinedly committed to instituting procedural and legislative reforms to wrestle control of the economy. Practically, this policy/view meant that an elaborate array of agencies, committees, and advisory councils was established to serve as channels of communication and policy adjustment. Many of these bodies — such as the Private Sector Consultative Committee of the National Development Planning Committee (NDPC) and the Wage Council

— were relatively unimportant. Others were specialized organizations that were recognized and approved by the government to function as instruments of policy implementation. The most important of these organizations were the Foreign Investment Committee (FIC) and the Capital Issues Committee (CIC) (Ho 1993).

Industrial Legislation

The Industrial Co-ordination Act (ICA) was one of the legislations that the Chinese business community complained against most vigorously. It extended to the entire manufacturing sector and provided the framework for the licensing and regulation of industrial investment in the country. The principal objectives of the ICA were to enable the ministry charged with industrial development to coordinate various aspects of the manufacturing sector, so as to ensure orderly industrial development in the country, orderly development and growth of industries, and to facilitate the collection of industrial information.

While these objectives seem harmless in a broad sketch, a closer look reveals the important intentions of many of the policy-planners. First, the ICA stipulates that all manufacturing activities with a minimum of US$250,000 in shareholders' funds and at least twenty-five full-time paid employees, must apply for a manufacturing licence. Second, the legislation gave the Ministry of Trade and Industry the authority to decide whether an application for a licence should be approved or refused. In short, the ICA gave the public bureaucracy vast power to control and regulate private industry.

The Chinese business community objected vigorously to this legislation. They argued that enough legislation had been enacted to govern or regulate manufacturing activities, for example, the Sales Tax Act, the Excise Tax Act, the Employment Ordinance, the Environment Quality Act etc. As far as the collection of data was concerned, industrial data and information could be easily obtained through the stipulation of the Statistics Act of 1965. More importantly, industrial development did not require legislation to guide any specific development because it was not as haphazard as the government claimed (Ho 1988). The Chinese business community, through the Associated Chinese Chambers of Commerce and Industry of Malaysia (ACCIM), claimed that the ICA acted as a disincentive to investment. While the fulfillment of the targets for the private sector required the maintenance of a conducive investment climate, the implementation of the ICA constituted the primary impediment that dissuaded the private sector (a majority of which were indeed Chinese businesses) (Ho 1988).

IMPACT AND SIGNIFICANCE

In June 1979, the ICA was further amended in response to criticism from the private sector. This time the Industrial Advisory Council was established. In 1985, further amendments were announced by Trade and Industry Minister, Tengku Razaleign Hamzah. There were two important provisions added. First, the government raised the level of exemption from licensing of manufacturing activities from $250,000 ringgit to $1 million ringgit and the number of workers from twenty-five to seventy-five. Companies with shareholders' funds of less than $2.5 million ringgit would no longer need to seek approval prior to any expansion of their production capacities or diversity. Second, the government agreed to issue a "clearance letter" to those companies who wanted to comply with the NEP, but were unable to find a suitable *Bumiputera* partner. This letter was to facilitate dealings with the ministries and government agencies.

The relaxation of the ICA requirements, however, did not mean that the aims of the NEP are to be taken any less seriously. Political stability and economic growth advance when all sectors and groups have opportunities to share the wealth. The spirit of the ICA lies in its intention to promote fair access to economic opportunities. Indeed, the trade and industry minister has said that such a relaxation should not be considered as an exemption from the equity conditions (Ho 1988; Nobuyuki 1991; Fujio 1991).

In sum, the ICA with its derivative regulations had an adverse impact on the Malaysian manufacturing sector during the 1970s. The share of real private investment total investment declined from about 70 per cent in 1970 to 50 per cent in 1985 (Malaysia, *Fifth Malaysia Plan*, p. 13). In 2003, The International Trade and Industry Ministry (MITI) reviewed the Industrial Co-ordination Act (ICA) and the Promotion of Investments Act (PIA) to ensure their continued relevance.

THE NATIONAL DEVELOPMENT POLICY (NDP)

The National Development Policy (NDP) replaced the NEP in 1991. The Malaysian government noted that the NEP fell short of its 30 per cent target since only 20.3 per cent of the country's corporate assets had been transferred to the Malays. In view of this development, the new plan continued to create conditions conducive to the creation of a Malay commercial and industrial community. It stressed that while the 30 per cent quota would definitely be realized in the future, a specific date should not be given for its attainment (Ho 1992*a*).

The National Vision Policy (NVP), implemented in 2001, replaced the New Economic Policy (NEP) and its successor, the National Development Policy (NDP). The Eighth Development Plan, covering the period 2001–05, incorporates strategies, programmes, and projects designed to achieve the NVP objectives for sustainable growth. The Malaysian Government also increased funding, which was made available under the Eighth Development Plan, with a focus on new spending for education, healthcare, and small-scale infrastructure, thus marking a shift from the previous focus on "mega-projects". The policy towards government-linked corporations (GLCs) was also reformed with the aim of improving their competitivenes.

During the 1980s and 1990s, a period that coincided with the Mahathir administration, the focus shifted from restructuring the economy (which still dominated economic policies) to the use of political resources to create a *Bumiputera* class of entrepreneurs (Ho 1992*b*). Money politics in UMNO and political patronage for *Bumiputera* and non-*Bumiputera* businesses were two major issues that attracted scholarly attention (Jomo, 1997; Gomez, 1999). The UMNO government has been using pro-*Bumiputera* policy to dispense contracts to their own allies; a policy that many observers have termed as political cronyism.

ETHNIC CHINESE RESPONSES

Corporatization Movement

In response to the NEP, which was perceived as being discriminatory toward the Chinese, Chinese-based political parties initiated a movement of self-help programmes, the most important of which was the Malaysian Chinese Association (MCA)-led Multi-Purpose Holdings Berhad (MPHB). Its objective was to accumulate Chinese capital in order to compete effectively with large state enterprises, such as the State Economic Development Corporations (SEDCs), Pernas and Permodalan Nasional Berhad (Heng 1997; Jesudason 1989). It also had the declared aim of assisting Chinese businesses to restructure their capital and modify their business practices. A similar movement was launched by the Associated Chinese Chambers of Commerce and Industry of Malaysia (ACCCIM), which incorporated UNICO Holdings as its own investment company. Similar holding companies were launched by other Chinese businesses. However, according to Heng, "These holding companies have failed to emerge as active corporate players in Malaysia." (p. 273).

The corporatization movement emerged at a time when politics and business was becoming intimately intertwined in Malaysia. The MCA went through a bitter period in the 1980s. Lee San Choon's retirement as party president in 1983 was followed by a twenty-month acrimonious struggle between Deputy President, Dr. Neo Yee Pan, and his challenger, Tan Koon Swan. Tan won the party presidency in 1985, but the political party was plunged into an even deeper crisis. A week after Tan became party president, he was arrested by the Singapore Government for his role in the Pan-El debacle, which had triggered a stock market collapse in both Singapore and Malaysia. The 1985 recession also brought down several deposit-taking cooperatives headed by well-known MCA personalities. Some 580,000 customers, mostly MCA members and lower-income Chinese, lost considerable sums of money. As a result of its failures in business ventures and the criminal breach of trust involving the management of Multi-Purpose Holdings, MCA began to lose the political support of the Malaysian Chinese community.

Sino-Malay Business Alliance

One survival strategy employed by the Malaysian Chinese business in such a discriminatory environment was to ally themselves with the powerful Malay bureaucrats and politicians. Heng argued that "well-connected Malay patrons serving as company directors opened doors to licences, permits, contracts, and other business opportunities regulated by the state." (1997, p. 274). She further divided Chinese businesses that utilized the Malay patronage system into three groups: "old money", "new money" and "declining money".

The most common Chinese-Malay business venture in the 1970s and 1980s was the Ali-Baba partnership, where the Chinese (Baba) were the active partner and the Malay (Ali) were partner-in-name but had the political connections and influence. This kind of partnership is most common in small and medium-scale industries and enterprises. It was obvious that this kind of partnership benefited both the Chinese and the Malays, but in the long run, it was unlikely to sustain or create a Malay entrepreneurial class. Recent studies have shown, however, that this pattern of Malay-Chinese partnership is beginning to be replaced by "genuine joint ventures" involving two equally active and genuine partners, although the venture/concept is limited to the middle class (Chin 2004). Such a transformation of the nature of the Ali-Baba alliance would mean a class-based rather than an ethnic-based coalition in the future development of the Malaysian political economy.

ETHNIC CHINESE: POLICY (IR)RELEVANCE, POLITICAL PATRONAGE, AND MARKET DETERMINANTS

During the last two decades, the Malaysian Chinese business community has been under tremendous pressure to compete with the local Bumiputera business community and the MNCs in Malaysia. So far, evidence suggests that despite the constraints imposed by legislation and failures of incorporation of Chinese capital by political parties, the Malaysian business class has not diminished in its vitality. In fact, studies suggest that the Chinese business community has been extremely "resilient" (Lee and Lee 2003). Heng also argues that "Chinese fears regarding an erosion of business control in enterprises that include Malay capital and management have largely been unfounded to date." (Heng 1997: 276).

There are a few observations to make about the development of Malaysian Chinese businesses.

First, Malaysian Chinese capitalists with political resources have surged ahead and maintained their edge in the rapidly expanding capitalist class. Indeed those with political connections, especially with top Malay bureaucrats and politicians, continue do very well. Some examples are Resorts World, Genting and YTL Corporations. Some of these powerful Chinese business groups reportedly helped bankroll UMNO; in return, UMNO protected them and allowed them to acquire the resources they required. The Chinese-based political parties, such as the MCA and Gerakan, are supposed to negotiate with the top Malay political leadership to ensure a better bargain/scenario (Tan 2000).

Second, those Malaysian Chinese entrepreneurs with little or no political connections are also surviving, and some are doing equally well. This group includes small and medium Chinese businesses, which one would expect to be particularly vulnerable to discriminatory state policies. Many of these Chinese businesses find the state policies unfavourable, but play the game and obey the rules to endure. "Businessmen, particularly Chinese entrepreneurs, who have little or no links with politicians, appear to have been able to retain control over their companies, mainly by conforming to state policies." (Gomez 2003).

Third, some segments of the Malaysian Chinese business community appear to be surviving and to a certain extent thriving as a result of their resilience in the period of capitalist development. It is difficult to say if there is a cultural explanation for such elasticity, but the community's emphasis on hard work, risk-taking, marketing skills, competitive spirit, ability to handle money, etc. certainly are factors that have contributed to their continued survival. Gomez offers this explanation: "They key factor explaining their capacity to thrive in the Malaysian economy is that they have been forced to compete." (Gomez 2003). For non-*Bumiputera* who cannot find employment in the federal government's public service, which at present is 83.7 per cent *Bumiputera*, 8.2 per cent Chinese, 5.2 per cent Indian and 3.3 per cent others, the search for self-employment or employment in the private sector is the only option.

Fourth, in recent years, Chinese-based political parties, such as the MCA and Gerakan, have begun to approach the discussion of the Malaysian economy from a national perspective rather than the ethnic perspective. Ethnic Chinese politicians within the state's economic bureaucracy are advocating views that can only be construed as Malaysian view. Issues of trade surplus, capital control, FDI, environmental standards, and competitiveness were some of the non-ethnic based issues appearing in the public dialogue. Their audience is the "outsider" rather than the ethnic groups within the country. Perhaps with the exception of the DAP and the Chinese Chamber of Commerce, the dual plights of ethnic Chinese economic rights and deprivation are seldom heard.

Fifth, government regulations enacting a quota for *Bumiputera* shares seem out of place "in the age of globalization"; thus, criticisms from the political oppositions seemed more justified. For example, in March 2005, the Domestic Trade and Consumer Affairs Ministry required all eateries wholly owned by foreigners to have a minimum capital of one million ringgit with 30 per cent of that capital being Bumiputera equity. This regulation was heavily criticized by the DAP. Another example is the continuous ban on allowing non-*Bumiputera* contractors to participate and bid for government contracts. Despite the fact that Prime Minister Datuk Seri Abdullah Ahmad Badawi had announced that $28 billion ringgit was to be allocated for construction projects in early 2005 to boost the construction sector, government contracts were only awarded to *Bumiputera* contractors.

Sixth, massive state assistance in the NEP and NDP have provided what some Malay political leaders call *tongkat* (crutches) for the Malay community. The Malay leaders have ironically realized the political, psychological and social risk as well as the "disadvantages" of over-relying on special privileges. It is protective government policies that are holding back the progress of the Malay community. The issue of *"mentaliti tongkat dan subsidi"* dominated Malay political discourse in the 1990s when the Malay mood was particularly reflective. For example, Prime Minister Datuk Seri Abdullah Ahmad Badawi, in his maiden speech as UMNO President to the UMNO general assembly in 2004, appealed to the Malay supporters by saying: "Let's not use the crutches for support all the time, the knee will become weak." However, when questioned and challenged by the non-*Bumiputera*, the Malay political position remained steadfast. In 2000, former Prime Minister Mahathir Mohammad was quoted to have said a similar statement on his view on the confrontation of the Malay and Chinese communities over special preferences for the Malays: "The government will not back down, not even by one step, in defending the Malays as we are aware they are still weak." The Chinese, on the other hand, with their survival instinct and commercial wits, were able to thrive in spite of government policies that remained unfavourable toward them.

THE PRESENT AND FUTURE: CHINA AS A DESTINATION

The emergence of China as an economic power in Asia offers yet another opportunity for the Malaysian Chinese business class to continue to thrive. In the 1970s and the 1980s, Malaysian Chinese businessmen were already investing in China but their business trips to China were limited to trade delegations to Canton trade fairs organized by the Associated Chinese Chamber of Commerce and the Industry of Malaysia or the Kuala Lumpur/ Selangor Chinese Chamber of Commerce and Industry. These trips had to be led by Pernas and the Ministry of International Trade and Industry (ACCCIM 2000).

In January 1988, the Malaysian Government abolished the AP system (Approved Permit) under which importers of Chinese goods had to apply for permits from the then government agency Pernas. This AP system was much loathed because it charged a fee of 0.5 per cent against the invoice value of imports. The abolition of this system allowed a rapid increase in the trade volume between China and the Malaysian Chinese business community (ACCCIM 2000).

With a freer flow of trade between Malaysia and China and a vast improvement in government bilateral ties, as well as the opening up of China's economy to the world, the Malaysian business community, led by the newly formed Malaysia-China Chamber of Commerce (formed in 1990), has been able to consolidate the opportunities in an open manner without any fear of a backlash from Malay nationalists who doubted Malaysian Chinese loyalty. The exceptionally huge delegation that accompanied Prime Minister Abdullah Badawi to Beijing to commemorate the thirtieth anniversary of Sino-Malaysian relations in 2004 attested to this new trend.

CONCLUSION

This chapter has surveyed the policy instruments used by the Malaysian state to restructure Malaysian society and redistribute corporate wealth to examine how and why many have perceived these policies to have adverse effects on the ethnic Chinese business community. In the last thirty years, a complex array of development in Malaysia has emerged: Corporate wealth has indeed been restructured, but it has yet to reach the desired objective; state enterprises are only functioning to a certain extent, and therefore, need to be reformed; regulations to promote *Bumiputera* equity and ownership have produced negative consequences, which the state had to modify; and privatization became an important instrument for the new competitive economy. Despite the growth and encouragement of the private sector and policy moves toward privatization, Malaysian economic policy is still geared toward the reinforcement of the state's apparatus for power and growth. Through that policy, there has been extension of its intervention *vis-à-vis* the private sector, as it extends its political control through further implementation of the pro-*Bumiputera* policies.

What has been the impact of these policy developments on the ethnic Chinese community? It is clear now that Malaysian economic development does not depend on ethnic capital alone. Malay and non-Malay businesses "swim and sink" together. When the NEP was implemented, many sceptics criticized the objective of the "expanded economic cake". Paradoxically, it can be argued that all the ethnic communities have contributed to the expansion of the economic cake, and in the process, everyone has benefited. If that were indeed the case, state policies protecting Malay businesses would then be irrelevant in the future — *Bumiputera* would no longer require state protection for their business ventures, and non-*Bumiputera* would not be prevented from participation in the national economy. In the past decade, the country witnessed the emergence of a Malay business elite community that could compete with the economically dominant Chinese community in Malaysia. The demise of the Ali-Baba ventures and the emergence of a genuine Malay-Chinese partnership in businesses is another trend that has widespread implications. The business opportunities in an emerging China are now available to both Chinese and Malay businesses. But do Chinese businessmen regard their *Bumiputera* counterparts as equals and do the ordinary *Bumiputera* feel economically secure enough for the pro-Malay government to drop all discriminatory programmes? This is a political question that Malaysians themselves will still have to answer.

References

Associated Chinese Chambers of Commerce and Industry of Malaysia (ACCCIM). 2000. *The Associated Chinese Chambers of Commerce and Industry of Malaysia (ACCCIM) Survey Report on Economic Recovery in Malaysia for the First Half of the Year 2000*. Kuala Lumpur.

Chin, Yee Whah. 2004. "Ethnicity and the Transformation of the Ali Baba Partnership in the Chinese Business Culture in Malaysia". In *The Challenge of Ethnicity*, edited by Cheah Boon Kheng (Singapore: Marshall Cavendish Academic).

Gomez, Edmund Terence. 1999. *Chinese Business in Malaysia: Accumulation, Ascendance, Accommodation* (Richmond: Curzon).

_____. 2003. "Corporate Malaysia under Mahathir: Where Have All the Capitalists Gone?" *Aliran Monthly*, no. 10.

Hara Fujio. 1991. "Malaysia's New Economic Policy and the Chinese Business Community". *The Developing Economies* 29, no. 4 (December): 350–70.

Heng Pek Koon. 1992. "The Chinese Business Elite of Malaysia". In *Southeast Asian Capitalists*, edited by Ruth McVey (Ithaca, New York: Cornell University Press).

_____. 1997. "The New Economic Policy and the Chinese Community in Peninsular Malaysia", *The Developing Economies* XXXV, no. 3 (September): 262–92.

Ho Khai Leong. 1988. *The New Economic Policy and the Bumiputera State in Peninsular Malaysia*, Ph.D. Dissertation, Ohio State University.

_____. 1992*a*. "The Dynamics of Policy-making in Malaysia: The Formulation of the New Economic Policy and the National Development Policy". *The Asian Journal of Public Administration* 14, no. 2, pp. 204–27.

_____. 1992*b*. "Aggrandizement of the Prime Minister's Power. The Transformation of the Office of the Prime Minister in Malaysia",

Internationales Asienforum [International Quarterly for Asian Studies], 23, no. 3–4, pp. 227–43.

_____. 1999. "Politics and Institutions in Economic Policy Implementation in Malaysia". In Fred Lazin (ed.), *The Politics of Policy Implementation in the Developing Nations* (Connecticut: AEI Press).

_____. 2002. "Reinventing the Bureaucracy? Malaysia's New Administrative Reforms Initiatives". *The Journal of Comparative Asian Development* 1, no. 1 (Spring): 87–104.

Jesudason, J. 1989. *Ethnicity and the Economy: The State, Chinese Business, and Multinationals in Malaysia* (Singapore: Oxford University Press).

Jomo, K.S. 1997. "A Specific Idiom of Chinese Capitalism in Southeast Asia. Sino-Malaysian Capital Accumulation in the Face of State Hostility". In *Essential Outsiders. Chinese and Jews in the Modern Transformation of Southeast Asia and Central Europe*, edited by Daniel Chirot and Anthony Reid (Seattle and London: University of Washington Press).

Lee Kam Hing and Lee Poh Ping. 2003. "Malaysian Chinese Business: Who Survived the Crisis?", *Kyoto Review of Southeast Asia*, no. 3 (October).

Malaysia. 1971. *Second Malaysia Plan, 1971–1975* (Kuala Lumpur: Government Press).

Malaysia. 1986. *Fifth Malaysia Plan, 1986–1990* (Kuala Lumpur: Government Press).

Tan, Eugene Kheng-Boon. 2000. "Success Amidst Prejudice: Guanxi Networks in Chinese Businesses in Indonesia and Malaysia". *Journal of Asian Business* 16, no. 1.

Yasuda Nobuyuki. 1991. "Malaysia's New Economic Policy and the Industrial Co-ordination Act". *The Developing Economies* 29, no. 4 (December): 330–49.

8

Malaysian Chinese Businesses in an Era of Globalization

Leong Kai Hin

1. INTRODUCTION

People often see globalization as the formation of a global village. The advent of information and communication technology (ICT) has shortened the distance between different parts of the world. We have closer contact and speedier flows of information, enabling the creation of a global civilization, with freer trade, freer flows of people, of capital and of technology. IMF defines globalization as "the growing economic interdependence of countries worldwide through increasing volume and variety of cross-border transactions in goods and services, freer international capital flows, and more rapid and widespread diffusion of technology".

The recognition of comparative advantages conferred to each country leads to increasing specialization of nations in exports, and pressure to trade liberalization, such as ending protective tariff and other barriers to trade.

In the nineteenth century, trade liberalization was facilitated by adoption of the gold standard along with the growth of industrialization. Globalization has been disrupted since World War I. In the era since World War II, globalization has been driven by trade negotiation rounds, which led to a series of agreements to liberalize trade. The Uruguay Round led to a treaty to create the World Trade Organization (WTO) to mediate trade disputes. Other bilateral trade agreements and regional trade treaty such as the ASEAN Free Trade Area has also been signed in pursuit of the goal of reducing tariffs and barriers in trade.

Since World War II, globalization has manifested itself through the reduction of trade barriers, increase in international trade and foreign direct investments besides increase in international cultural exchanges, international travel and tourism and immigration.

In this era of information and communication technology, globalization is here to stay. The advent of information and communication technology such as Internet enables vast amount of information to be processed and transmitted speedily through an e-commerce portal. Producers can access to global sources of inputs and screen for the most cost-effective producers of such inputs. Thus, the components of a product can be sourced from several different countries. The producer just has to integrate these inputs to produce his final products for his consumers. Not only can the producers take advantage of the ICT, consumers can also purchase through an e-commerce network. Thus in this era, competition becomes global. A firm will not be able to survive the competition if it is not globally competitive.

Globalization brings both advantages and disadvantages. To a nation, globalization increases competition which makes the firm more innovative in order to adapt to the changes and compete in the market. Globalization eliminates the middlemen and the firm can directly source for the most efficient suppliers. This will cut down the cost of production. The reduction in the cost of production coupled with the global competition will benefit the consumers who will be able to enjoy cheaper goods.

The disadvantages of globalization are that a firm might not be able to survive the global competition. The cheaper imported goods will kill the domestic industry. This will bring about problems of unemployment and current account deficit to the affected country. The import of cheap shoes and garments from China into the Southeast Asian countries is an example. The domestic industry could be wiped out by such an impact.

Malaysia is an open economy, with international trade constituting 200 per cent of its GDP. The major trade partners of Malaysia are Singapore, Japan and the United States. These countries are also the major contributors of FDI to Malaysia.

Malaysia is a member of the ASEAN FTA. This free trade area has a population of 500 million and a total GDP of US$683,891 million in 2003. The intra-trade among the ten member countries has been increasing significantly. The rise of China in the recent decades has also had an impact on this region. We have seen increasing trades between China and Malaysia. In 1999, the trade between China and Malaysia was only US$5.2 billion. In 2003, it reached US$20.1 billion. It is an increase of about four times. The full implementation of the Ten+1 (ASEAN + China) Free Trade Area in 2010 will produce a market with a population of 1.8 billion.

Malaysia is the chair country of the NAN (Non-Alignment Nations) organization and the OIC (Organization of Islamic Countries). Malaysia has a good relationship with the developing and the Islamic countries. This relationship provides a good opportunity for the country to trade with these countries. With its well-known racial harmony and its political stability, together with its currency peg to the U.S. dollar, Malaysia was able to have 6 per cent growth in 2004. It has surplus in its current account and continuous increase in its foreign reserves. Its foreign reserve is sufficient to support 8.5 months of imports.

The Malaysia Chinese businesses in Malaysia have been playing important roles in the economy, especially in the small and medium manufacturing industries and the retailing and wholesale industries. There are also large Malaysia Chinese corporations such as the Genting Group in the entertainment and hotel industries, IOI Group in the plantation industry and the Public Bank and Hong Leong Bank in the banking industry.

2. OBJECTIVES AND METHODOLOGY

This chapter intends to study the impact of globalization on the Malaysian Chinese businesses and the strategies adopted by them to face such challenges. The impact could be measured by looking at their financial performance over this period of globalization. Their reaction to the phenomenon of globalization could be studied by looking at their involvement in global business. Since there are both big tycoons and small and medium firms among the Chinese businesses, it is necessary to study both these groups of Chinese businesses.

For the group of big Chinese tycoons, a sample of six prominent tycoons is selected. The global perspective and performance of the conglomerates of these six tycoons will be studied. For the small and medium industries, the most badly affected industries and the industry that benefited most will be studied. The shoes and garment industries have been selected for it is well known that they are the most badly affected industries. For the industry that benefited the most, the rubber glove industry has been selected for its outstanding performance.

The data are collected from the company websites, company annual reports, magazines and newspaper.

3. THE IMPACT ON THE CHINESE TYCOONS

The table below lists the six Chinese tycoons selected and their conglomerates.

TABLE 8.1
Six Selected Chinese Tycoons and their Conglomerates

Tycoon	Group	Estimated Wealth
Tan Seri Quek Leng Chan	Hong Leong Group	RM8.17 billion
Tan Seri Lee Shin Cheng	IOI Corporation Bhd	RM3.5 billion
Tan Seri Lim Goh Tong	Genting Bhd	RM6.89 billion
Tan Seri Teh Hong Piow	Public Bank Bhd	RM3.62 billion
Tan Seri William Cheng	Lion Group	NA
Tan Seri Yeoh Tiong Lay	YTL Corporation Bhd	RM3.13 billion

3.1 Hong Leong Group

Hong Leong Group comprises fourteen listed companies in various stock exchanges around the world. Its total market capitalization was US$12 billion in 2004. Hong Leong's business focuses in three main core business activities — manufacturing and distribution, financial services, and property and development industries.

MANUFACTURING AND DISTRIBUTION SECTOR

In the manufacturing and distribution sector, Hong Leong's listed companies are Hong Leong Industries Berhad, Malaysian Pacific Industries Berhad, Hume Industries Berhad, OYL Industries Berhad and Narra Industries. Their operations span the globe and the products are represented and distributed by a worldwide network of branches, appointed distributors and agents.

Hong Leong Industries Berhad is principally an investment holding company for the companies in this sector. Activities of its subsidiaries include the manufacture, testing and sale of integrated circuits, semiconductor devices, electronic components and lead frames, manufacture, and assembly of motorcycles, electric scooters and related parts and products, distribution of motorcycles and motorcycle components, manufacture and sale of ceramic tiles, manufacture and sale of polypropylene and polyethylene products, duplex board boxes and flexible packaging products.

The manufacturing and distribution activities can be divided into the following segments:

(a) Heating, Ventilation, Air-conditioning and Refrigeration
OYL Industries Berhad owns AAF-McQuay in the United States and
J&E Hall in the United Kingdom.

(b) Semiconductor Assembly and Testing
Malaysian Pacific Industries Berhad is one of the top six
semiconductor sub-contracting assembly operators in the world. It
owns Carsem in Suzhou, China.

(c) Motorcycle Manufacturing, Assembly and Distribution
Hong Leong distributes Yamaha motorcycle and it owns a German
motorcycle brand "MZ".

(d) Building Materials
Hong Leong group manufactures and distributes a diverse range of
building materials such as floor and wall tiles, fibre- and cement-
based particleboard products, roofing tiles, steel products, and medium
density fibreboard products.

(e) Newsprint
Hong Leong's Malaysian Newsprint Industries produces newsprint.

(f) Furniture
Hume Furniture Industries manufactures and exports furniture to the
United States.

TABLE 8.2
Financial Performance of Hong Leong Industries Berhad, 2002–04

	2004 RM'000	2003 RM'000	2002 RM'000
Revenue	2,438,572	2,044,420	1,950,268
Profit after tax	199,249	58,117	(80,822)
Basic Earnings per share (Sen)	45.95	0.28	(36.21)
Dividends (Sen)	6.25	2.50	14.70

Source: Company's annual reports.

FINANCIAL SERVICES

Hong Leong Credit Berhad is the investment holding company for the firms in this sector. Its subsidiaries are Hong Leong Bank Berhad, Hong Leong Assurance Berhad and HLG Capital Berhad. Hong Leong Bank Berhad is one of the ten anchor banks in Malaysia. It has 179 branches in Malaysia, and one branch each in Singapore and Hong Kong. Hong Leong Assurance Berhad is in the life and general insurance services. HLG Capital Berhad is involved in stocks and shares broking, agent and nominee for clients, corporate advisory services, fund management, unit trusts, share financing, futures and options broking.

PROPERTY AND DEVELOPMENT INDUSTRIES

Hong Leong Properties Berhad has significant interests in properties located in the United Kingdom, India, Malaysia, Singapore and China. In the U.K., its Thistle Hotel has 56 hotels in key U.K. locations and 24 in

TABLE 8.3
Financial Performance of Hong Leong Credit Berhad, 2002–04

	2004 RM'000	2003 RM'000	2002 RM'000
Revenue	2,539,628	2,460,978	2,554,698
Profit after Tax	546,000	563,416	553,120
Basic Earnings per Share (Sen)	37.3	36.0	37.9
Dividends per Share (Sen)	11.3	8.6	11.5

Source: Company's annual reports.

TABLE 8.4
Financial Performance of Hong Leong Properties Berhad, 2000–04

	2004 RM'000	2002 RM'000	2000 RM'000
Revenue	199.0	439.1	255.9
Profit Attributable to Shareholders	33.9	25.6	57.7
Net Earnings per Share (Sen)	4.8	3.7	(8.2)
Net Tangible Assets per Share	1.06	1.02	0.97

Source: Company's annual reports.

London. In Singapore, it has sold 20 residential projects yielding more than 6,800 apartments and homes. In China, it has property development projects in Shanghai and Beijing. Its Guoman Hotel and Resort Holdings Sdn. Bhd. own Guoman Hotel in Hanoi.

Hong Leong group has extended its manufacturing and distribution activities to the United States and United Kingdom to acquire more advanced technology and to gain entry into foreign markets. Its entry into China enables it to gain advantage from the cheap labour supply and the large market. Its property development in the United Kingdom, Singapore and China are successful and profitable. Its financial performance in all the segments is encouraging and shows good growth over the past five years.

3.2 The IOI Group

The IOI Group comprises three listed companies: IOI Corporation Berhad, IOI Properties Berhad and IOI Oleochemical Berhad. Its core businesses are in palm oil plantation, oleo chemicals, and property development.

IOI has acquired Loders Croklaan from Unilever to integrate forwards the downstream palm oil-based manufacturing capabilities into producing specialty oil and fats. Then Loders Croklaan further consolidated its position in the growing palm ingredients market by acquiring Soctek, a Malaysian palm oil specialties company. Loders Croklaan has announced the building of Europe's largest palm oil-processing plant in Rotterdam in the second half of 2004. This will position itself as a preferred supplier to its global customers and enable it to be more competitive in an evolving and challenging global market.

In 2004, the group has an operating profit of 1.16 billion *ringgit*, which shows a 33 per cent growth over the previous year on the back of good performances from all the three core business segments.

In Table 8.5, the 17.5 per cent growth of the plantation segment is due to higher crude palm oil prices and higher production volume contributed by recent acquisition of other plantations.

The 32 per cent growth in the property segment is due to improving economy and buoyant property market. The 50.8 per cent growth in the resource-based manufacturing is due to volume growth, improved cost efficiencies, raw material price hedging and improved results from specialty fats business unit.

IOI has expanded its business globally by acquiring Loders Croklaan, which will enable it to expand into the palm oil-based specialty oil and

TABLE 8.5
Growth of Operating Profit by Core Segments
of IOI Group, 2003–04

Core Segments	2003 Operating Profit (RM Million)	2004 Operating Profit (RM Million)	Growth (%)
Plantation	543.4	638.7	17.5
Property	255.2	336.8	31.8
Resource-based Manufacturing	123.5	186.2	50.8

Source: IOI Company website.

fats market in Europe. The 50.8 per cent operating profit growth of the firm in this segment indicates the gain of the firm from this globalization strategy.

3.3 Genting Group

The Genting Group comprises the following five listed companies: Genting Berhad (US$3.7 billion); Genting International PLC (US$0.33 billion); Resorts World Berhad (US$2.9 billion); Asiatic Development Berhad (US$0.35billion) and Star Cruises Limited (US$1.6 billion).[1] Its key business activities are in leisure and hospitality, power generation, plantation, properties, paper and packaging, and oil and gas.

During this era of globalization, Genting group has extended its business globally. In 2002, Star Cruises acquired Norwegian Cruises Lines and became the third largest cruise line operator in the world comprising a fleet of twenty cruise ships. Through Genting International, Genting expanded its casino business to Australia, Bahamas, Philippines, the United Kingdom, Egypt, Lebanon and South Africa. In 2004, Genting International acquired Maxims Casino Club, a top-end casino in London's West End. It has also extended into a joint venture with Stanley Leisure, the largest casino operator in the United Kingdom with 41 casinos and over 600 betting shops.

Table 8.6 shows that although there was a steep fall in the business in 2000, it recovered since 2001. This indicates that during this era of globalization, Genting has adopted an appropriate strategy to expand to foreign markets to sustain its growth.

TABLE 8.6
Financial Highlights of Genting Group

	1999	2000	2001	2002	2003
Profit before Taxation (RM'million)	1,521.4	(322.7)	1,034.6	1,559.6	1,562.3
Total Assets Employed (RM'million)	9,440.2	9,307.2	10,230.0	11,445.8	14,207.4
Basic Earnings per Share (Sen)	156.40	(34.96)	64.20	107.41	101.34
Tangible Assets per Share (RM)	8.26	7.68	8.18	9.12	10.00

Source: Genting Group website.

3.4 Public Bank Group

The group provides all banking and financing services that include commercial banking , hire purchase, merchant banking, credit cards, cash management services, leasing and factoring, stock-broking, sale of trust units and management of unit trust funds, and related financial services such as nominees and trustee services. The group also provides a wide range of Islamic banking products and services. As at 31 December 2003, the bank's market capitalization stood at 18.7 billion *ringgit*, representing a 70 per cent increase from 11.0 billion *ringgit* as at 31 December 2002.

The group has overseas presence in five Asian countries. It has branches in Hong Kong, Sri Lanka and Laos and subsidiaries in Hong Kong and Cambodia. In Vietnam, it has a joint venture bank. Its international operations contributed 248 million *ringgit* or 13 per cent of the group's pre-tax profit for 2004. Its Cambodian Public Bank Limited was voted "the Best Bank in Cambodia" for the fourth consecutive year in 2004. The group's profit before tax has increased from 1,415 million *ringgit* in 2003 to 1,848 million *ringgit* in 2004, that is, an increase of 30.6 per cent.

JCG is the investment holding company for all the overseas and offshore companies of the group. Table 8.7 shows that the group gains the most from JCG, with a tremendous growth of 89.8 per cent. This indicates how much the group gains from its globalization strategy.

TABLE 8.7
Profit before Tax by Company

	2004 (RM Million)	2003 (RM Million)	Growth (%)
Public Bank Berhad	1,512	1,111	36.1
JCG Holdings Ltd.	241	127	89.8
Public Mutual Berhad	65	55	18.2
PB Securities Sdn Bhd	32	26	23.0
Public Merchant Bank Berhad	15	14	7.1

Source: Company's website.

3.5 The Lion Group

The group's core activities comprise five manufacturing activities: Steel division, motor division, tyre division, computer anbd communication division, and pulp and paper and plantation division. The group is also involved in two service activities — retailing, distribution and trading division, and property and community development division. The group has operations in several countries.

(a) Steel Division: It has steel operations in Indonesia, Singapore and Malaysia. In 2004, the division had a total sales value of 8,505 million *ringgit*.

(b) Motor Division: Its countries of operation are China and Malaysia. In 2004, its total sales value was 14,889 million *ringgit*.

(c) Computer and Communications Division: This division has operations in China, Mexico, The Netherlands, Singapore, the United States and Malaysia. In 2004, its total sales value was 2,294 million *ringgit*.

(d) Pulp and Paper, and Plantation Division: This division has operation only in Malaysia. The main crops of the plantations are forest, oil palm and rubber. Its total sales value in 2004 was 922 million *ringgit*.

(e) Property and Community Development Division: It has operations in China, Hong Kong, Singapore and Malaysia. Its total gross development value was 11.8 billion *ringgit*.

(f) Retail and Trading Division: It has operations in China and Malaysia. In 2004, its department stores and super-centres contributed total sales revenue of 3,751 million *ringgit*. Its trading activities contributed a sales value of 254 million *ringgit*.

The group has operations in foreign countries, especially in China and Singapore. Due to its high debt, it was facing financial distress after the financial crisis. Lately, after its asset and financial restructuring, it has recovered and re-emerged. This large conglomerate has survived the financial crisis and has benefited from its early entry into the China market.

TABLE 8.8
The Financial Performance of Lion Group, 2000–04

	2004 (RM'000)	2002 (RM'000)	2000 (RM'000)
Revenue	2,445,442	1,205,105	525,852
Profit after Tax	55,118	(138,355)	(265,036)
Dividend per Share (Sen)	–	–	15.2
Net Tangible Assets per Share (Sen)	4.6	(267.6)	(113.7)
Earnings per Share (Sen)	4.7	(50.2)	(141.4)

Source: Company's website.

3.6 The YTL Group

The YTL group comprises the following listed companies: YTL Corporation Berhad, YTL Land & Development Berhad, YTL Cement Berhad, YTL Power International Berhad and YTL E-Solutions Berhad (Mesdaq Market). The YTL group's core businesses are in construction contracting, property development, cement manufacturing, power generation, water and sewerage services and IT and e-commerce initiatives.

YTL's power division owns 33.5 per cent stake in ElectraNet Private Limited, which owns and operates the electricity transmission network of South Australia under a 200-year concession. ElectraNet's transmission network provides electricity supplies to over 99 per cent of the state's population. YTL has acquired Wessex Water, which provides water services to 1.2 million customers and sewerage facilities to 2.5 million customers over an area of approximately 10,000 square kilometres in the southwest of England. Wessex Water's Regulatory Asset Base increased by 7.2 per cent to £1,580 million in the last regulatory year ended 31 March 2004, from £1,474 million in the previous year. YTL E-Solutions Berhad has one company in Singapore in its stable of incubates: Hipmobile Singapore Pte. Ltd.

YTL has expanded its power transmission business to Australia and its water and sewerage services to England. Table 8.9 shows that, over the years from 2000 to 2004, YTL has performed very well, with more than 100 per cent improvement in its revenues, and profit after tax. Its earnings per share have also increased by about 88 per cent.

The above study on the businesses of the six selected tycoons shows that, in this era of globalization, these tycoons have also ventured into the global markets. They have built up their core competitiveness in the home country. They acquire foreign firms for their technology and their market network. This in turn improves their competitiveness. An example is the acquisition of Loders Croklaan by the IOI Group.

TABLE 8.9
Financial Performance of YTL Group, 2000–04

	2004	2002	2000
Revenue (RM'000)	4,409,344	2,547,941	2,189,096
Profit after tax (RM'000)	1,012,410	588,163	551,160
Total Assets (RM'000)	26,546,010	21,774,569	10,117,436
Earnings per share (Sen)	48.31	25.06	25.69
Gross Dividend per Share (Sen)	16.00	15.00	10.00
Net Tangible Assets per Share (RM)	3.34	2.70	2.70

Source: YTL Group website.

4. THE CHINESE SMALL AND MEDIUM INDUSTRIES

For the Chinese small and medium industries, some industries benefit from the globalization while some are badly affected. Top Glove Berhad, which is a rubber glove manufacturer, is selected for illustration for its marvellous performance in the global market. The most badly affected industries are the shoes and garments industries.

4.1 The Industry that Benefited Most

Top Glove Berhad

Top Glove claims to be the largest natural rubber glove manufacturer in the world. It has eleven factories, with two in Thailand, one in China, while the rest are located in Malaysia. It has 164 production lines (as at 1 April 2005). Its total capacity can produce 13.38 billion pieces of rubber gloves and it is running at 85–90 per cent utilization rate. With its current capacity, Top Glove accounts for 13.4 per cent of the global market share. Currently, its products are exported to 160 countries. Its

FIGURE 8.1
Top Glove's Growth between 2003 and 2004
Year-to-Year Comparison (12 months)

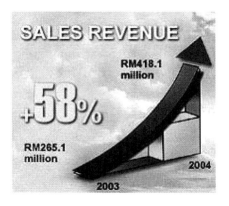

Source: Company's website.

plan is to increase to fourteen factories by December 2006, with 260 production lines, producing 24 billion pieces of gloves for exporting to 175 countries. Top Glove aims to increase its current market share to 24 per cent by December 2007.

Table 8.10 shows that over the nine-year period from 1996 to 2004, the sales of the company have increased from 29.1 million *ringgit* to 418 million *ringgit*, showing a growth of 13.4 times.

In 2004, the firm achieved more than 50 per cent annual growth in its sales revenue, net profit and earnings per share. The global markets have given the company performance a big boost. In fact, about 70 per cent of the production of the firm is original equipment manufacturing (OEM) for most famous brands in the world. This is an example of a Chinese small and medium firm growing to be a multi-million giant in the manufacturing industry in this era of globalization.

TABLE 8.10
Sales Turnover of Top Glove, 1996–2005 (RM Million)

	1996	1997	1998	1999	2000	2001	2002	2003	2004	2005*
Sales Turnover	29.1	35.5	48.5	70.2	103.2	138.9	181	266	418	590

* Estimate
Source: Company's website.

4.2 The Most Badly Affected Industries

Malaysia has been losing its competitive edge in industries that are labour intensive such as the shoes and garments industries. Malaysia now has to depend so much on foreign labour that officially it has about 1.5 million foreign workers in the country, mostly from Indonesia and Pakistan. These foreign workers have also created social problems.

The emergence of China and its entry into the WTO has enabled it to embark onto the globalization bandwagon. It has abundant supply of cheap labour which has given China a competitive edge in the labour-intensive industries. The Malaysian market has been flushed with imports of cheap shoes and garments from China, making a very big impact on the shoes and garments industries in Malaysia. Many of them found that their production cost is higher than the selling price of the imported goods. Take one example. Bata is a household shoe brand in Malaysia. It used to employ more than a thousand workers in its factory to produce canvas shoes for schoolchildren and has also subcontracted its shoe production to the small shoe cottage industry around its factory in Klang. At one time, a small shoe cottage industry flourished in Klang. This scenario has now disappeared; the same thing happened to the garment industries too. Many of them find that they are no more competitive in the market.

Bata has changed its strategy and has transformed itself into a trading company. It does not produce most of the shoes now as it contracts its production to countries with cheap labour such as China and Vietnam. Most of Malaysia's Chinese firms in these industries resort to this strategy, although they still do the designing but outsource the production to the manufacturing firms in China or other low labour cost countries.

Some firms have joint ventures and open their own factories in China. This strategy sometimes does not work due to both management and partnership problems. A shoe components manufacturer opened ten factories in China within one year. However, due to some management problem, he lost about ten million *ringgit* in the end. He has since sold all these factories and resorted to outsourcing. By doing this, he does not have to worry about management problems and can now choose to buy from the cheapest suppliers.

Indeed, the Chinese small and medium industries have adapted to the challenge and adopted changes to face the impact of globalization. They either moved their factories to countries with lower production cost or outsourced their production. In fact, the falling prices of shoes and garments have benefited the consumers. Recently due to the increasing price of petroleum, there is an upward trend in inflation. The June 2005 inflation was a record high of 3.2 per cent. All the components of the consumer price index show an upward trend except for shoes and garments, which shows a negative trend of −1.1 per cent.

5. CONCLUSION

This study shows that the Chinese tycoons have actually taken full advantage of the opportunity arising from globalization. They have acquired foreign firms or entered joint ventures with foreign firms to improve their technology or gain access into the global market network. Their groups show sustainable growth.

For the Chinese small and medium industries, not all are equally lucky. Some are badly hit, such as the shoes and garments industry. However, they have adapted to the changes and adopted a strategy to stand on their feet again. They have either moved their factories to countries that have lower cost of production, or have outsourced their production. They found that outsourcing is a better strategy than relocation. However, some have become traders and have no more headaches in production. The lucky one benefits from globalization. Like the tycoons, they take full advantage of the opportunities arising from globalization. Their firms flourish and achieve tremendous growth.

Note

[1]   The figures in brackets refer to the market capitalization of the companies in 2004.

References

1.   Companies' annual reports of various years.
2.   Companies' websites.
3.   <http://www.klse.com.my/>.

9

China, the "Chinese Economy" and the Ethnic Chinese in the Philippines

Teresita Ang See
Go Bon Juan

1. INTRODUCTION

In the last decade, much has been written about globalization, the rise of China as an economic power, the impact of China's entry into World Trade Organization (WTO), the Asian Century, Southeast Asia's ethnic Chinese economy, and related topics. Conferences, workshops, and seminars on the topic have been convened in all parts of the globe. This highlights the growing interest and concern over China and its entry into the big league of global powers. This volume examines these three issues that impact on one another — globalization, the rise of China as an economic power, and the ethnic Chinese economy in Southeast Asia.

As a caveat, just like many academics, especially from China and Hong Kong who have explored and written about this topic, the chapter contributors are neither economists nor business practitioners. At best, the authors are participant-observers who have closely monitored and have been deeply involved in concerns and issues affecting China and the Chinese-Filipino community in mainstream Philippine society. It is on these grounds that this chapter is presented. Past research and studies on the topic tend to draw general conclusions based on meagre data, which have led to greater misconceptions and muddling of the issues and have been a drawback towards a better understanding of the issue. Edmund Terence Gomez and Michael Hsiao Hsin-Huang organized a seminar workshop in 1997 at the Academia Sinica in Taipei and published *Chinese Business in South-East Asia* (Gomez and Hsiao 2001, Preface, pp. 1–4) also as an attempt to understand the Southeast Asian situation better.

Gomez pointed out that the presumption that ethnic Chinese businessmen in Southeast Asia will use their racial and cultural ties and influence with China to pour in huge "overseas Chinese capital" that will have tremendous impact on the global economy in the twenty-first century is not supported by empirical data (Gomez and Hsiao 2001). Henry Yeung and Kris Olds' book, *Globalization of Chinese Business Firms*, likewise contains articles that provoke critical thinking on "Chinese capitalism", "Chinese business", and "internationalization of ethnic Chinese-owned enterprises", (Yeung and Olds 2000) as well as some theoretical perspectives on the topic.[1] There are many more recent publications and discourses on this topic and through this workshop, different perspectives and insights will hopefully give rise to a better and more critical understanding of the issues at hand. (Chan 2000, pp. 234–60).

2. ETHNIC CHINESE ECONOMY?

In this connection, at the outset, the use of the term "ethnic Chinese economy and business" especially as it refers to Southeast Asia must be put into perspective. It is probably only in Singapore that the use of the term "Chinese economy" can be valid. In all other Southeast Asian countries, and most particularly in the Philippines, an "ethnic Chinese economy" does not and cannot exist. The ethnic Chinese-owned businesses, enterprises, and industries cannot be isolated exclusively as "Chinese". In the Philippines particularly, they can be sustained and be viable only as part and parcel of the Philippine domestic economy.

On top of the non-existent "ethnic Chinese economy", the much-vaunted "overseas Chinese network" or *huaren* global network and its supposed impact on the global economy is likewise an exaggeration. The so-called *huaren* global network is a heterogeneous, non-cohesive and non-collective aggrupation of ethnic groups, each with their own interests to protect. The presumption that a powerful *huaren* economic force exists is stretching reality too far. Citing the case of the Chinese in the Philippines, this chapter also challenges this notion on the existence of the so-called "overseas Chinese capital" and "overseas Chinese networks" that are supposed to wield enormous influence or impact on the global economy. The chapter will discuss the role and impact of the presence of an economically dynamic Chinese-Filipino business community *vis-à-vis* the Philippines' own shift in terms of its economic relations with China and *vis-à-vis* China's rise to economic power. However, the participation of these Chinese-Filipino businessmen in China's economy has all been on individual initiatives and not as a collective community with an organized effort to take a bite out of China's economic pie. In the same vein, rather than as a unified force, the participation of other Southeast Asian ethnic Chinese communities in the newly opened Chinese economy are distinct and disparate efforts.

This chapter raises some of the limitations that have led to erroneous conclusions to some of the problems earlier written about or presented in relation to this issue. In fact, more questions may be raised than it can answer but it is hoped that this book will be read with an open mind to mutually explore and analyse the problems so that a greater understanding of the issue can be arrived at. Some of the questions raised at the outset are:

1. How big a capital lies in the hands of the Southeast Asian Chinese? How much of this capital is tied up in their own businesses? How much is the surplus capital that can be invested in China?
2. Some writers, who use the term "overseas Chinese capital" that flows into China, often include capital from Hong Kong and Taiwan. What really is the actual percentage of the foreign direct investments into China that comes from the ethnic Chinese in Southeast Asia?
3. Of the investments of the Southeast Asian Chinese into China, how much really come from their own money? How much of that capital come from loans from China's banks and accommodations from Chinese officials?
4. How big a percentage is the ethnic Chinese share in the overall investments of their country into China? For example, out of the estimated 200,000 ethnic Chinese-owned businesses in the Philippines, how many have investments in China? Is it significant enough to be called Chinese capital or is it more prudent to say investments of Lucio Tan, John Gokongwei, Henry Sy, Carlos Chan, Tony Tan Caktiong, and not ethnic Chinese investment?
5. Corollary to the above question, how many of these businessmen went into China because of their affinal and cultural ties? How many invested in their own hometowns and villages? How many invested elsewhere? How many invested because of privileges and incentives offered by the special economic zones or Chinese officials?
6. What is the effect of the Southeast Asian Chinese capital in the overall performance of China's economy? Is the inflow big enough as to validate the claim that "overseas Chinese capital" will have an enormous impact in the twenty-first century global economy?

The search for references on Southeast Asian Chinese economy and business in order to answer the questions above has largely been futile. The figures found do not satisfactorily answer the questions raised. In short, empirical data is simply too limited to conclude with certainty that there really exist a Southeast Asian Chinese capital that is being poured into China, much less is the so-called Chinese capital having an enormous impact on the global twenty-first century economy.

3. CHINESE-FILIPINO BUSINESS MAGNATES

Most of the Chinese Filipino-owned businesses in the Philippines are SMEs (small- and medium-scale enterprises). Few have truly become conglomerates in terms of overseas or global expansion. The "taipans" or the Chinese-Filipino magnates in the Philippines, to a certain extent, fit into the globalized operations. But none of these companies can compare to the operations of the transnational companies in the West or in developed countries. Below is a brief summary of the business concerns of the five acknowledged leading Tsinoy (colloquial term for Chinese Filipino) magnates to give an idea of the extent of their operations (see Table 9.1).

4. CHINESE-FILIPINO INVESTMENTS IN CHINA

4.1 The Less Successful Cases

All the prominent Tsinoy business leaders mentioned in Table 9.1 are influential and well connected politically, both in the Philippines and in China. They have poured millions of dollars of investments into China. However, they are finding out it is not at all easy to make money there. Most of the interviews the author conducted with those who have done business in China revealed that there are simply too few success stories so far. Some of the investors, in fact, regretted to find out that their cultural and familial ties to the homeland could even be a drawback rather than an advantage. Some of those who went in early, like in real estate development, especially in Xiamen or in Fujian, made a handsome profit. Unfortunately, later expansion and the real estate development glut led to big losses in the end.

John Gokongwei's Universal Robina Corporation, JG Summit's food arm, established a manufacturing plant in Guangzhou early 2000 to produce snacks and wafers. But up to now, Lance, son and heir of John Gokongwei, admits operations have not been profitable. "We made a

TABLE 9.1
Chinese-Filipino Conglomerates

Main Companies	Banking and Financial Businesses	Other Investments/Joint Ventures
Lucio Tan 陳永栽 (b1934, Fujian province) — Lucio Tan Group of Companies		
Fortune Tobacco Corp., Philippine Airlines, Century Park Hotel, Formost Farms Inc., Asia Brewery Inc., Tanduay Distillers Inc., Himmel Industries Inc.	Allied Banking Corp. (formerly General Bank), Philippine National Bank	Oceanic Bank (California and Guam), Eastern Pacific Bank and Mercury Drug (Canada), Melanesian Tobacco Pty. Ltd., PNG Atlas Steel (Papua New Guinea), Micronesia Shopping Center and Bakery Monopoly (Guam), Allied Capital Resources Ltd. (Hong Kong), Several breweries and cigarette factories in the People's Republic of China, Dynamic Holdings Limited (Hong Kong), Lotte Philippines, Landcom Realty Corp., Manufacturing Services and Trade Corp., Lucky Travel Corp., Charter House; Grandspan Development Corp.
George Ty 鄭少堅 (b1933, Hong Kong) — Metrobank Group of Companies		
Toyota Motor Philippines Corp., Thomas Cook Phils. Inc., Systematic Technology Services Inc., Federaland	Metropolitan Bank and Trust Co., Philippine AXA Life, Philippine Axa Life Insurance Corp., Unibancard Corp., Philippine Savings Bank, First Metro Investment Corp., Sumigin Metro Investment Corp., Philippine Charter Insurance Corp., Orix Metro Leasing and Finance	International Bank of California (LA), First Metro International Investment Co. Inc. (HK), MB Remittance Centre Ltd., Asia Money Link Corp., Asialink (New York), Metrobank branch in Shanghai, Metrobank branches in Taipei, Tainan, Taichung and Kaoshung
Henry Sy 施至成 (b1924, Xiamen) — SM Group of Companies		
SM Investments Corporation SM Prime Holdings Inc. Shoemart Inc. SM Department Stores SM Development Corp. Highlands Prime, Inc.	Banco de Oro Universal Bank, China Banking Corp., Equitable PCI Bank, General Pilipinas Holdings Inc.	Supervalue Inc., Super Shopping Market Inc., Hardware Workshop Inc., Homeworld Shopping Corp., International Toy World Inc., Ace Hardware Philippines Inc., Star Appliance Center Inc., Watsons Personal Care Stores (Phils) Inc., Pilipinas Makro Inc., Intercontinental Development Corp., SM Foundation Inc.

continued on next page

TABLE 9.1 — *continued*

Main Companies	Banking and Financial Businesses	Other Investments/Joint Ventures
John Gokongwei 吴亦辉 (b1926, Fujian province) — JG Summit Holdings, Inc.		
Universal Robina Corporation, Robinsons Land Corporation, Robinsons Department Store, Robinsons Supermarket Corp., JG Summit Petrochemicals Corp., Cebu Air Inc., Digitel Telecommunications Phils. Inc., Sun Cellular	Robinsons Savings Bank and JG Summit Capital Markets Corp., Unicorn Insurance Brokers Corp., JG Summit Capital Services Corp., Express Holdings Inc.	Premier Printing Co. Inc., Terai Industrial Corp., Hello Snacks Food Corp., Litton Mills Inc., Westpoint Mills Industrial Corp., Big R Supercenter, Robinsons Movieworld, Robinsons Homes Inc., Handyman/Do it Best, Summit Publishing Co., Apo Cement Corp., Trion Homes Development Corp.
Alfonso Yuchengco 杨应琳 (b1923, Manila) — Yuchengco Group of Companies		
Rizal Commercial Banking Corporation and Malayan Insurance Co. Inc.	Rizal Commercial Banking Corp., RCBC Bankard Inc., RCBC Forex Brokers Corp., RCBC Capital Corp., RCBC Savings Bank, RCBC Securities Co. Inc., RCBC Realty Inc., Malayan Reinsurance Corp., The First Nationwide Assurance Corp., Malayan Insurance Co. Inc., Great Pacific Life Assurance Corp., Pacific Plans Inc., Grepaland Inc., First Malayan Leasing and Finance Corp., House of Investments Inc., GPL Holdings Inc., Mico Equities Inc.	RCBC International Finance, Ltd. (HK), RCBC California International Ltd. (US), RCBC Telemoney Europe (Italy), Malayan Insurance Co. Ltd. (HK), Malayan Insurance Co. Ltd. (UK), Malayan International Insurance Corp. Ltd., Honda Cars—Quezon City, Kalookan, Manila, Isuzu Manila. Inc., EEI Corp., Philrock Inc., Landev Corp., iPeople, Inc., Mapua Institute of Technology, E.T. Yuchengco Inc., Y Realty Corp., Pan Malayan Travel and Tours Inc., Mona Lisa Development Corp., Seafront Resources Corp., Yuchengco Center for East Asia, RCBC Plaza Satellite Properties Estate Corp.

couple of mistakes going in. We hired managers from Hong Kong who had no familiarity with our product range and processes", Lance says in a recent magazine interview. The young Gokongwei says his experience has taught him that China is a high-involvement market. "You cannot run it by remote control. You don't go into China unless you're willing to send in the best people and you have the time." Lance now goes there once a month and spent some time there early this year to oversee the start of operations of their new plant in Shanghai. The plant will produce mainly candies, particularly their Maxx's brand (Torrijos 2002).

Lucio Tan recently bought a new brewery in Xiamen, reportedly for a very low price, but the purchase is more for the purpose of acquiring the prime land where the brewery stands rather than running the brewery itself. Tan, through Asia Brewery, has about ten breweries across China, but they are ready-made factories that continue manufacturing the local Chinese brands of beer. Tan has opened banks in Xiamen and Chongqing and also ventured into cigarette manufacturing which is his principal business in the Philippines. In aggregate, Tan reportedly has not broken even on them and has sold off some of the concerns due to losses. The success of businessman like Carlos Chan in cosmopolitan Shanghai seems to entice Lucio Tan who recently purchased a 25,000 square metre piece of land in the new district of Pudong to build a hotel and department store.

Henry Sy's first venture into China, the Xiamen Plaza Hotel, incurred huge losses before it was finally sold off. Despite the fact that he hired the Manila Hotel to run the Xiamen Plaza, he found that proxy operations just would not work. At one point, Sy had to send Filipino engineers and managers to China to oversee the construction and supervise the Chinese workers who gave them a hard time and would not follow instructions, causing losses due to delays. He also found out that the practice of malling in China is different from the Philippines. In Jinjiang, the huge ShoeMart (SM) structure has been a white elephant for more than a decade. Henry Sy discovered that retailing in China is restricted and is quite different from the Philippines. Thus, though the building carries the name SM, the department store never opened in the mall and thus was unable to attract other lessors to occupy the space. Today, because of the big hall, the structure is now used merely for exhibitions. Shishi, Quanzhou and Jinjiang cities are known for their brand-name goods — shoes, handbags, luggage, ready-to-wear, and others that often have trade fairs and fashion shows that make use of the convenient location of Sy's SM. His second mall in Xiamen had to tie up with the

Taiwanese Lai Ya retail group, which already existed and thus was able to follow the required government regulations. It is now called the SM-Laiya, and has recently re-opened.

George Ty and Lucio Tan both put up banking and finance operations in China, and Alfonso Yuchengco set up his insurance operations there. The three taipans found out that China's liberalization is not moving all that fast for banking, finance and insurance. Alfonso Yuchengco's Malayan group has set up a unit in China but cannot operate fully until it has been there for at least seven years. George Ty has invested in real estate in China. His Metropolitan Bank and Trust Co. of the Philippines opened its branch in Pudong financial district in Shanghai and is set to open Metrobank in Beijing and Xiamen soon. Both banks place key focus on trade financing. Lucio Tan was in fact outbid by George Ty in putting up the first full banking in China although Tan was ahead in putting up the Bank Center in Xiamen. In both cases, however, the main concern is that earlier, they could not do local currency lending because at that time, the Chinese Government has not fully opened up the financial structures and foreign exchange systems. It was only recently that they were allowed to do so (Torrijos 2002).

An overview of the business concerns of these five taipans will show that whether in the Philippines or abroad, there is no indication that the prominent Tsinoy businessmen established business linkages in China on the basis of common ethnic ties. Most joint ventures they have set up involve non-Chinese multinationals, usually forged because the latter provided the needed capital and technological expertise (Cariño 2001, pp. 101–23). In fact, except for Lucio Tan, none of the other four (Gokongwei, Sy, Ty, and Yuchengco) are active members of any of the local organizations like the Federation of Filipino-Chinese Chambers of Commerce or the family and hometown associations, except as honorary members, an unsolicited position given to them by these organizations. Sy and Gokongwei are ardent rivals in the supermalls business while Ty and Yuchengco are rivals in the insurance business. All five were rivals in banking and finance until Gokongwei sold his shares in the Far East Bank and Philippine Commercial and Industrial Bank.

4.2 The More Successful Cases

Antonio Tan Caktiong was chosen as the World Entrepreneur for 2004 by Ernst and Young. His Jollibee Foods Corporation commands 65 per cent of the fast food stores in the Philippines, and has outstripped even the multinational fast food corporations like McDonald's and Kentucky Fried Chicken. A survey undertaken by the regional magazine Asia, Inc. (June 1997), shows that of the top fifty most competitive businesses in Asia, the only Philippine business that made it into the list was Jollibee Foods Corp. (Gomez and Hsiao 2001, p. 27). However, Tan Caktiong's franchisee closed its branch in Xiamen because of labour problems and pilferage. Likewise, many of the Chinese-Filipino businessmen there learned that work ethics in China does not go beyond the pay check and the hard-working ethic of the old immigrant Chinese can nowhere be found. In fact, many soon discovered that at Jollibee in the Philippines, even waiters are more willing to just get the mop and wipe spilled drinks without having to call their attention several times to do it, unlike in China.

Jollibee is present in countries where there are big Filipino communities. It has stores abroad: Jollibee (United States) 9, Jollibee (Hong Kong) 2, Jollibee (other Asian countries) 12, Chowking (United States) 8. Tan Caktiong recently bought Yonghe King (China), which has an eighty-nine-store network nationwide. Yonghe King is China's leading fast food chain and Tan made a good move to reposition his fast food chain by buying the prime locations of the Yong He stores. He was also able to fast track the stringent government requirements for the retail food trade by buying ready-made stores and capitalizing thus on the locations. Not content with bringing Jollibee to foreign shores, Tan Caktiong also acquired other leading fast food outlets like Chow King, Delifrance, and Greenwich. With the acquisition of Yonghe King in China, Jollibee is well on its way to becoming the dominant food service company in the country (De la Cruz 11, no. 9, 2004).

Criselda Yabes in Shanghai wrote recently about the first ethnic Chinese Filipino to make a name for himself in Shanghai. Carlos Chan's Liwayway Food Industries, known by the brand it sells, Oishi (Japanese for "delicious") prawn cracker, is the most successful venture in China. The ubiquitous Oishi products have found a solid niche, a 15 per cent market share in China in the snacks food market, especially in Shanghai. Chan was able to capitalize on the reputation of cosmopolitan and discriminating tastes of Shanghai. Producing Oishi in Shanghai definitely beats the original in the Philippines. Operations in Shanghai started in September 1993. Now, more than ten years later, Liwayway has three factories in Shanghai, seven in other parts of China, and two more set to open later this year in Jiangxi and Hubei. The seven factories outside Shanghai are in Harbin, Suzhou, Ningbo, Xuzhou, Changsha, Zhengzou, and Kunming. Harbin is the capital of Heilongjiang province, next to Russia in the northeast region of China. In winter, the temperature can drop to a low of –40 degree Celsius (Yabes 2005, pp. 19–21).

The company has also expanded to Vietnam and Myanmar, Thailand and Indonesia. Moreover, Liwayway exports its snacks to Japan and Korea. Chan also bought a chain store selling traditional Chinese food, Honai foods, but with licence to sell cigarettes and hard drinks. This again is a brilliant positioning to acquire stores with a good location. Oishi itself maintains a dormitory for Filipino managers and personnel, and Chan's son, Larry, himself manages the operations there.

On the other hand, Carlos Chan's brother, Ben Chan, has also brought his trademark, Bench, abroad. In 2002, Ben Chan opened an outlet in mall magnate Henry Sy's Micronesia Mall in Guam, and the same year, Ben's Bench Body store carrying his innerwear, cosmetics, and perfumes at the SM mall in the Coastal City of Xiamen, in South China, on Sy's personal invitation. In 2003, his success in Xiamen led Ben to open a second outlet at the World Trade Center in the same city, and another at the SuperBrand Mall in Shanghai. Also in November 2004, he opened Bench Body's seventh outlet at the Ascendas Mall in Shanghai, his first American outlet at the Serramonte Mall in Daly City, California. Like his brother Carlos, who plans to put the Philippines on China's map, Ben also believes: "We should export our creative designs and strive to be among the world's best Fashion Houses." (Lee-Flores 2004). Dr. Rosalinda Hortaleza's Splash Manufacturing and its line of cosmetics, Chit Juan's coffee chain Figaro, Dy Cho Im's carton and diaper manufacturing concerns, and Tan Cho Chiong's real estate development ventures and other speculative but lucrative buy-and-sell ventures are likewise some of the new successful forays into the China market.

4.3 Factors Affecting Chinese-Filipino Investments in China

So far, aside from Carlos Chan, few of the Philippine's most prominent business leaders have quite succeeded, although they are hoping that their experiences there are preparing them for future breakthroughs into the China market. The Chinese Filipinos' ventures into China, in fact, are stacked more on the side of losses. For every success story like that of Carlos Chan, sad stories abound on how expectations to capitalize on their affinal, kinship and cultural ties with their hometowns were dashed.

In my personal interviews with the Shijen villagers in China and at the Shijen Hometown Association in Manila, made up of the Lee, Dee, Li, or Dy family, most of them said that they thought it more prudent to invest elsewhere than in their hometowns because of bad experiences of their predecessors. "If you open a business here, all your relatives would expect that they will be given high managerial positions. Even those who will be labourers would expect preferential treatment like sick leaves or educational benefits for their children. "*Kay ki lang* (自己人: we're relatives)" is not an ingredient that you could easily discard by claiming the need to hew to purely business (as against personal) transactions (Ang See 2004).

Another prominent family that had close ties with China suddenly found themselves cheated by their own cousins based in Xiamen after the eldest and second family patriarch died. The family started first by exporting construction, hardware, and related materials to China as early as 1995; and since they were doing well, by 1999 they had built their own warehouse, with a cousin in Xiamen in charge of operations. The family decided to expand and thus prepared the grounds to build their own factory. Unfortunately, when the two older patriarchs died, successively in 2001 and 2002, the Xiamen cousins not only stole the inventory left at the warehouse but also the money set aside to build the factory. They were forced to scale down operations considerably and now, only the first generation shareholders of the company wanted to continue their China operations, all the second generation descendants wanted to pull out entirely from China (Ang See 2005).

Another business concern, a Cebu-based soap maker, tied up with local (China) partners but despite the fact that his manufacturing plant was doing well in China, he was forced to abandon the business because his local partners had sold the property to a Singaporean group that was building a hotel. From experiences of other Chinese-Filipino businessmen in China, bringing cases to court would just end up with the Philippine side losing even more. Alex Go, who was in China for seven years as former administrative officer of the Philippine consulate-general in Xiamen, clinches these tales of woe. He says that many businesses fail there because investors take a lot of things for granted. Despite labour being cheap, the cost of doing business is high. "Many people go there thinking that China is a vast market — when you go in you will make money quickly. That is not so," Go says. To succeed, businessmen should know the market conditions (such as conditions for opening a current account) and be technically competent and aware of what they are doing. Moreover, he emphasizes, "they must be diligent about monitoring their businesses, otherwise they may end up with a container of defective products from China." (Torrijos 2002)

The stories of both success and failure described above emphasize the hypothesis posited at the beginning of the chapter, that the focus on supposed Chinese networks and institutions in connection to entry into the China market is exaggerated. Most of the businesses described above found a niche in China or failed in their ventures not as a result of their cultural or kinship ties with China but mostly from their own personal initiatives. Moreover, despite the fact that the profits and earnings can be quantified, the amount of capital brought into China is still difficult to assess.

For example, a businessman interviewed by the author revealed that when he expressed a desire to start a business in Hunan, the local government there offered him anything he needed — capital from the banks, land to build his factory, and all kinds of incentives just so they can enter into their accomplishment report card that an overseas Chinese ventured into their place. There was no need to bring in capital at all. Another interview elicited the information that a Chinese-Filipino businessman who ventured into China's version of build-operate-transfer scheme earned one billion *renminbi* just because of the very cheap concessions sold to him, which he in turn sold off ten times the cost of purchase. These were done due to personal connections with local officials.

Carlos Chan of Oishi had the same experience. Once his profit figures became quite impressive, he received a number of official invitations to different provinces just to look around. He received surprising and unsolicited offers of extremely favourable business incentives (like interest-free loans) and tax rebates (like waiving property taxes and licences), just so he would consider investing in these places. Chan's is not an isolated case. This scenario holds true for many other newcomers who venture into the less developed areas of China, which the government is bending backwards to open up. Interviews with two other businessmen revealed that Chinese officials seem willing to give them anything they wanted or needed.

5. CHINESE INSTITUTIONS AND NETWORKS

The separate efforts of the Tsinoy businessmen and conglomerates in venturing into China's economy show that they compete and clash with one another rather than hew to a collective effort in their attempts to penetrate the Chinese market. However, the existence of numerous, overlapping and inter-connected organizations and institutions gives rise to a deceptive appearance of a functional and cohesive network. A look at these organizations and their response to the various economic crises that confronted the community showed instead that the Chinese-Filipino community has not drawn strength from organized, planned and cohesive strategies that help address many of the pressing concerns of the community as they relate to mainstream society.

Gomez writes: "It is now increasingly being questioned whether a few business deals by a handful of Asia's leading Chinese businessmen can be used as the empirical base to support the notions of "Chinese commonwealth", "global tribes", and "co-ethnic business networks". The most prominent example of such criticism is that by Dirlik (1996), in his article, "Critical Reflections on 'Chinese Capitalism' as a Paradigm", wherein Dirlik not only challenges the widely-accepted argument that the spirit that drives Chinese entrepreneurial behaviour is strongly associated with a Confucian ethic, but even draws attention to "the vagueness of the notion of 'Chineseness'. For Dirlik, the strategic location of Chinese entrepreneurs in the Asia-Pacific region is the primary structural explanation for their capacity to tap into emerging business opportunities and develop their corporate base." (Gomez and Hsiao 2001).

5.1 The Federation and Trade Organizations

The Chinese-Filipino businessmen appear to be well-organized in an impressive network of nearly 170 trade groups and regional chambers of commerce nationwide under the lead umbrella organization — the Federation of Filipino-Chinese Chambers of Commerce and Industry Inc. (菲华商联总会) or Federation for short. The Federation celebrated its fiftieth anniversary in March 2004, and on 8–10 April, it just concluded its twenty-fifth biennial convention. If we talk of "Chinese capital" or "Chinese economy" in the Philippines, especially in relation to investments in China, then, the Federation should be the best representative institution since it is made up of the more prominent and most well-connected businessmen, as far as both the Philippines and China is concerned. The Federation has been one of the active participants of the World Chinese Entrepreneurs Convention (世界华商会议) initiated in Singapore in the 1990s and similar global overseas Chinese business forums. It has also led many trade delegations to the ASEAN countries and to China. However, the Federation has not played an active role, much less formed itself as an economic network, to carry out trade and form business partnerships as a by-product of such trade forums and exchanges. In a paper on ethnic Chinese social organizations presented by this author at the fourth ISSCO conference in Taipei, the interviews conducted revealed that none of these trade delegations and exchanges or even the world business forums gave rise to the formation of business partnerships or trade deals.

Aside from the Federation, two other Tsinoy business groups also adopted the word "zong (总会)" or Federation to signify that they are also umbrella organizations. One is the General Association of Filipino-Chinese Chambers of Commerce (中华总商会), which was organized way back in 1904, and the other is the Chinese-Filipino Business Club (工商总会), which split out of the Federation in 1999. Most businessmen join organizations like the Federation or the smaller trade organizations more for reasons of prestige and to establish connections than for economic gain. Membership and leadership in bigger organizations can be rather costly since the members, especially those who aspire to be officers, are required to give generous contributions to social and charitable projects of the organization, not to mention contributions to politicians and political parties to fund election campaigns. This bears out the contention that in the conduct of business by the Chinese, personalistic rather than kinship ties have been more important. The unsuccessful businessmen tended to rely on ties related to clans, lineage and hometown associations, indicating that social networks with an ethnic base do not in themselves guarantee business success. (Cariño, in Gomez and Hsiao 2001, pp. 112–14) While the business community appears to be neatly organized and well-knit on the surface, neither one of the three organizations or collectively as a group, have wielded a homogeneous and unified action in many of the key economic issues affecting them directly.

In fact, the issue of globalization, entry of China into the WTO, trade liberalization, and such crucial concerns seem to be a non-issue, even for such a prominent group as the Federation. Although individual members may be affected or may take such issues as crucial, the Federation and the other umbrella organizations, as an organized group, have not seriously tackled these problems in the agenda of their meetings or nationwide conventions. In fact, the Federation had not come up with any research regarding this topic of economic globalization. How their own members should respond to the challenges of globalization is their own lookout. The most important practical consideration is that after all, although globalization is around, they still have business to do and have money to earn. So far, these business federations have not been a force to contend with as far as entry to the Chinese economy or in influencing economic policy are concerned. Dr. Theresa Carino, in writing about Philippine-Chinese businesses, said: "One cannot conclude that Chinese-based organizations and their business networks have been primarily responsible for Chinese corporate development. While they can function as a medium for social contacts, prestige-building and networking, most of the largest Chinese firms have had to develop strategic linkages with the indigenous political elites and non-ethnic links appear more crucial than intra-ethnic ties in explaining Chinese business development in the Philippines." (Cariño 2001, pp. 120–23).

5.2 Response to Various Economic Crises

From the 1970s to the present, specially during the 1980s, the Philippines experienced grave economic and political crises which also coincided with big international events and global changes. These include the critical economic crisis in the Philippines from 1983 to 1985 as a result of the assassination of returning opposition leader, the late Senator Benigno Aquino, the 1997 Asian financial crisis, globalization, trade liberalization, financial liberalization, as well as the opening up of the China economy and the establishment of ASEAN free trade zone.

In the face of these changes and critical events, the Chinese-Filipino businessmen, or the community as a whole, generally failed to take a collective stand to respond to the crisis or to take any proactive measures and strategies to alleviate the situation. Inflation reached more than 40 per cent during the economic crisis of 1983 to 1985. What some of the traders and the chambers of commerce did was to field mobile stores that sold basic goods at a low cost to help alleviate the tense situation arising from the high cost of living. These measures again were reactive and palliative in nature and were done to prevent the assault of Chinese-owned stores due to the high cost of basic commodities. In short, only stopgap measures could be adopted and nothing was done about the more serious problems in the economic and financial crisis. Of course, it should also be considered that the magnitude of the problems was also beyond the ability of the Chinese-Filipino community to address.

5.2.1 Market and Retail Trade Liberalization

In the local domestic economy, even the lead organization, the Federation, has seldom taken the initiative of using its organized network to influence government policies, especially at the time when the Philippines has outpaced other ASEAN countries in terms of opening up and liberalizing its markets, to the detriment of local manufacturers and the agricultural sector.

In the liberalization of retail trade, for example, the biggest retail businesses like Shoemart, Robinsons, Fairmart, Abenson, and others, had to conduct their own policy studies and work out their own strategies in finding a win-win solution to the entry of the big retailers from the United States in particular. In the 1950s, the Chinese traders in the Philippines started to turn into larger-scale manufacturing. On the one hand, the change was affected by nationalization of the retail trade in 1954; but more importantly, the change was brought about by the implementation of the import control laws in the 1950s in order to spur the development of national industries. At that time, the Manila Chinese Chamber of Commerce (which was founded in 1904) and the newly founded Federation of Filipino-Chinese Chambers of Commerce and Industry Inc., both adopted passive resistance and protest as the main strategy in dealing with the biggest blow to the Chinese businessmen in Philippine history — the nationalization of retail trade. They failed to take the initiative to work out more long-term and viable solutions to the problem. It was fortunate that the retail trade restrictions became a blessing in disguise when the retailers turned the misfortune into opportunity to become manufacturers. Today, the same passive, reactive stance was taken and most of the retailers opted to just flow with the tide and adjust to whatever drastic changes may result out of the new liberalization trend.

5.2.2 Market Competitiveness

It has also not used its network to find alternatives to make the Philippine businesses more competitive, for example, by working together to bring down production costs. One of the former top Philippine entrepreneurs, Elena Lim of Solid Industries, the leading producer of Sony brand television, tape recorders, radios, videoke systems, and other electronic appliances, had to close down its last plant in 2003 because the landed costs of such products from Indonesia and Malaysia are much cheaper than the production costs in the Philippines. She said in an interview with the author that, "Our nation of manufacturers is now reduced to become a nation of traders because of too rapid liberalization." But, there is no coherent or cohesive organization to thresh out such crucial problems, much less to form an economic network to lobby for the delay of implementation or soften the impact of liberalization. Businessmen here have to fend for themselves and solve their own problems rather than rely on such organized networks as the Federation to address crucial and common concerns.

5.2.3 Influx of Cheap Imported Goods

The aspect of economic globalization which affects the Chinese-Filipino traders more severely, is that of trade liberalization. The abrupt lowering of tariffs resulted into a flood of cheap imported goods and products causing a lot of difficulties and anxieties to local Chinese manufacturers. The agriculture sector is adversely affected too — the vegetable and fruit growers, chicken farms, and even the producers of the mundane everyday table salt and sugar complain about the dumping of cheap imports from China. These manufacturers and traders have requested for strict compliance of the anti-smuggling law, with little success. The Federation, as a counter-measure, launched the "Buy Pinoy" (buy Philippine-made goods) movement to urge consumers to patronize Philippine-made products. The businessmen in favour of the Buy Pinoy movement represent just a portion of the Chinese-Filipino businessmen; they are most probably just the portion engaged in the manufacturing business. Chinese-Filipino businessmen engaged in import trading have a different outlook and reaction to this problem. As long as they make profits, it does not matter where they import the products from or what products they import. The liberalization of trade and the low tariffs create more opportunities for importation and make import business easier to conduct. Thus, they welcome such opportunities and will not oppose it. Those who have little background on economic liberalization will even come up with beautiful "theories" on the free competition and its advantages to the consumers to support their claims. As for small and big store owners or shopping malls, there is even less worry as regards the problem of sources of the products that they sell. Whether Philippine-made or imported, as long as the products can be sold easily and the profit they make is bigger, the rest do not matter. In fact, because of the pressure caused by the low-priced imported products, some Chinese-Filipino manufacturers have turned themselves into importers, or have bought some of the products which they originally manufactured from the importers because quite often, the landed costs of the imported goods are lower than the manufacturers' own production costs.

For the past years, there has been an influx of new immigrants from mainland China who are engaged in the trade of this kind of low-priced imported goods from China. Although many Chinese-Filipino manufacturers keep complaining, the businesses of these new immigrants are getting bigger and their lucrative business in the Philippines entice even more new immigrants to come. Secretary-General Lim Keng, of

Valenzuela Chinese Chambers of Commerce, said in an interview that "every time a kind of Chinese product enters the Philippines from China, one Chinese factory has to close down." Although this may be exaggerated, it still highlights the fact that globalization and its resultant trade liberalization are indeed pressing concerns especially since the Chinese-Filipino owned businesses are predominantly in the SMEs category. Unfortunately, the community is without a common direction or position about the issue, or a common stand or unified strategy to deal with the onslaught of cheap imported goods, many of which do not even generate revenues for our government because they are smuggled.

5.2.4 The 1997 Asian Financial Crisis

In essence, the financial crisis is a consequence of the disastrous effect of the financial liberalization brought by the economic globalization. This crisis elicited the same kind of response from the Tsinoy community. A number of Chinese-Filipino businessmen and enterprises were adversely affected by the crisis but again, there was no collective effort to respond and help cope with the crisis. The Tsinoy community as a whole, including the many business organizations and chambers of commerce in the country, failed to come up with positive measures that could have provided the affected businessmen with some coping mechanisms or to lead the constituents into taking a collective response to help alleviate the crisis. Unlike in other Asian countries such as Korea and Thailand, basically, the businessmen fended on their own and addressed their own problems individually and settled their own affairs the best way they could, without any coordination, much less cooperation with one another.

Actually, because of the depth and magnitude of this financial crisis and its large-scale effect on so many sectors, the crisis, in reality, was not something that the Chinese-Filipino traders themselves, not even the whole country on its own, can address. In a crisis of such magnitude, the Chinese-Filipino traders cannot be isolated from the rest of the country and they could not address such a crisis independently from the rest of the country. The Chinese-Filipino economic strength has always been part and parcel of the Philippine domestic economy and it could not stand alone nor survive independently from the rest, especially during times of crisis.

The different crises situation cited above gives rise to the conclusion that the Chinese-Filipino community, generally, have been passive and reactive and they find it difficult to adjust to new circumstances or threats. Second, in the face of crisis, they seem unable to be unified or take collective action, hence, they have quite limited power. They often take the more difficult path of coping by themselves when organized effort could possibly have brought better relief.

5.3 Attracting More Capital from China

The Federation has been looked upon by the Philippine Government as a force that will help in attracting more capital from China or even from ASEAN countries. The government thought that directly or indirectly, the ethnic Chinese links with the Chinese-speaking communities all over the world should be a decided edge towards attracting the much-needed foreign capital inflow. However, although there have been consultations and mutual exchange, the Federation has not maximized these ties to produce better results as far as joint partnerships with Chinese business groups are concerned. Executive Secretary Eduardo Ermita, in addressing the opening of the Federation's biennial convention on 8 April 2005, highlighted the government's hope that the local businessmen here can entice more foreign direct investments from China. The recent opening of the mining sector looks promising and maybe the Federation, indeed, can use its influence in attracting China's investments into the exploration of the country's rich mineral resources. Dr. Cariño made the same observation: "Chinese based institutions can be good vehicles for attracting more capital to the Philippines, but other conditions have to be in place for them to operate effectively. ...There are evidently limits to the usefulness of Chinese networks. An increasingly internationalized environment, Chinese businessmen will seek new ways of doing business more effectively and successfully. This would probably entail greater inter-ethnic linkages, and there is a need to determine at what levels this is happening. Rohwer (1996) has noted that Lim Sioe Liong of Indonesia's Salim Group has allowed a Filipino professional manager Manuel Pangilinan to run a subsidiary, First Pacific, and turn it into a conglomerate, even to the extent of sometimes overriding family decisions. It should be noted, however, that Pangilinan was a classmate of Salim's son, an indication that 'old school ties' may be more important than ethnic ties." (Cariño 2001, p. 123).

There is a big Spanish Filipino and sizeable Indian-Filipino communities in the Philippines but there never was any claim of an Indian economy or Spanish economy. Although the American-controlled multinational companies wield a high economic position, there never was any mention of a so-called American economy and in the same vein, nowhere can there be a claim of an existence of a Chinese economy. Most of the ethnic Chinese, whether in the Philippines or in Southeast Asia, who invested in China did it on their own individual initiative and not collectively as an organized group. The capital that they poured into the Chinese economy should not be lumped together as Chinese capital. It is capital that originated from Lim Sioe Liong, from the Kuoks, and Lucio Tan individually, but none of these big capitalists decided to organize themselves and pool together their resources as a conglomerate (财团) or collectively made a decision to invest in China. In fact, instead of lumping them together as Chinese capital, it is more accurate to pinpoint the investors as Chinese Filipinos, Chinese Indonesians, Chinese Malaysians and so on and so forth.

6. *HUAREN* GLOBAL NETWORK

The preceding sections presented the response of the ethnic Chinese in the Philippines *vis-à-vis* the opening up of China and their lack of collective or organized action in addressing various economic problems. The succeeding sections will in turn discuss the issue of the global *huaren* network on two aspects: First is the global *huaren* network of *huashang* or ethnic Chinese businessmen, including the ethnic Chinese in the Philippines, and the other is the response and strategy of the *huaren* towards economic globalization. One unique and common trend of these two aspects is the view that the *huaren* are a homogeneous or unified bloc, and that their racial and cultural origins are a common denominator that binds together the Chinese of the world into a global network. However, as already stated in the beginning of this chapter, the worldwide *huaren*, especially the case of the Philippines, do not and cannot have a common or unified stand or response towards economic globalization.

It is assumed that the *huaren* global network exists. But this network of *huaren* is highly heterogeneous, is made up of varying kinds and groups of Chinese differentiated by their regional origins, their new homes and identities, orientation and education and a myriad other factors that separate, rather than unite, the Chinese in the world. (Li 2000, pp. 261–82) Unfortunately, a false view or an impression of a unified and organized network arises out of the phenomenon of worldwide aggrupation or regional networks of business, family, hometown of origins, alumni or school associations and the like. International conventions like the World Chinese Entrepreneurs Convention and other types of global overseas Chinese business forums and that of World Hakka Culture conference held in Taipei in 2002, which gathered the worldwide Chinese of Hakka origins from all parts of the globe, is one example that gives rise to an erroneous perception of a potent and powerful globalized force of ethnic Chinese. Qiu Liben in writing about Chinese Networks in Southeast Asia (Chan 2000) observed that "Since the end of 1970s, more than 60 dialects, clans, professional associations have emerged in Taiwan, Hong Kong and Southeast Asia. From the early 1990s, the World Chinese Entrepreneurs Convention has been held once every two years." Qiu concluded that such "Chinese networks" formed as a part of the process of globalization to help push forward the respective agenda of the organizers, do not really quite result in the transnational connections these conventions and federations desire (Qiu 2000, p. 202).

6.1 Differing Stance on the Global *Huaren*

However, even our perceptions, acceptance or non-acceptance of the nature of such global Chinese networks are coloured or affected by our different standpoints or positions, our background, objectives, or agenda. For example, on the side of Chinese Government, propagation of a global Chinese network is advantageous from the standpoint of its desire to obtain the support and entice the attention of such an aggrupation for its economic development and business expansion. On the side of the West and developing countries, especially Japan, a close attention and better understanding of the global Chinese networks is a necessity arising out of their anxiety that such network could become a potential rival or competitive threat. In the academic field, there is a belief that such a global network has a great impact on the economic development or business of ethnic Chinese, and even on the world economy, hence, there arises a great interest and attention in pursuing further research on the phenomenon (Department of Foreign Affairs and Trade, Australia 1995).

The Taiwan Government was the first to propagate this idea of a global Chinese network because of political expediency. Seeing the looming entry of the People's Republic of China in the United Nations and its increasing recognition in the community of nations, as early as the beginning of the 1970s, Taiwan has aggressively pushed forward the agenda of forming international or global Chinese aggrupations, along the lines of business or trades, school or alumni, and clan or lineage. Taiwan supported the organization of world conventions of Chinese from regional origins, world clan or family associations. But from actual outcome of such gatherings, there really had been no significant results in unifying these groups into a global network that can push a common agenda, except perhaps for the success in the establishment of the World Overseas Chinese Commercial Bank (世华银行). To say that this global network of Chinese from different groups, origins and orientation can result out of concerted moves to internationalize the *huaren* and *huashang* through world conferences and the like is stretching the reality too far.

The overall impact of such internationalization of the economic development or even business growth of different groups of ethnic Chinese appears to be miniscule, much less is it realistic to quantify its impact on economic globalization itself. The different international conventions have produced a lot of noise because of their magnitude and nature, but such has in fact also produced a false sense that there is something substantial that comes out of these gatherings.

6.2 Lack of Coping Strategies to Globalization

The resources of the Chinese-Filipino business organizations, led by the Federation, are much greater compared to those of the Philippine Chambers of Commerce and Industry (PCCI) and the Makati Business Club (MBC), leading business groups in the mainstream Philippine society. The money spent each year by the Federation is much more than the two organizations. However, the impact the Federation has on the national economy, especially on the economic policies, is very much inferior compared to the two other groups. The Chinese-Filipino businessmen have never considered as their priority and their primary obligation to undertake research on economic development and they seldom give their inputs and suggestions on various government economic policies, primarily because their capability on this aspect is weak. Most Chinese Filipinos know how to do business, but only a few know economics, much less on the level of economic policies.

The primary concern and the major problems of the Chinese-Filipino businessmen and the chambers of commerce are often confined to taxes and labour problems. On these matters that affect their daily operations, they have expressed their collective positions. They are seldom concerned about other major topics like the issue of globalization, much more undertake research on it. It is not surprising if they cannot come up with any suggestion or strategic response to it. Even the people from the academe who attempt to do research on the impact of globalization find it very difficult to pursue, with the ethnic Chinese businessmen as their respondents. Empirical data are not only difficult to find, there is practically not much statistics to offer. A case in point is the experience of Singapore University Ph.D. student Ren Na who stayed in the Philippines for a month to study this *huaren* global network and the ethnic Chinese in the Philippines. She interviewed Chinese-Filipino businessmen and associations about the existence and role of such a network but after her one-month interviews, she concluded that nothing much can be gathered on this aspect because such a network really does not exist.

If research really has to be done, probably it can only be conducted by collecting data on the individual businesses, and then come up with necessary comparisons, surveys, analyses and syntheses. In other words, it can only be done on individual Chinese-Filipino businessmen, to learn their experiences and see how they adjust their businesses to the globalization of economy, so as to come up with an analysis of statistics, and some kind of a quantitative conclusion, which can somewhat present a clearer picture.

The Chinese-Filipino businessmen have never been a united economic force or entity. (This may also be true in other Southeast Asian countries.) For the Chinese-Filipinos, what kind of business to engage in is a matter of personal interest, and is handled individually. In the 1970s, the Philippines started to implement the policy on encouragement of exports, and it started boosting the opening of several export processing zones. Though some Chinese-Filipino businessmen started to engage in exports, the actual number of those who ventured into the export processing zones was not high, much less were there any efforts at all to pool resources and go into joint enterprises to develop export processing zones, which the government at that time was pushing forward. Despite government encouragement, the Chinese-Filipino businessmen, as a group, made no collective effort or strategy to undertake a large scale joint enterprise, like the development of an economic zone or industrial park. In the mid 1970s, many Chinese-Filipino businessmen surged into the real estate business. This was a natural effect of the mass naturalization in 1975. However, there was no special concerted effort to consciously take the lead in developing the national economy after the door was opened when the majority of the Chinese Filipinos then acquired Filipino citizenship.

In short, the Chinese-Filipino businessmen may seem to be a strong economic force in terms of number, but they are in reality scattered and disunited. From the historical and contemporary point of view, they still play an objective economic role but they have not yet drawn strength from their economic positions and numbers to be a force to contend with. There has been no effort to harness or organize the so-called economic power of the Chinese-Filipino businessmen as a strategic potential to boost the development of the Filipino domestic economy.

6.3 Small Impact of *Huaren* on Global Scale

Marie-Sybille Du Vienne, in her paper, "For a Tentative Modelization of the Economics Weight of Overseas Chinese at the beginning of the 3rd Millennium," presented at the fifth ISSCO conference in Copenhagen, 10–14 May 2004, gave some figures to compare the impact of the *huaren* on the global economy. Since the paper is still an unpublished one, this paper will cite only two figures relevant to our own study. These are presented here just for reference purposes, which can help in validating other data provided on this subject. Du Vienne first cited the percentage of gross national product (GNP) sourced from the *huaren*. The figures are fairly representative: Singapore has 81 per cent GNP, Malaysia has 42 per cent, Indonesia 10 per cent, sourced from *huaren*. (Du Vienne 2004).

Table 9.3 shows that the Overseas Chinese share in the total foreign direct investments into China is indeed quite small. Even if the figures have been extrapolated for the past few years to give an average for the last ten years, the figures indeed still validate the observation that the share of overseas Chinese direct investment into China is not as big as

TABLE 9.2
Huaren's Share in Southeast Asian Country's GNP, 2002
(US$ Billion, current)

Country	GNP	Huaren "GNP"	% GNP	% Huaren Regional GNP
Southeast Asia	**625**	**183.6**	**30**	–
Burma (Myanmar)	20.5	2.5	12	1.3
Brunei	4.25	2	40	1
Cambodia	3.67	0.26	10	0.1
Indonesia	172.91	17.20	10	9.4
Laos	1.68	0.16	9.43	0.09
Philippines	77	6.5	8.4	3.5
Malaysia	95.15	40.3	42	22
Singapore	87.8	71.2	81	38.7
Thailand	126.4	41.38	33	22.7
Timor-Lorosa	0.388	0.01	3.8	0.1
Vietnam	35.11	1.6	4.5	0.8

the other multinational companies, especially when it is compared with the gross fixed capital formation (GFCF). Du Vienne's paper challenges the belief that the PRC would succeed in capitalizing on the presence of overseas Chinese communities for its own benefit. Likewise, she also challenges the belief that there can be an "overseas Chinese domination" or that there exists an "overseas Chinese as a superpower or a threat. The authors agree with her view and have also written on this aspect in earlier papers (Ang See 2004, pp. 14–36). In fact, Dr. Leo Suryadinata writes, "In many countries Chinese companies are having to become public rather than remain family based and ethnic Chinese businessmen and women increasingly are having to form partnerships with indigenous Southeast Asians." (Suryadinata 2001, p. 72).

Du Vienne also argues that the wealth of the overseas Chinese is quite limited relative to the global average. Although in Southeast Asia, the per capita income of the ethnic Chinese is nearly five times the average in the region, the average gross per capita income for developed countries is 2.7 times those of overseas Chinese and their average wealth remains behind that of developed countries. Suryadinata gave the same conclusions: "The economic strength of ethnic Chinese in Southeast Asia is not very impressive when put on global or East Asian scales. In comparison to Asia's top 500 banks in 1997, the aggregate assets of the 135 ASEAN banks were reported as US$442 billion. This was less

TABLE 9.3
Huaren's Share in Direct Foreign Investments
over Capital Formation, end 2002
(US$ Billion, current)

	China	Hong Kong	Macao	Taiwan
Inwards DFI/Total investments (GFCF %)	11.0	34.2	3.3	3.3
Overseas Chinese inwards direct Investment/total FDI (%)	8.5	2.7	1.9	10.0
Overseas Chinese GNP Produced in… (Billions US$)	12.0	2.0	4.0	2.1
Overseas Chinese Share Of GNP (%)	0.9	1.2	0.06	0.7

Source: Chinese World, GNP, 2002.

than the total assets of one Japanese bank — Sanwa Bank, the fifth largest bank in the country at the time, which amounted to US$456.7 billion (Suryadinata 2001, p. 59). Above all, the Chinese in Southeast Asia do not comprise a homogeneous bloc. They are heterogeneous in their religions, culture and traditions, in their socio-economic class, and in their political ideologies. There can therefore be no threat from a non-existent world of overseas Chinese. Clearly Du Vienne points an important validation of the author's hypothesis that the export of "Chinese capital" to China is miniscule and is not something that we have to be concerned about, especially since the economic activities are not done through organized efforts of these businessmen.

7. CHINA-PHILIPPINES ECONOMIC RELATIONS

7.1 Investment and Trade Cooperation

The bigger picture of Philippine-China relations must also be taken into consideration. This year marks the thirtieth anniversary of diplomatic relations between the Philippines and the People's Republic of China. Although volume of trade and investments have increased phenomenally the past five years, such trading is still miniscule compared to the trade volume with other Southeast Asian countries (Baviera 2001, p. 249).

Two years ago, the Philippines had its first exposition at the Shanghai Exhibition Centre in China on 27–30 March 2003, signalling the Philippines' first concerted attempt to tap the list of China's procurers and suppliers of a wide array of goods and thus to strengthen a newly-found niche for Philippine exports in the diverse Chinese market. The solo exhibition was also timed to meet the projected needs of China for the 2008 Summer Olympics in Beijing and the World Expo 2010 in Shanghai. Albeit coming in a bit late, this first exhibition highlights the growing importance the Philippines has now given to China as a potential market for its exports and as a source of foreign direct investments to the Philippines. There is also an increasing interest on the business opportunities available in mainland China.

Trade has grown dramatically in volume and increased beginning in 1995 and there has also been a substantial bilateral direct foreign investment (DFI). In general, however, Philippine DFI into China has been miniscule, accounting for less than 1 per cent of total DFI. Hong Kong and Taiwanese businessmen have held the lion's share, posing stiff competition (Palanca 2001, pp. 103–59).

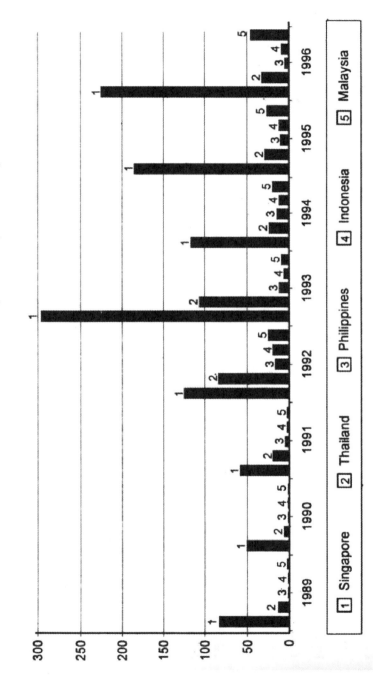

FIGURE 9.1

ASEAN-5's Investments in China, 1989–96 (US$ Million)

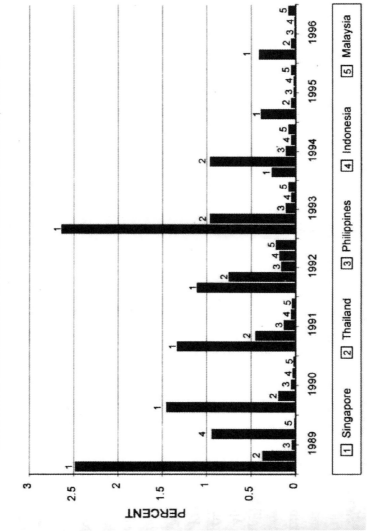

FIGURE 9.2
ASEAN-5's Investments in PRC as Share in Total DFI, 1989–96

1 Singapore   2 Thailand   3 Philippines   4 Indonesia   5 Malaysia

Source: General Administration, P.R. China.

TABLE 9.4
China's Trade with Selected Asian Countries, 2002

Country	Total Trade with China (US$ billion)	Exports to China (US$ billion)	Imports from China (US$ billion)	Trade with China as a % of total trade
Indonesia	4.0	2.2	1.8	4.6
South Korea	31.2	18.4	13.5	11.0
Malaysia	7.6	3.8	3.8	4.7
Philippines	1.7	0.8	1.0	2.8
Singapore	12.5	8.3	7.2	5.3
Taiwan	39.5	31.7	7.8	17.1
Hong Kong	157.6	76.5	87.5	40.3
India	3.5	1.5	2.1	3.8

Source: CLSA Emerging Markets (From *Far East Economic Review*, 20 March 2003, p. 28).
Cited in Dr. Palanca's "China's WTO Entry: Effects on its Economy and Implications for the Philippines", a research project of the Philippine APEC Study Center Network (PASCN) and the Philippine Institute for Development Studies (PIDS), 2003.

In 2004, bilateral trade volume reached US$13.33 billion, representing a growth rate of 41.8 per cent over the figure of US$9.4 billion in 2003. In the past five years, bilateral trade volume grew at a healthy annual average of 43.78 per cent, with the Philippines gradually selling more to China than it buys from China.

The trade structure is positive and beneficial to both sides. Top Philippine exports to China include semi-conductor devices, electronic data processing units, copper, petroleum and other resource-based products, automotive parts and fresh fruits. On the other hand, China's top exports to the Philippines include semiconductors, electronic data processing parts, textile yarns, petroleum products, telecommunication equipment parts, and consumer electronics.

There is a growing concern, however, especially in the manufacturing sector in the country that since it is so much cheaper to import from China than to produce locally, more and more manufacturers may consider moving their operations there. Manufacturing their products there will also allow them to sell to the over one billion Chinese. This has significant implications for the Philippines. On the positive side, a robust and economically stable China can complement the growth of the domestic economy but on the negative side, it may mean the loss of much needed employment and exacerbation of capital outflow.

TABLE 9.5
Philippine's Bilateral Trade with China, 1980–96

Year	EXPORTS			IMPORTS		
	Values (In US$ million)	% of Total Exports	% of ASEAN's Exports to China	Values* (In US$ million)	% of Total Imports	% of China's Exports to ASEAN
1980	45	0.78	6.49	258	3.11	21.57
1981	78	1.36	14.47	255	3.01	18.40
1982	105	2.09	13.53	236	2.86	18.45
1983	22	0.45	3.83	143	1.79	12.54
1984	60	1.12	9.10	223	3.47	11.27
1985	81	1.76	8.71	314	5.75	11.20
1986	101	2.10	8.08	157	2.91	8.36
1987	88	1.54	4.80	245	3.43	10.60
1988	67	0.95	2.54	268	3.07	9.61
1989	50	0.64	1.76	239	2.14	8.25
1990	62	0.76	2.40	205	1.57	5.33
1991	128	1.45	4.06	253	1.98	6.13
1992	114	1.16	3.02	209	1.35	4.92
1993	167	1.48	3.37	281	1.50	6.01
1994	164	1.22	2.51	476	2.11	7.47
1995	216	1.25	2.56	1,030	3.63	11.44
1996	328	1.61	3.43	1,015	2.97	11.50

*Values are China's exports to the Philippines.
Source: International Monetary Fund (Quoted in Palanca's "China's WTO Entry: Effects on its Economy and Implications for the Philippines," a research project of the Philippine APEC Study Center Network (PASCN) and the Philippine Institute for Development Studies (PIDS), 2003.

TABLE 9.6
The Philippines' Total Trade and Bilateral Trade with China, 1993–2002

	Exports to China	% Share in Total Exports	Imports from China	% Share in Total Imports	Total Trade with China	% Share in Total Trade	Total Exports	Total Imports	Total Trade
1993	173.87	1.53	180.66	1.03	354.54	1.22	11374.81	17597.40	28972.21
1994	164.48	1.22	294.27	1.38	458.75	1.32	13482.90	21332.57	34815.46
1995	213.97	1.23	578.62	2.18	792.58	1.80	17447.19	26537.48	43984.66
1996	327.92	1.60	684.20	2.07	1012.12	1.89	20542.55	33028.72	53571.27
1997	244.41	0.97	871.59	2.43	1116.00	1.82	25227.72	35933.82	61161.54
1998	343.68	1.17	1198.89	4.04	1542.57	2.61	29496.35	29659.88	59156.23
1999	574.81	1.64	1038.43	3.38	1613.24	2.45	35032.67	30723.14	65755.81
2000	663.26	1.74	767.67	2.45	1430.93	2.06	38077.95	31386.84	69464.79
2001	792.76	2.47	952.92	3.18	1745.68	2.83	32150.20	29550.81	61707.01
2002	1352.90	3.86	1231.19	3.68	2584.08	3.77	35066.02	33467.13	68533.15
Average Annual Growth	25.60		23.77		24.70		13.33	7.40	10.04

Source: Department of Trade and Industry, Republic of the Philippines.
Quoted in Palanca's "China's WTO Entry: Effects on its Economy and Implications for the Philippines", a research project of the Philippine APEC Study Center Network (PASCN) and the Philippine Institute for Development Studies (PIDS), 2003.

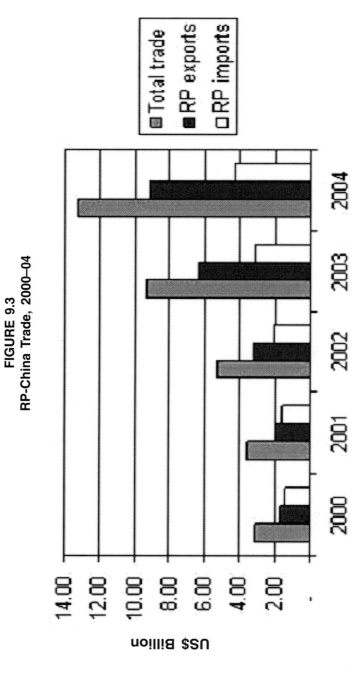

FIGURE 9.3
RP-China Trade, 2000–04

Source: General Administration, P.R. China

For the domestic market, however, "The effects of growth in China is not felt by the upper class of the Filipinos, but by the poor — the young ones are enjoying the good life of buying cheap DVDs and CDs. Even the workers are enjoying buying cheaper tools like hammers, spade, even more prohibitive Stanley power tools, chain saws, motorcycles, bicycles and the like. China has money and is willing to help the Philippines but the country has to decide whether it is prudent to side with China and antagonize the United States, especially Bush, who feels that China may threaten the foundation of Asian security (Ang See 2005). The government in recent years have gradually tried to rationalize the liberalization of its trade in order to safeguard, especially the agricultural sector, from cheap goods originating from China.

Telecommunications is a primary area of reform and development, especially for purposes of improving interconnectivity. The passage of the Power Industry Reform Act of 2001 is a government initiative towards restructuring the country's power sector, with the goal of reducing electric costs and consequently, the overall cost of doing business in the Philippines. To date eight foreign (including China) and three local companies have signified their interest to take part in the privatization of the assets of the Philippine National Power Corporation. Chinese companies may also take advantage of the Philippines' Build-Operate-and-Transfer laws to invest in telecommunications infrastructure to support high-speed connectivity at low costs, or perhaps explore the use of satellites for the country's Internet backbone especially that the country is made of 7,000 islands.

Another promising investment area for the Chinese companies is in the agriculture sector. Henry Lim Bon Liong, one of the Vice Presidents of the Federation of Filipino-Chinese Chambers of Commerce, has successfully introduced China's hybrid rice technology into the Philippines. Despite the lack of a network of support, which could have fast tracked the development of the technology to ensure rice sufficiency and increase the rice farmers income, Lim has persisted and has made significant inroads on his own initiative. This is one of the most significant and positive highlights of technology-exchanges with China and on this aspect, perhaps the fact that Lim is a Chinese Filipino has been the deciding edge.

The opening up of the mining sector had given another investment opportunities. Mining and/or exploitation of natural resources was strictly limited to Filipino citizens before the passage of the new law allowing foreign investments. On this aspect, interviews with some Chinese-Filipino businessmen reveal that there had already been positive feelers from China's side to offer joint partnerships in this new industry that would entail huge and long-term capitalization.

7.2 China Not a Competitor for Foreign Direct Investment

A growing concern among Southeast Asian countries is the competition with China for foreign direct investment that they face. Dr. Ellen Palanca's paper, "China's Economic Growth: Implications to the ASEAN and to the Philippines", cites that although it poses as a challenge to ASEAN countries, China's growth can also be a positive factor for its neighbouring countries, especially with the new trend in outsourcing of goods and the growing purchasing power of China's consuming public (Palanca 2001, pp. 1–26). Hong Kong economic strategist, Chi Lo, echoes the same observation in his book, *When Asia Meets China in the New Millennium*, that "The DFI inflow outlook need not be dim for Southeast Asia. Southeast Asia is not competing with China for foreign capital. It is facing a challenge of reinventing itself to attract foreign investment and local factors in individual economies would play an important role in attracting capital inflow." More fundamentally, Lo says, if Southeast Asia could pursue appropriate economic policies to nurture a stable, transparent, and fair institutional and regulatory base for foreign businesses, capital will flow in even if it is also going to China. The trend of global outsourcing, driven by specialization and comparative advantage of different economies means that investment opportunities are not restricted to China." (Lo 2003, pp. 87–91) Such significant observations likewise bolster the earlier contention that the ethnic Chinese in Southeast Asia need not fear the backlash of China's growing economy and their own countries likewise can capitalize in fact on the spill over of China's growth.

CONCLUSION

The phenomenon of China's growth and expansion of its economic power has been a cause of concern to many countries. The workshop organized by ISEAS highlights the importance it has given to this phenomenon. However, from the analysis of recent developments *vis-à-vis* the local ethnic Chinese businessmen in the various countries in Southeast Asia, we can tentatively draw a conclusion that China's growing economy poses no threat to the Southeast Asian Chinese. The opposite is also correct, the Southeast Asian Chinese investments into China should pose as no threat to their own country's economy, contrary to the fears of some of the Southeast Asian governments. One role the ethnic Chinese in Southeast Asia can undertake is to try to use their direct and indirect links with China to encourage flow of investments into Southeast Asia to create a synergy of mutually beneficial economic activities that would generate greater growth in the region. At the recently concluded biennial convention of the leading organization in the Tsinoy community, the Federation of Filipino-Chinese Chambers of Commerce and Industry Inc., most of the speakers from the government side emphasized that fact — the Philippine domestic economy needs investment inflows from China and though there is no direct mention of the local businessmen's investments in China, they are causing concern in the Philippines that is suffering from slow economic growth and poor job creation.

One important lesson, however, that the ethnic Chinese in Southeast Asia must carefully consider is that they continue to be vulnerable, especially in times of economic crisis. The racial riots in Indonesia and Malaysia are too fresh to be forgotten. Even if we present studies and research like this one, pointing to the fact that in the case of Tsinoy investments in China, the failures so far out-rank the successes, perception still predominantly colours people point of view. The fear that China is competing with the Philippines for much needed foreign direct investments remains a pressing one.

This study also points to the significant fact that a collective, cohesive and unified network forming a "Chinese economy" does not exist. The lack of a coherent proactive agenda among the Chinese Filipino big trade organizations, even on such crucial issues as economic globalization and trade liberalization, belie the fears that a cartelized, distinct and separate ethnic Chinese economy exist, independent of the mainstream.

Workshops and studies that are being conducted, just like this ISEAS workshop, are meant to clarify the true role and impact of the Southeast Asian Chinese and explain whether the existence of their so-called "mother country" is a threat to their own Southeast Asian countries. Such fears and accusations are unjustified and outputs of our studies should be disseminated not just to the academe but also to the governments and media so that public opinion can also be influenced by the true picture.

References

Ang See, Teresita. 2004. "Cultural Influence of the Chinese Overseas on the *Qiaoxiang* — The Case of Shijen (Chio-Chun) Migrants to the Philippines". Interviews with Shijen villagers.

———. 2004. "Globalization and Ethnic Chinese: The Philippine Perspective". In *Chinese in the Philippines — Problems and Perspectives* 3, edited by Teresita Ang See (Manila: Kaisa Para Sa Kaunlaran Inc.)

———. 2005. Interview with Prof. Benito Lim of the Ateneo Centre for Asian Studies, Ateneo de Manila University, Loyola Heights, Quezon City.

Baviera, Aileen S.P. 2001. "The Political Economy of China's Relations with Southeast Asia," in Ellen Palanca, ed., *China's Economic Growth and the ASEAN* (Quezon City: Philippine Apec Study Center Network).

Chan, Kwok Bun, (2000). *Chinese Business Networks: State, Economy and Culture* (Singapore: Prentice Hall).

Cariño, Theresa Chong. 2001. "Chinese Business in Southeast Asia — the Philippines". In *Chinese Business in South-East Asia*, edited by Gomez, Edmund Terence and Michael Hsiao Hsin-Huang (Richmond, Surrey: Curzon Press).

Commonwealth of Australia, Department of Foreign Affairs and Trade, East Asia Analytical Unit, *Overseas Chinese Business Networks in Asia*, 1995.

De la Cruz, Annie. 2004. "The Buzz behind Jollibee", *Philippines Business*, Vol. 11, No. 9.

Du Vienne, Marie-Sybille. 2004. "For a Tentative Modelisation of the Economics Weight of Overseas Chinese at the Beginning of the 3rd Millennium". Paper presented at the fifth ISSCO conference held in Copenhagen.

Gomez, Edmund Terence and Michael Hsiao Hsin-Huang (eds.) 2001. *Chinese Business in South-East Asia* (Richmond, Surrey: Curzon Press).

Lee Flores, Wilson. 2004. "Meet the Next Taipans — Ben Chan". *Entrepreneur* 4, no. 46.

Li, Peter. 2000. "Overseas Chinese Networks — A Reassessment". In *Chinese Business Networks: State, Economy and Culture*, edited by Chan Kwok Bun (Singapore: Prentice Hall).

Lo, Chi. 2003. *When Asia Meets China in the New Millenium — China's Role in Shaping Asia's Post-Crisis Economic Transformation* (Singapore: Prentice Hall).

Mackie, Jamie. 2000. "The Economic Roles of the Southeast Asian Chinese: Information Gaps and Research Needs". In Chan, 2000.

Qiu Liben. 2002. "The Chinese Networks in Southeast Asia". In Chan, 2000.

Palanca, Ellen (ed.) 2001. *China's Economic Growth and the ASEAN* (Quezon City: Philippine Apec Study Center Network).

———. 2001. "China's Changing Trade Patterns: Implications for ASEAN-China Trade". In Palanca (ed.), 2001.

———. 2001. "China's Economic Growth: Implications to the ASEAN and to the Philippines". In Palanca (ed.), 2001.

———. 2003. "China's WTO Entry: Effects on its Economy and Implications for the Philippines". A research project of the Philippine APEC Study Center Network (PASCN) and the Philippine Institute for Development Studies.

Suryadinata, Leo. 2001. "Ethnic Chinese in Southeast Asia and their Economic Role". In *Chinese Populations in Contemporary Southeast Asian Societies: Identities, Interdependence and International Influence*, edited by Armstrong, Jocelyn, R. Warwick Armstrong and Kent Mulliner (Surrey: Curzon).

Torrijos, Elena. 2002. "Doing Business in China". *Newsbreak.*

Yabes, Criselda. 2005. "The Rising Taipan". *Newsbreak* 5, no. 5.

Yeung, Henry Wai-chung and Kris Olds (eds.) 2000. *Globalization of Chinese Business Firms* (London: Macmillan Press).

10

Public Policy, Political Culture, and Ethnic Chinese Businesses in the Philippines

Ellen H. Palanca

1. INTRODUCTION

The ethnic Chinese have been active players in Philippine business for centuries. Until a few decades ago, however, other than the multinational corporations, large business establishments in the country mostly belonged to the elite families composed primarily of Spanish Filipinos and Chinese *mestizos*[1] (Palanca 1977). Due to their economic and political power, for centuries this group of elites has had strong influence on public policy. In the Southeast Asian region where in most countries the ethnic Chinese have been the most dominant group in business, in the Philippines, the presence of a powerful non-Chinese group in business is a unique feature. Towards the end of the nineteenth century, there were a few successful businessmen,[2] but none of them could compare with the wealth of the propertied elite families. Nevertheless, even then, the Chinese had an established commercial network, although most were engaged in petty trading or small-scale manufacturing.

It was only since the liberalization of the naturalization process in the seventies when ethnicity distinction started to blur that we saw a significant expansion of the ethnic Chinese business. The rise in economic status of many ethnic Chinese, as well as their integration into the mainstream of Philippine society, has placed them in the same social and economic class as the traditional oligarchs, a class that has been able to influence policy- and decision-making of the government.

The rise of East Asian economies in the last few decades has again brought attention on Chinese culture as an explanation for entrepreneurial success. With Hong Kong, Korea, Singapore and Taiwan having gained the "newly industrialized" status, "Chineseness" as an explanation of business success regained focus. Hong Kong and Taiwan are part of what is called Greater China. Singapore is 80 per cent ethnic Chinese while Korea is very Confucian in its cultural orientation. The countries that followed suit in the pursuance of such export-driven growth are Malaysia, Thailand, the Philippines and Indonesia wherein the major business players are the ethnic Chinese. China joined the league after adopting market reform and opening up its economy. While the factor of vibrant Chinese entrepreneurship is common in all these cases, there are intra-regional and temporal differences in the growth of these Asian economies due to difference in institutional structure, politics and policies. This is very evident in the case of China, whose phenomenal growth started only after it adopted the open door policy.

The experience of East Asian countries in recent years shows that Chinese culture is an important factor for entrepreneurship, although it is also evident that culture alone is by no means sufficient in explaining Chinese entrepreneurship. Institutions typical of Chinese business community such as networking and credit access also play important roles in the development of Chinese business (Brown 1996). Other than culture and institutions, the state and its policies have strong influence on business development. These governmental factors determine the business environment, which can provide business opportunities or restrict entrepreneurial activities. Globalization and its effect on capital market liberalization, however, have lessened the effect of the state on business. Investors can easily move capital out of the country when business opportunities are lacking.

The business environment faced by the ethnic Chinese in the Southeast Asian countries has been characterized as patrimonial, a system which began during the colonial eras and, in most of these countries, continued in the post-colonial period. In such a system, it is not just the public policies which determine the business environment, but the overall political setting as well. Patrimonial polity in the Philippines, however, is different from the kind practised in the other countries (Hutchcroft 1998). In Indonesia and Thailand, for example, patrimonialism is of the administrative state, where the elites belong to the bureaucracy. On the other hand, patrimonialism in the Philippines has been that of the oligarchic state, where the elites are the oligarchs. The presence of a powerful oligarchic class (its development to be explained in the next section), which, until recently, the Chinese were not part of, has been a feature of the Philippine political setting. A patrimonial oligarchic state is said to be more difficult to reform,[3] while the state regulation weak. Hence despite modernization and reforms, we do not see the system receding and in fact observe a stronger oligarchic force, exerting their control on government institutions. Many government regulatory agencies are being captured by the companies they are supposed to regulate.

This kind of political economy, coupled with the political culture of patronage and emphasis on personal loyalty, has caused poor and weak governance as well as a very unequal distribution of economic benefits within the Filipino population. Economists have asserted the lack of growth and transformation of the Philippines economy in the last half century to be caused by such a political economic environment (ACERD 2005).

This chapter looks at the business environment, as determined by public policies and political setting, faced by the Chinese in the Philippines since the colonial period and how it affected their business. In the Philippines, before mass naturalization was granted in 1975, the business environment under which the ethnic Chinese operated was rather volatile and generally unfavourable as nationalistic policies restricted the types of business and even the professions they could enter. The adverse business environment existed since the colonial period as the Chinese were not favoured by the colonial masters, both the Spanish and American. The group that enjoyed favours was the landed aristocracy that dominated the economy. It was only when the Chinese obtained their Filipino citizenship in the mid-seventies and gained equal economic footing with the other Filipinos that they rose to become super-rich, engaging in business lines which had been territories of the traditional elite group.

2. PHILIPPINE POLITICAL ECONOMY

The presence of a powerful oligarchic class and politics based strongly on the patronage system and interpersonal relations are two features of Philippine political economy. The powerful oligarchic class dominates the country's economy as well as its politics. As such, the oligarchic business class can easily extract rent from the government bureaucracy. On the other hand, the political culture is such that personal relations are important in securing favors and privileges, which are granted with expectation of political loyalty. Business entrepreneurs had to seek political benefactors especially in cases where the rules are not clear. Hence windfalls and rent incomes accrue to businesses that have connections to people in power.

2.1 Oligarchic Class

The Philippine political economy is a colonial heritage. A patrimonial oligarchic economic system developed under the two colonial regimes. It was built up by the three-and-a-half centuries of Spanish regime, which dated from 1521 to 1898, and perpetuated by the half-a-century of U.S. rule, which followed immediately the Spanish rule. During the Spanish period, the colonial administration had to rely on private landowners for agricultural production to meet the demand of world trade. These landowners in turn developed close and predatory connections with the state, thus becoming oligarchic. They were mostly Spanish *mestizos*, and Chinese *mestizos* who were assimilated towards the Hispanic culture. Up to now these traditional elite families still have a strong hold on the government. In fact many of them participate in politics and so have been ruling the country. For example, Fernando Lopez, whose family owns large tracts of sugar lands, was the vice president when Marcos was president before he declared martial law; while Salvador Laurel, from a landed, elite family in Batangas Province, was Corazon Aquino's vice president. Aquino herself came from the Cojuangco clan, a Chinese *mestizo* family, which still owns a large sugar hacienda, the Philippine long-distance telephone monopoly, among many other business interests.

The American occupation (1898–1946) did not reform the system, but in fact aggravated it (Putzel 1992). The objectives of the United States in colonizing the Philippines were to make the Philippines its gateway to China's markets and secure the Philippines' export crops for the United States. The easiest way to fulfil these objectives was to allow the continuation of land concentration and maintain the patrimonial oligarchic system. The American regime further strengthened the oligarchic base and power with the creation of more enrichment opportunities: The preferential access for agricultural products in American markets, and the means by which local officials could control the access to natural resources (de Dios and Hutchcroft 2003).

In the Philippines, for centuries, the oligarchs have dominated the country's political and economic arenas, working for their vested interest. They lobbied for protection for their business activities — high prices for their products and services and low tariffs for the inputs they need. Their interests are usually put ahead of public interest, even among public servants. President Corazon Cojuangco Aquino, who fought against the Marcos dictatorship and succeeded him, disappointed the Filipino population when she chose to protect her family's large sugar estate instead of reforming the land distribution. Because the institutions are weak, the country continues to experience a political economy wherein the state policies work around the vested interests of the oligarchs. For example, the most vibrant industry in the Philippines today is the telecommunication industry, which is dominated by traditional oligarch families, the Ayalas and the Lopezes. The proposal to tax the sending of SMS (called texting in the Philippines) to help solve the country's fiscal deficit problem was met with much opposition and could not get to be filed as a bill in congress. These same families dominating the telecommunication sector were given concession for water service distribution in 1998 despite their dive bids (Bello 2004), which of course was unfair to other participants who gave more realistic bids. Because their bid proposals were not realistic, their actual operations resulted in revenues not being able to cover cost. This loss was then solved by allowing them to raise prices. These families continue to get concessions, including, very recently (in 2004), the right to maintain the main superhighways linking Manila to the north and the south. The concession, which was awarded to the Lopez family, plus weak regulatory control, led to an increase in toll rates by hundreds of percent.

Over the last several decades, the oligarch class has become more diverse. Today, aside from the traditional elite families, many indigenous and Chinese Filipinos who have become wealthy and/or powerful due to windfalls from business or political connections, form part of the oligarch class. Although the Chinese are not active in politics, they are no longer under the shadows of the traditional oligarchs. Most of them have adjusted and integrated well into the country's political culture. Given their economic power, many now have political connections while some in fact have reached the level of oligarchic importance. For those without such influence, their voices are being heeded through business and civic organizations.

2.2 Political Culture

The other feature of Philippine political economy is the culture of patronage politics. This means that people in power use their political power to grant favours to loyalists or to those who they expect will be able to return the favours. Such a culture, where the linkage between political and economic power is very close, allows for rampant bribery. Personal loyalty to politicians is important in gaining favours. Although the oligarchs are invariably part of the recipients of favours due to the pressure they can exert, to some extent, this patronage culture within the government offsets the effect of the patrimonial oligarchic system. For example, the political culture of patronage and personal connection was very apparent during the industry protection period in the fifties when foreign exchange and imports were under control through the licensing system. This resulted to some degree in the dilution of wealth concentration. The elite group expanded to include industrialists who profited from the protection under the industrialization programme.

The patrimonial patronage system was indeed the basis of cronyism in the seventies when the business of the country was in the hands of a few personalities whose loyalty to Marcos and his family was absolute during the martial law period (Hawes 1992).

Presently, with this kind of political culture still deeply entrenched, many Chinese Filipinos have been able to establish political connections and utilize their economic power to attain their objectives. Still, the Chinese are generally politically vulnerable and play safe by maintaining good relationships with all political groups. To quote Hutchcroft (1998), "Those least public in their political affiliations, of course, are most adept at cultivating ties across political divides and adjusting to changing political fortunes. Chinese-Filipino entrepreneurs, historically more vulnerable to exactions and more reliant on extra-familial links to the political machinery, have earned a particular reputation for their ability to cultivate ties with more than one side in any political contest." They, as individuals and business organizations, are known to contribute to the coffers of all the strong contenders in every national election.

3. CHINESE BUSINESS DURING THE COLONIAL PERIOD

The Spanish settled in the Philippines in the second half of the sixteenth century and developed the Manila-Acapulco galleon trade, which lasted for more than two centuries. Manila was an entrepôt as goods of silks and porcelain were brought from China, loaded on the Manila galleon, and shipped to Mexico. More and more Chinese merchants and artisans came in the ships carrying goods for the galleon trade. The Spaniards regarded this development with mixed feelings. They feared the increasing number, especially since the Spanish population was much smaller in size. However, they had come to depend on the Chinese most of who were artisans whom they found skilled and industrious, and merchants whom they found to be performing an important function of bringing goods to the provinces. Hence there ensued very volatile policies towards the Chinese — expulsion and massacre on the one hand, and tolerance and accommodation on the other (Wickberg 1965).

In the nineteenth century, the Spaniards developed the export crop economy to replace the declining Manila galleon trade for foreign exchange. The landed class consisting of Spanish Filipinos, Chinese *mestizos,* and a few indigenous Filipinos benefited from such an economy and emerged as the elite and oligarchic class. Only a few Chinese, who were involved in the trading of raw materials and imported manufactured products, profited from the export crop economy.

The export crop economy grew even faster after the American regime took over in 1898 as the Philippine export crops were very much in demand in the U.S. home market. A boom in the external trade resulted when the Philippines-United States free trade was established under the 1909 Payne-Aldrich Act. This relationship was strengthened in 1913 with the abolition of the quota system for sugar export.[4] Rapid export-led economic growth continued up to 1929 when the Great Depression set in. Unfortunately, this kind of economic growth failed to develop the structure of the Philippine economy as it was based on the cultivation of the same export crops of the nineteenth century. Manufacturing was limited only to the processing of some export crops as the United States wanted to keep the Philippines as a market for its own manufactures.

The capitalists then were the landed oligarchs, who benefited greatly from the export trade boom. The wealthy land-based elite dominated in the collection and exportation of the exportable commodities. The participation of the Chinese in the very profitable export trade during this period was limited only to a few rich enough to be capitalists (Wong 1999). Most Chinese at that time were poor struggling migrants from southern China. Moreover, agricultural export processing had become more sophisticated and required more capital. In this respect the Chinese in the Philippines were considered an anomaly when compared with their counterparts in Southeast Asia (Wong 1999). At that time in Indochina, Malaya, and Siam, the Chinese dominated the trade in primary produce such as rice, tin, rubber and sugar.

With the growth in domestic market and pioneering settlements during the American period which presented opportunities for distributing goods to the new settlements, the Chinese went into domestic trade instead (Wong 1999). Such business engagement was very practical for the Chinese as it did not require much initial capital outlay and generated high liquidity in asset disposal. Many engaged in the simplest retail business by being owners and storekeepers of small convenience stores called *sari-sari* stores, which formed a large base in the pyramid of the Chinese distribution system. With its easy entry since little capital and only simple business skills were needed, the *sari-sari* store concept was very attractive to new migrant Chinese. Skills were easily acquired while the potential store owner worked as an employee in a retail store owned by his patron relative.

Commerce was the dominant activities of the Chinese in both colonial regimes. A number of them engaged in the exchange of export crops for manufactured goods, but the majority of the Chinese simply engaged in small-scale retail trade business or household-type factories. Very few were engaged in large-scale manufacturing.[5] Accumulation of wealth was primarily through thrift and industriousness. By the 1920s, more Chinese became settled in the country as they could bring in their families. Thus formal organizations and institutions of the Chinese community such as schools, newspapers, a general hospital, and the Chamber of Commerce were established. Important to the business community was the establishment of the China Banking Corporation in 1920.[6]

4. POST-COLONIAL PERIOD

The Philippines gained independence from the United States in 1946 and gradually recovered from the devastation of World War II. The plight of the Chinese in the country was, however, less hopeful as they continued to face difficulties and uncertainties due to events that were happening in China and the rising nationalism in the Philippines. Expecting to return to their native land after accumulating some wealth, the immigrant Chinese now found it undesirable to do so because of the economic and political turmoil in China. The thirties and the forties saw the bitter and destructive Sino-Japanese war as well as the civil war between the Kuomintang government and the Chinese communists. The wars, coupled with corruption of the Chinese national government, aggravated the deterioration of its economy. Finally, the victory of the Chinese Communist Party led to a radical change in China's political situation. Going back to the homeland was certainly not an attractive option. In fact many Chinese in the mainland got out of China during these tumultuous decades.

In the meantime, in the Philippines, the sentiment of nationalism grew fiercely. It started to brew since the American period, as manifested in the nationalization of inter-island shipping in 1923 and logging in 1930. The 1935 constitution drafted during the Commonwealth period was generally nationalistic with particular provisions targeting the Chinese. It limited citizenship with a strict and stringent naturalization law, requiring an arduous process and a big sum of money. Aside from the stringent requirements, the Chinese were not eager to adopt Philippine citizenship due to their spirit of patriotism towards their homeland and their resentment towards the anti-Chinese sentiment of the Filipinos. The social gap between the Chinese and the Filipinos at that time was huge.

The worst discrimination measure targeting the Chinese was the Nationalization of Retail Trade Act in 1954. Since the Chinese business was mostly in the trade sector, this act created uproar in the Chinese community, although, given its weak social and political standing then, there was nothing it could do.[7] The strict interpretation of the law also meant that traders at almost all levels of the Chinese trade pyramid network were affected (Yoshihara 1985). In 1960, the rice and corn business, another industry dominated by the Chinese, was also nationalized. Other restrictions to the non-Filipinos were the practice of certain professions such as medicine, accounting, architecture, and engineering, as the government examinations for the professional licences were limited to Filipino citizens only.

Meantime, as a newly independent nation, the Philippines focused on industrialization, which was neglected during the colonial period. Most of the manufactured products consumed were imported. Soon after independence, the national government undertook an active role in the investment and management of firms in the heavy and basic industries as well as the service sector.[8] Light industries were promoted with the adoption of the import-substitution industrialization (ISI) strategy, that is, producing commodities purchased by the local market. Manufacturers were given protection in terms of tax exemption, favourable credit terms, and preferred foreign exchange allocation, as well as the control of imports of products produced by them. Through the foreign exchange and import controls, the government hoped also to solve its serious balance of payments crisis, even as it tried to promote the industrialization programme.

The protected industrial sector provided a convenient refuge for the many Chinese businesses displaced by the nationalization of retail trade and rice and corn industries. High tariffs, restrictive quotas and foreign exchange and import controls made doing business difficult for wholesale traders as well. For the Chinese merchants, engaging in domestic production was the most rational thing to do. The ISI protectionist policies did not exclude the entry of foreign capital. Hence other than the traditional elites and other Filipinos, the participation of foreign and domestic Chinese investors was also significant. Foreign investments in manufacturing came in as subsidiaries of multinationals, other wholly foreign-owned firms, or joint ventures with Filipinos and local Chinese.

Attracted by the incentive policies, the landed elite families diversified into ISI manufacturing. They shunned the heavy industries which were riskier and had longer gestation period. But because they had more capital and/or better access to it, the ISI investments they engaged in were more large-scale and capital intensive. The participation of the landed elites in industry, however, did not contribute much to economic development. The result of their participation, described as the "feudalization of the industry" (O'Connor 1990), resulted in the traditional elites becoming not just landowners, but also owners of urban industrial business.[9] Because wealth from land was not converted to capital for the manufacturing sector, Philippine industrialization did not have the class transformation which in other countries such as Taiwan and South Korea, resulted in significant industrial growth and development (Rivera 1998).

The ISI protectionist policies also attracted non-landed Filipinos, many of who were professionals who had worked in American firms as managers, accountant, etc. and could develop connections with the ruling class. The size of their firms was, however, expectedly much smaller compared to those owned by the traditional landowning elites.

Under the new industrial policy in the fifties, the Chinese also enjoyed many of the government incentives in their import-substitution manufacturing endeavours. Such opportunities provided escape from the difficulties they faced in the trade sector, although low-interest credit and other privileges available only to Filipinos made it difficult for them to engage in large-scale production activities. It became apparent that the acquisition of citizenship was important although, given the cost and procedure involved, not many could avail of it. The use of dummies as front for their businesses and ownership of properties was prevalent.

The ISI policies resulted in a rapid growth of Philippine manufacturing in the fifties and sixties. The share of manufacturing in GDP grew from 10.7 per cent in 1948 to 17.9 per cent in 1960 (Putzel 1992). Since manufacturing provided an attractive alternative to trade which had become restricted to them, Chinese participation in this sector increased significantly. The Filipino Chinese firms occupied a third in number among the top 250 Philippine manufacturing firms for 1968 with the foreign and Filipino groups each occupying a third as well (Yoshihara 1985). Firms owned by the domestic Chinese were, however, relatively smaller in size while the foreign-owned ones were largest in size.[10] A great majority (75 per cent) of these top manufacturing firms were established after 1950, to take advantage of the government's industrial policy. This was more evident for the Chinese firms, where 73 (90 per cent) of the eighty-one firms owned by the Chinese were established after 1950. This percentage could actually be higher since many of the sampled Chinese firms with establishment year before 1950 were engaged in trading before then but diversified into manufacturing only after the import-substitution industrialization policy took effect.[11] Keeping the same corporate name, they went into manufacturing products of the same business lines they traded. For example, firms engaged in textile trading went into textile manufacturing while hardware merchants went into the manufacturing of nails, bolts and nuts, etc. There were some joint ventures with foreign investments, mostly Japanese and American. These were larger in scale, and used more advanced technology.

Despite the significant growth of the sector, the manufacturing during this period was criticized to be very simple, last-stage type of production, involving simply mixing, packaging, or assembly (Power and Sicat 1971). Thus the reliance on imports of raw materials and semi-processed materials, let alone machinery and equipment, was significant. Because of government protection, those who went into the industrial sector realized great windfall profits. Those who benefited most from the import and foreign exchange controls were the politically powerful oligarchs.[12] What developed was a very oligopolistic structure of manufacturing sector which limited innovation and competition (de Dios 1991). Rampant corruption in the government bureaucracy also resulted from the controls.

While the import-substitution strategy benefited many industrialists, it did not contribute to economic development but instead resulted in many negative effects on the Philippine economy. The balance of payments crisis grew worse as the over-valued currency discouraged exports while the demand for imported raw materials, machinery and equipment, and semi-processed materials for manufacturing drained the foreign exchange reserve excessively. Moreover, manufacturing, which was essentially assembly processes, had little value-added. Instead it relied heavily on foreign exchange and had little effect on employment creation. The implementation of foreign exchange controls and import quota resulted in rampant bureaucratic corruption. The use of government economic power was essentially "determined by patronage relationships between politicians and entrepreneurs" (Hawes 1992). Unemployment increased since the credit incentive given to manufacturers made the use of capital-intensive methods of production more attractive than the labour-intensive ones. Income disparity grew with the manufacturers enjoying windfall income while labour suffered unemployment and low wage rate. Above all, the low income and purchasing power of the domestic market restricted the growth of the import-substitution manufacturing activities.

The government post-war industrialization plan was hence not very successful. Aside from the many negative effects of the ISI on the economy, most of the public investments in capital-intensive industries and operation of national corporations in utilities and other services resulted in losses due to corruption and poor management. The failure of national corporations and investments in the Philippines in the fifties and sixties contrasts significantly with the case of Korea, where the large government-subsidized manufacturing corporations (*chaebols*) have enabled Korea to face global competition with Japan and the United States due to their large-scale production capability today (Fukuyama 1995).

In 1962, the Philippine currency was devalued and the foreign exchange and import controls lifted when Diosdado Macapagal took office. However, due to pressure from the industrialists and clamor from the nationalistic left-wing sector, the government, using the "infant" industry rationale, continued to protect the local industries with high import tariffs, thus creating monopolistic element in many manufacturing industries. "Successful" manufacturing entrepreneurs included both traditional landowning elites and non-landed Filipinos and Chinese. The political culture made it easy for the industrialists to be rent-seekers and to lobby for protection.

The history of Philippine manufacturing reveals that protection has been responsible for the stagnant economic structure and the lack of industrial competitiveness in the Philippines. Monopolistic power in Philippine manufacturing industry as measured by the average four-firm concentration ratio has increased from 70.88 per cent in 1988 to 80.55 per cent in 1998, while effective protection rates in agriculture and manufacturing sectors have increased significantly since 1998 (Aldaba 2005). The trend could have worsened after 1998 as the Estrada (1997–2001) and Arroyo (2001–) administrations have reversed many of the liberalization efforts made in the eighties and nineties.

5. MARTIAL LAW

Marcos declared martial law in 1972 as a means to perpetuate his rule since he had been elected to the presidency twice (1965 and 1969) and under the constitution then could no longer run for another term. The time was opportune because at that time the country was experiencing social and political tension created by the problems of corruption, income inequality, unemployment and serious balance of payments deficit — problems that had resulted from the exchange and import controls as well as protection of the manufacturing industries. The economy was perceived to be controlled by American MNCs and the oligarchs. Rallies organized by students and the leftists protested against imperialism and oligarchy. Anti-Sinicism was, nonetheless, not an issue at that time.

The martial law period under President Ferdinand Marcos displayed the worst of Philippine political economy with patrimonialism being centralized under the dictatorship. Crony capitalism characterized the business and economic environment during the fourteen years of authoritarian rule. The economy was run by a very miniscule segment of the private sector composed of Marcos's friends, relatives, and other loyalists. The traditional landed oligarchs lost power, as they were branded enemy of the state.[13] It was convenient for Marcos as the oligarchs, together with U.S. imperialism, had been the target of attacks by student activists and the left-leaning sector of society.

To justify his authoritarian government, Marcos actually had a comprehensive development plan for the country, vowing to undertake export-oriented industrialization. With the economy run by cronies, the plan was never followed. It, however, satisfied the international institutions (World Bank and IMF), from which credit and development funds were secured. Patrimonialism and the patronage politics were stretched to the limit under one absolute dictator. Corruption became even more entrenched while the economy stagnated and the poverty situation worsened. Eventually, like most absolute rules, corruption and cronyism brought the Marcos regime to its end.

The impact of Marcos's dictatorship on the ethnic Chinese business was, however, rather favourable. The Chinese were generally apolitical and without political power. They did not pose any threat to Marcos's political ambition. Moreover, one of Marcos's few legacies, the liberalization of the naturalization procedure instituted in 1975, greatly benefited the Chinese. Solving the legal status of the Philippine ethnic Chinese had to be done in preparation for establishing Philippine diplomatic ties with China, which was done in the same year. The liberalization of the naturalization process was a great turning point for the Chinese. Most of the ethnic Chinese then, despite the fact that they were born in the Philippines and were culturally assimilated, remained

Chinese citizens due to the high cost and legal complexity of the naturalization procedure. The presidential decree liberalizing the naturalization process allowed qualified aliens — those over age twenty-one, of good moral character, literate, and had resided in the Philippines for at least ten years — to apply and acquire Filipino citizenship easily. The ethnic Chinese responded enthusiastically and took advantage of the opportunity to become Filipino citizens.

The new citizenship increased greatly the ethnic Chinese's business-doing capability, including those in the lower economic classes. Before the mass naturalization, only a few wealthy Chinese who could afford the citizenship had access to the economic privileges limited to Filipino citizens. With respect to their business activities, during the martial law period, like all other people engaged in business at that time (except for the cronies), the Chinese were very low-key. Businesses which were conspicuously profitable took the risk of government or military takeover. The Chinese in business basically looked for inconspicuous opportunities that would not attract the attention of Marcos and his cronies. This was generally the attitude and approach taken by the business people at that time. The traditional oligarchs and other *nouveau riche* Filipinos were also as quiet and inconspicuous as possible in their businesses (Hawes 1992).

Cronyism during the martial law period bred a new class of economically powerful Filipino elite. The new oligarchs were the cronies who included relatives and friends of Marcos and his wife. They monopolized the sugar and coconut industries and dominated the large business conglomerates that emerged during this period. Some of the non-landed entrepreneurs who had benefited from the industrial protectionism in the previous period became cronies during the Marcos regime through their reliance on the state as well as their history of personal and working ties with elite politicians in the state apparatuses (Rivera 1994).

A few ethnic Chinese were among the cronies. The most prominent among them was Lucio Tan and Jose Yao Campos. Lucio Tan built his business empire, which started with tobacco manufacturing but extended to animal husbandry, beverages, banking and hotels, through his connections with Marcos. He is one of the few cronies who continue to thrive under all administrations after Marcos and has become the wealthiest person in the Philippines and one of the wealthiest in the world. Up to now he has been able to elude the tax evasion charges filed against him more than a decade ago. Jose Yao Campos, who was in the pharmaceuticals business, was given the monopoly of pharmaceutical distribution in government hospitals during the martial law period.

The martial law rule devastated the country, setting back the political gains and economic development achieved earlier.[14] With his attention focused on how to stay in power and amass wealth, Marcos ignored attempts that would lead to the country's economic transformation, which many neighbouring countries were going through at that time. Instead, plundering, over-borrowing and mismanagement of funds by the government resulted in financial difficulties that were felt by 1981 and further aggravated by the political instability caused by the assassination of the opposition leader Benigno Aquino in August of 1983. An unprecedented economic crisis brought the economy to a virtual standstill. External debt, which could not be serviced, led to the termination of credit lines. The dictator and his family were finally deposed in a People Power revolution in February of 1986 and Corazon Cojuangco Aquino was sworn in as president.

6. POST-MARTIAL LAW ERA

With the economy saddled with a huge external debt left by the ousted government and marked by political instability caused by the rightist reform movement, the leftist National People's Army, and the Muslim rebels in the south, the Philippines during President Aquino's term (1986–92) was very unstable. Several natural disasters[15] also cost the economy much damage. To top it all, in the last couple of years of her term, the country experienced a very serious energy crisis. Moreover, Aquino did not use the power she had to institute reforms that the civil society, the left, and the population in general were expecting to happen after the dramatic revolution.[16]

Aquino did, however, undertake some major economic reforms that set the groundwork for recovery which occurred after she had left office. These reforms, which her successor President Fidel Ramos continued, included tax reform, the dismantling of the agricultural monopolies, and trade liberalization. With the economic liberalization programme that opened the country to more exports and foreign investments, after her term, the economy began to experience recovery, which was sustained until 1997 when the Asian economic crisis occurred.

The economic and political crises during the Aquino's term were very severe and prompted many Filipinos to leave the country. The ethnic

Chinese, however, reacted differently. They saw investment opportunities in the midst of the turbulence and atmosphere of hopelessness.[17] They took advantage of the cheap asset prices and diversified their business portfolios. The really wealthy Chinese even bought out some of the sequestered businesses and properties of the Marcos government. The Filipino citizenship they now had allowed them to own lands and become majority owners of businesses. In contrast, the non-Chinese Filipinos, both from the traditional elite and the middle class, tended to escape the pessimistic and depressed economic situation by migrating abroad. This was observed by Roberto Tiglao (1990), who wrote in the *Far Eastern Economic Review*: "In the 1980s, when many Spaniard *mestizo* and Filipino professionals and businessmen were fleeing to the U.S. and Canada, Chinese-Filipinos mostly remained at home and expanded their businesses."[18] In the last decade, however, the ethnic Chinese have started to migrate out of the Philippines due to the kidnapping spate which targeted them. For safety, many left for Canada, Australia, Singapore and even China. Capital outflow by the Chinese was observed for the period of 1992–93, with much of it going to China, due to the economic boom occurring there then (Ang See 1994).

The significant and conspicuous rise of Philippine ethnic Chinese business in the post-martial law era can be traced only to the last few decades. According to Wickberg (1997), "In the early 1970s, the situation of the Philippine Chinese was still much as Weightman[19] had described it in the 1950s — that of a marginal trading community" (p. 170). This was still the general perception of Filipinos on the Chinese based perhaps on their social status. The industrialization programme of the government in the fifties and sixties provided protection to manufacturing entrepreneurs. The Chinese businesses, banned from the trade sector, shifted to manufacturing and realized windfall profits due to the protection given to it. It was the citizenship they secured in the seventies which allowed them the same economic rights and privileges as the Filipinos. They also took advantage of the business opportunities the post-martial law transitional political and economic situation presented. These developments, coupled with their high propensity to save and business acumen, led to the emergence of large Chinese business conglomerates. Starting in the early nineties, conspicuous edifices owned by the ethnic Chinese such as huge shopping malls, office buildings which house the banks of the building owners on the ground floor, residential condominium buildings, and luxurious hotels, started to rise one after another. The owners of these conspicuous businesses and edifices were mostly self-made entrepreneurs, completely unknown half a century ago. The ethnic Chinese business also diversified extensively, as it moved towards the services, particularly finance, insurance and real estate (Palanca 1995).

At the same time there arose a different generation of ethnic Chinese, whose identity was more Filipino than Chinese. Socially, the ethnic Chinese have also become more integrated into the mainstream of society, enjoying respectable social position due to their higher educational status and economic standing. Increasingly, many are engaged in professions such as medical doctors, lawyers, accountants and architects[20] other than business. The number of Chinese engaged in politics and government service is, however, still very small.

Despite the improvement in their social and legal position, however, due to their minority status and lack of political clout, the economic success of the Chinese in the Philippines has not been without cost. In the early 1990s, kidnappings targeting the ethnic Chinese became rampant. The Ramos administration, which followed that of Aquino, targeted them for government revenue, citing "to promote fair competition" as the motive. In 1993, six prominent Chinese Filipino tycoons[21] were handpicked by President Ramos to accompany him in his state visit to China. At the same time, these multi-billionaires (called *taipans* by the media) were asked to form a corporation that would undertake infrastructure projects to speed up the country's economic growth. Six months after this, tax investigation cases were filed against these same tycoons. Because the traditional business Spanish *mestizo* elites did not get the same treatment, it was concluded that "it is likely that the Chinese business community was targetted not only because of its ability to pay but also because, as part of a tiny ethnic minority under a democratic political regime, it lacked both the electoral clout and the state protection to fight back" (Lim and Gosling 1997, p. 302).

7. INTEGRATION OF CHINESE AND FILIPINO ELITE BUSINESSES

The growth of Philippine Chinese business in the second half of the century, which accelerated in the last couple of decades, placed the Chinese at par with the traditional elites in terms of wealth accumulation by the 1990s. The six *taipans* (targeted by Ramos) are wealthy by any standard. Two of them, Henry Sy and Lucio Tan, are among the three Filipinos in the 2005 Forbes list of top 500 wealthiest in the world. The third Filipino, Jaime Zobel de Ayala, is from a traditional Spanish-descent elite family, which owns the lands in Makati and has developed it to become a very upscale commercial and financial centre. Both Sy and Tan, who migrated from China after World War II, are rags-to-riches cases.

The traditional elites have dominated the economic and political arenas of the country since the Spanish era except for the martial law period when most of the traditional elites were not in Marcos's circle of cronies.[22] Except for a couple, however, most of the traditional elites were not severely persecuted, and they tried to stay as inconspicuous as possible (Hawes 1998). Despite the years of low-key activities of the traditional elites during those years, their latent economic strength was still very strong. This can be seen from the case of the Lopez family whose electricity monopoly in Metro Manila, two television stations and a newspaper were taken over by the government when martial law was declared, but was able to again take control of all these within a few months after the ouster of the Marcoses.[23]

In the last few decades, the Chinese excelled in business areas which were traditionally dominated by the Spanish Filipinos. They hence pose challenges to the Filipino elites in areas of business such as banking, food production and real estate development. In banking, aside from the foreign banks, the larger ones were owned by the traditional Filipino elites.[24] Chinese-owned banks such as China Banking Corporation and Philippine Bank of Communications were small by comparison. The largest and strongest bank had for a long time been the century-old Bank of the Philippine Islands owned by the Ayalas, a Spanish Filipino family. In the last decade, however, this bank has been strongly challenged by the ethnic Chinese-owned Metropolitan Bank and Trust Company. Founded by George Ty (one of the six *taipans*) in 1960, the Metropolitan Bank has since the mid-nineties occupied the first place in deposits, assets, and portfolio. Banco de Oro, owned by Henry Sy, which started only as a savings bank in 1980, has also been growing very fast and caused a stir when it bought out another Chinese Filipino bank, the Equitable-PCI Bank in July 2005. A large share of the Philippine National Bank has since 2000 been owned by Lucio Tan, who is planning to merge it with his own bank (Allied Bank). All these will certainly result in the Chinese dominating and taking the lead position in the banking industry.

In the food and beverage industry, San Miguel Corporation (SMC), another gigantic Spanish Filipino-owned corporation founded in 1851, had enjoyed a monopoly position in the beer, and other food and beverage product markets for more than a century. It now faces tough competition from Lucio Tan's breweries and Gokongwei's Universal Robina Corporation, and a couple of other beverage companies, which produce food and beverage products similar to SMC's.

The Chinese are also involved in the real property business which for a long time had been controlled by the Spanish Filipinos, who acquired vast lands during the Spanish time. Owning most of the lands in the cities, they have been credited for having developed cities in Metro Manila. On the other hand, the majority of the ethnic Chinese could not own lands till they acquired their citizenship in the seventies. Presently, however, many big-time real property developers are Chinese Filipinos. For huge development projects, the Chinese Filipinos have joined forces with other ethnic Chinese in Southeast Asia. The Shangri-La Plaza mall in Mandaluyong and Tagaytay Highlands Golf Club development in Tagaytay City were such joint projects. The biggest show of force of the Chinese was the consortium involving Indonesia's Liem Sioe Liong, Robert Kuok of Malaysia and Chinese Filipino tycoons Andrew Gotiunun, Henry Sy, Lucio Tan, and George Ty, when it won a bid against the Ayalas (the Spanish Filipinos known for the development of Makati City and to own practically the whole city) to develop the 214-hectare Fort Bonifacio tract of land in Makati City in February of 1995 (Ang and Palanca 2000).

In the midst of competition with each other, the Chinese tycoons and Filipino elites now also cooperate with each other, pooling together resources. The growing cooperation between the two groups follows the merging and acquisition phenomenon prevalent in the international business arena. The globalization and liberalization trend demands greater competitiveness of business firms. In order to increase their competitiveness, Philippine business firms have merged with other domestic businesses or with foreign ones. In this respect, alliances have also been formed because the Filipino and Chinese business groups recognized the mutual advantage in such. There have been several significant joint ventures between the present Chinese *taipans* and the elite indigenous and Spanish Filipinos. For example, John Gokongwei has alliances with the Lopez family in several businesses — banking, power generation, and telecommunication; while Henry Sy, has since the eighties been linking up with the Ayalas on several property development projects. Chinese affiliation with large Filipino firms such as the Philippine Long Distance Telephone Company and San Miguel Corporation has also been done through significant purchase of their stocks and eventually joining their boards. Indigenous professional elites have integrated into the Chinese business sector by being officers of Chinese firms.

The mutual advantage realized by the Chinese and traditional elite groups in combining their resources goes beyond increasing competitiveness through size. Such alliances combine the aggressiveness of the Chinese business people with the business tradition and experience of the Filipino elite group. They also realize the advantages in the combined connections with the international financial communities and other networks of both groups. The merging of two Chinese firms would not have such advantages because their competitive edges are similar. Moreover, merging between Chinese firms in the same line of business are not likely cases because of the rivalry between them. Examples are John Gokongwei and Henry Sy in the retail business, Lucio Tan and John Gokongwei in the airline business, and Lucio Tan and Alfredo Yao in the beverage industry. The recent acquisition by Henry Sy's Banco de Oro of Equitable-PCI, a bank owned by the Go family,[25] involved fierce struggle. This situation is also true for the traditional Filipino elite families. The Cojuangcos and the Lopezes are keen competitors in the telecommunication industry. Both groups have involved the ethnic Chinese to expand their capability and increase their competitive edge. Such alliances, coupled with the social integration of the ethnic Chinese into the Philippine society, have gradually blurred the ethnic distinction between large Filipino and Chinese businesses.

8. CHINESE FILIPINOS: THE NEW ELITES

The last few decades saw the gradual integration of the ethnic Chinese into the mainstream of Philippine society, both in business and in the social circles, and their emergence as a strong elite group. Six Chinese Filipino businessmen have been given the status of super-rich *taipans,* two of whom are in the 2005 Forbes list of the top 500 wealthiest in the world. Aside from these identified super-rich ethnic Chinese, there are many others whose wealth and social stature are comparable or not too far behind.[26] Having equal legal rights as the other Filipinos after gaining citizenship, the Chinese took advantage of the business and investment opportunities presented during the crisis years in the eighties. In addition, the globalization trend has presented more international investment opportunities. Capital market liberalization in the last couple of decades makes it easy to move capital around the world. The rise of China since the eighties also presents more opportunities to the ethnic Chinese, as their cultural and language affinity makes doing business with the mainland Chinese easier for them than for the other Filipinos. Investments of the *taipans* in China are growing and very visible. One can find an SM mall in Xiamen and Metrobank branches in Beijing and Shanghai.

8.1 Oligarchic Power

Although oligarchy is generally associated with the traditional landowning elite families, there is now a blurring of ethnic distinction as many Chinese now join the ranks. The Chinese and the foreign investors are considered "newer forces" which the traditional oligarchs now have to compete with (de Dios and Hutchcroft 2003). There is, however, no obvious discriminatory distinction between the traditional and the ethnic Chinese elites. The stark social division is along economic class, that is, between the very miniscule percentage of the wealthy class and the impoverished majority of the population. Because the wealthy are not exclusively represented by the Chinese, but include the traditional elites, in the Philippines, the resentment of the poor against the rich is not defined by ethnicity.

The economic position of the six *taipans* and a few other Philippine Chinese put them in the oligarchic class that can lobby for their interests. Except for the case of Lucio Tan, the tax investigation filed against the *taipans* did not prosper. The influence of their businesses more than compensates for their lack of political clout. For example, the presence of a SM mall exerts tremendous effect on the land value and development of the surrounding area. When Henry Sy started to build his SM shopping malls in other cities outside of Metro Manila in the nineties, many town mayors wooed him to have one built in their place. In another instance, the threat of labour to strike was quelled by the threat of Henry Sy to close down his business.

With little direct political connections, the Chinese elites have a different way of achieving such connections. One practice common to the large business conglomerates of the *taipans* is the hiring and retention of retired high-ranking government officials, military generals, and retired judges in their corporations. These well respected and educated indigenous Filipinos act as liaison between their business and the government. They also give prestige to their companies, provide convenience, and improve the level of professionalism.

Another common feature of the wealthy Philippine Chinese is that the extensive charity and civic works they do, are much more than what the traditional elites do. Through these, they integrate with the mainstream society and gain its goodwill.

The Chinese elites can and have exerted their oligarchic power and capitalized on their citizenship. A significant and very obvious case that illustrates the oligarchic power of the Chinese was the sale of Manila Hotel in 1997. Known for its grandeur and illustrious past, the hotel was built and run by the national government since 1912. In 1997, when the government decided to privatize it, a Malaysian business group won the bid, but instead, the hotel was sold to a wealthy ethnic Chinese, Emilio Yap. Mr. Yap lost the bid for the historic hotel; however, he appealed to the Supreme Court and was able to have the decision on the sale reversed to favour him. His claim was that the hotel is a patrimonial property and should be awarded to a Filipino citizen. The hotel unfortunately has lost its grandeur since the transfer of ownership.

The slow pace of retail trade liberalization might be another case of oligarchic pressure. There were insinuations by newspaper columnists of lobbying effort of the dominant players in the industry, who were mostly prominent Chinese Filipinos, although there is no strong evidence regarding it. The industry was open to foreigners only in 2000 with the passage of the Retail Trade Liberalization Act even though many other industries of the service sector had already been liberalized. The Retail Trade Liberalization Act replaced the half-a-century old Retail Trade Nationalization Act of 1954, which seriously affected the Chinese then as most were non-citizens. But now that the Chinese had become Filipino citizens, they naturally preferred that the sector remained nationalized, to limit competition from foreigners in the retail business. Although the industry is now denationalized, protection continues to some extent with a high minimum capital requirement of US$2.5 million for foreign retailers, the highest among the Asian economies. However, the high degree of competition among the major players such as Henry Sy and John Gokongwei in the industry has kept the monopoly power rather low (Aldaba 2005).

8.2 Patronage Politics

For those with economic power not the calibre of the *taipans*, the patronage system is being exploited for government favours and concessions. Historically the Chinese had obtained favours and concessions through patronage politics and bribery. Many lumber concessions were secured in such manner in the sixties and seventies. Patronage politics during the martial law period, extensive in the form of cronyism, did not involve many Chinese. This might be due to the fact that the Chinese then had little military connections or perhaps because they preferred not to be involved with the military and hence did not care to develop such connections during the fourteen years of martial law.

Cronyism made a comeback during Joseph Estrada's administration. Film actor Estrada was duly elected in 1998, but abused his power and was removed from office before his term ended. Among his cronies were his Chinese friends from way back in the 1970s when he was mayor of San Juan, a Metro Manila municipality. These cronies introduced more Chinese into this crony circle. Estrada's most prominent Chinese crony was Lucio Tan, his largest campaign contributor. People (both Filipinos and Chinese) who wanted to be in Estrada's circle generally do not have oligarchic power, and so tried to get favours and protection through presidential connections.[27] But this was not so for Tan, who, no doubt an oligarch, needed to get favours directly from the president. His tax evasion case was one reason why he needed such direct protection. The case was indeed suspended based on a minor technicality point, and aside from that, he got other favours. The government very openly protected Philippine Airlines which Tan owns by reversing the country's airline liberalization policy and refusing landing right to planes coming in from Taiwan in 1999. This abrogation of air services agreement with Taiwan hindered competition and, because of the inconvenience it caused, meant loss for the Philippines in the number of tourists. The Chinese Filipino cronies made use of Estrada's power for illegal wealth accumulation, the most prominent case of which was the manipulation of the stock market for BW Resources issue. Estrada also facilitated in corporate merging and buyouts which benefited his cronies and in turn earned him huge commission.

Estrada allowed the exploitation of the political economic system and its weak institutions to the fullest (de Dios and Hutchcroft 2003). In the end he fell in the hands of one of his own associates, governor of a province in the north, who testified that Estrada received *payola* for the running of an illegal gambling game at the national level. Other scandals were exposed. His term was cut short by another People Power, which protested against the proceedings of the impeachment process, since the senate, which was dominated by his allies, was blocking it. The result was the installation of Gloria Macapagal-Arroyo, then vice president, to finish his term.

The involvement of the Chinese Filipinos as cronies during the short presidency of Joseph Estrada showed that, compared to Marcos's time, there were more Chinese who had the temerity and capability to be close to people in power, or to go along with those who are willing to exploit the system. The people (both Filipinos and Chinese) who wanted to be in Estrada's circle generally lacked real oligarchic power, and hence, they tried to get favours and protection through presidential connections.[28] Despite the fact that quite a number of Estrada's cronies were Chinese, ethnicity of the cronies was never an issue. Estrada's Chinese accomplices, Dante Tan, Charles Atong Ang, George Go, and Jose Dichaves, were condemned together with Mark Jimenez and other Filipinos for their illegal business activities, with no special remark on their ethnicity.

8.3 Community Organizations

A more legitimate way for the Chinese to get their voices heard is through organized groups. Individually most Chinese do not have economic clout or political connection to get the attention of policymakers. However, they are listened to as major organizations representing the Chinese community. Through these organizations, they have asserted their role in the mainstream society and have influenced policy-making and government decisions.

The half-a-century old Federation of Filipino Chinese Chambers of Commerce and Industry represents the interests of its 170 association members all over the countries in confronting the government on business issues. Established in 1954, the year Retail Trade Nationalization bill was passed and several other nationalist policies were proposed, it was an effort of the Chinese community to unite the Chinese business groups in dealing with the government. For a long time, the organization was controlled by the Taiwan Kuomintang Party, which promoted its agenda, even after the Philippines shifted its One-China recognition from the Republic of China to the People's Republic of China in 1975. This caused much divisiveness in the Chinese community. Now because many in the Chinese business community do business with China, plus the fact that the leaders of the organization belong to the generation of ethnic Chinese who were born in the Philippines, are well-educated, and have little affiliation to China, either the mainland or Taiwan. With such leadership, the organization, instead of looking inward, has extended its activities outside of the Chinese community, becoming more integrated into the mainstream society. It undertakes development projects, the most prominent of which is the construction of school buildings all over the country. Its importance can be seen from the fact that one of the first things President Gloria Macapagal-Arroyo did after assuming the presidency was to visit Binondo (Chinatown in Manila), and was received by the officers of the Federation. It is an open secret that individual Chinese businessmen and the various business groups continue to be the objects of extortion. The Federation is approached during times of economic crises and is perennially expected to contribute to various government development funds.

Another important organization that has become a strong voice of the Chinese community is the Kaisa Para sa Kaunlaran (Unity for Progress) particularly on social issues and cultural promotion. Established after the first People Power revolution in 1987, it is composed of young Chinese Filipino members interested in playing a more active and important role in nation-building. It aims to promote integration of the Chinese into the Philippine society, at the same time preserving the Chinese culture. Since the nineties when kidnapping of ethnic Chinese became very rampant, this organization has become an important civic organization safeguarding peace and order in the country, particularly in the fight against kidnapping of the ethnic Chinese. The organization now links up with government agencies and policymakers on issues related to the Chinese community. A few years ago, in order to appease the Chinese community when there was uproar over another surge in kidnapping incidents, President Macapagal-Arroyo reversed her decision to suspend the death penalty.

Presently civic and charity works of the ethnic Chinese are directed at the Philippine society as a whole and not just the Chinese community. In this respect, the effort of the Chinese Filipinos have been much more than the traditional elite families. Through charity and civic projects towards the Filipino community, the Chinese Filipinos hope to promote goodwill and to assert their stature in Philippine society. The Chinese organizations have regular education and medical projects, while the *taipans* and other wealthy businessmen each has his foundation to take professional care of his charity projects.

The present Philippine Chinese represents a transitional generation that is concerned with national interests and not just those that affect their community. Many of them are now engaged in vocal sectors such as the mainstream media and non-government organizations. There are also a few who now join the government or are in elective posts.

9. CONCLUSIONS

This chapter shows how the ethnic Chinese have emerged from being a vulnerable minority group in Philippine society to the present when most are comfortably integrated into the mainstream. They suffered the effect of the adverse colonial policies aimed at them and the nationalist policies in the post-independence period when the political situation in China did not leave them with much alternative option. They started to enjoy equal economic rights under the law when mass citizenship was granted in mid-1975. More opportunities were made available to them when in the 1980s, the Philippine Government adopted economic liberalization policies and China opened its economy. Globalization and China's economic boom provided even more investment opportunities. Since then we saw the rise of *nouveau riche* Chinese, most of who rose from practically nothing. They now form part of the elite group that can lobby for government protection and influence government legislation, regulation, and policy-making.

The Chinese have adjusted to the Philippine political setting, which is characterized by the dominance of a powerful elite class and the practice of a patronage culture within the government. The traditional Filipino oligarchs with both economic and political power remain the main societal elites. However, although the political power of the Chinese *taipans* and others of similar economic stature is still very insignificant, definitely they are now considered part of the elite class. Patronage system, which usually involves corruption, is being exploited by those who are not as powerful as the oligarchs.

The political economy, which influences doing business in the Philippines, has also explained the country's lack of development and poverty in the last quarter of the twentieth century. The social divide is no longer along ethnicity, it is the glaringly unequal distribution of wealth in the country and the lack of government services for the poor. There is an urgent need to reform the political economy in the Philippines in order to solve this serious social problem. True and long-term ethnic harmony will occur only when the majority of the population are well educated to understand the issue and when eking a living is not their main concern.

Notes

[1] Offspring of intermarriage between Chinese and Filipino during the Spanish era. These offspring were active in Philippine politics and business and were generally more Hispanized, rather than Filipinized or Sinicized.

[2] For example, Dee C. Chuan, Yutivo, and Uychaco.

[3] First, the reforms are difficult to be implemented given the strong

power of the oligarchs with their entrenched interests. Second, new social forces to challenge the oligarchic power are not likely to rise given the weak bureaucracy (Hutchcroft 1998).

4   Sugar was the most desired commodity as can be seen from the fact the eighty per cent of American manufacturing activities in the Philippines at that time was sugar milling.

5   A couple of the more prominent manufacturers were the distillery of Carlos Palanca and the sawmill of Dee C. Chuan.

6   The China Bank was founded by Dee C. Chuan, the head of the Chamber of Commerce then. Unlike most Chinese establishments at that time which were family-owned, the bank had as its stockholders businessmen of different nationalities and was very professionally run. When it first opened, it hired an American as its manager.

7   It was during this critical period that the Federation of Filipino Chinese Chambers of Commerce and Industry, Inc. was established. This organization, representing the Chinese business sector, attempted to petition and lobby against the Retail Trade Nationalization Act, but to no avail.

8   According to Golay (1961), "By the early 1950s, it (the government) was operating railroads, hotels, electric power, gas, and waterworks as well as producing coal, cement, fertilizer, steel, textiles, yarns, and operating a shipyard and engineering shops."

9   With their control over congress, the landed elite were able to deflect the attempts of the government at any comprehensive land reform after independence.

10   Of the largest 25 firms, 13 were foreign-owned while Filipinos and domestic Chinese each owned 11 of them. On the other hand, of the smallest 50 firms, 24 belonged to domestic Chinese, 14 to domestic Filipinos and 12 to foreigners.

11   One good example is Yutivo Hardware Corporation which was incorporated in 1917 as a trading firm but was considered a manufacturing firm when it went into car assembly in the fifties.

12   As analysed by Hutchcroft (1998), "In historical context, the period of controls can be seen as one more source of booty for an oligarchy whose strategies of capital accumulation had long depended on favourable access to the state apparatus. Given the weak capacity of the state apparatus, it is not surprising that the controls were far less a tool of state industrial planning than an object of oligarchic plunder. As a rule, what the oligarchs grabbed from the state was theirs to keep, not only was there massive corruption in the allocation of licenses, but

the beneficiaries of the system had no obligation to make even the most minimal contribution to larger developmental objectives. In some cases, so-called industrialists requested a foreign exchange licence to support manufacturing ventures and then diverted the proceeds to import finished goods."

[13] Being in politics for a long time, Marcos knew the power and predatory nature of the traditional oligarchs in Philippine society and economy. In fact, for financial support for his two presidential elections, he allied with the oligarchs by having as his running mate Fernando Lopez who became vice president in his two terms of elected presidency.

[14] In the fifties and sixties, despite the numerous economic problems it faced, the Philippines was relatively more developed than most of the Asian countries then.

[15] Three major ones were the earthquake in Baguio, eruption of Pinatubo volcano, and tsunami in Ormoc.

[16] President Corazon Aquino could have changed much of the Philippine political economy then through a change in the land distribution. Instead, coming from an elite landed family, she chose to let the landowners-dominated congress institute a very much watered-down form of land reform.

[17] The attitude of seeing opportunities in crises among the Chinese can be seen in the two characters used to express the word crisis. The characters, *wei* and *ji,* mean danger and opportunities respectively.

[18] The willingness of the Chinese to take risks and seize opportunities paid off when property boom followed the crisis years.

[19] From endnotes in Wickberg (1997): George H. Weightman, "The Philippine Chinese: A Cultural history of a Marginal Trading Community" (Ph.D. Dissertation, Cornell University, 1961).

[20] These professions were restricted to the Chinese before when they did not have the Filipino citizenship.

[21] Identified as *taipans* by the media, they were: Henry Sy of SM shopping malls; John Gokongwei whose conglomerate includes food production, banking, and telecommunication; Lucio Tan with a host of business in tobacco, banking, and breweries; George Ty, owner of Metropolitan Bank; Alfonso Yuchengco whose primary business is insurance and banking; and Andrew Gotianun, a prominent real-estate developer.

[22] One exception was Eduardo Cojuangco, an estranged cousin of President Corazon Cojuangco Aquino.

[23] The Lopez family went all out to support Mrs. Corazon Aquino in the snap election in 1986 called by Marcos (Bello 2004).

24 In 1993, 9 out of the 28 domestic private commercial banks were owned by the ethnic Chinese. The largest was Metropolitan Bank and Trust Corporation, ranked third among all 34 commercial banks, including foreign and public ones (Go 1993). The other eight Chinese banks ranked from the 9th to the 31st places.

25 Equitable Bank was established by the patriarch, Go Kim Pah, in the fifties. It took control of PCI Bank with the help of President Estrada. The bank had been with the Go family up till July 2005 when the Sy family strategically acquired it.

26 Examples are Emilio Yap, owner of shipping lines since the fifties, who right after the fall of Marcos, bought the *Manila Bulletin,* the crony-owned newspaper that had the largest circulation then, and in 1997, bought out the Manila Hotel from the government; Tan Yu, a poor immigrant from Fujian, who started as a textile trader in Bicol, a region south of Manila, and established a real estate empire that extended from the Philippines to Taiwan and Canada; the Ramos family, who owns the ubiquitous National Book Store and has developed shopping malls and hotels jointly with the international Kuok group of property developer. Other outstanding names are Angelo King in the motel business, the Coyiutos in the insurance industry, and Leonardo Ty in the paper business.

27 Presidential power, used to the fullest extent, can quell the power of the elites. During Estrada's administration, this is seen in the case of the Philippine Long Distance Telephone Company, owned by elite families (the Cojuangcos and the Yuchengcos), being taken over by the government using presidential power.

28 Except for Lucio Tan, who seemed not to be satisfied with his oligarchic power, but wanted also "closeness" to the seat of power.

References

Abrenica, Ma. Joy and Gilberto Llanto. 2003. "Services". In *The Philippine Economy: Development, Policies, and Challenges*, edited by Balisacan, Arsenio and Hal Hill (Manila: Ateneo de Manila University Press).

ACERD (Ateneo Center for Economic Research and Development). 2005. "Beneath the Fiscal Crisis: Uneven Development Weakens the Republic". Unpublished draft.

Aldaba, Rafaelita. 2005. "The Impact of Market Reforms on Competition, Structure and Performance of the Philippine Economy". Paper presented at the "Workshop on Policies to Strengthen Productivity in the Philippines", sponsored by the Asia-Europe Meeting (ASEM) Trust

Fund, Philippine Institute for Development Studies and the World Bank, Makati City, 27 July.

Ang, Rodolfo and Ellen Palanca. 2000. "Management in the Philippines". In *The Regional Encyclopedia of Business and Management: Management in Asia Pacific*, edited by Malcolm Warner (Thomson Learning).

Ang See, Teresita. 1995. "The Socio-Cultural and Political Dimension of the Economic Success of the Chinese in the Philippines". In *China, Taiwan, and the Ethnic Chinese in the Philippine Economy*, edited by E.H. Palanca (Philippine Association for Chinese Studies).

Balisacan, Arsenio and Hal Hill (eds.) 2003. *The Philippine Economy: Development, Policies, and Challenges* (Manila: Ateneo de Manila University Press).

Bello, Walden, Herbert Docena, Marissa de Guzman, and Marylou Malig. 2004. *The Anti-Development State: The Political Economy of Permanent Crisis in the Philippines*. University of the Philippines Department of Sociology.

Brown, Rajeswary Ampalavanar. 1995. "Introduction: Chinese Business in an Institutional and Historical Perspective". In *Chinese Business Enterprise in Asia*, edited by R.A. Brown (Routledge).

_____, ed. 1995. *Chinese Business Enterprise in Asia* (Routledge).

Chirot, Daniel and Anthony Reid (eds.) 1997. *Essential Outsiders: Chinese and Jews in the Modern Transformation of Southeast Asia and Central Europe* (Seattle: University of Washington Press).

De Dios, Emmanuel. 1991. *Three Essays on Nationalist Industrialization* (Manila: Philippine Center for Policy Studies).

De Dios, Emmanuel and Villamil, Lorna (eds.) 1990. *Plans, Markets and Relations: Studies for a Mixed Economy* (Manila: Philippine Center for Policy Studies).

De Dios, Emmanuel and Paul Hutchcroft. 2003. "Political Economy". In Balisacan, Arsenio and Hal Hill (eds.) 2003.

Fukuyama, Francis. 1995. *Trust: The Social Virtues and the Creation of Prosperity* (Penguin Books).

Go, Bon Juan. 1995. "Ethnic Chinese in Philippine Banking". In *China, Taiwan, and the Ethnic Chinese in the Philippine Economy*, edited by E.H. Palanca (Philippine Association for Chinese Studies).

Golay, Frank. 1961. *The Philippines: Public Policy and National Economic Development* (Ithaca, N.Y.: Cornell University Press).

Hawes, Gary. 1992. "Marcos, His Cronies, and the Philippines' Failure to Develop". In *Southeast Asian Capitalists*, edited by McVey (Cornell University Southeast Asia Program).

Hicks, George (ed.) 1995. *With Sweat and Abacus, Economic Roles of the Southeast Asian Chinese on the Eve of World War II* by Fukuda Shozo in Japanese and translated by Les Oates to English (Singapore: Select Books).

Hutchcroft, Paul. 1998. *Booty Capitalism: The Politics of Banking in the Philippines* (Manila: Ateneo de Manila Press).

Lim, Linda and Peter Gosling. 1997. "Strengths and Weaknesses of Minority Status for Southeast Asian Chinese at a Time of Economic Growth and Liberalization". In Chirot and Reid (eds.).

McVey, Ruth (ed.) 1992. *Southeast Asian Capitalists* (Ithaca, N.Y.: Cornell University Southeast Asia Program).

O'Connor, David. 1990. "Industry in a Mixed Economy". In Emmanuel de Dios and Lorna Villmil (eds.).

Palanca, Ellen. 1977. "The Economic Position of the Chinese in the Philippines". *Philippine Studies*, first quarter.

———. 1995. "Business Families in the Philippines". In Brown (ed.).

———. 1995. "An Analysis of the Top Corporations in the Philippines". In *China, Taiwan, and the Ethnic Chinese in the Philippine Economy*, edited by E. Palanca (Philippine Association for Chinese Studies).

Putzel, James. 1992. *A Captive Land: The Politics of Agrarian Reform in the Philippines* (Manila: Ateneo de Manila University Press).

Rivera, Temario. 1994. *Landlords and Capitalists: Class, Family, and State in Philippine Manufacturing* (Center for Integrative and Development Studies and University of the Philippines Press).

Tiglao, Rigberto. "Gung-ho in Manila". *Far Eastern Economic Review*, 15 February 1990, pp. 70–71.

Wickberg, Edgar. 1965. *The Chinese in Philippine Life, 1850–1898* (New Haven: Yale University Press).

———. 1997. "Anti-Sinicism and Chinese Identity Options in the Philippines". In *Essential Outsiders: Chinese and Jews in the Modern Transformation of Southeast Asia and Central Europe*, edited by Chirot, Daniel and Anthony Reid (Seattle: University of Washington Press).

Wong, Kwok-chu. 1999. *Chinese in the Philippine Economy, 1898–1941*. (Manila: Ateneo de Manila University Press).

Yoshihara, Kunio. 1985. *Philippine Industrialization: Foreign and Domestic Capital* (Manila: Ateneo de Manila University Press).

———. 1988. *The Rise of Ersatz Capitalism in Southeast Asia* (Oxford University Press/Ateneo de Manila University Press).

11

Ethnic Chinese Business in an Era of Globalization: The Singapore Case

Ng Beoy Kui

1. INTRODUCTION

Globalization is not a new phenomenon. As far back as the Tang Dynasty in the seventh century, trade routes of the Silk Road had brought together Eastern and Western civilizations through trade. Since the visit of Marco Polo to China in the thirteenth century, global economic integration had accelerated, amidst interruptions during World Wars I and II in the early part of the twentieth century. However, globalization continues to be a rising trend, with occasional outbursts of protectionism and anti-globalization rhetoric. From the historical perspective, World Bank (2002) identifies three major waves of globalization. The first wave of globalization occurred in the period 1870–1914, resulting from decreases in tariff barriers and transportation costs with the advent of steamships and railways. The progress of globalization ended abruptly with the outbreak of World War I, starting from 1914. International trade was severely disrupted. After the war in 1918, the Great Depression of the 1930s gave rise to protectionism among major trading countries. Again, globalization was in disarray when World War II broke out in 1942. After the war in 1945, the second wave of globalization which took place between 1945 and 1980 ignited a hope for acceleration in economic integration at a global scale. With falling transportation costs and a reduction in trade barriers among developed countries, there was a sharp increase in international trade in manufactured goods, apart from the usual primary commodity trade. Of significance was the spread of agglomeration economies arising from clustering of related industries in specific locations, thus facilitating vertical and horizontal integration within an industry. The other important occurrence during this period was the emergence of multinational corporations (MNCs) in facilitating international trade and capital flows. Globalization process went into a new peak after 1980 when information and communication technologies breakthroughs cut communication costs dramatically. Together with digitalization, information-based activities are "weightless" so that inputs and outputs can be traveled vast distances at virtually not cost. At the same time, transportation costs were cut further with the rise of containerization and airfreight. All these led to the third wave of globalization since 1980. This wave of globalization was characterized by a spread of trade and financial liberalization not only in developed countries but also in developing nations. The consequence of this liberalization was the massive capital flows in the form of direct foreign investment (DFI) and portfolio investment from developed countries to emergent economies. The international trade also focuses more on manufactured goods and services. While globalization brings benefits to many countries, it has also brought about financial crises, poverty and inequality among and within countries.

In the face of globalization, Singapore, which is a small open economy, has taken the challenge by further liberalizing its financial sector since the Asian financial crisis in 1997. The country also has signed several Free Trade Agreements (FTAs) with a number of its major trading partners, notably the United States, Japan and Australia. Negotiation on FTAs with China has just begun in 2005. Apart from trade and capital movement, Singapore has been adopting an open-door policy of attracting foreign talents. MNCs also play a vital role in the national economy, contributing significantly in output, employment and economic restructuring since Independence in 1965.

Nonetheless, the most important impact of the third wave of globalization was the intense competition at a global scale, and the occurrence of financial crises with their contagion effects. Against this background, there are a number of issues raised as regard to the sustainability of overseas Chinese business[1] in general, Singapore's ethnic Chinese business in particular, as viable business organizations, especially after their setback in the Asian financial crisis (AFC) in 1997. Overseas Chinese businesses have been characterized by their inherent structural weaknesses, such as family-ownership, over-reliance on "*guanxi*", conservatism and investment concentrating in traditional sectors such as real estate and property, banking and hotel industry. With globalization and its stiff competition on a global scale, it is doubtful that these overseas Chinese businesses are able to withstand such an onslaught.

The purpose of this chapter is, therefore, to examine the impact of globalization in general, and the rise of China in particular, on ethnic Chinese business in Singapore. Generally, public policy in Singapore has been tilted towards economic liberalization and the immediate challenge facing ethnic Chinese business here is how to adapt to such an increasingly competitive environment. Secondly, with the rise of China, it is interesting to find out how do these ethnic Chinese businesses in Singapore exploit "ethnic advantage", if any, in their investment in China. The chapter is divided into five parts. After the Introduction, the chapter examines the extent to which ethnic Chinese businesses in Singapore have been affected by globalization, and their adjustment in the face of such challenge. The third section gives an account of possible threats and opportunities that China may pose as a global economic power to ethnic Chinese businesses in Singapore. In the face of globalization and the rise of China, the fourth section reviews existing government policies in enhancing capabilities of ethnic Chinese businesses through upgrading and restructuring efforts. Finally, several concluding remarks are made in the last section.

2. GLOBALIZATION AND ITS IMPACT ON ETHNIC CHINESE BUSINESS

The pace of economic globalization has accelerated since the first half of 1990s, with the launching of the World Wide Web (WWW). Specifically, economic globalization, as defined by the International Monetary Fund (IMF) (2000), is "a historical process, the result of human innovation and technological progress. It refers to the increasing integration of economies around the world, particularly through trade and financial flows. The term sometimes also refers to the movement of people (labour) and knowledge (technology) across international borders. There are also broader cultural, political and environmental dimensions of globalization..." With technological advances, especially in information and telecommunication technologies, economic globalization is characterized, among others by the following features:

- High degree of mobility in factors of production
- High level of connectivity through internet and telecommunication
- Economic integration of markets, especially financial markets
- Economic inter-dependence among nations

- Economies of scale and specialization
- High degree of standardization and homogenization
- Important role of MNCs in trade and investment
- More information being produced and transmitted with high speed
- Markets are highly competitive on a global scale
- Formation of virtual markets.

Mussa (2000) has identified three major factors that have affected the process of economic globalization. The first is the sharp reduction of transportation and communication costs through marked improvements in technology and innovation. This has facilitated trade of goods and services, as well as factors of production on a larger global scale. Communication of useful knowledge and technology through telecommunications and the internet also intensifies with increasing momentum and greater speed than ever before. Secondly, tastes of individuals and societies for the benefit of economic integration have also taken the advantage of lower costs of transportation and communication. Finally, public policies such as economic liberalization also exert influence on the pace of economic globalization. A classic example is the open-door policy of China which has helped integrate its economy with that of the world since 1978. Apparently, globalization exerts its main impact through four channels, namely (1) through trade in goods and services; (2) through movement of capital and integration of financial markets; (3) through human migration; and (4) through communication of knowledge and technology.

With this rapid increase of globalization in the 1990s, views were that overseas Chinese businesses with their structural weaknesses would not be able to withstand the onslaught of severe competition on a global scale. Chan, Ronnie (2000) notes that ethnic Chinese firms with their problematic cultural traits, especially hierarchical management style and distrust of non-family members, are expected to encounter various problems amidst an increasingly more competitive international environment. These problems include lack of positioning in global industries, lack of growth drivers such as technology, brand name, etc., and succession problems. Moreover, overseas Chinese businesses, in their state-business relations, were implicated for corruption, nepotism and cronyism. Some writers (Backman 1999) have even argued that the Asian financial crisis in 1997 was due to the secretive and corrupt Chinese business networks as well as the inherent structural weaknesses of overseas Chinese family businesses.

All in all, the overseas Chinese business system, as typified in the literature (Chan 2000; Hamilton 1996; Redding 1990); Weidenbaum, Murray, and Hughes 1996; Yoshihara 1988) has the following major characteristics:

- Basically family-owned with pervasive ownership and control;
- Owners display overwhelmingly entrepreneurial spirit;
- Attach importance to establishing business networks through "*guanxi*";
- Small to medium size under direct control of the family;
- Big business conglomerates are under family control, and each of these conglomerates comprises a network of small to medium enterprises; and
- Investment tend to confine to traditional sectors such as wholesale and retail trade, banking, real estate and property sector, and hotel industry.

2.1 Characteristics and Structure of Singapore Chinese Business

The above characterization of overseas Chinese business implies that ethnic Chinese firms are homogenous, no matter where they operate, including Singapore. Such a stereotypical description about overseas Chinese business is, more often than not, gravely misleading.[2] As Gomez and Benton (2004) observed, there is "a large assortment of Chinese business firms in terms of size, types of ownership and management, and areas of operations". Ethnic Chinese business in Singapore is a classic example.

In Singapore, ethnic Chinese business may be classified into three categories (Chan and Ng 2004), depending on their respective cultural traits. The more culturally-oriented Chinese group belongs to the first and second generations of Chinese immigrants from mainland China, and their outlook as a group is predominantly traditional and conservative. Some of these firms may have absorbed non-family members only after their long service in the company. Even then, the final business decisions of these firms ultimately hinge on family members. A majority of this type of ethnic Chinese businesses are small in size and traditional in outlook. According to a survey conducted by the Singapore Chinese Chamber of Commerce and Industry (SCCCI), they spend less than 2 per cent of their business expenditure on IT (*Straits Times* 2004).

The second group has a long business history and has evolved into big business conglomerates. Once they are listed on the stock exchange, family ownership may be diluted somewhat but their management control is still in the hands of the founding or family members. These ethnic

Chinese business enterprises are involved in a host of industries ranging from light manufacturing, real estate and property, to hotels and banking. An increasing number of these big business conglomerates even diversify their business into computer technology, telecommunication and e-business. Socially, these ethnic Chinese businesses are long-time members of SCCCI, clan associations and alumni bodies of previous Chinese schools. These associations provides a vast business networks through which they get their clients, contractors and suppliers.

The big ethnic Chinese conglomerates in Singapore usually expand their business operations mainly through mergers and acquisitions. A classic example is the United Overseas Bank (UOB) owned by Wee Cho Yaw family (Tschoegi 2001). UOB was founded in 1935 by Wee Keng Chiang (Wee Cho Yaw's father) and his six friends under the name of the United Chinese Bank (UCB). UCB changed its name to UOB in 1965 when Wee Cho Yaw was the managing director. In 1971, UOB acquired 53 per cent of Chung Khiaw Bank (CKB) and then 55 per cent of Lee Wah Bank in the following year. In 1974, Wee Cho Yaw took over the chairmanship of UOB. In its drive for expansion, UOB acquired 70 per cent of the Far Eastern Bank in 1984. To further expand its banking business, UOB acquired 87 per cent of the Industrial and Commerce Bank in 1987. By 1999, all the banks acquired earlier were merged under the umbrella of UOB group. In 2002, UOB, in its tussle with the Development Bank of Singapore (DBS), a government-linked corporation, over the acquisition of the Overseas Union Bank (OUB), finally turned out to be the victor. UOB is one of the big three banks in Singapore.

Apart from mergers and acquisitions, ethnic Chinese business conglomerates in Singapore have also been expanding their business operations by venturing abroad since 1970s. The general strategy adopted is through multiplication of their parent firms in other parts of the world. For instance, food courts were set up in cities in China and Australia, emulating the mode of operation of a typical food court in Singapore. OSIM and BreadTalk have also expanded their business in healthcare equipments and bakery business respectively in China. Other modes of expansion include joint ventures, chain stores and franchise.

The third group of ethnic Chinese businesses in Singapore, in contrast to the previous two groups, is less culturally oriented, and mostly does not depend on traditional family lineage. Most of them are English educated with engineering background. They may have worked previously with multinational corporations (MNCs) or government-linked corporations (GLCs), and now they venture out on their own to become subcontractors or suppliers to their former employers. Their core businesses include mainly computer technology, e-commerce and knowledge-based operations. They belong to the emerging group of technopreneurs whom the Singapore Government is anxious to nurture.

Because of its heterogeneous characteristics, ethnic Chinese business in Singapore as a group displays three distinct types of management practices (Tsang 2002). Traditional Chinese family business (CFBs) depends very much on family lineage in terms of ownership and control. The owner of a CFB has the final say as he is considered as knowledgeable about all aspects of business operations. The traditional CFB would normally send its family members abroad to be in charge of its overseas operations. Networking is an essential part of business operations and is done mostly by family members, usually the boss. The approach of traditional CFBs to investment overseas, notably in China, is considered as "informal and unstructured". Unlike CFBs, the non-CFB approach to business displays a high degree of formalization and structured in business organization and operations. Management decisions are usually made at their respective headquarters based on detailed and systematic reports sent from their subsidiaries overseas. There is also a systematic rotation of assigning expatriate managers overseas. In between CFBs and non-CFBS lies the semi-CFBs. The semi-CFBs normally recruit professionals to be in charge of business operations. The top management of these enterprises usually adopts group decisions made by both family and non-family members.

2.2 Opportunities, Threats and Financial Crisis

Globalization poses both threats and opportunities to the ethnic Chinese businesses in Singapore. With globalization, ethnic Chinese businesses can exploit cheaper labour and resources in any part of the world for their business expansion and diversification. Secondly, with economic liberalization on a global scale, the world is the market. Globalization provides ample opportunities for ethnic Chinese businesses to exploit in the knowledge-based economy. Unfortunately, CFBs are not ready to exploit the full potential of e-commerce and e-business, because of their conservatism. Unlike CFBs, semi-CFBs and non-CFBs (especially the larger ethnic Chinese businesses) are making significant in-road to commit to their investment in computer technology, information and telecommunication industry.

Globalization also poses threats to ethnic Chinese business in Singapore. With rapid growth in the information and communication industry, they have to face more severe competition in the domestic as well as host countries' markets. This is because of the increasingly competitive environment arising from the new technology which enables MNCs to constantly seek new or unexploited markets. They also create new needs among different target consumer groups. Of no less significance is the penetration of virtual market on the internet. Their potent force is the intensification and acceleration of commodification through international branding. Specifically, MNCs place a heavier focus on seeking to condition children and young people to construct their identities around brands. However, these threats can turn into opportunities for ethnic Chinese businesses if they join alliance with MNCs as partners, suppliers or even subcontractors. If possible, the ethnic Chinese business should also attempt to establish its own brands, just as what their counterparts in some of GLCs did. A good example is Singapore Airline.

The more serious threat of globalization is the occurrence of economic crisis. The Asian financial crisis in 1997 for instance has been called the "first crisis of globalization" (Higgott 1998, p. 2). The crisis with their contagious and systemic effect, spread from Thailand to other parts of East Asia. The crisis was a combination of simultaneous currency attacks, banking crisis and stock market crash. Despite the ferocious nature of the crisis, most of the ethnic Chinese businesses in Singapore were able to weather the crisis, in part with assistance from the Singapore Government through cost-cutting policy measures.[3] Yeung (2000) argues that their embedded business networks had helped them to diversify their business beyond their core businesses and also across borders well before the eruption of the crisis. They operate like MNCs and compete without fail in the global market. For instance, Kwek Leng Beng and his Hong Leong Group have expanded their business worldwide well before the crisis. The business conglomerate's activities range from banking and finance, real estate and property to hotel industry. In particular, Kwek family made a significant inroad into global hotel businesses through acquisitions of hotels in the United Kingdom, the United States and New Zealand (Yeung 2002b). His CDL Hotels International now owns 117 hotels, spanning 13 countries in Europe, the United States, Australia, New Zealand and Asia.

The two prominent ethnic Chinese family-controlled international banks, the Oversea-Chinese Banking Corporation (OCBC) and the United Overseas Bank (UOB) also made their marks in the business history of Singapore. These two banks own a vast number of bank subsidiaries and branches all over Asia, Australia and Canada (Tschoegl 2001). According to a survey of 2000 largest multinational corporations published in 2005, there were thirteen Singapore corporations in the list of which OCBC, UOB and City Development owned by Kwek family, were the only three privately owned business enterprises; the rest were GLCs owned by the Singapore Government (*Lianhe Zaobao*, 4 April 2005, p. 1).

Some of these ethnic Chinese firms in Singapore also engaged in pre-emptive measures through product and geographical diversification, tapping into the global capital market and using non-equity investments. These measures have enabled the ethnic Chinese businesses to continue to grow despite the crisis.

Tracy (2000) attributes the success of ethnic Chinese businesses in overcoming the adversity during the crisis to the transformation and restructuring of these Chinese enterprises from "*ersatz* capitalism" to technopreneurship, involving high-tech and high value-added industries. Such metamorphosis does not just cover the big ethnic Chinese business corporations such as Creative Technology, but also numerous start-up companies seeking to exploit the new computer and Internet-based economy. Although the extent of the metamorphosis in Singapore is way behind Taiwan, the emergence of such a trend is encouraging, especially with the support and assistance of the Singapore Government since 1990.

A majority of ethnic Chinese businesses were able to weather the storm for another two reasons. One was the concentration of new investments to China since 1996, with the Singapore Government taking the lead in that direction. Such a move is considered as fortunate in that China was not adversely affected by the crisis. The other reason is that, unlike *chaebols* in South Korea, ethnic Chinese businesses (especially Chinese SMEs) do not traditionally rely much on international financial markets for their funding (Lever-Tracy and Ip 2002). Their main sources of funds come from their own family business resources and through public fund by listing on the stock exchange. The issues of currency mismatches and the moral hazard problem arising from international lending were not much of a concern to the ethnic Chinese businesses. At most, they suffered loss of business deals in those countries that were adversely affected by the crisis, especially in Indonesia and to a lesser extent, Malaysia. According to Tracy (2000), the vast majority of the largest Chinese business families in the Southeast Asian region have survived the crisis, albeit with a reduction in wealth as well as in both the size and scope of their business conglomerates.

3. RISE OF CHINA AS AN ECONOMIC POWER AND ITS IMPACT

Globalization has given China a golden opportunity to become an international economic power through the latter's open-door policy since December 1978. Initially, China abolished trade plans, decentralized trade, reduced tariffs and more importantly, unified its dual exchange rate system in 1994. China also allows convertibility of its currency for current account transactions. However, the most crucial step was its accession to the World Trade Organization (WTO) on 11 December 2001. With the accession, China made wide-ranging commitments to liberalize its markets in exchange for the various rights it now enjoys under WTO rules. These commitments include lower trade barriers. Tariff reduction in China has, indeed, shown a long-term decline between 1982 and 2002. According to one estimate cited by Rumbaugh and Blancher (2004), unweighted average tariffs declined significantly from 55.6 per cent in 1982 to 12.3 per cent in 2002. On a weighted average basis, the tariff reduction was even more spectacular, from 40.6 per cent in 1992 to 6.4 per cent in 2002. Apart from lower tariffs, the trade regime in China has become more transparent (Yang 2003). As a result, China's trade expanded remarkably, with exports expanding from US$10 billion on average in the late 1970s to US$593 billion in 2004. Imports to China also increased rapidly, from US$42 billion in 1985 to US$561 billion in 2004. In 2004, China overtook Japan as the third largest trading nation after the United States and the European Union. Its exports amounted to 9 per cent of total world exports and its imports contributing 8.1 per cent of the total world imports (see Table 11.1).

China also embarked on an ambitious policy programme to attract foreign direct investment (FDI) for its economic growth. After its first introduction of a law governing joint ventures in 1979, China began to attract an increasing inflow of FDI, notably from the Newly Industrialized Economies (NIEs), comprising Hong Kong, Korea, Singapore and Taiwan. Special Economic Zones (SEZs) with generous tax incentives were set up in the southeast coast of the country as its first experiment in attracting FDI. The experiment was extremely successful and the model was emulated in other provinces. The surge of inflows of FDI to China only started in the early 1990s, following Deng Xiaoping's tour of the southern coastal areas where he reaffirmed China's commitment to economic reforms and open-door policies to the outside world (Tseng and Zebregs 2002). In 2002, total FDI inflows reached US$53 billion, as compared to an average of US$28.3 billion for the whole of 1990s, and only US$2.3 billion on average per year in the second half of 1980s.

TABLE 11.1
World Trade: 2004 Leading Exporters and Importers
(Excluding intra-EU (25) trade)

Rank	Exporters	Value (US$ Billion)	% share	Annual % change
1	Extra-EU(25) exports	1,203	18.2	20
2	United States	819	12.4	13
3	China	593	9.0	35
4	Japan	566	8.5	20
5	Canada	322	4.9	18
6	Hong Kong	266	4.0	16
7	South Korea	254	3.8	31
8	Mexico	189	2.8	14
9	Russia	183	2.8	35
10	Taiwan	181	2.7	21
11	Singapore	180	2.7	25
12	Malaysia	127	1.9	21
13	Saudi Arabia	120	1.8	28

Rank	Importers	Value (US$ Billion)	% share	Annual % change
1	United States	1,526	22.0	17
2	Extra-EU(25) imports	1,280	18.4	20
3	China	561	8.1	36
4	Japan	455	6.5	19
5	Canada	276	4.0	13
6	Hong Kong	273	3.9	17
7	South Korea	224	3.2	26
8	Mexico	206	3.0	16
9	Taiwan	168	2.4	32
10	Singapore	164	2.4	28
11	Switzerland	112	1.6	16
12	Australia	108	1.5	21
13	Malaysia	105	1.5	26

Source: World Trade Organization (WTO).

3.1 Economic Impact on Singapore Ethnic Chinese Business

China's success in promoting trade and investment has been a concern not only to developed countries such as the United States, but also developing countries, especially its neighbours in East Asia. This is because China, with its huge domestic market and cheaper cost of labour, is able to attract huge amount of FDIs, to the disadvantage of the Southeast Asian region (Phar 2002*a*). China also poses as a formidable competitor in the international market. Apart from trade and FDI diversion, some of the economies, such as Taiwan and the Southeast Asian nations also suffer from "hollowing out" of their domestic investment. Moreover, developed countries and NIEs lose jobs with significant increases in unemployment in certain sectors, following a rise in outsourcing some of their jobs to China.

One serious concern with the rise of China is the potential competition in the international market place for manufactured goods either for consumption or as intermediate inputs in third countries' markets. Lall and Albaladejo (2004) use correlation coefficients between export structure of China and that of East Asian countries as a measure of competition among them (see Table 11.2). From the table, mainland China's export structure had changed drastically between 1990 and 2000. By 2000, its export structure resembled almost that of Taiwan in 1990. In relation to Singapore, China's export structure was totally different from that of Singapore in 1990. However, by year 2000, the correlation coefficient rose sharply from 0.1 in 1990 to 0.42 in 2000. This implies that China has become increasingly a potent competitor to Singapore in the international market as China moves up the technology ladder. The competition between the two countries is not so much in the resource-based and low technology sector (see Table 11.3). Singapore lacks of natural resources, and its resource-based industry which comprises mainly oil refineries and food and beverage processing, depends largely on imported raw materials. The oil refineries are, indeed, a source of energy supplies to China. As for the low technology sector, Singapore had re-allocated this sector to its neighbouring countries in the 1970s and 1980s. Apparently, the real competition between the two countries occurs mainly in the medium technology sector. As China catches up in the high technology sector, such upgrading will represent a challenge to Singapore in general and ethnic Chinese businesses in particular. According to Lall and Albaladejo (2004), 23.5 per cent of Singapore exports encountered direct threat from China in 2000, while another 40.4 per cent faced partial threat from the same competitor.

With regard to FDI, Singapore has not suffered much from a diversion in FDI as experienced by other Southeast Asian countries, nor has it experienced a severe "hollowing out" effect as has happened in Taiwan and Hong Kong. Little diversion in FDIs in the Singapore case is mainly due to the different types of foreign investment that Singapore has attracted,

TABLE 11.2
Correlation Coefficients of Mainland China and
Regional Export Structure
(3-digit SITC)

	Mainland China 1990	Mainland China 2000
Korea 1990	0.38	0.64
Korea 2000		0.43
Taiwan 1990	0.34	0.83
Taiwan 2000		0.53
Singapore 1990	0.10	0.42
Singapore 2000		0.41
Malaysia 1990	0.28	0.24
Malaysia 2000		0.44
Thailand 1990	0.30	0.52
Thailand 2000		0.51
Indonesia 1990	0.38	0.07
Indonesia 2000		0.33
Philippines 1990	0.23	0.38
Philippines 2000		0.33

Source: Lall and Albaladejo (2004) Table 4.

as compared to that of China. Singapore attracts mostly high-tech and high value added type of investment while China is more interested in industries with relatively low technology and most of these FDIs are labour intensive. In fact, the two different types of foreign investment that each country attracts are complementary to each other resulting in vertical integration and an increase in intra-trade between the two countries. Goldman Sachs (2003) reports that about 80 per cent of intra-regional exports to China are intermediate and capital goods and raw materials, with the remainder directly for domestic consumption. Rumbaugh and Blancher (2004) also report that about half of China's imports are for processing and re-exporting. Ethnic Chinese businesses that are suppliers or subcontractors to MNCs in Singapore have somewhat benefited indirectly from this vertical integration and intra-regional trade.

The case of "hollowing-out" effect is not much of an issue in Singapore either. The phenomenon of "hollowing out" had already occurred in the 1970s and 1980s when the labour-intensive industries and light manufacturing such as textiles and garment industries were forced to re-structure or re-allocate to the neighbouring countries, notably Malaysia and Indonesia. During that time, ethnic Chinese businesses which were

TABLE 11.3
Technological Structure of Manufactured Exports 2000 (%)

	China	Korea	Taiwan	Singapore	Malaysia	Thailand	Indonesia	Philippines
Resource-based	9.5	11.7	4.4	14.9	13.1	18.4	33.7	6.5
Low-technology	44.9	17.1	23.8	6.5	9.6	21.5	31.3	11.9
Medium-technology	21.2	34.0	25.5	17.4	17.8	23.8	17.5	11.6
High-technology	24.4	37.1	46.3	61.2	59.4	36.3	17.4	70.0

Source: Lall and Albaladejo (2004) Table 3.

actively involved in these sectors were adversely affected. Secondly, the "hollowing-out" phenomenon is restricted to those electronics industries of a lower level in the supply chain where MNCs and not ethnic Chinese business are heavily involved. However, the outsourcing issue is severely felt in the IT sector, although the outsourcing to China is somewhat less serious as compared to that to India which has a high standard of English. But, as China's standard of English improves, ethnic Chinese businesses involved in the IT sector are expected to be adversely affected.

The rise of China as an economic powerhouse also gives rise to vast opportunities to Singapore in terms of trade and investment. Ethnic Chinese businesses with their cultural affinity with mainland China can exploit these opportunities through deployment of their "ethnic advantage" (Chan and Tong 2000; Dahles 2005). In addition, the Singapore Government took the initiative in promoting Singaporean investment into China, after its regionalization drive in 1993. GLCs with support from the government provided the much needed leadership in investing in China. Through government-to-government relations, Singapore used its reputation of "honesty and straightforwardness" in business dealings (Bolt 2000) to display its "political entrepreneurship" in investing in China.

The classic example is the establishment of the Suzhou Industrial Park (SIP) in Jiangsu Province through the cooperative effort of the two governments. As a result, total direct investment in China rose significantly from S$1.7 billion in 1994 to S$16.5 billion in 2001.

Historically, ethnic Chinese business in Singapore has been investing in China since the 1970s. For instance, Hock San Yuen Food Manufacturing which manufactures food and beverages, invested in Qingdao as early as 1975 (Yeung 2002a). Sunwa Construction and Interior Pte. Ltd., another Singapore Chinese firm, also set up a garment factory in Guanzhou in 1979. The firm then moved its plant to Shenzhen in 1981. However, most of these investments are confined to light manufacturing, such as appliance manufacturing and food processing. After the strong encouragement from the Singapore Government in early 1990s, large ethnic Chinese enterprises began to exploit such opportunities in a big way. However, they were again involved mainly in low-cost manufacturing, hotels and real estate (see Table 11.4). Only in recent years did these companies forge strategic alliance with GLCs and MNCs in high-tech industries such as computer technology and electronics. Of significance is the increasing investment on the part of large ethnic Chinese business conglomerates, in the services sector of China, especially in tourism, education, medical

TABLE 11.4
Singapore's Distribution of FDI to China by Activity

Activity	1990		2000	
	S$ (Million)	% of activities	S$ (Million)	% of activities
Manufacturing	115.4	48.1	7,999.1	68.3
Construction	0.3	0.1	84.2	0.7
Commerce	49.1	20.5	561.3	4.8
Transport and communication	48.3	20.2	590.6	5.0
Financial services	1.7	0.7	547.9	4.7
Real estate	–	–	1,366.5	11.7
Business services	6.2	2.6	90.2	0.8
Others	18.7	7.8	477.6	4.1
Total	239.7	100.0	11,717.4	100.0

Source: Singapore's Investment Abroad, 1990–91 and 2000–01.

and transport services as well as infrastructure. Bolt (2000) notes that the sectoral pattern of Singapore's investments reflects both China's domestic needs and Singapore's economic strengths. He also notes that unlike Taiwan and Hong Kong, Singapore investment has not resulted in widespread network of manufacturing operations, mainly because of a lack of domestic entrepreneurs who are actively engaged in manufacturing. This is understandable as Singapore was originally a trading nation which developed later into an international financial centre. Manufacturing activities, especially electronics, are conducted mainly by MNCs while labour-intensive industries were re-allocated out of Singapore since the 1970s.

Singapore will benefit further from the ongoing liberalization in China's services sectors, following its commitments under the WTO accession. According to the original schedule, China will fully open all of its markets to full international competition from foreign service providers in a number of key services areas over a span of five years, from 2002 to 2007 (Whalley 2003). These areas include distribution, financial services, telecommunications, professional business and computer services, motion pictures, environmental services, accounting, law, architecture, construction, and travel and tourism. All barriers to entry and all conduct barriers for domestic and foreign entries will be removed subsequently. China is also planning a progressive approach towards foreign ownership and geographical coverage of licences for the liberalization of services sector. Doubt has been cast on the feasibility of the full implementation of these commitments, especially in the areas of banking, insurance and telecommunications. Even then, such liberalization represents ample opportunities for Singapore ethnic Chinese businesses to exploit through direct investment. Prior to China's accession to WTO, a significant number of the ethnic Chinese businesses already have substantive investments in some of the services sectors, especially in banking, tourism and hotel businesses, and distribution and transport services. For instance, UOB and OCBC have four bank branches each in major cities such as Shanghai, Beijing and Guangzhou (Tschoegl 2001). Ethnic Chinese businesses can make a significant stride in the services sector of China but this requires a strategic alliance among GLCs, the big ethnic Chinese enterprises and MNCs to penetrate into the Chinese services market, especially in the areas of banking, insurance and telecommunications.

3.2 Ethnic Advantage and Investment in China

The emphasis on investment in China in Singapore's regionalization drive in the 1990s was due to the four major factors. The first factor was the rapid rise of China as an economic powerhouse and the rise would provide ample opportunities for Singapore to create its external wing. Secondly, Singapore has a long history of investing in the Southeast Asian region and any impetus to increase investment further would not lead to much headway. Thirdly, investment in India would not lead anywhere either as the economic reform there is still in its infant stage. More importantly was the realization on the part of the government that "the fast-growing relationship and contact with China soon began to transform the Chineseness[4] of Singapore from an unavoidable and unfortunate liability to an important and immensely profitable asset" (Vasil 1995, p. 133). This is illustrated in a speech by the Minister of Home Affairs Wong Kan Seng who stated that Singapore could take advantage of its familiarity with the Chinese culture and language by investing in China. He added, "Singapore's policy towards China is based only on the simple fact that China is a geopolitical reality. We must live with it and it is in our national interest to have good relations with China. It is also where the greatest economic opportunities lie. If we invest in China, it is because there is money to be made there" (*Petir* 1994, p. 51). This provides excellent opportunities for ethnic Chinese enterprises in Singapore to exploit their dual identity as ethnic Chinese and Singaporean (Chan and

Tong 2000; Dahles 2005). On the one hand, they can play out their Chinese identity to enhance *guanxi* with Chinese Government officials and mainland Chinese businesses. At the same time, they, as Singaporeans, can exploit the fact of their being different from mainland Chinese, and pose themselves as attractive business partners and associates. On top of that, Singapore ethnic Chinese business can even use "brand state"[5] to enhance their business reputation (Tan 2003).

As noted earlier, the shift from de-Chineseness in the 1960s and 1970s to re-engagement of Chineseness since 1990s is, in part, motivated by economic factors relating to the rise of China (Tan 2002). In addition to tapping on cultural affinity and good political ties with China, the other strength of Singapore is its straddling between the East and the West. In this way, Singapore can serve as a gateway between China and the West (which includes mainly Europe, the United States and Australia) to serve its national economic interest. With the rise of India as an economic power, Singapore again attempts to exploit both its Indian and Chinese cultural affinity on each side respectively to serve "a gateway for China and a bridge to India" (Buenas 2004). As Senior Minister Goh Chok Tong said, "Just as our Chinese businessmen enjoy special *guanxi* in China, our Indians too have special knowledge, understanding of local culture and family, and business connections with India" (Koh 2005, p. 9). In fact, India (with an average growth rate of 7.5 per cent between 2002 and 2005) has stamped its mark as the third preferred foreign investment destination after China and the United States. This excellent economic performance represents ample opportunities for the Singapore business community to take advantage of a middleman and serve the two giant economies, a bridge to boost more economic co-operation among the three countries. Singapore can also serve a facilitator and even collaborator to the two economies in their respective regionalization drives (Chuang 2005*b*). In 2004, there were 1,100 mainland Chinese companies (150 in 1995) that have their registered offices in Singapore, with fifty-four of them or 9 per cent of total companies listed in the Singapore Exchange (*Lianhe Zaobao* 2004*a*; 2004*b*). High-tech Chinese companies such as Cytech, Biotreat, ChinaCast, China Petrotech and Guangzhao have also raised substantial amount of funds in Singapore by issuing their Initial Public Offers (IPOs) in the Singapore Exchange (*Lianhe Zaobao* 2004*c*). In 2004, fourteen Singapore listed Chinese companies conducted roadshows in Hong Kong, London and New York (*Lianhe Zaobao* 2004*d*).

In short, Singapore is well-placed to serve as a conduit for Chinese companies venturing into international markets. Mainland Chinese companies can leverage on Singapore's extensive regional and global distribution networks to reach out to markets in Southeast Asia and beyond. Singapore-based Chinese companies with substantial high value-added activities anchored in Singapore can also enjoy greater access to other markets by leveraging on Singapore's network of FTAs with New Zealand, Australia, Japan, EFTA and the United States.

The exploitation of ethnic advantage by the Singapore Government and ethnic Chinese businessmen for economic interest seems to work well in the case of investment in China. According to an international survey conducted by Grant Thornton International, one-in-five Singapore companies polled have a business presence in China, among the highest in the region (Chuang 2005a). However, there are economic and social costs involved (Chan and Tong 2000). The most glaring example is the Suzhou Industrial Park (SIP) which started in 1994. By 1997, it had become obvious that the project was not doing well. In December 1997, Lee Kuan Yew publicly expressed dissatisfaction with the Chinese side, citing "different work habits" and competition from the Suzhou New District (Bolt 2000). By 1999, dissatisfaction on the part of Singapore came to a head. George Yeo claimed that the problems in Suzhou were due to cultural differences, demonstrating how different Chinese and Singaporeans really are. He concluded that China would always be different from Singapore. "Thus a project initially dubbed as 'Singapore II' came to symbolize the stark differences between Singapore and China...." (Bolt 2000, p. 141).

Tension and differences between Singapore and China are not limited to SIP. The more Westernized government officials and businessmen in Singapore are generally bureaucratic and cautious in their investment decisions. This inhibits Singaporean entrepreneurship and investment in an unstructured environment such as that of China. This differentiates Singapore ethnic Chinese companies from other overseas Chinese companies from Taiwan and Hong Kong. For instance, ethnic Chinese business firms from Singapore will invest mainly in those projects that are supported by the Singapore Government or negotiated by local ethnic Chinese business conglomerates. This is in direct contrast to Taiwanese investments which tend to involve less capital, are made by small- to medium-sized companies, are flexible and lower in profile. More importantly, there is a conspicuous absence of their government involvement in investments in China.

From a national perspective, the Singapore Government cannot play the Chinese card all the time. It has to take into account the internal imperatives and external implications. Internally, Singapore must not let its involvement with China and Chinese culture alienate its non-Chinese population. Externally, it has to be sensitive to its neighbours, especially Malaysia and Indonesia. Even though Singapore now is more confident than before, it still needs to rebalance its act. As a matter of sensibility and political correctness, while encouraging ethnic Chinese Singaporeans to invest in China, it never fails to mention that India also represents an incredible market for Singapore to invest. Prior to the Asian financial crisis in 1997, Indonesia was often mentioned as another key area for investment opportunities. However, after the crisis, little mention was made with regard to investment in Indonesia as the economy has not fully recovered, amidst adverse consequences arising from the tsunami in December 2004. In the ASEAN forum, Singapore also never fails to encourage other ASEAN countries to invest in China for their benefit. Such a call is to address suspicion on the part of its ASEAN neighbours about Singapore's investments in China. In a nutshell, Singapore has to prove beyond doubt that its investments in China are purely based on economic grounds and also for its national interests. Nothing emotional is involved.

4. GOVERNMENT POLICY TOWARDS ETHNIC CHINESE BUSINESS

In Singapore, the People's Action Party (PAP) government's attitude towards ethnic Chinese business has shifted from one of non-intervention and political alienation in the 1960s and 1970s into a closer one with firm commitment to strengthen the latter's capabilities since 1990. The shift is due to economic, political and social imperatives in the development process of Singapore.

4.1 Three Legs with an External Wing

In the first decade since Independence in 1965, the ruling PAP government adopted a non-interference policy with political alienation towards ethnic Chinese business (Vasil 1995; Rodan 1989; Huff 1994; Ng 2002; Chan and Ng 2004). This was due to a differing view on Chinese culture and language between the PAP government and the Chinese clans and associations as well as the Chinese Chamber of Commerce and Industry (SCCCI) as a group. The latter group considered the promotion of Chinese culture and language to be part and parcel of a multi-racial and multi-cultural society. The PAP government, on the contrary, considered such a move as racially sensitive in view of "internal ethnic imperatives as well as the regional geographical compulsions" (Vasil 1995, p. 34). This led to the government to adopt a "two-legged policy" with emphasis on GLCs and MNCs as the two pillars for promoting economic development. Ethnic Chinese businesses were left alone with non-interference from the government.

After a successful industrialization drive in the 1960s and 1970s, the problem of labour shortage became increasingly serious. Economic restructuring was badly needed to address this issue as the success of economic restructuring hinged on the close cooperation of local private enterprises, which had been involved heavily in labour intensive industries. A majority of these local enterprises were owned by ethnic Chinese, who were still somewhat unhappy with the government's cultural and language policy. Any restructuring of these industries would definitely lead to grievances which, if not handled carefully, could be exploited by opposition parties for their political gains. The PAP government took the initiative in 1976 to engage these ethnic Chinese businesses by providing financial and technical assistance. However, local private enterprises still played as a "second fiddle" to the MNCs and GLCs in economic development during the period 1976–84. Only after a deep recession in 1985 did the government realize the importance of developing local private enterprises for economic growth. Firstly, the labour shortage problem still lingered with no sign of abatement. Secondly, over-dependence on MNCs could be dangerous as these MNCs might re-allocate their plants to elsewhere if the business costs were to rise further. Finally, local private enterprises especially SMEs could be restructured and upgraded to become potential co-partners, suppliers and subcontractors to GLCs and MNCs. Such a tripartite alliance would enhance the resilience and competitiveness of the Singapore's national economy.

The three-legged strategy was finally adopted in 1989 by implementing the SME Plan to nurture local SMEs into more viable enterprises so that they could become effective co-partners in the development process. In the meantime, the government also announced the setting up of the Growth Triangle which covers Singapore, the Riao Archipelago of Indonesia and Johor of Malaysia. One of the purposes of the Growth Triangle is to allow local enterprises (including MNCs) to re-allocate their labour intensive plants in neighbouring countries to relieve domestic labour pressure. In 1993, the Singapore Government, after deliberating over the choice between globalization or regionalization for over more than half a decade, finally decided to adopt a regionalization drive with emphasis on investment in China. The promotion of outward investment to the region was necessary for Singapore as Singapore had completed the "factor-driven" phase of economic development whereby domestic resources, especially labour resources, had been fully utilized. It was ready for Singapore to enter into the next phase of economic development which is the investment-driven stage whereby outward investment is promoted to form an "external wing" of the national economy.

4.2 Government Assistance to SMEs

As noted earlier, the Singapore Government has been providing financial and technical assistance since 1976 to SMEs, which were owned mainly by ethnic Chinese. However, most of these assistance were either *ad hoc* in nature or under-utilized because of their bureaucratic procedures in application. In 1989, the government introduced the SME Master Plan with a more systematic approach towards assisting SMEs. The promulgation of the plan was to address a number of issues. Firstly, it is important to recognize that SMEs comprise more than 90 per cent of total establishments, employ 51 per cent of the workforce and generate 34 per cent of total output and yet their productivity is about half that of non-SME establishment. Any increase in the productivity of this sector will release a significant amount of labour and land resources for other productive uses. Secondly, SMEs are now recognized as the third "leg" of the national economy. This third "leg" is expected to serve as suppliers, service providers and subcontractors in the national supply chain. This "leg" is also expected to be part of the strategic alliance in the creation of the external wing. Any weakness in this leg will make the country a limp. Finally, SMEs could join GLCs and MNCs in the regionalization drive. With the majority of SMEs being Chinese family owned, they possess some sort of cultural affinity which can be exploited for creating a viable external wing. As most of these SMEs had significant influence on the HDB heartland, any initiative to assist them will help improve regime maintenance. When the master plan was promulgated, the promotion of entrepreneurship was not such an urgent issue yet.

However, with rapid development in computer and telecommunications technology, especially the World Wide Web (WWW), the economic landscape has been drastically transformed from the old economy to the new economy, called the knowledge-based economy (KBE). With this new development, the KBE presents vast opportunities to be exploited and at the same time poses serious threats to SMEs. In a KBE environment, entrepreneurship is critical for generating innovation and creativity. However, Singaporeans, especially the younger ones (because of their comfortable and stable jobs with MNCs and government services), have lost their entrepreneurial drive that their forefathers had a few decades ago. They tend to be *"kiasu"* or loss averse. The KBE environment also brought with it pockets of structural unemployment in various industries. One source of the structural unemployment arises from re-allocation of MNCs' plants to low-cost countries such as China and Vietnam. The high-tech industries which still remain in Singapore require different and higher as well as new levels of skills which the Singapore workers are not well-equipped. The increase of productivity through innovations as a result of the exponential growth in information and communications technologies, especially in the field of knowledge management, could also be translated into retrenchment of outmoded employees, and at the same time, the better use of more productive ones. The more serious type of structural unemployment is the retrenchment of white-collar workers following a widespread of outsourcing either within the economy or to other countries. If this issue of structural unemployment is not resolved amicably, it may have serious repercussions on regime maintenance.

Experience in the 1990s, especially after the Asian financial crisis, exposed the structural weaknesses of SMEs, in particular their capabilities in coping with the KBE environment. With these structural weaknesses, SMEs could not be effective partners in venturing abroad and play a supporting role in the industry cluster. The government is therefore committed to develop and build up the capabilities of SMEs to enhance their competitiveness. With this background, SME 21 (www.spring.gov.sg) was announced in January 2000 with three major targets for the year 2010, as follows:

- Doubling of productivity of the retail sector from S$28,000 to S$56,000 per worker;
- Trebling of local SMEs with sales turnover of S$10 million and above from 2000 to 6000; and
- Quadrupling of local SMEs with e-commerce transactions from 8,000 to 32,000.

In implementing SME 21, the first step is to restructure the institutional framework to facilitate assistance to SMEs. Foremost, the Standards, Productivity and Innovation Board (SPRING Singapore)[6] has been appointed as the champion agency for SMEs. All the previous assistance schemes to SMEs were consolidated into eight schemes under SPRING Singapore.[7] Any matters relating to investment abroad are under the purview of International Enterprises Singapore (IE Singapore). One good example is the International Partners Programme (iPartners) whereby IE Singapore tries to be a matchmaker between local and foreign partners. However, any investment incentive schemes such as the Overseas Investment Incentive will be under the Economic Development Board's (EDB) purview.

In their latest move, IE Singapore and SPRING Singapore have teamed up to launch BrandPact which will help local enterprises to use branding as a tool for enhancing competitiveness. The programme is also aimed at raising the understanding and awareness of branding among SMEs in Singapore (Hooi 2005). In addition, the Enterprise Development Centres (EDCs), which is a joint initiative between SPRING and six major business chambers and industry associations, will also be established over the next few years. In this case, the government would provide funding to defray up to 70 per cent of the set-up costs for the EDCs. These EDCs will also offer consultancy and advisory services to help SMEs upgrade, expand and venture overseas, and also organize activities to help enhance the capabilities of SMEs.

On the whole, the government has been adopting a holistic approach in nurturing SMEs (Lim 2005). Broadly, there are three dimensions to the approach. At the national level, the government will strive to improve the business environment in Singapore with an aim to foster a pro-business environment. Secondly, the government would provide broad-based assistance to SMEs to help them build up their capabilities and expand business opportunities. Under this framework, the government will launch the Enterprise One-Stop Service (or EOS) at the end of 2005 to better assist SMEs. EOS will enable the government to reach out to more SMEs and increase their awareness of the assistance schemes available to them. Finally, the government seeks to develop vibrant industry clusters in which key players across the entire value chain can work closely together. The aim is to enhance the capabilities of the industry cluster as a whole and in this instance, the industry and business associations will be asked to be heavily involved.

5. CONCLUDING REMARKS

Unlike the stereotype of overseas Chinese business as typified in the literature, ethnic Chinese business firms in Singapore are not homogenous.

Any attempt to characterize overseas Chinese business into a stereotype would be gravely misleading. Moreover, any exaggeration and glorification of Chinese business success arising from Chinese business networks, would only lead to unnecessary jealousy, anxiety and political tension in the Southeast Asian region. This is especially true when one tries to link monetary wealth with political powers (Phar 2002b).

Yoshihara's (1988) penetrating analysis on overseas Chinese business may be incisive and enlightening. However, his observation of overseas Chinese business system as "*ersatz* capitalism" may not be at all true. As Winn (1998) has shown, large Chinese enterprises in Hong Kong and Taiwan have invested heavily in information and telecommunication industries. Even Singapore Chinese companies which have invested in the real estate previously have also diverted part of their resources to invest in high-value and high-tech industries. Nevertheless, Yoshihara's observation may still apply to many traditional small family businesses whose capability in coping with globalization may be in question.

With globalization, opportunities are abundant but threats can be suicidal. As the Asian financial crisis in 1997 has shown, globalization induces global integration which may carry with it systemic and contagious effect of a financial crisis. Such effects may be able to cause a total collapse of the world economy. Surprisingly, ethnic Chinese businesses in Singapore, in particular the larger ones, were able to withstand the onslaught of the Asian financial crisis. The main reasons are that ethnic Chinese businesses have diversified their businesses long ago not only in terms of geographical areas, but also in terms of industry. In other words, they "don't put all eggs in one basket". Of no less importance is their relative concentration of their investment in China which happened to be insulated from the contagion effect of the Asian financial crisis.[8]

Investment in China by ethnic Chinese enterprises in Singapore was considered as politically sensitive in the 1960s and 1970s. Internally, Singapore is a multi-racial and multi-cultural society. Any tilt towards Chineseness might cause uneasiness and tension among the non-Chinese constituents. Only after the establishment of diplomatic relation with China in 1990,[9] did Singapore make a bold move in encouraging ethnic Chinese businesses to invest in China, especially after 1993 when the regionalization initiative was officially launched. The official argument for such a move is that the decision to invest in China is based purely on economic ground. The use of cultural affinity and ethnic advantage is instrumental for pursuing Singapore's national interest. Despite the re-engagement of

Chineseness, Singapore is still very cautious in its endeavour and finds ways to rebalance its act whenever opportunities arise.

The past experience of Singapore's investment in China in the 1990s indicates that the investments were not without tension and conflict. The case of the Suzhou Industrial Park illustrates clearly how different Singapore Chinese are from those in mainland China. Chan and Tong (2000) note that "...a Singaporean Chinese is like them and not like them; or he is like them now, but not like them later...." Culturally they are the same and yet they are not exactly the same. The exploitation of "ethnic advantage" for investment in China in this respect may be over-exaggerated.

The Singapore Government's attitude towards ethnic Chinese businesses has changed from one of political alienation to one of firm commitment to assist them. A holistic approach has been adopted to ensure its effectiveness. The success of converting traditional Chinese family business (also include other ethnic businesses) into viable and resilient business structures hinges on the business enterprises' sheer determination in developing their capabilities. These capabilities will be tested in the marketplace with global competition in the rapidly changing environment. In this case, globalization may bring vast opportunities to these business enterprises but it can also destroy them within a short span of time with lightning speed.

Drawing experiences from Hong Kong, Taiwan and Thailand, Winn (1998) cautions that with the rapid pace of globalization, the market environment has constantly changed, and more often than not, in a drastic manner. The immediate challenge for these ethnic Chinese businesses, especially those in the category of "builders"[10] is to expand their business operations into new markets, notably outside Asia. However, the regulatory environment in the new markets is totally foreign. The Chinese business networks which have been a key factor in achieving business success in Asia may become less useful in the new environment. Winn observes that "the strength and insulation of the Bamboo Network in Asia as well as the lack of market competition has given Chinese companies as Asia-focus myopia and has actually inhibited overseas Chinese business to globalize." It is therefore not uncommon that "the heads of the largest overseas Chinese companies may be one of the richest men in the world, but few have created a global product or an international brand name, let alone command strong market share in an area outside Asia." One way to overcome such constraints is through acquisitions of existing non-

Chinese firms with products or services of international brands, but the costs of such acquisitions can be enormous.

Ethnic Chinese businesses have been diversifying their businesses with horizontal integration (or "structurers"). In the face of globalization, they may still have to compete with MNCs that constantly produce new products and services of high quality and international brands. With rising income and sophistication, as well as greater exposure to advertisement, consumers in Asia have become more informed and discriminating in their purchases. The main issue facing ethnic Chinese business in Singapore in years to come is how to compete successfully with their own branded goods and services on a global scale, given their existing comparative advantages.

Notes

[1]   In this chapter, I use the phrase "overseas Chinese firms or businesses" to refer to those ethnic Chinese businesses or firms outside mainland China. For firms or businesses owned by ethnic Chinese in Singapore, "ethnic Chinese firms or businesses" will be used to differentiate them from "Chinese firms or businesses" owned by mainland Chinese. The phrases are chosen just for convenience, and do not carry any connotations.

[2]   Chan and Ng (2000) and Menkoff and Sikorski (2002) provide clarifications on some of the myths about overseas Chinese business in Southeast Asia.

[3]   The measures included, among others, a drastic cut in employers' contribution to the Central Provident Fund (CPF) and a general wage cut.

[4]   According to Tan (2003, p. 751), Chineseness refers to the Singaporean perspective of the political elite placing increasing importance and prominence on the Chinese language and culture within the political and social-cultural discourse.

[5]   A state uses its own history, geography, and ethnic motifs to construct its own distinct image that can be utilized for transnational influence and knowledge arbitrage (Peter van Ham 2001).

[6]   A statutory board previously known as the Productivity and Standards Board (PSB).

[7]   The schemes include Local Enterprise Finance Scheme (LEFS), Micro Loan Programme, Variable Interest Loan Scheme (V-Loan), Local Enterprise Technical Assistance Scheme (LETAS), Loan Insurance

Scheme, Domestic Sector Productivity Fund, Enterprise Investment Incentive (EII) Scheme and SPRING SEED.

8   China was insulated from the crisis mainly because of its exchange control, that is, non-convertibility of the *renminbi* for capital account transactions. In other words, short-term capital flows were prohibited such that currency speculators had no way to attack the currency.

9   Singapore was the last country among the ASEAN nations to establish diplomatic relations with mainland China. This was to avoid suspicions that Singapore would be the "Third China Republic" after mainland China and Taiwan.

10   Chu and MacMurray (1993) classify large Chinese enterprises into "structurers" and "builders". Structurers are diversified conglomerates based on horizontal integration while "builders" concentrate on certain specific business areas and keep a tight ring of businesses around their core business.

References

Backman, Michael. 1999. *Asian Eclipse: Exposing the Dark Side of Business in Asia* (Singapore: John Wiley & Sons).

Bolt, Paul J. 2000. "Economic Co-operation Between China and Singapore". In *China and Southeast Asia's Ethnic Chinese: State and Diaspora in Contemporary Asia* (Westport, Connecticut and London: Praeger). Chapter 7, pp. 131–52.

Buena, Daniel. 2004. "S'pore: Gateway to China and Bridge to India". *The Business Times*, 7 April.

Chan, Kwok Bun (ed.) 2000. *Chinese Business Networks: State, Economy and Culture* (Singapore: Prentice Hall and Nordic Institute of Asian Studies).

Chan, Kwok Bun and Ng Beoy Kui. 2000. "Myths and Misperceptions of Ethnic Chinese Capitalism". In Chan (ed.), 2000, pp. 285–302.

Chan, Kwok Bun and Ng Beoy Kui. 2004. "Singapore". In *Chinese Business in Southeast Asia: Contesting Cultural Explanations, Researching Entrepreneurship*, edited by Gomez, Edmund Terence and Hsin-Huang Michael Hsiao (London and New York: RoutledgeCurzon), pp. 38–61.

Chan, Kwok Bun and Tong Chee Kiong. 2000. "Singaporean Chinese Doing Business in China". In Chan (ed.), 2000, pp. 71–85.

Chan, Ronnie. 2000. "Overseas Chinese Management Styles: Some Reflections". In *Management and Organizations in the Chinese Context*, edited by Li, J.T. Anne S. Tsui and Elizabeth Weldon (Houndmills: MacMillan Press), pp. 325–36.

Chu, T. C. and Trevor Murray. 1993. "The Road Ahead for Asia's Leading Conglomerates". *The McKinsey Quarterly* 3, pp. 117–26.

Chuang, Peck Meng. 2005*a*. "Mid-sized S'pore Firms Cash in on China Boom". *The Business Times*, 22 March.

Chuang, Peck Meng. 2005*b*. "S'pore Can Help Boost China-India Business: Top Execs". *The Business Times*, 9 April.

Dahles, Heidi. 2005. "Culture, Capitalism and Political Entrepreneurship: Transnational Ventures of the Singapore-Chinese in China". *Culture and Organization* 11, no. 1: 45–58.

Gomez, Edmund Terence, and Gregor Benton. 2004. "Introduction: De-essentializing Capitalism: Chinese Enterprise, Transnationalism, and Identity". In *Chinese Enterprise, Transnationalism and Identity*, edited by Gomez, Edmund Terence, and Hsin-Huang Michael Hsiao (London and New York: RoutledgeCurzon), pp. 1–19.

Goldman Sachs. 2003. "What is Driving Asia's Exports to China?" *Asia Pacific Economics Analyst*, January 17.

Haley, George T., Tan, C.T. and U.C.V. Haley. 1998. *New Asian Emperors: The Overseas Chinese, Their Strategies and Competitive Advantage* (Oxford: Butterworth).

Hamilton, Gary G. (ed.) 1996. *Asian Business Network*s (Berlin: de Gruyter).

Higgott, R. 1998. "The International Relations of the Asian Economic Crisis: A Study of the Politics of Resentment". ARC Workshop.

Hooi, Joyce. 2005. "Tie-up to Raise Brand Awareness Among SMEs". *Straits Times*, 8 April.

Huff, W.G. 1994. *The Economic Growth of Singapore: Trade and Development in the Twentieth Century* (Cambridge: Cambridge University Press).

IMF. 2000. "Globalization: threat or Opportunities". <http://www.imf.org/external/np/exr/ib/2000/041200.htm>.

Kao, John. 1993. "The Worldwide Web of Chinese Business". *Harvard Business Review* (March/April): 24–36.

Koh, Leslie. 2005. "Build Bridges with India, SM tells Indians Here". *Straits Times*, 3 April, p. 9.

Lall, Sanjaya and Manuel Albaladejo. 2004. "China's Competitive Performance: A Threat to East Asian Manufactured Exports?" *World Development* 32, no. 9: 1441–66.

Lever-Tracy and David Ip. 2002. "Small Chinese Businesses after the

Asian Crisis: Surviving and Reviving". In *Globalization and SMEs in East Asia*, edited by Charles Harvie and Boon-Chye Lee (Cheltenham: Edward Elgar), pp. 253–73.

Lianhe Zaobao. 2004*a*. "Bilingual Singaporeans Have Opportunity to Exploit Comparative Advantage in China". 12 October, p. 27.

Lianhe Zaobao. 2004*b*. "Singapore Exchange Continued to Regulate Listed Chinese Companies". 12 October, p. 27.

Lianhe Zaobao. 2004*c*. "S'pore and China Contemplating Hedge Fund to Invest High-tech Chinese Companies". 13 October, p. 28.

Lianhe Zaobao. 2004*d*. "14 Singapore Listed Chinese Companies having Road Shows in HK, London and New York". 7 October, p. 34.

Lianhe Zaobao. 2005. "Citibank, the Largest Corporation in the World". 4 April, p. 1.

Lim, Hng Kiang. 2005. Speech at the Opening of the Enterprise Development Centre (EDC) at the Association of Small and Medium Enterprise (ASME), 28 March.

Menkhoff, T. and Douglas Sikorski. 2002. "Asia's Chinese entrepreneurs between Myth-making and Renewal". In *Chinese Entrepreneurship and Asian Business Networks*, edited by Thomas Menkhoff and Slovay Gerke (London and New York: RoutledgeCurzon), pp. 23–42.

Mussa, Michael. 2000. "Factors Driving Global Economic Integration". Paper presented at a Symposium on "Global Opportunities and Challenges," held at Jackson Hole, Wyoming, sponsored by Federal Reserve Board of Kansas City. <http://www.imf.org/external/np/speeches/2000/082500.htm>.

Ng, Beoy Kui. 2002. "The Changing Role of Ethnic Chinese SMEs in Economic Restructuring in Singapore: From 'Two-legged' Policy to 'Three-legged' Strategy". In *Ethnic Chinese in Singapore and Malaysia: A dialogue between Tradition and Modernity,* edited by Leo Suryadinata (Singapore: Times Academic Press), pp. 255–76.

Peter van Ham. 2001. "The Rise of the Brand State: The Postmodern Politics of Image and Reputation". *Foreign Affairs* 80, no. 5: 2–6.

Petir. 1994. "The Keys to Successful Regionalization" (January/February): 51.

Phar, Kim Beng. 2002*a*. "Southeast Asia Losing FDI Flight to China". *Asia Times*, 12 November.

Phar, Kim Beng. 2002*b*. "Overseas Chinese: How Powerful Are They?" *Asia Times*, 10 December.

Redding, S. Gordon. 1990. *The Spirit of Chinese Capitalism* (Berlin: de Gruyter).

Rodan, G. 1989. *The Political Economy of Singapore's Industrialization: National State and International Capital* (Kuala Lumpur: Forum).

Rumbaugh, Thomas and Nicolas Blancher. 2004. "International Trade and the Challenges of WTO Accession". In *China's Growth and Integration into the World Economy: Prospects and Challenges*, edited by Eswar Prasad (Washington, D.C.: International Monetary Fund), pp. 5–13.

Seagrave, S. 1996. *Lords of the Rim: The Invisible Empire of the Overseas Chinese* (London: Corgi Books).

Straits Times. 2004. "Fewer SMEs Investing in IT Due to Downturn". 16 October.

Tan, K.B., Eugune. 2002. "Reconceptualizing Chinese Identity: The Politics of Chineseness in Singapore". In *Ethnic Chinese in Singapore and Malaysia: A dialogue between Tradition and Modernity*, edited by Leo Suryadinata (Singapore: Times Academic Press), pp. 109–36.

Tan, K.B., Eugune. 2003. "Re-engaging Chineseness: Political, Economic and Cultural Imperatives of Nation-Building in Singapore". *The China Quarterly*, pp. 751–74.

Tracy, Noel. 2000. "Weathering the Storm: Structural Changes in the Chinese Diaspora Economy". In *Chinese Business and the Asian Crisis*, edited by David Ip, Constance Level-Tracy and Noel Tracy (Aldershot: Gower), pp. 163–82.

Tsang, Eric W.K. 2002. "Learning from Overseas Venturing Experience: The Case of Chinese Family Business". *Journal of Business Venturing* 17: 21–40.

Tschoegi, Adrain E. 2001. "The International Expansion of Singapore's Largest Banks". Working Paper Series, Financial Institutions Center, The Wharton School, University of Pennsylvania.

Tseng, Wanda, and Harm Zebregs. 2002. "Foreign Direct Investment in China: Some Lessons for Other Countries". IMF Policy Discussion Paper No. 02/03 (Washington, D.C.: International Monetary Fund).

Vasil, Raj. 1995. *Asianising Singapore: The PAP's Management of Ethnicity* (Singapore: Heinemann Asia).

Weiderbaum, Murray and Samuel Huges. 1996. *The Bamboo Network: How Expatriate Chinese Entrepreneurs Are Creating A New Economic Superpower in Asia* (New York: Martin Kessler Books).

Whalley, John. 2003. "Liberalization in China's Key Service Sectors Following WTO Accession: Some Scenarios and Issues of Measurement". NBER Working Paper Series, Working Paper no. 10143, <http://nber.org/papers/w10143>.

Winn, Peter. 1998. "Tomorrow's Tigers: The Transformation of Asia's Leading Overseas Chinese Enterprises". Unpublished mimeograph, 20 April, The Joseph H. Lauder Institute.

World Bank. 2002. *Globalization, Growth, and Poverty: Building an Inclusive World Economy* (New York: World Bank and Oxford University Press).

Yang, Yongzheng. 2003. "China's Integration into the World Economy: Implications for Developing Countries". IMF Working Paper, WP/03/245.

Yeung, W.C. Henry. 2000. "Managing Crisis in a Globalizing Era: The Case of Chinese Business Firms in Singapore". In *Chinese Business and the Asian Crisis*, edited by David Ip, Constance Level-Tracy and Noel Tracy (Aldershot: Gower), pp. 87–113.

Yeung, W.C. Henry. 2002a. "Transnational Entrepreneurship and Chinese Business Networks: the Regionalization of Chinese Business Firms from Singapore". In Menkhoff and Gerke (eds.), 2002, pp. 184–216.

Yeung, W.C. Henry. 2002b. *Entrepreneurship and the Internationalization of Asian Firms: An Institutional Perspective* (Cheltenham: Edward Elgar).

Yoshihara, Kunio. 1988. *The Rise of Ersatz Capitalism in South East Asia* (Singapore: Oxford University Press).

<www.spring.gov.sg>.

12

The Changing Dynamics of Thailand CP Group's International Expansion

Pavida Pananond

The Charoen Pokphand (CP) Group of Thailand had been one of the most studied Thai firms both in the vernacular press and the academic circles. Among best-selling books on leading domestic personalities, those on the CP Group's chairman, Dhanin Chearavanont, probably ranked second, only after the prime minister, Thaksin Shinawatra. In the academic literature alike, CP had been the case study favoured by scholars from different fields, ranging from agri-business (for example, Burch and Goss 2005) to business history (for example, Suehiro 1989, 2003).

One stream of academic inquiry that had always featured CP as its main case was the study of the "overseas Chinese" capitalism in Southeast Asia.[1] The CP Group had been frequently referred to as one of the major Thai representatives of the "overseas Chinese" business (see, for example, Gomez 2002, 2004; Suehiro 1989, 2003; Brown 1998, 2000; Yeung 2004). CP's characteristics of family ownership and management, large size, conglomerate diversification, and extensive relationships with politicians, made the group fit under the stereotypical model of Chinese capitalism. The myth of CP as an "overseas Chinese" business was further reinforced after the group and the U.S.-based Continental Grain formed the first foreign joint venture in Shenzen Economic Zone in 1979. Since then, China had been the second most important country for the CP Group after Thailand. Of all the group's 400 subsidiaries worldwide, 213 were located in China (<www.cpgroup.cn>, July 2005).

The over-emphasis on the ethnicity of CP's founder might have divested some attention from the group's business operations. CP had been regarded more as the Thai face of the "overseas Chinese" capitalism than as a regular business corporation. As a result, most studies overwhelmingly stressed how CP's characteristics resembled other ethnic Chinese businesses throughout Southeast Asia, rather than unveiled the group's behaviour from an economic or business perspective. The weight given to the group's Chinese ethnicity was further emphasized following the group's extensive expansions in China. Studies on CP's international activities had therefore been dominated by what CP had done in China, thus reinforcing the perception of the group as an ethnic Chinese business. Not much had been said, however, on the group's strategic directions behind its overall development. Even less was known about the group's extensive international activities, pre- and post-crisis alike.

Although there were some attempts to explain the pre-1997 international expansion of the CP Group (see Handley 1997; Brown 1998; Pavida 1998, 2001*a*, *b*), not much had been said on whether and how the group's internationalization behaviour changed after the crisis. This chapter therefore aims to analyse CP's post-crisis changes, as well as to discuss the changing dynamics of the group's international expansion. While this chapter acknowledges the contribution of the literature on ethnic Chinese business, it argues that this stream of research would benefit from integrating other theoretical perspectives in their analysis. It therefore incorporates the views from the Third World multinational literature to analyse the changing dynamics of the CP Group's international expansion. The chapter is divided into six parts. The first critiques the literature on the ethnic Chinese business. The second and third parts document CP's pre- and post-crisis development, while the fourth section analyses the changing dynamics of the group's international expansion. Prior to the conclusion, the fifth section discusses major challenges that CP is facing.

1. CRITIQUE OF ETHNIC CHINESE BUSINESS LITERATURE

Since China opened its doors to foreign investment in 1979, the "overseas Chinese" had been the largest source of foreign investment in China, with Hong Kong ranking as the number one investor (EAAU 1995). Southeast Asian firms became an additional important source of investment in the 1990s (Brown 1998, p. 612). Close ties between Southeast Asia, Hong Kong, Taiwan and China attracted much attention, and exotic terms, such as the "bamboo network" (Weidenbaum and Hughes 1996) or the "worldwide web of Chinese business" (Kao 1993) were coined to describe these links. Many scholars suggested that these "overseas Chinese" networks provided entrepreneurs with necessary business intelligence, alternative sources of capital, and necessary political linkages (for example,

Hamilton and Biggart 1988; Biggart and Hamilton 1990; Redding 1990, 1995; Ch'ng 1993; EAAU 1995; Brown 1998). These resources served as competitive advantages for "overseas Chinese" entrepreneurs in their domestic development (Haley, Tan, and Haley 1998), as well as their expansion in East and Southeast Asia.

With regard to "overseas Chinese" investment in China, some common notions and characteristics had been widely discussed. First, it was suggested that the shared ethnic background and language contributed largely as competitive advantages of these ethnic Chinese firms *vis-à-vis* their Western competitors (for example, Limlingan 1986; Redding 1990, 1995; EAAU 1995). Some further argued that the initial investment of these overseas Chinese was led by links to their ancestral villages and provinces (for example, Brown 1998, p. 620; Weidenbaum and Hughes 1996). Second, most scholars agreed that doing business in China required much use of *guanxi* — personal relationships and connections. Luo and Chen (1997) suggested that these personal connections contributed significantly and positively to the performance of firms operating in China. They stated that, compared with their Western counterparts, the overseas Chinese investors were more at ease using these *guanxi*, and that in turn had benefited their ventures in China. Third, it was acknowledged that Hong Kong played a major role in foreign direct investment in China. Hong Kong served not only as a major financial source, but also as trading links into China (Mackie 1992). In an attempt to explain Southeast Asian business expansion, Ch'ng (1993) suggested that after having expanded domestically, these entrepreneurs often set up a representative office in Hong Kong before investing in China and other Southeast Asian countries.

Although the above paragraphs addressed some common features of the ethnic Chinese capitalism, they were not meant to be a detailed review of the existent literature. Such exercise had been undertaken in various works, whose primary purpose was to evaluate the current status of this field of research.[2] Rather than repeating those points in detail, this part discusses the main criticism of the literature on ethnic Chinese business.

The strongest criticism on studies of ethnic Chinese business in Southeast Asia had been its over-emphasis on the cultural and institutional perspectives (for example, Dirlik 1997; Fan 2002; Shapiro, Gedajlovic, and Erdener 2003; and Yeung 2004, Gomez and Hsiao 2004). The primary argument under these perspectives was that institutions, cultural norms, and practices of ethnic Chinese had been the key factors shaping their emergence, growth, and behaviour. As a result, issues such as

Confucianism, *guanxi*, trust, family, and ethnic networks, were put forward as key explanatory variables for the spread of ethnic Chinese capitalism. Such an emphasis carried both methodological and theoretical implications.

On methodology, the most important consequence of an over-dependence on the cultural and institutional perspectives was the difficulty these value-based variables posed on the empirical analysis (Gomez and Hsiao 2004, pp. 19–20). Several concepts that were associated with Chinese capitalism, or even the concept of "Chineseness", had been criticized as too vague and too complex to be sufficiently captured in empirical analysis. As succinctly put by Dirlik in his critical paper on "Chinese capitalism" (1997, p. 311), "the fundamental problem with the idea of a 'Chinese capitalism' is the vagueness of the notion of 'Chineseness' ". He argued against culturalist explanations that focused on unique characteristics of "Chinese capitalism" and proposed instead that the flourishing of "Chinese capitalism" in East Asia was to be understood in reference to developments within capitalism globally. Some multi-faceted concepts, such as *guanxi*, had been simply used to refer to interpersonal relationships, despite its complex nature and different types. Fan (2002) strongly criticized this over-simplified interpretation of *guanxi* and noted that the lack of understanding of these differences often resulted in the confusion in the literature.

The difficulty in interpreting these value-based concepts often led the literature on ethnic Chinese business to be fraught with generalized observations that were rather difficult to refute (Yeung 2004). Moreover, the tendency to over-generalize the characteristics of ethnic Chinese businesses in East and Southeast Asia inevitably implied that they formed a homogeneous community. The notion that Chinese business organizations were similar within the same home economies, and across different countries, had been met with strong criticism (for example, Jomo 2003; Yeung 2004; Gomez and Hsiao 2004). In their review of the Chinese business research in Southeast Asia, Gomez and Hsiao (2004, pp. 5–9) identified various reasons that prevented the Chinese from being a collective unit. These factors included the different timing of their immigration, their generational differences, as well as their sub-ethnic groups. More importantly, the different context in which ethnic Chinese capitalists developed in each country led to different path of capital accumulation (Jomo 2003). Thus, assuming that there was a collective group of ethnic Chinese capitalists throughout Southeast Asia was gravely misleading.

In addition to the methodological shortcomings resulting from the over-emphasis on the cultural and institutional perspectives, the ethnic Chinese capitalism literature also suffered from its shortage of empirical evidence. Gomez and Hsiao (2004, p. 23) pointed out that, despite the fact that most ethnic Chinese firms in Southeast Asia were small- and medium-sized enterprises, most analysis of Chinese enterprises were drawn from a few largest companies in the region, making many conclusions more applicable only to large companies. Even among the largest enterprises, studies of ethnic Chinese business in Southeast Asia were predominantly based on a number of key groups, like the CP Group in Thailand or the Salim group in Indonesia. The authors also drew attention to the lack of in-depth studies that unveiled the formation and development of other enterprises, not only the selected few that had long been the focus of analysis of this literature. They therefore called for more firm-level empirical studies that put greater attention on management and entrepreneurship.

On top of methodological problems, the ethnic Chinese business literature was characterized by a deficiency of theoretical perspectives. Much of the existing literature predominantly placed emphasis on cultural and institutional explanations. Although the main unit of analysis of the existing literature concerned the ethnic Chinese capitalism, few studies had examined this phenomenon from the business and economic perspectives (Shapiro *et al.* 2003). This inclination often brought about sentimental descriptions of how the ethnic Chinese across Asia felt united through their common ancestry, or how ethnic Chinese capitalists "returned home" to invest in China. Many scholars had argued against these culturalist explanations. In explaining why Southeast Asian Chinese capitalists invested in China, Suryadinata (1997, p. 16) clearly pointed out that they did so primarily to reap economic benefits, and only partly because of ethnic links. Similarly, Dirlik (1997) stressed that Chinese capitalism had to be interpreted as part of the global capitalist developments.

Furthermore, the view that the organization and behaviour of ethnic Chinese business firms were results of their cultural and institutional environments led to a static interpretation that, once established, these business organizations were unlikely to change "as if they have a particular fate or destiny, depending very much on their cultural origins and/or institutional structures that almost leave a permanent imprint on these capitalist organizations" (Yeung 2004, p. 31). But the reality of business environment in Asia had not remained the same over the past few decades. Factors such as generational changes among the ethnic Chinese business families, the threat of the new Internet economy, the maturing of Asia's legal and regulatory systems, and more importantly, the 1997 crisis which had made big Asian businesses more reliant on the equity capital, had all forced these ethnic Chinese entrepreneurs to adopt a more "Western" style of conducting business (*The Economist*, 29 April 2000). The sea change that Asia's competitive environment has gone through in the aftermath of the 1997 crisis made it necessary for business organizations, locals or multinationals alike, to rethink and adapt their behaviour like never before (Williamson 2005). It is therefore crucial that studies on ethnic Chinese capitalism be understood as dynamic and changing over time (Gomez and Hsiao 2004). Moreover, emphasis should also be placed on comparing the post-crisis practices of the major ethnic Chinese business groups to their pre-crisis behaviour to better examine their dynamics of change.

Following this view, this chapter examines the pre- and post-crisis growth and development of the CP Group. It focuses, in particular, on the group's international expansion activities that started in the late 1970s and became a significant strategic direction for the group's overall development. Although CP had been one of the most often selected case to discuss the "overseas Chinese" capitalism in Thailand, studies on the CP Group were no exception to the limitations discussed above. CP characteristics that had been most discussed included the group's ethnicity, family ownership and management, large size, extensive relationships with Thai and Chinese politicians, and the group's voracious appetite for a conglomerate style of unrelated diversifications. These features were very much in line with the celebrated characteristics of other "overseas Chinese" business groups in Southeast Asia. Not much, however, had been elaborated on the mechanism behind the group's business expansions that rendered CP the thirty-eighth largest non-financial multinational enterprise (MNE) from developing countries (UNCTAD 2004). Even less had been discussed on how the group undertook its restructuring in the post-crisis years to cope with many new challenges that included China's increased integration in the world economy.

This chapter explores CP's international development through the lens of the theory of the "third-world multinational".[3] By integrating this framework, it intends to point out how the group had achieved its growth in the years before the crisis, how it had adjusted during the post-crisis years, as well as what remained to be the group's future challenge as an emergent multinational. The next two parts summarize CP's development in the pre- and post-crisis years.

2. CP'S PRE-CRISIS GROWTH AND INTERNATIONAL EXPANSION: A HISTORICAL BACKGROUND[4]

Beginning modestly in 1921 as a seed supplier, the CP Group has grown into a multinational conglomerate with subsidiaries in twenty countries, employing more than 100,000 people and generating an estimated total group turnover of US$13 billion in 2002 (<www.cpthailand.com>, April 2005). At its peak before the 1997 crisis, the group's affiliated companies total more than 200, with fourteen listed in seven stock exchange markets around the world, that is, Bangkok, Jakarta, Hong Kong, Taipei, Shanghai, London and New York (*Corporate Thailand*, May 1996, pp. 12–80). Before the 1997 crisis, the group's operations were organized under nine different business groups: Agro-industry; aquaculture; seeds, fertilizer and plant protection; international trading; marketing and distribution; real estate and land development; petrochemical; automotive and industrial products; and telecommunication. After the major corporate restructure following the 1997 crisis, however, the group streamlined their structure by adhering to three core industries, namely agri-business, telecommunications, and logistics and retailing (<www.cpthailand.com>, April 2005). Pavida (2001*a*) divided CP's growth before 1997 into five stages: Early start in international trading (1921–54); animal feed production (1954–70); vertical integration (1970–97); conglomerate diversification (1980–97); and international expansion (1972–97).

2.1 International Trading (1921–54)

The origin of the CP Group dates back to 1921 when two brothers, Chia Ek Chor (1895–1983) and Chia Seow Hui (1905–90), who emigrated from Guangdong to Thailand in search for better economic opportunities. The two brothers set up a small shop called "Hang Chia Tai Chung" to trade eggs and vegetable seeds with Hong Kong. Commercial trading of seeds and some agricultural chemicals remained their main business until Ek Chor's eldest son started chicken feed milling in 1954.

2.2 Animal Feed (1954–70)

After returning from schooling in China, Jaran Chearavanont, Ek Chor's eldest son, set up his own feed shop named Chareon Pokphand in 1954.

The name meant "prosperous feeds" in Thai. The family business became divided into two lines, with Jaran running the feed business, while his uncle took care of the original trading business of seeds, fertilizers and insecticides.

Their feed business grew with the rise in commercial chicken farming in Thailand after 1955. The growth enabled CP to set up their branch in Hong Kong in 1959 to serve as a distribution centre for food products into China. After Dhanin Chearavanont, the group's chairman, returned from his education in China and later took over the leadership of the family firm in 1963. He modernized the feed production through the recruitment of non-family staff, the development of compound animal feeds and investment in new machinery. At the end of 1960s, the company became an important player in animal feed industry, holding 90 per cent of the market in 1968 (Wichai 1993, p. 62). Animal feed milling remains the core activity of the group until today.

2.3 Vertical Integration (1970–97)

A major milestone for CP's poultry operations was its joint venture in 1970 with an American agricultural multinational, Abor Acres. The 60:40 joint venture, Abor Acres (Thailand) was established to import chicken breeds from the United States. Since then, CP placed great emphasis on vertical integration to integrate animal feed production, livestock farming, chicken slaughtering, and meat processing. The success in integrated poultry industry led CP to replicate their vertical integration in swine and shrimp production in 1980 and 1988 respectively.

With the production side of the agro-industry pretty much under control, the CP Group was looking for further expansion along the distribution line. Attempts at retail level included selling grilled chicken under the Five Star brand, and later starting a fast food chain called Chester's Grill. In 1984, CP and the Central Group became the Thai franchisee for KFC restaurant, to which CP also supplied chicken (Yuthasak 2001). In addition to restaurant outlets, CP strengthened its retailing and distribution through a number of investments in supermarkets, and hypermarkets. These investments included: Siam Makro, a joint venture with the SHV group of the Netherlands, the owner of cash-and-carry Makro store in 1988; a licensing contract with Southland Corporation for the 7-Eleven convenience store in 1989; Sunny supermarket, and the Lotus Supercenter hypermarket chain in 1994.

2.4 Conglomerate Diversification (1980–97)

While CP's first wave of diversification concentrated on agri-business and distribution, the group's next phase in diversification focused on infrastructure sectors that were being liberalized or privatized, such as petrochemicals and telecommunications. CP entered the petrochemical industry through a joint venture with a Belgian firm, Solvay, in 1988. The joint venture, named Vinythai, produced PVC and vinyl chloride monomer, the main raw material for PVC. In addition, CP joined with the Thai state-owned Petroleum Authority of Thailand (PTT) in 1993 to establish a petrol station network under the name Petro Asia. Failure to overcome stiff competition led to persistent losses, and CP announced in 1996 that it wanted to leave the petrochemical industry (*Business in Thailand*, March 1998).

The most well-known, yet controversial, diversification of the CP Group was in telecommunications. CP set up a new subsidiary, CP Telecommunications, which was later renamed TelecomAsia, and again changed to True in 2004, to bid for a fixed-line concession from the Telephone Organization of Thailand (TOT). TelecomAsia (TA)'s winning of the concession in 1990 triggered a heated and prolonged conflict that became one of the most controversial episodes in Thailand's privatization history (Nukul 1996, Sakkarin 2000). CP's further expansion in the telecommunications industry was carried out through Telecom Holding (TH), the group's telecommunications investment arm. Through TH, CP had investments in at least forty subsidiaries covering a wide range of communications and media-related industries, including cable television, satellite-based communication services, and submarine fibre-optic cable network (*TelecomAsia Annual Report* 1997).

2.5 International Expansion

Although CP could claim that it was international from its beginning when the founding brothers were trading seed in the Asian region, CP's committed international expansion did not begin until 1972 when the group set up its first overseas feed milling operation in Indonesia. Further investment in poultry farming and fisheries later followed in 1974 and 1976. During the same period, CP expanded its feed mill investment to Hong Kong in 1974, Singapore in 1976, and Taiwan in 1977 (Wichai 1993, pp. 269–74). International investment during the 1970s also included an insurance company and at least three investment and finance companies in Hong Kong. All these investment companies served as sources of funding in CP's China ventures because Thailand still imposed a strong control over currency outflows during that time.

Investment in China started soon after the open-door policy was implemented. In 1981, Conti Chia Tai,[5] a joint venture between CP, Continental Grain Co., Ltd. of the United States, and a local Chinese authority was set up. This venture was the first foreign joint venture in the newly established Special Economic Zones (SEZ) of the Shenzen area (*FEER*, 21 October 1993, <www.cpthailand.com>).

CP's investment in China followed its formula which had proved successful in Thailand and Indonesia. Feed milling was used as pioneer before poultry farming and meat processing were later introduced. In 1997, CP operated feed mills in twenty-seven out of thirty provinces in China (*FEER*, 23 January 1997). The group's first diversification away from the agro-industry came in 1985 when a motorcycle manufacturing plant was set up in Shanghai. Despite its lack of experience, CP nonetheless started the operation by licensing technology from Honda. This pattern of finding suitable technological partnership characterized CP's non-agri-business activities.

CP's activities in China during the 1980s were mainly concentrated in agri-business and motorcycle manufacturing. The group expanded its activities to include aquaculture, downstream petrochemical and real estate projects in the 1990s. Most of these activities were concentrated in the Shanghai area. CP initially operated its real estate investment through Hong Kong Fortune, a joint venture with a Thai real estate group, Univest. Announced projects included a US$2 billion-dollar Shanghai satellite town project comprising office buildings, hotels, shopping arcades and sport facilities (*Bangkok Post*, 12 July 1993). However, the joint venture did not work out and two groups parted way and split up the properties (Handley 1997).

Other manufacturing investments in China included two beer breweries. Shanghai Mila Brew was a joint venture with the Heineken Group (announced in 1993), while Trillion Brewery (announced in 1994) was a joint venture of CP with the Boonrawd Brewery Group and the Siam Commercial Bank. CP later expanded its retailing activities to China. Together with the Netherlands-based SHV Holdings, CP opened its first Makro outlet in 1992. The two partners, along with a Taiwanese partner, had also operated Makro outlets in Taiwan since 1989 (*FEER*, 3 November 1994). In addition, CP introduced its own warehouse outlet, Lotus Super Centre, to China in 1996 after a planned joint venture with the U.S.-

based Wal-Mart collapsed. Wal-Mart, on the other hand, entered China by itself in the same year (Handley 1997). By 1995, the number of CP's retail outlets in China reached fourteen (Brown 1998, p. 629). Other retailing projects in China included shopping malls, a jewellery exchange centre, and a seafood restaurant. All were joint ventures with both Thai and Chinese partners (*The Nation*, 22 November 1995).

CP's international investments in telecommunications were again concentrated in China, although the group held a 15 per cent interest in Kopin Corporation, a Nasdaq-listed electrical equipment company, and a 16 per cent equity in the Fibre-optic Link Around the Globe (FLAG), an international project led by Nynex.[6] CP's telecommunications investments in China included a 10 per cent equity in APT Satellite, a satellite transponder controlled by the Chinese government; a 40 per cent holding in Chia Tai Vision (Shanghai), a television programme producer; and a 49 per cent equity in a joint venture with a Chinese authority to manufacture telecommunications equipment (*TelecomAsia Annual Report* 1997).

On top of the above projects, CP was involved in banking and finance activities. In 1994, the group took a 20 per cent stake in TM International Bank, which was established in 1992 as a joint venture between the M Thai group and Thai Military bank in the southern province of Swatow. Moreover, CP's diverse expansion in China included smaller projects, such as factories making shoes, toys, raincoats, and luggage (Handley 1997).

Because of its wide-ranging international investments, the CP Group was often referred to as Thailand's first and foremost multinational corporation (see *Corporate Thailand*, May 1996; *Institutional Investor*, October 1996; *FEER*, 23 January 1997; Wichai 1993; Handley 1997; Suehiro 1997; and Brown 1998). It should be emphasized, however, that these diverse international projects took place only in China. CP's investments elsewhere were mainly concentrated on its core activity — the agri-business industry. Moreover, not all planned projects materialized. Many projects that were announced with fanfare either never took place or had limited success. For example, announced petrochemical projects in Hainan and Shanghai never came through. Nor did projects to invest in power generation, computer chip fabrication, and heavy truck production in China. Despite these failed expansion efforts, CP still remained at the forefront of Thai multinationals. Figure 12.1 summarizes locations of CP's international projects under each business group prior to 1997.

FIGURE 12.1
Location of CP's Pre-Crisis International Activities

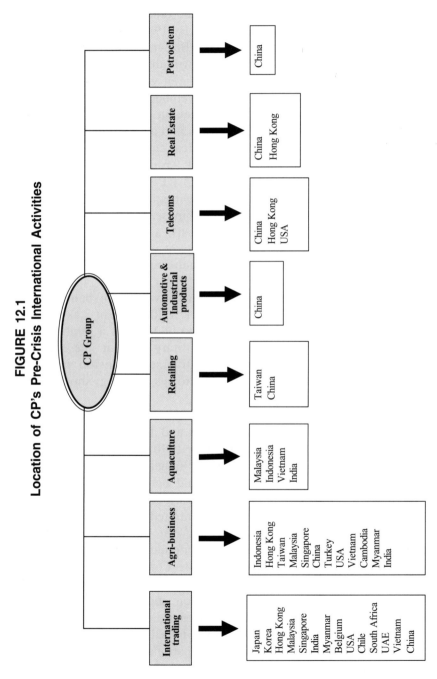

Note: * Investment Company

Source: Pavida (2001, Figure 6.4)

3. POST-CRISIS ADJUSTMENTS

Like many other companies in Thailand, CP's rapid pre-crisis growth since the late 1980s was financed mainly through domestic and international loans. For example, TelecomAsia's debt to equity ratio increased from 0.53 in 1994 to 1.8 in 1996 and 11.6 in 1997 (*TelecomAsia Annual Report*, 1997). The high level of leverage was also practised in its overseas subsidiaries, as the debt to equity ratio of the group's major Hong Kong subsidiary, CP Pokphand (CPP), shot up from 0.69 in 1993 to 4.08 in 1997 (CPP Annual Report, 1997). Such a high level of debts, most of which was foreign currency-based, led to a disastrous financial problem after the Thai currency was floated in July 1997. The CP Group was faced with a total debt of US$1.2 billion, US$800 million of which belonged to TelecomAsia alone (*The Nation*, 28 July 1998). CP's operations in Indonesia suffered the same fate, as most of their loans were also based on the U.S. currency. CP's executives stressed that the financial difficulty CP suffered after 1997 was not caused by its operations in China, but by the increased value of foreign debts in its Thai, Hong Kong, and Indonesian operations (Interviews, January–February 2005).

The flotation of the *baht* affected CP in both positive and negative ways. While the weaker currency triggered the growth of exports during the post-crisis years, CP's foreign currency loans almost doubled in value. CP's post-crisis restructuring was therefore concentrated in three areas: Business consolidation, debt restructure, and export promotion. These three objectives led to major adjustments of CP's domestic and international activities. Because the primary purpose of this chapter is to examine the post-crisis dynamics of CP's international operations, only the business consolidation of CP will be explored in detail. The most significant change CP has undertaken since 1997 is its decision to focus on three core industries: Agri-business and food industry; retail, logistics and distribution services; and telecommunications and multimedia services (<www.cpthailand.com>, April 2005). Despite this strategy, CP still maintains its involvement in many areas that the group had started prior to the 1997 crisis. The following discussion looks at CP's adjustments in the core and non-core sectors.

3.1 Core Industries: More Focused and More Value-added

Having realized that it had expanded too fast, CP decided to forego some of the non-core industries and some international projects to save the group from insolvency. For the first time, CP was forced to decide which of its extensive wide-ranging activities were most crucial to the group. CP divided its businesses into two streamlines: Production and processing (agri-business and food industry) and services (telecommunications, logistics and retailing) (see <www.cpthailand.com>). With the focus on three main areas, CP tried to reduce its exposure in other industries both in Thailand and China. The biggest sale at home was when CP sold 75 per cent of shares in Lotus Supercenter, its home-grown hypermarket chain, to Britain's Tesco for US$365 million (*FEER*, 8 April 1999). In China, CP sold or withdrew from approximately sixty to seventy subsidiaries in various sectors (Interview, 16 February 2005).

Agri-business was the most outstanding area of CP's post-crisis adjustments. CP took a long-deserved attempt to consolidate its vast empire of subsidiaries under one main roof, Charoen Pokphand Food (CPF). Despite being the group's core sector, agri-business's operations in Thailand and elsewhere had been the most difficult area to trace prior to the crisis. In Thailand, CP's agri-business was organized under nine key subsidiaries, including four listed ones in the Stock Exchange of Thailand (SET): Charoen Pokphand Feedmill (CPF), Charoen Pokphand Northeastern (CPNE), Bangkok Agro-Industrial Products (BAP), and Bangkok Produce Merchandising (BKP). After the consolidation, the three were delisted from the SET (CPF Notification to SET, 8 June 1998). Charoen Pokphand Feedmill also changed its name to Charoen Pokphand Food, in order to reflect its mission to become the "kitchen of the world" (*CPF Annual Report* 1999). For overseas subsidiaries in agri-business, most were consolidated under the Hong Kong-listed CP Pokphand (CPP).

One important factor that prompted CP to consolidate its agri-business operations was the need to attract investment funds in its listed companies (*Phujadkarn Rai Duen*, February 2000). CP and all other Thai companies that were heavily leveraged learned their lesson on the risk of foreign currency loans after the *baht* flotation almost doubled their debt value. The dire need for cash and the risk of debt financing made the capital market and direct cash injection from foreign partners two of the most viable options for many Thai companies, including the CP Group.

Rather than going through details of CP's post-crisis structural changes, which are summarized in Table 12.1, this part discusses two key strategies that underlie CP's adjustments in the food and retails sectors: Concentration on value-adding activities; and a more serious integration into retailing and distribution.

TABLE 12.1
Summary of CP's post-crisis changes

Business Group	Subsidiary	Country	Changes
Agri-business	Charoen Pokphand Foods (CPF)	Thailand	• Consolidated 9 agri-business units, including 3 listed ones under CPF (*1998–99*)
	CP-KFC	Thailand	• Sold its 51 per cent equity to KFC International (*2001*)
	Charoen Pokphand Foods (CPF)	Thailand	• Extended the vertical integration into processing to swine (*2002*)
	Seafoods Enterprise (SFE)	Thailand	• SFE invested a 100 per cent equity in Aqua–Agri Foods International, Inc. in the United States. CPF invested 99.99 per cent in two newly set up companies in Thailand, Universal Food and Marketing Co. Ltd. and International Pet Food Co. Ltd. (*2003*)
	C.P. Standard Gida Sanayi ve Ticaret A.S. (CPS)	Turkey	• CPF bought shares in C.P. Standard Gida Sanayi ve Ticaret A.S. (CPS), resulting in CPF's taking 84.49 per cent control (*2004*)
	Charoen Pokphand (USA), Inc.	U.S.A.	• Ceased operations by selling all the company assets (previously held 99.95 per cent of equity) in March 2004
	CP-Yonekyu	Thailand	• CPF formed a food venture with Japan's Yonekyu Corporation to manufacture processed meat products for both domestic sales and export. The new company, CP-Yonekyu Co, will be established with 200 million *baht* in registered capital, 80.5 per cent held by CPF (*2004*)
Petrochemicals	PetroAsia	Thailand, China	• Sold most of its petrol stations in Thailand to joint venture partner, the Petroleum Authority of Thailand. Terminated operations in Thailand
	Vinythai	Thailand	• Vinythai will invest 2.3 billion *baht* next year to double the production capacity of vinyl chloride monomer (VCM) to 400,000 tonnes a year at its Map Ta Phut plant. The project, using technology of the company's major shareholder, Solvay SA of Belgium, will be financed by local banks (*2004*)

continued on next page

TABLE 12.1 — continued

Business Group	Subsidiary	Country	Changes
Telecoms	TelecomAsia (TA)	Thailand	• KFW, a German bank, converted TA's debt into a 24 per cent equity and became a TA shareholder, resulting in the dilution of ownership of CP and Nynex (2000)
	Apstar Satellite	China	• Sold 10.7 per cent to Chinese partners (1997)
	Kopin	U.S.A.	• Sold 15 per cent (worth US$19 million) (1999)
	UTV Cable Network	Thailand	• Merged with its sole competitor, IBC, and held 60 per cent in the merged venture.
	TA subsidiaries	Thailand	• Closed and sold several TA subsidiaries, including a paging unit, equipment distributor, software consultancy, and TV programme production unit
	n.a.	Indonesia	• CP established a cell-phone operation in Indonesia Cyber Access Communications. This became its first overseas telecom venture since the 1997 financial crash. It would provide GSM 1800 MHz frequency phone services and 3G mobile-phone technology. Under the BTO deal, the Indonesian Government gave it three years to develop the system. Once the service starts, the firm would pay 1 per cent of revenue to the Indonesian Government (2003)
	TA Orange	Thailand	• Orange, which had invested more than 20 billion *baht* in the joint venture with TelecomAsia to date, sold a 39 per cent stake in the company to TA for just one baht following a debt restructuring. Under the deal, Orange would sell 819 million shares in Bangkok Inter Teletech Co. (Bitco) to TA for just one *baht*. Bitco was a holding company controlling TA Orange, and was 44 per cent owned by TA and 7 per cent by the Charoen Pokphand Group (2004)
	TelecomAsia Corp	Thailand	• TA unveiled its new corporate identity, changing its name to True Corporation and assuming red as its corporate colour (2004)

Retailing	Lotus Supercenter	Thailand	• Sold 75 per cent to Britain's Tesco for US$350m, but kept its name for the Chinese market (1999)
	Sunny Supermarket	Thailand	• Sold to Belgium's Delhaize Group
	7-Eleven	Thailand	• Sold 11 per cent to Singapore's Government Investment Corp, leaving CP with a 65 per cent ownership
	Chia Tai Group	China	• CP opened Super Brand Mall, Asia's biggest mall in China that had cost around 20 billion *baht* to build (2002)
	Shanghai Lotus Supermarket Chain Store Co., Ltd (SLS)	China	• Established new branches of Lotus Supercentre from 1997 onward. In 2004, 14 branches (56 per cent) had been set up in Shanghai, and 11 others (44 per cent) in the towns along the Yangtze river (2004)
Brewery	Heineken Shanghai Brewery	China	• Sold 35 per cent in Heineken Shanghai Brewery to Heineken (1998)
	Shanghai Boonrawd Brewery	China	• Sold 50 per cent in Shanghai Boonrawd Brewery to various partners (1998)
Motorcycle	Shanghai Ek Chor	China	• Sold 50 per cent to Chinese partner, the state-run Shanghai Automotive Industry, for US$12.8million (1998)
	Ek Chor China Motorcycle	China	• Disposed of entire equity interests in February 2004
	Echo Autoparts (Thailand)	Thailand	• Ek Chor China was privatized and became a wholly-owned subsidiary of CP in June 2003. Net profit attributable to the group was US$6.2 million (2003) • CP formed auto-parts venture with Japan's Kodarma Chemical Industry to manufacture plastic parts for the automotive industry. Echo is 49 per cent owned by Thai Kodama — in which CP has a stake — and 47 per cent by Kodama Chemical Industry, with 2 per cent each owned by Nagaset (Thailand) and SBCS Co. (2004)
Insurance	Ayudhya Allianz C.P. Life	Thailand	• The Allianz group held a 62.58 per cent stake in AACP, Thai-German joint venture

Source: Pavida (2001*a*), Information disclosure reports 2004 (Form 56-1), Stock Exchange of Thailand (SET), newspapers and magazines.

3.1.1 Concentration on Value-added Products

Many factors were instrumental in pushing CP to concentrate on more value-added food products, that is, processed and cooked meat. First, Thai chicken exporters were facing a strong competition in the frozen meat category from cheaper producers like China and Brazil (Yuthasak 2001). In addition, stricter food standards imposed by major importing countries, like Japan, the European Union and Australia, made it harder and more expensive for exporters to meat such requirements. Third, the commodity-like price instability of frozen chicken reduced the profitability of exporters (Interview, 16 February 2005). Most importantly, the Severe Acute Respiratory Syndrome (SARS) and the avian flu outbreak that spread throughout China, Thailand and Vietnam during 2002–04[7] led importing countries to avoid frozen meat and to buy cooked products instead. Tables 12.2 and 12.3 show that the sharp decline of Thailand's frozen poultry exports after 2003 was substituted by the increase of prepared and preserved meat exports. The cooked and processed meat had become the priority of CPF and the company was pursuing this strategy in other meat categories including pork. In late 2004, CP formed a joint venture with Japan's Yonekyu Corp, a company that specialized in food processing technology, to accumulate their technological skills as well as to benefit from the Japanese firm's distribution networks in Japan (*Phujadkarn Rai Duen*, March 2005).

In addition to focusing on cooked and processed products, CP's value-adding strategies included the adoption of a single corporate brand "CP". Starting in 2005, CP integrated all its products under the CP brand for the domestic market and planned to adopt the same brand name for its export markets (*Phujadkarn Rai Duen*, March 2005). CP's creation of its own brand signified the attempt in shifting its role as OEM supplier toward becoming a food company with its own products.

3.1.2 Integration into Retailing and Distribution

CP had already started its downstream integration into retail and distribution prior to the crisis. However, the group's decision to focus on the retail sector led to several major changes. First, CP expanded its retail operations in Thailand and China through various formats, ranging from hypermarket to convenience store. Although CP relinquished most of its stake in Lotus Supercenter in Thailand,[8] the group maintained its hypermarket operations in China. CP operated twenty-five Lotus

TABLE 12.2
World Exporter of Frozen Poultry (HS 0207.14) (US$ Millions)

Ranking	Country	1999	2000	2001	2002	2003	2004
1	Brazil	451.27	445.01	789.56	881.28	1,092.36	1,692.07
2	United States	1,112.91	1,332.21	1,603.53	1,178.11	1,311.83	1,475.26
3	Netherlands	404.41	390.69	424.35	452.53	543.10	547.73
4	Germany	87.59	84.96	85.08	158.34	257.54	206.53
5	U.K.	105.56	86.84	98.19	90.78	132.84	164.01
6	Belgium	71.81	87.42	110.11	102.80	103.07	134.37
7	Hong Kong	522.63	522.16	456.64	382.98	361.07	108.80
8	France	85.31	70.33	74.59	80.30	87.12	79.16
9	China	463.00	494.58	499.89	338.85	249.67	78.65
10	Chile	7.99	10.93	24.10	14.65	33.78	76.14
11	Canada	26.55	29.87	38.42	39.63	34.48	60.17
12	Poland	12.50	7.29	11.25	15.02	33.35	56.79
13	Thailand	399.08	388.98	537.34	533.12	598.66	44.45
	Others	234.08	212.20	269.20	270.99	313.93	211.85
	Total	3,984.70	4,163.46	5,022.24	4,539.38	5,152.80	4,935.98

Source: Global Trade Atlas (2005).
Note: Commodity 0207.14 are Chicken Cuts And Edible Offal (Including Livers) Frozen.

TABLE 12.3
World Exporter of Prepared or Preserved Chicken Meat
(HS 1602.32) (US$ Million)

Rank	Country	1999	2000	2001	2002	2003	2004
1	Thailand	156.20	216.87	259.28	305.97	383.15	515.44
2	China	171.06	274.31	368.55	441.52	447.47	460.16
3	Netherlands	189.67	186.04	233.25	258.78	311.31	273.08
4	Germany	59.97	59.04	88.64	100.10	143.52	154.80
5	United States	122.78	136.19	166.84	134.22	133.59	132.06
6	Belgium	66.49	59.38	69.68	80.26	106.55	117.86
7	Brazil	17.38	23.01	42.14	57.76	89.21	100.95
8	France	159.85	145.10	127.38	121.94	152.57	99.22
9	United Kingdom	39.58	35.33	44.21	56.34	71.57	93.75
10	Ireland	10.86	15.21	30.14	55.11	78.29	88.14
	Others	89.62	117.12	149.49	174.22	239.22	210.20
	Total	1083.44	1267.61	1579.59	1786.22	2156.46	2245.66

Source: Global Trade Atlas (2005).
Note: Commodity 1602.32 are Prepared or Preserved Chicken Meat, Meat Offal or Blood, N.E.S.O.I.

Supercenter stores in 2004, and planned to increase the number of stores to a hundred by 2006 (Interview, 7 February 2005).[9] In addition to hypermarket stores, CP strengthened its operations of the 7-Eleven convenience stores in both Thailand and China. There were 3,000 stores in Thailand by the end of 2004. In China, CP won the franchising right to operate the 7-Eleven stores in 1997 (*Phujadkarn Rai Duen*, February 2000). CP's expansion in the retailing industry also included the creation of its own retail outlet in Thailand, CP Fresh Mart, which carried only CP food products. Five branches had been set up by 2005, and the group set a target of 200 branches by 2008 (*Phujadkarn Rai Duen*, March 2005). The fast food industry was another target for CP's expansion in retailing and distribution. In 2001, CP sold its fifty-one per cent share in CP-KFC Development (Thailand), the major KFC franchisee, to its partner (Yuthasak 2001). Although CP continued to be a major supplier to KFC, this sale terminated the group's seventeen-year right to the KFC franchise that started in 1984. It also signified CP's attempt to develop its own fast food chains that might include fried chicken.[10]

The second change toward CP's strengthening of its retail operations in international markets was the transfer of control of CP's trading offices. Prior to the crisis, CP's trading arms were under the management of CP Intertrade. However, the consolidation of CP's food businesses led to the transfer of trading offices that were mainly responsible for meat products to the management of CP Foods, the group's main subsidiary in the food industry. As a result, CP Intertrade's responsibilities were shifted toward providing logistical services to the group's international trade operations and handling the trade of non-group products, such as rice (Interview, 14 January 2005). This shift affected only the management control, but not the number of the group's trading offices. In 2005, the group had twenty trading offices spreading throughout the world.[11]

3.2 Telecommunications

CP's adjustments in the telecommunications sector can be summarized under two main strategies: Reduction of international orientation, and expansion into mobile telephone, broadband internet, and other content-related areas. Contrary to the pre-crisis years, during which the group invested in several overseas projects, CP's post-crisis international strategy in telecommunications was primarily to get rid of them. CP sold its equity in the Apstar satellite in China in 1997 and later sold its stake in the Nasdaq-listed Kopin Corporation in 1999 (*TelecomAsia,*

Information Disclosure Reports (Form 56-1), 1999). Following this direction, CP's interest in telecommunications was shifted to focus mainly on domestic operations.

After three years of debt restructure that included the sales of subsidiaries and the conversion of debt into a twenty-four per cent equity of the group's largest debtor, Kreditanstalt für Wiederaubau (KfW), TelecomAsia or True,[12] expanded its activities from fixed-line telephony to include mobile telephone services in 2001. Since then, True focused on expanding its Internet/broadband operations, as well as other content related areas such as web development solutions and online games (<www.truecorp.co.th>, March 2005). With most of the network provision reaching its saturation in Thailand, True's future expansion strategy would be based more on the software- and application-related services (Interview, 19 January 2005).

CP's strategy in telecommunication resembled that in the food sectors. It confirmed the group's push toward more value-added and downstream activities in each line of its businesses. These moves also reflected the group's consolidation and integration attempts to restructure its vast business empires into a more transparent and less complex structure. However, CP's selection of its core industries did not mean that the group would divest from its non-core sectors. Apart from the changes that took place in the three core sectors, most of the group activities remained unchanged (see Figure 12.2). The next part takes a closer look at CP's non-core sectors.

3.3 Non-core Sectors: Still There

Although CP set its priority on the three previously mentioned sectors, the group still maintained its involvement in many other industries that are vaguely related to their core sectors. In Thailand, the group continued with its investment in petrochemicals through its joint venture with Belgium's Solvay group, Vinythai, in which CP's holding companies together held more than 24 per cent equity (see <www.vinythai.com>).

Other non-core activities included real estate and land development, automotive and industrial manufacturing, and e-procurement services (see <www.cpthailand.com>). More investment projects had also been periodically reported, such as Internet service provision in India and China (*The Nation*, 2 February 2000), a joint venture with a Taiwanese group that operated department stores in China (*The Nation*, 4 August 2003), and a reported plan that the CP group might take over seventy-five

FIGURE 12.2
Location of CP's Post-Crisis International Activities

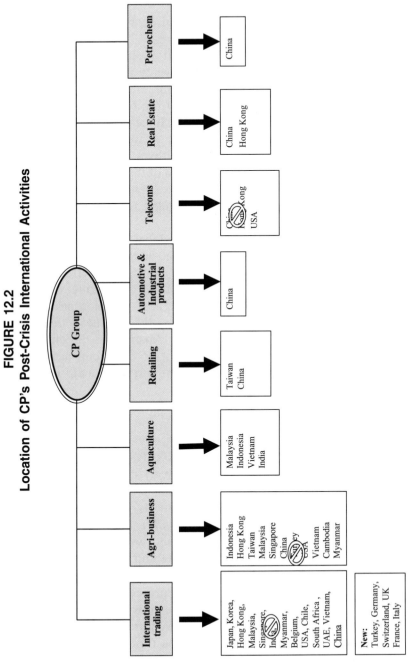

Notes:

* Investment Company

The "no entry" sign indicates that those locations are given up after the crisis.

Source: Information disclosure reports 2004 (Form 56-1), Stock Exchange of Thailand (SET) and CP Pokphand's Annual Report 2003.

per cent of the troublesome TPI Group (*Dokbia*, February 2004). It should be noted, however, that these non-core activities were located only in Thailand and China.

While details of CP's adjustments are presented in this part, the next section discusses the dynamics of changes that explain CP's post-crisis behaviour.

4. CHANGING DYNAMICS: FROM A LOCAL CONGLOMERATE TO A MULTINATIONAL CORPORATION

4.1 CP as a "Third World Multinational": Technological and Networking Capabilities

The international expansion of firms from developing countries has attracted scholarly interest since the early 1980s. The literature on "Third World multinational" can be broadly categorized under two different waves, based on the timing of their emergence and their views on the nature of the competitive advantages of these firms. The first wave, or those that emerged in the late 1970s and the early 1980s, argued that the competitive advantages of developing country multinationals were derived from their ability to reduce costs of imported technology through "descaling" techniques such as reducing operation scale, substituting machinery with human labour, and replacing imported inputs with cheaper local ones. The sustainability of these firms was thought to be bleak as their cost advantages would erode over time once local firms caught up. Proponents of this view included Wells (1977, 1981, 1983), O'Brien (1980), Aggarwal (1984), Lecraw (1977, 1981), and Kumar (1982).

Though attention in the subject faded in the late 1980s, a renewed interest surged since the early 1990s. The second-wave literature on Third World multinational enterprises (MNEs) particularly focused on the capability of these firms to catch up with their developed-country counterparts through the learning-by-doing technological accumulation process. It was suggested that developing country multinationals built their competitive advantages from the incremental learning process that started with lower value-added activities and worked their way up the value chain. Proponents of this view included Lall (1983*a*, *b*), Vernon-Wortzel and Wortzel (1988), Cantwell and Tolentino (1990), Tolentino (1993), Lecraw (1993), Ulgado, Yu, and Negandhi (1994), Dunning, Hoesel, and Narula (1997), and Hoesel (1997). Despite their differences, both groups shared a strong emphasis that, without their own proprietary technology, the competitive advantages of multinationals from developing countries lay in their ability to gradually adapt and accumulate technological skills from the technology originally imported from the more advanced economies.

In her in-depth studies of four Thai multinationals, namely, the CP Group, the Siam Cement Group, the Dusit Thani Group and the Jasmine Group, Pavida (2001a) concluded that the pre-crisis internationalization process of these firms was guided not only by their accumulated technological skills, but also by their networking capabilities, or the ability to draw from complementary resources of different partners and to turn them to the firm's benefits. While industry-specific technological skills were fundamental in creating these Thai multinationals' competitive advantages, networking capabilities served as an additional source of advantage that could be exploited across industries during these firms' growth and expansion. The three key sources of network relationships that contributed greatly to these multinationals' domestic growth and international expansion were close ties with financial sources, links with foreign technology partners, and political connections. Among these, the first two types of networks were crucial in the international expansion of the four selected Thai multinationals.

Although most studies on CP have highlighted the group's strong networking capabilities, the group's strength and competitive advantage in agri-business cannot be overlooked. The major factor that contributed to the CP's pre-crisis growth in agri-business was its scale and scope. While CP's scale economies were derived from the group's vertical integration along all the stages of livestock production, starting from animal feed supplies to processed meat distribution and retailing channels, its economies of scope stemmed from the group's diverse range of products, including livestock, swine and aquaculture. The key advantage of vertical integration in the poultry industry was the ability to reduce the problems of variation in: Input quality, fluctuations in the demand for products at various stages, and fluctuations in input supplies and their prices. Most importantly, vertical integration allowed the transaction costs that occurred between various stages to be minimized (Nipon et al. 1985). Boyd and Watts (1997, pp. 203–05) called the overall process of the broiler industry *filière*. According to them, the broiler *filière* comprised two main functions: Production, and distribution. While production covered breeding, hatching, feed milling, and processing, distribution was concerned with bringing processed meat to end consumers through different channels, such as restaurants, retail outlets, or exports. CP's expansion in agri-business covered the whole length of *filière*, starting from producing feeds to farming, slaughtering, meat processing, and retailing.

With success in the poultry industry, CP replicated the vertical integration system to its swine and shrimp industries, albeit not on a similar scale. CP invested in shrimp farming, feed milling and other supporting research and development activities. Aquaculture was becoming more and more significant for the group, as shrimp feeds fetched four times the price of chicken feeds and two times the profit margin (*Than Setthakij*, 8 August 1992). Shrimp farming was also the fastest growing sector in agribusiness during the late 1980s, and shrimp exports from Thailand had been enjoying a tremendous growth until the mid-1990s when the United States and the European Union reduced imports from Thailand due to environmental concerns on shrimp farming techniques (*Bangkok Post*, 7 December 1996). Unlike the poultry industry, in which most production was for domestic consumption,[13] 80 per cent of shrimp production was exported (Goss, Burch, and Rickson 2000). CP's international operations in the shrimp industry were much more export-oriented. The flexibility in shifting export bases from one country to the next in was therefore a key competitive advantage of the CP Group (ibid.).

CP's international expansion prior to the crisis was driven by the search for new markets that the group could exploit its competitive advantages based on its accumulated technology in agri-business. Growth opportunities in the host country's market were the main attraction for CP's early international expansions, most of which were concentrated in neighbouring countries. Developing countries not only offered more opportunities for growth. They also shared some institutional similarities with which the group had been familiar. The understanding of how developing-country markets work was an important part of CP's knowledge. It allowed the group to be more tolerant to and flexible with the unpredictable environment that characterized these markets.

In sum, most of CP's international expansions in agri-business were undertaken to supply the growing demand in the host countries. There were only few locations, namely China, Turkey and Portugal, which CP intended to use as export bases. While CP's main source of advantage in Thailand was the scale economies achieved through its vertical integration, only a selected number of operations outside Thailand, namely Taiwan, Indonesia, and Turkey, was that vertically integrated. The majority of international investments in other countries were concentrated in the production and sales of animal feeds (see *CP Pokphand Annual Report*, various years). Despite CP's vast investments in China, there were only two subsidiaries — Heilongjiang Chia Tai and Qingdao Chia Tai — which were involved in meat processing production. The main activities of CP's other 100-plus subsidiaries in China were production and sales of animal feeds and chicken (*CPP Annual Report* 2003). Given this nature of CP's investments, Thailand remained the key export base, while Shanghai contributed toward some exports to Japan (Interview, 16 February 2005).

CP's post-crisis adjustments in agri-business were characterized by the move downstream toward retailing and distribution of more value-added products. The intensified integration into retailing and distribution was the main drive behind CP's post-crisis growth both in Thailand and China. CP had not expanded its feed and poultry activities in China since 1997, but had focused instead on motorcycle trading, retailing and distribution. The group expected its industrial activities to contribute as much as fifty per cent of its turnover in China by 2015 (Interview, 16 February 2005). Such increase was not small, given that seventy per cent of the group's 2004 turnover was attributed to agri-business (Interview, 16 February 2005).

Although vertical integration remained the key to CP's pre- and post-crisis competitive advantages in agri-business, its nature differed. While CP's pre-crisis integration was concentrated in the production and sales of animal feeds and chicken, the post-crisis strategy placed a much stronger emphasis on the production and sales of processed meat, and the retailing and distribution activities. The extensive integration into retailing served as a strong competitive advantage for CP's international expansions, as few other agri-business multinationals were able to integrate into retailing activities (Burch and Goss 2005). The emphasis on retailing appeared to be the main engine of growth of the CP Group, especially in China.

The other key dynamics in CP's post-crisis international expansion is the group's production flexibility. Since the crisis, a clearer direction emerged to enhance the CP Group's overall global efficiency in agri-business productions. Instead of replicating its vertically integrated production chain in every country, CP appeared to change its strategy to focus more on using each production base for a specific role. For example, Thailand had been positioned as the group's "experiment centre" and main export base for processed and cooked meat, while China's majority of production sites targeted the local market, with some exports to Japan

(Interview, 16 February 2005). Japan remained one of CP's biggest markets, in addition to the EU. Of the 60,000 tonnes of Japan's chicken imports in the first half of 2003, Brazil ranked as the number one exporter (24,000 tonnes), followed by Thailand (18,000 tonnes), China (12,000 tonnes), and the United States (6,000 tonnes) (*Phujadkarn Rai Duen*, March 2005).

CP's flexibility in using different production bases around the region to supply export markets was more evident in aquaculture. CP's shrimp exports grew 300 per cent in 2004, thanks to its guarantee of a 100 per cent traceability. CP guaranteed that it could trace every lot of its shrimp exports to every stage of production, heightening the level of the group's quality control. CP also claimed to be the "only company in the world that can offer this level of guarantee" (Interview, 16 February 2005). CP's shrimp export bases were located in Malaysia, Indonesia, Vietnam, and India (see Figure 12.2). Since the downturn of the shrimp industry in Taiwan in the 1980s, CP had been able to benefit from the globalization of shrimp production in Southeast and South Asia, spreading its investments to new export "stars" like Vietnam and India (Goss, Burch, and Rickson 2000).

In sum, the post-crisis dynamics of CP's international operations had been led by the group's changing focus from the production of lower value-added products, like animal feeds and frozen chicken meat, to the retailing and distribution phase of the broiler value chain, and the increased efficiency gained from division of responsibility among the group's overseas production bases. This strategic direction showed that CP had been in the process of integrating its vast agri-business operations into a complementary system. Rather than focusing separately in each market, CP appeared to make better use of its production bases by designating appropriate role for each one, making its global activities more coordinated. However, it is still too early to determine whether this strategy will be adapted throughout its overseas operations. The more obvious changes only are taking place in Thailand. Moreover, the division of responsibility among overseas production base did not always succeed. The group's attempt to establish a production base in the United States failed miserably and the group withdrew from all its U.S. operations in 2004, ending a five-year struggle to break into the white meat-dominated market of the United States (*CPF Annual Report* 2004). CP earlier attempted to use the U.S. production base to supply the white meat for domestic consumption, while using dark meat as raw material for processed food products for the Japanese market (Interview, 12 January 2005). CP's failure in the United States suggested that the group had yet to acquire the skills needed to compete successfully in highly competitive markets.

The difficulty the group faced in more mature markets limited the group's international expansions to developing economies in the region. In fact, CP's overseas activities were mostly concentrated in one market, China. As discussed earlier, CP's sizeable investments in China has earned the group the representative status of the "overseas Chinese" firm from Thailand. Therefore, to understand CP, one needs to look closely at CP's operations in China. The next part examines specifically CP's pre- and post-crisis changes in China and discusses how the group's ethnicity contributed to the group's performance in China.

4.2 CP in China: The "Overseas Chinese" Factor?

Although CP's general profile fits the stereotype of "overseas Chinese" capitalism, it would be dangerously simplistic to characterize CP's investment in China as arising out of ethnic ties and ancestral loyalty. Although there was no doubt that common cultural backgrounds and language made it easier for CP to invest in China, it was more the mutual benefits that lay beneath the relationship between the CP group and the Chinese state apparatus. Tony Asvaintra, CP Pokphand's chief financial officer, put it succinctly:

> The point is not whether you are an overseas Chinese or a fair-haired Westerner, it is the bottom line that counts. We invest in China because of business opportunities, not out of sentiment.
>
> Quoted in *FEER,* 21 October 1993

As earlier discussed, China offered a variety of locational advantages for CP's agri-business production. A gigantic domestic market where the majority of people then remained in agriculture could more than absorb CP's products. On top of agri-business, China's newly opened economy also provided numerous opportunities in many industrial and service sectors. From China's viewpoint, the most important things the country needed when it first opened its doors were foreign technology and foreign investment. It was the ethnic Chinese from East and Southeast Asia that were the first to enter China in the 1980s before Western multinationals rushed there in the 1990s. CP's experience in agri-business was much welcome in China, where modern technology in farming was urgently needed. Moreover, CP did not come alone, but brought along Continental

Grain, an American multinational. The prospect of gaining technology from these multinationals contributed to China's warm reception of the group. Since its first entry to China in 1979, CP was able to extend its business to cover a wide range of activities, including agri-business, motorcycle production, real estate development, retailing and distribution, as well as telecommunications (see Figure 12.1).

The group's rapid expansion in China was characterized by its ability in combining its technological capabilities in agri-business with its networking skills. Similar to the way CP built its political clout in Thailand, CP's connections in China were cultivated from the grass-roots level of municipal authorities in agriculture (Wichai 1993). Thirayut Phitya-Isarakul, president of agro-industry business group, was quoted claiming in 1994 that: "After 14 years in China, we have all the connections from the top of the government down to the local county level. And they are all willing to support us in all our businesses." (Cited in *Asian Business*, February 1994). That claim was not an exaggeration. Both CP's chairman Dhanin and his brother Sumet, who supervised CP Pokphand in Hong Kong, served as economic advisers to the Chinese Government. They also sat on the advisory board overseeing Hong Kong's handover to China in July 1997. The CP Group also enjoyed equally strong connections in Shanghai, where most of the group's industrial activities were located (*FEER*, 23 January 1997). Brown (1998, p. 627) claimed that Dhanin's close ties with the city mayor had assisted the group's various investments in Shanghai. CP's extensive connections in China were certainly helpful in some cases. For example, CP was selected over many competitors to join the China-supported satellite project, APT Satellite, as one of the founding shareholder (*FEER*, 18 August 1994).[14] But network-based expansion had its limits and CP did not always get what it wanted. An example was the group's failure to obtain a passenger-car-assembly licence from the Chinese Government (*FEER*, 20 April 1989). China's denial reflected CP's weakness in lacking its own technology, especially when the other licensees were Volkswagen, Chrysler, Peugeot, Citröen, Suzuki, Subaru, and Daihatsu. This incident proved that without concrete technological knowledge, CP's extensive connections did have their limits.

As China became more open to the world, the level of competition increased. Neither CP's early entrance, nor its extensive networks, could prevent the changing nature of business environments in China. Even in animal feeds, which had long been CP's growth engine in China, the group was facing more and more competition from newly emerging local firms, like the Hope Group.[15] The rise of Chinese firms that benefited from the state's help through funding and subsidies squeezed out CP's control in one of its strongest areas — animal feeds. Despite its market-share leadership, CP had been facing an intensive local competition that forced the group to close more than fifty per cent of its animal feed production facilities (Interview, 16 February 2005). Its main local rival, the New Hope group, proudly announced on its website of how its feeds *"broke the monopoly by foreign feed manufacturers"* <www.newhopegroup.com>.

A closer look at the accounts of CP Pokphand, the group's main Hong Kong-listed subsidiary, also confirmed that CP's operations in China since 1997 had not been rosy. In agri-business, the group's sales drastically dropped, following the avian flu outbreak, leading to heavy losses in 2003–04. Motorcycle production was the only sector that showed a positive performance. Tables 12.4 and 12.5 present CP Pokphand's profits by industry and by country from 1992 to 2004. It is also evident from Table 12.5 that CP's profits from its international operations had nosedived since the late 1990s.

CP's post-crisis difficulty in China indicated that the group's ethnic Chinese root may have helped facilitate its early expansion, but could not be accounted for as the group's main source of competitive advantage. CP's operations in China stand at an important crossroad. Under the current competition from both local and multinational competitors, CP's changing in dynamics of turning toward retailing and distribution still needed to be proven, while the answer to whether and how the group could sustain its competitiveness in its broad range of industrial activities and real estate projects remained doubtful. The next part discusses some challenges that the group is facing in its quest to become a true global player.

5. FUTURE CHALLENGES

CP is facing challenges both as an ethnic Chinese company and as an emergent multinational. As an ethnic Chinese business group, CP should ponder how long its ethnic card can be played. When China first opened its doors to foreign investment in 1979, ethnic Chinese firms from East and Southeast Asia received a warm welcome partly because there was little interest from Western multinationals at the time. Ethnic ties, common cultural traits, and those ethnic Chinese firms' experience accumulated in their respective home countries, certainly made them attractive then. But as China continued its path toward global integration and became the

TABLE 12.4

CP Pokphand Profit by Business Type, 1992–2004 (US$' 000)

Business Type	1992	1993	1994	1995	1996	1997	1998	1999	2000	2001	2002	2003	2004[2]
Trading	1,626	431	(727)	326	(687)	1,468	(3,118)	n.a.	n.a.	n.a.	n.a.	n.a.	n.a.
Investment Properties	430	417	4	45	(816)	(1,832)	(5,075)	n.a.	(4,334)	(660)	(3,429)	(902)	(399)
Motorcycle	10,760	14,215	21,501	21,891	2,871	(54,436)	11,227	n.a.	2,394	3,232	4,369	6,224	22,189
Investment Holding	1,673	8,486	268	1,294	863	(4,869)	(6,658)	n.a.	(36,256)	(17,753)	(14,553)	(26,536)	(12,389)
Agribusiness	31,926	23,650	50,966	58,178	15,704	72,470	83,420	n.a.	(12,958)	4,883	106,215[1]	(41,544)[1]	(26,425)[1]
Retail & Distribution	–	–	(1,706)	(4,243)	(7,713)	(7,935)	(6,687)	n.a.	n.a.	n.a.	n.a.	n.a.	n.a.
Total	46,415	47,199	70,306	77,491	10,222	4,866	73,109	n.a.	(51,154)	(10,298)	92,602	(62,758)	(17,024)

Source: CP Pokphand Annual Report, various years.

[1] Feedmill and poultry operations.

[2] Six months ended 30 June 2004.

TABLE 12.5

CP Pokphand Profit by Country, 1992–2004 (US$' 000)

Country	1992	1993	1994	1995	1996	1997	1998	1999	2000[1]	2001[1]	2002	2003	2004[2]
Turkey	1,867	2,901	2,351	4,905	4,652	8,633	12,322	n.a.	(4,194)	(3,901)	8,019	(8,509)	–
Hong Kong	(921)	7,863	(2,230)	(6,018)	(17,575)	49	(23,470)	n.a.	n.a.	n.a.	(17,982)	(11,793)	(5,105)
Thailand	15,548	11,680	13,671	11,517	12,634	(6,609)	26,897	n.a.	17,048	6,300	579	–	n.a.
China	26,049	19,374	50,396	61,023	7,478	57,299	57,360	n.a.	(25,812)	4,462	100,694	(45,223)	(4,236)
Indonesia	3,872	5,381	6,118	6,064	3,033	(54,506)	–	n.a.	–	(1,978)	1,292	2,767	(7,683)
Total	46,415	47,199	70,306	77,491	10,222	4,866	73,109	n.a.	(51,154)	(10,298)	92,602	(62,758)	(17,024)

Source: CP Pokphand Annual Report, various years.

[1] Agri-business operations only.

[2] Six months ended 30 June 2004.

single most important destination for foreign investment, an ever increasing number of Western multinationals has entered the race to capture the opportunities available in the Middle Kingdom. Moreover, the increased competition also comes from the inside, as China nurtured its own firms through various state support schemes. Competition from both Western and Chinese multinationals certainly makes it necessary to question whether common cultural background would be sufficient to sustain the competitive position of ethnic Chinese capitalists. While CP tried to stress its ethnic Chinese origin by claiming on its China website that "two founders of CP group and the second generation of its management team have deep feeling and a 'Blood is thicker than water' affection with China", it is clear that the increasing competition CP faced from state-supported local firms that the Chinese blood is even thicker than an ethnic Chinese one. Although common ethnic ties may have contributed to the group's investment earlier on, it is questionable how long these cultural traits would remain helpful.

Second, while CP claimed that the group's long-term experience, knowledge and understanding of the Chinese market, contributed to its competitive advantages in China, it remains to be seen whether CP can translate these first-mover advantages that the group cultivated through its agri-business operations to other activities that the group is currently pursuing. For example, the group suggested that its cross-country networks of small feed merchants would serve as an unrivalled network of suppliers and distributors for its retail operations (Interview, 16 February 2005). Doubts continue, however, whether these networks of small-scale merchants could match the sophisticated logistics management that are proprietary knowledge of giant retail multinationals like Makro and Wal-Mart, who are making their presence felt in China. CP's earlier fall out with Wal-Mart and its recent termination of its thirteen-year partnership with Makro in Thailand might signify a more direct and fiercer competition CP is facing in the race for Chinese retail spaces.[16]

CP's ultimate challenge, however, is whether the group would be able to increase its competitive advantages in its selected core industries, particularly agri-business, and truly become a global player as stated in its "Kitchen of the World" slogan. This challenge poses questions on several aspects of the group's operations. The first one concerns the level of technology required in today's agri-business industry. Agri-business today has become increasingly driven by advanced technology, like global positioning system, geographic information system, biotechnology, and the Internet (Weick 2001). These technological developments lead the way agri-business is done, starting from crop production to livestock production, food processing, and worldwide marketing. The need to keep up, let alone catch up, with these technological advances poses a serious challenge to CP's quest to become a global player in the food industry.

The second hurdle CP confronting CP is whether the group would be able to integrate its operations in different countries to a level that would enhance its global efficiency. The changing nature of global competition demands that today's multinationals maximize their cross-border synergies among different subsidiaries. This question carries a strong implication on whether CP would remain a regional player that is competitive only in developing countries where agri-business competition is not based on cutting-edge technology, or a true global player whose competitive advantage is derived from efficient integration of its worldwide operations.

6. CONCLUSION

This chapter has argued that the literature on ethnic Chinese businesses would benefit from integrating other theoretical perspectives in their analysis. It is also pointed out that research on ethnic Chinese capitalism needs to reduce its static interpretations and focuses more on how the behaviour of ethnic Chinese capitalists has changed. The chapter therefore integrates the views from the Third World multinational literature to analyse the changing dynamics of the CP Group's international expansion. Being among Thailand's most well-known "overseas Chinese" business groups, CP has drawn much attention on how its ethnicity contributed to its behaviour. With its conglomerate structure, family ownership and control, extensive investments in China, and expertise in cultivating networks with those in power, CP has often been known as the Thai representative of ethnic Chinese business. Not much has been said, however, on the group's strategic directions. Even less is known about the group's extensive international activities, pre- and post-crisis alike.

The chapter examined the changing dynamics of the CP Group's international operations, arguing that in the agri-business and aquaculture sectors, CP's post-crisis adjustments have indeed strengthened its status as an agri-business multinational company. Through the process of downstream integration into retailing and distribution, value addition to its products, and division of responsibility among overseas production bases, the CP group emerged as a more globally focused and integrated agri-business multinational. However, the group's adherence to its pre-crisis conglomerate expansions, particularly in China, posed a significant question to the group's future. Although the group's ethnicity and extensive networks in China may have contributed to the group's success earlier, the previous section already contends that the immediate challenges facing CP have less to do with ethnicity issues but more with business competence.

Acknowledgement

This chapter is part of my research project on post-crisis changes of Thai multinationals, sponsored by Thailand Research Fund (TRF). I would like to thank the TRF for their financial support. An earlier draft was presented at the ISEAS workshop on "Ethnic Chinese Economy and Business in Southeast Asia in the Era of Globalization" in April 2005. Comments from Dr. Leo Suryadinata and other participants contributed to the improvement of this chapter. The excellent research assistance provided by Veerayooth Kanchoochat and Patchareewan Boriboonsate is highly appreciated.

Notes

[1] The term "overseas Chinese", or *huaqiao*, had long been a subject of debate. The connotation implicit in the term was that the Chinese nationals overseas were still regarded as Chinese nationals and would eventually return to their ancestral land. The accuracy of this implication was increasingly questioned since the end of World War II, when Southeast Asian countries became independent and embarked on their nation building process. Assimilation policy adopted in each Southeast Asian country gradually led these Chinese nationals and their descendants to identify themselves as nationals of their adopted countries. The term *huaren*, or "ethnic Chinese", therefore became more widely accepted as the accurate reference to the Chinese in Southeast Asia (see Suryadinata 1997).

[2] Four recent volumes that focused specifically on Chinese capitalism and its existence in Southeast Asia were Jomo and Folk (2003), Gomez and Hsiao (2004), Yeung (2004), and Menkhoff and Gerke (2002). Several chapters and papers in these volumes provided critical reviews of the literature. For example, Jomo (2003) discussed a number of common "myths" of Chinese capitalism, while Gomez and Hsiao reviewed in their introduction chapter the areas of research on Chinese capitalism in Southeast Asia and Yeung (2004) deconstructed the

Chinese business systems. For reviews on the ethnic Chinese capitalism in Thailand, Mackie (2004) provided a summary on what had been written, while Phuwadol (2003) historically traced the existence of the "overseas Chinese" in modern Southeast Asia in different aspects, including the development of the "overseas Chinese" capitalism in Thailand.

3   Yeung (1994, pp. 302–03) strongly criticized the term "Third World multinationals" as "imperialistic" and "not a theoretically fruitful way to conceptualise the nature of international business and production". He suggested that a more unbiased and less derisory term, "developing-country multinationals" be used instead. However, the term "Third World multinationals" has been associated with the established stream of literature that date back to the 1970s. This chapter uses this term specifically as a reference to this existing literature.

4   Unless stated otherwise, the historical background of the CP group is based on Wichai (1993), and the company's own document, *From Opportunity to Opportunity* (1993).

5   Chia Tai was the original Chinese name of the CP group. It is based on the local Chinese dialect of the Chia (Chearavanont) family. In China, the group is known as the Chia Tai group, or Zheng Da Ji Tuan in Mandarin pronunciation (Wichai 1993, p. 113).

6   Nynex is the major foreign partner in TelecomAsia, CP's key subsidiary in telecommunications. CP diluted its shareholding in FLAG down to ten per cent after the latter was listed in Nasdaq in February 2000 (*The Nation*, 1 February 2000).

7   The first cases of Severe Acute Respiratory Syndrome (SARS) were known to have emerged in the Guangdong province of China in November 2002. After the diseases moved out of southern China, the areas that became "hot zones" included Hanoi, Singapore, Hong Kong, and Toronto (WHO 2003).

8   CP sold seventy-five per cent of its stake to Tesco in 1999. Since then, the group had gradually reduced its holding in the company and owned less than one per cent in 2005 (Interview, 16 February 2005).

9   Of the twenty-five Lotus Supercenter stores in China, fourteen were located in Shanghai, three in Wuxi, three in Wuhan, and one each in Nanjing, Hangzhou, Xuzhou, and Kunsun (7-Eleven, Information Disclosure Reports (Form 56-1), 2004).

10   CP had to remove fried chicken from its Chester's Grill menu, as it was against the franchise agreement with KFC (Yuthasak 2001).

[11] The locations of CP's trading offices were: China (4), the United States (2), European Union (6), Asia (7), and Africa (1).

[12] TelecomAsia changed its name to True Corporation Public Company Limited in 2003.

[13] Of all the 42.6 million tonnes of chicken production in 2000, only 6 million tonnes (14 per cent) was exported (Kanchana and Salaya 2001).

[14] There were seven founding shareholders in APT Satellite. Four were China's state enterprises. The rest were Singapore Telecom, a Macau company owned by a subsidiary of Beijing-controlled China Travel Service and a pro-China businessman, and Orient Telecom and Technology (OTT), the Hong Kong-listed subsidiary of the CP group (*FEER*, 18 August 1994). In 1996, the shares were transferred to Chia Tai International Telecommunications, a newly set up wholly owned subsidiary under Telecom Asia (*TelecomAsia* Form 56-1 1997).

[15] The four brothers who established the Hope group have built it into one of China's largest private enterprises. Business operations started in 1982 with the breeding of quails and chickens. The group later expanded into animal feeds, real estate, electronics, banking and insurance. In 1995, the mainstay animal feed business was split into two, East Hope in Shanghai, and New Hope in Sichuan <www.newhopegroup.com>.

[16] After the planned joint venture between CP and Wal-Mart collapsed in 1996, each entered China separately in the same year. CP also lured several high-ranking management personnel from Wal-Mart to work for its own hypermarket chain, Lotus Supercenter (Handley 1997). In May 2005, Charoen Pokphand Foods (CPF), the group's key subsidiary in agri-business, announced its divestment in Siam Makro Holding, ending its thirteen-year partnership with the SHV Holdings of the Netherlands (*Bangkok Post*, 27 May 2005).

References

Aggarwal, R. 1984. "The Strategic Challenge of Third World Multinationals: A New Stage of the Product Life Cycle of Multinationals?" In *Advances in International Comparative Management: A Research Annual*, vol. 1, edited by R.N. Farmer (Greenwich, Connecticut; London, England: JAI Press).

Biggart, N.W. and G.G. Hamilton. 1990. Explaining Asian Business Success: Theory No. 4. *Business and Economic Review*, 5: 13–15.

Biggart, N.W. and G.G. Hamilton. 1992. "On the Limits of a Firm-Based Theory to Explain Business Networks: The Western Bias of Neoclassical Economics". In *Networks and Organisations: Structure, Form and Action*, edited by N.N. a. R.G. Eccles (Boston: Harvard Business School Press).

Boyd, W. and M. Watts. 1997. "Agro-Industrial Just-In-Time: The Chicken Industry and Postwar American Capitalism". In *Globalising Food: Agrarian Questions and Global Restructuring*, edited by D. Goodman and M.J. Watts (London: Routledge).

Brown, R.A. 1998. "Overseas Chinese Investment in China — Patterns of Growth, Diversification and Finance: The Case of Charoen Pokphand". *The China Quarterly* (September): 610–36.

Brown, R.A. 2000. *Chinese Big Business and the Wealth of Asian Nations* (London: Palgrave).

Burch, D. and J. Goss. 2005. "Regionalisation, Globalisation and Multinational Agribusiness: A Comparative Perspective from Southeast Asia". In *Multinational Agribusiness*, edited by R. Rama (New York: Haworth Press).

Cantwell, J. and P.E.E. Tolentino. *Technical Accumulation and Third World Multinationals*. Discussion Papers in International Investment and Business, no. 139 (Reading: University of Reading).

Ch'ng, D. 1993. *The Overseas Chinese Entrepreneurs in East Asia: Background, Business Practices and International Networks*. CEDA Monograph M 100.

CP Group. 1993. *From Opportunity to Opportunity*. Bangkok: CP Group.

Dirlik, A. 1997. Critical Reflections on 'Chinese Capitalism' as a Paradigm. *Identities* 3, no. 3: 303–30.

Dunning, J.H., R. van Hoesel, and R. Narula. *Third World Multinationals Revisited: New Developments and Theoretical Implications*. Discussion Papers in International Investment and Management, Series B, no. 227 (Reading: University of Reading).

East Asia Analytical Unit (EAAU). 1995. *Overseas Chinese Business Networks in Asia* (Canberra: Department of Foreign Affairs and Trade, Australia).

Fan, Y. 2002. "Questioning Guanxi: Definition, Classification, and Implications". *International Business Review*, 11: 543–61.

Global Trade Atlas, 2005.

Gomez, E.T. 2002. "Political Business in East Asia: Introduction". In *Political Business in East Asia*, edited by E.T. Gomez (London: Routledge).

Gomez, E.T. and H.H.M. Hsiao. 2004. "Chinese Business Research in Southeast Asia". In *Chinese Business in Southeast Asia: Contesting Cultural Explanations, Researching Entrepreneurship*, edited by E.T. Gomez and H.H.M. Hsiao (London: RoutledgeCurzon).

Goss, J., Burch, D. and R.E. Rickson. 2000. Agri-food Restructuring and Third World Transnationals: Thailand, the CP Group and the Global Shrimp Industry. *World Development* 28, no. 3: 513–30.

Haley, G.T., Tan, C.T. and U. Haley. 1998. *New Asian Emperors: The Overseas Chinese, their Strategies, and Competitive Advantages* (Oxford: Butterworth Heinemann).

Hamilton, G.G. and N.W. Biggart. 1998. "Market, Culture, and Authority: A Comparative Analysis of Management and Organisation in the Far East". *American Journal of Sociology*, 94 (Supplement): S52–S94.

Handley, P. 1997. "De-mytologising Charoen Pokphand: An Interpretive Picture of the CP Group's Growth and Diversification". Paper presented at the Chinese Business in Asia, Kuala Lumpur.

Hoesel, R. 1997. *Beyond Export-Led Growth: The Emergency of New Multinational Enterprises from Korea and Taiwan* (Rotterdam: Erasmus University).

Jomo, K.S. and B.C. Folk. (eds.) 2003. *Ethnic Business: Chinese Capitalism in Southeast Asia* (London: RoutledgeCurzon).

Jomo, K.S. 2003. "Chinese Capitalism in Southeast Asia". In *Ethnic Business: Chinese Capitalism in Southeast Asia*, edited by K.S. Jomo and B.C. Folk (London: RoutledgeCurzon).

Kao, J. 1993. "The Worldwide Web of Chinese Business". *Harvard Business Review* (March–April): 24–36.

Karnchana Noppan and Salaya Aksornmat. 2001. "Sakkayapap Utsahakam Kai Praeroup Khong Thai Nai Tasana Poo Boriharn CP [Potentials of Thai Processed Chicken Industry in CP's View]". *Thailand Investment Promotion Journal* (August): 45–51.

Kumar, K. 1982. "Third World Multinationals: A Growing Force in International Relations". *International Studies Quarterly* 26: 397–424.

Lall, S. 1983*a*. "The Rise of Multinationals from the Third World". *Third World Quarterly* 5, no. 3: 618–26.

Lall, S. 1983*b*. *The New Multinationals: The Spread of Third World Enterprises* (New York: John Wiley & Sons).

Lecraw, D. 1977. "Direct Investment by Firms from Less Developed Countries". *Oxford Economic Papers* 29, no. 3: 442–57.

Lecraw, D. 1993. "Outward Direct Investment by Indonesian Firms:

Motivations and Effects". *Journal of International Business Studies* (Third Quarter): 589–600.

Lecraw, D.J. 1981. "Internationalization of Firms from LDCs: Evidence from the ASEAN Region". In *Multinationals from Developing Countries*, edited by K. Kumar and M.G. McLeod (Lexington, Massachusetts: D.C. Heath), pp. 37–51.

Limlingan, V.S. 1986. *The Overseas Chinese in ASEAN: Business Strategies and Management Practices* (Manila: Vita Development Corporation).

Luo, Yadong and Min Chen. 1997. "Does *Guanxi* Influence Firm Performance?", *Asia Pacific Journal of Management* 14, no. 1: 1–16.

Mackie, J. 1992. Changing Patterns of Chinese Big Business in Southeast Asia. In *Southeast Asian Capitalists*, edited by R. McVey (Ithaca: Southeast Asia Programme, Cornell University).

Mackie, J. 2004. "Thailand". In *Chinese Business in Southeast Asia: Contesting Cultural Explanation, Researching Entrepreneurship*, edited by E.T. Gomez and H.H.M. Hsiao (London: RouthledgeCurzon).

McCargo, D. and Ukrist Pathmanand. 2005. *The Thaksinization of Thailand* (Copenhagen: Nordic Institute of Asian Studies Press).

Menkhoff, T. and S. Gerke (eds.) 2002. *Chinese Entrepreneurship and Asian Business Networks* (London and New York: RoutledgeCurzon).

Nipon Poapongsakorn, Chirmsak Pinthong, Chitriya Pinthong and Dow Mongkolsamai. 1985. *Food Processing and Marketing in Thailand* (Geneva: United Nations Conference on Trade and Development (UNCTAD)).

Nukul Prachuabmoh. 1996. *Cheewit tee kumka* [*Fruitful Life: An Autobiography*] (Bangkok: Dokya Publishing).

O'Brien, P. 1980. "The New Multinationals: Developing-Country Firms in International Markets". *Futures*: 303–16.

Pan, L. (ed.) 1998. *The Encyclopedia of the Chinese Overseas* (Singapore: Archipelago Press and Landmark Books).

Pasuk Phongpaichit and C. Baker. 2004. *Thaksin: The Business of Politics in Thailand* (Chiangmai: Silkworm Books).

Pavida Pananond and C.P. Zeithaml. 1998. "The International Expansion Process of MNEs from Developing Countries: A Case Study of Thailand's CP Group". *Asia Pacific Journal of Management* 15, no. 2: 163–84.

Pavida Pananond, 2001a. *The Making of Thai Multinationals: The Internationalisation Process of Thai Firms.* Unpublished Ph.D. Thesis, University of Reading, Reading.

Pavida Pananond. 2001*b*. "The Making of Thai Multinationals: A Comparative Study of Thailand's CP and Siam Cement Groups". *Journal of Asian Business* 17, no. 3: 41–70.

Pavida Pananond. 2004*a*. "Thai Multinationals after the Crisis: Trends and Prospects". *ASEAN Economic Bulletin* 21, no. 1: 106–26.

Pavida Pananond. 2004*b*. "Mitigating Agency Problems in Family Business: A Case Study of Thai Union Frozen Products". *Family Business in Developing Countries: International Workshop Proceedings* (Chiba: Area Studies Centre, Institute of Developing Economies).

Phuwadol Songprasert. 2003. *Chine Pon Thalay Samai Mai [Overseas Chinese in Modern History]* (Bangkok: Thaicoon Higher Press).

Redding, S.G. 1990. *The Spirit of Chinese Capitalism* (New York: Walter de Gruyter).

Redding, G. 1995. "Overseas Chinese Networks: Understanding the Enigma". *Long Range Planning* 28, no. 1: 61–69.

Sakkarin Niyomsilpa. 2000. *The Political Economy of Telecommunications Reforms in Thailand* (London: Pinter).

Shapiro, D.M., E. Gedajlovic and C. Erdener. 2003. "The Chinese Firm as a Multinational Enterprise". *International Journal of Organizational Analysis* 11, no. 2: 105–22.

Suehiro, A. 1989. *Capital Accumulation in Thailand 1855–1985* (Chiang Mai: Silkworm Books).

Suehiro, A. 1997. "Modern Family Business and Corporate Capability in Thailand: A Case Study of the CP Group". *Japanese Yearbook on Business History*, 14: 31–58.

Suehiro, A. 2003. Determinants of Business Capability in Thailand. In *Ethnic Business: Chinese Capitalism in Southeast Asia*, edited by K.S. Jomo and B.C. Folk (London: RoutedgeCurzon).

Suryadinata, L. 1997. "Ethnic Chinese in Southeast Asia: Overseas Chinese, Chinese Overseas, or Southeast Asians?" In *Ethnic Chinese as Southeast Asians*, edited by L. Suryadinata (Singapore: Institute of Southeast Asian Studies).

Tisdell, C., T. Murphy and T. Kehren. 1997. "Characteristics of Thailand's Commercial Pig and Poultry Industries, with International Comparisons". *World Annual Review* 89, no. 2: 2–11.

Tolentino, P.E.E. 1993. *Technological Innovation and Third World Multinationals* (London and New York: Routledge).

Ulgado, F.M., Yu, C-M.J. and A.R. Negandhi. 1994. "Multinational Enterprises from Asian Developing Countries: Management and

Organisational Characteristics". *International Business Review* 3, no. 2: 123: 33.

United Nations Conference on Trade and Development. 2004. *World Investment Report: The Shift towards Services* (New York and Geneva: United Nations).

Vernon-Wortzel, H. and L.H. Wortzel. 1988. "Globalizing Strategies for Multinationals from Developing Countries". *Columbia Journal of World Business* (Spring 1988): 27–35.

Weick, C.W. 2001. "Agribusiness Technology in 2010: Directions and Challenges". *Technology in Society* 23: 59–72.

Weidenbaum, M. and S. Hughes. 1996. *The Bamboo Network: How Expatriate Chinese Entrepreneurs Are Creating A New Economic Superpower in Asia* (New York: The Free Press).

Wells, L.T. 1977. "The Internationalisation of Firms from Developing Countries". In *Multinationals from Small Countries*, edited by T. Agmon and C.P. Kindleberger (Cambridge, Mass. and London, England: MIT Press).

Wells, L.T. 1981. "Foreign Investors from the Third World". In *Multinationals from Developing Countries*, edited by K. Kumar and M.G. McLeod (Lexington, Massachusetts: D.C. Heath), pp. 23–36.

Wells, L.T. 1983. *Third World Multinationals: The Rise of Foreign Investment from Developing Countries* (Cambridge, Massachusetts: The MIT Press).

Wichai Suwanban. 1993. *CP: Turakij rai Promdan [CP: Borderless Business]* (Bangkok: Than Setthakij).

Williamson, P.J. 2005. "Strategies for Asia's New Competitive Game". *Journal of Business Strategy* 26, no. 2: 37–43.

World Health Organization. 2003. *Severe Acute Respiratory Syndrome (SARS): Status of the Outbreak and Lessons for the Immediate Future* (Geneva: World Health Organization).

Yeung, H.W-C. 1994. "Third World Multinationals Revisited: A Research Critique and Future Agenda". *Third World Quarterly* 15, no. 2: 297–317.

Yeung, H.W-C. 2004. *Chinese Capitalism in a Global Era* (London: Routledge).

Yuthasak Kanasawas. 2001. "Perd Tamnan Liang Kai Lok [Unveiling the Global Poultry Industry]". *Thailand's Investment Promotion Journal* (August 2001): 19–60.

Newspapers and Magazines

Asian Business
Bangkok Post
Business in Thailand
Corporate Thailand (in Thai)
Dokbia (in Thai)
The Economist
Far Eastern Economic Review
Institutional Investor (International edition)
The Nation
Phujadkarn Rai Duen (in Thai)
Than Sethakij (in Thai)

Index